# List of Tab

# THE LIFE AND MUSIC OF ERIC COATES

# The Life and Music of Eric Coates

MICHAEL PAYNE

Routledge
Taylor & Francis Group

LONDON AND NEW YORK

First published 2012 by Ashgate Publishing

Published 2016 by Routledge
2 Park Square, Milton Park, Abingdon, Oxfordshire OX14 4RN
711 Third Avenue, New York, NY 10017, USA

First issued in paperback 2016

*Routledge is an imprint of the Taylor & Francis Group, an informa business*

**British Library Cataloguing in Publication Data**
Payne, Michael.
  The life and music of Eric Coates.
  1. Coates, Eric, 1886–1957. 2. Composers–Great Britain–Biography.
  I. Title
  780.9'2-dc23

**Library of Congress Cataloging-in-Publication Data**
Payne, Michael, 1981–
  The life and music of Eric Coates / Michael Payne.
     p. cm.
  Includes bibliographical references and index.
  ISBN 978-1-4094-3408-5 (hardcover: alk. paper)
1. Coates, Eric, 1886–1957. 2. Composers–England–Biography. I.
Title.
  ML410.C68P38 2012
  780.92–dc23
  [B]
                                                              2011041167

ISBN 13: 978-1-138-27149-4 (pbk)
ISBN 13: 978-1-4094-3408-5 (hbk)

Bach musicological font developed by © Yo Tomita

# Contents

# List of Figures

# List of Music Examples

# Abbreviations and Library Sigla

**Bibliographical Abbreviations**

| | |
|---|---|
| Austin Coates, programme 1 | 05/08/1986 *Eric Coates – King of Light Music*: Programme 1, 1886–1923. Written and Presented by Austin Coates. BBC Radio 2 |
| Austin Coates, programme 2 | 12/08/1986 *Eric Coates – King of Light Music*: Programme 2, 1923–1931. Written and Presented by Austin Coates. BBC Radio 2 |
| Austin Coates, programme 3 | 19/08/1986 *Eric Coates – King of Light Music*: Programme 3, 1931–1940. Written and Presented by Austin Coates. BBC Radio 2 |
| Austin Coates, programme 4 | 26/08/1986 *Eric Coates – King of Light Music*: Programme 4, 1940–1957. Written and Presented by Austin Coates. BBC Radio 2 |

The transcripts of these programmes have been made by the author.

**Library Sigla**

| | |
|---|---|
| *GB-Bcbso* | City of Birmingham Symphony Orchestra, Birmingham |
| *GB-Cu* | University of Cambridge Library, Cambridge |
| *GB-HCKl* | Hucknall Public Library |
| *GB-Lam* | Royal Academy of Music, London |
| *GB-LAu* | University of Lancaster |
| *GB-Lbh* | Boosey and Hawkes, London |
| *GB-Lbl* | The British Library, London |
| *GB-Lcm* | Royal College of Music, London |
| *GB-Lprs* | Performing Right Society, London |
| *GB-Mhallé* | Hallé Orchestra, Manchester |
| *GB-NO* | University of Nottingham Library, Nottingham |
| *GB-Rwac* | BBC Written Archives Centre, Caversham Park, Reading |
| *US-Wc* | National Library of Congress, Washington DC, United States of America |
| *US-Wgu* | Georgetown University Library, Washington DC, United States of America |

Any manuscript referred to without a sigla denotes a source in private hands.

Unless otherwise stated, all material marked *GB-Rwac* is taken from Coates' personal files and all sources marked *GB-Lcm* refer to material in box 186 unless otherwise stated.

All dates used in this book are in the British format, i.e. 05/08/1986 is 5 August 1986.

# Preface and Acknowledgements

It was the redoubtable and formidable Ethel Smyth who, on being introduced to Eric Coates at Eastbourne, said in her brusque voice: 'You are the man who writes tunes? Come and sit down beside me and tell me how you manage to make your effects'![1] 'The man who writes tunes' sums up the legacy of Coates, a man who has written several of the most memorable and enjoyable light-orchestral works of the twentieth century – works that are still loved by millions.

This book seeks to provide a comprehensive account of the life and work of Eric Coates. It does not seek to be a salacious exposé of his private life, nor to put forward a case for the redressing the balance between light and serious music, but to discuss how and why he became one of Britain's most popular and successful composers.

My interest in the music of Eric Coates stems from playing *The Dam Busters* March at school. Around the time of choosing topics for my undergraduate dissertation, I had been introduced to the delights of British light music. Not wanting to choose a topic that was over-populated with research, I decided on Coates. The more I read, researched and listened to Coates' music, the more I was struck by the very high standard of construction of his scores, the brilliance of his melodic writing and the felicitousness of his orchestration. Furthermore, I was intrigued by his business acumen and his ability to embrace the new media of the time, namely the BBC and the gramophone, which enabled him to become one of the most popular and successful composers of his generation, if not the most successful. Inspired by this, my undergraduate research turned into a doctoral study that in turn resulted in this book.

It was whilst researching my undergraduate dissertation that I was struck by the absence of literature on Coates. Whilst there is the composer's own delightful autobiography, *Suite in Four Movements*, and Geoffrey Self's short centennial biography published in 1986, both books left important questions and ventures unanswered. With the current resurgence of interest in light music and the growing stature of Coates within the field of twentieth-century British music a fuller picture of his life and music was required.

I have been fortunate to have access to Coates' surviving papers and manuscripts as well as other important collections of Coates' material. I would like to thank the following for their assistance in the writing of this book: Hilary and Bill Ashton; Gareth Atkins; Geoffrey and Dorothy Atkinson; Paul Banks; Duncan Barker; Ray Bickel; Heidi Bishop, Laura Macy and all the staff at Ashgate; Malcolm Bulcock; George Capel; Andy Chan; Frances Cook; Marjorie Cullern and Gilles Gouset; Jeremy Dibble; Peter Edwards; Liz Fawcett; Katherine Gale; Michael Grey;

---

[1]   Eric Coates, *Suite in Four Movements* (London, 1953), p. 152.

Rod Hamilton and Ike Egbetola; Alan Heinecke; Peter Horton and all the staff of the Royal College of Music Library; Beresford King-Smith; Valerie Langfield; Daniel Leech-Wilkinson; Paul Lilley; Stephen Lloyd; Ray Luker; Ruth Mariner and Tom Creedy; Charlotte Mortimer; Thomas Muir; David Nathan; Louise North; Bridget Palmer; Michael Ponder; Libby Rice; Eleanor Roberts; the late Geoffrey Self; Geoff Sheldon; Harry and Ann Smith; the Syndics of Cambridge University Library to reproduce material in the Christopher Hassall Collection; Ernest Tomlinson and his late wife, Jean; Elizabeth Wardle; John Wilson.

Finally, I wish to thank all the members of my family, especially my parents, Alan and Christine Payne, who have supported all my research into Coates. My wife Anne has been a tower of strength, a valuable proofreader and has sacrificed so much to let me write this book. Sadly, my father did not live to see this book into print and it is to his memory I dedicate this book.

Michael Payne
Bristol, February 2012

# PART I
## The Early Years

# Chapter 1
# Light Music

It was a Viennese friend of mine, who years ago, was teasing me about English music.'What is all this about "light music"?' he asked. 'Are you still such a nation of shop keepers that you even sell music by weight'?[1]

The name of Eric Coates is synonymous with the genre of light music, a genre he practically defines. Mention light music and Coates is the first, and in many cases the only, name that people will think of. In discussing Coates' contribution to the genre one has to consider the history of light music and his place within that genre.

Light music has never attracted a proper, rigorous study as a genre. There is no 'Urtext' definition of light music; even the august *New Grove Dictionary of Music and Musicians*, second edition, does not have an entry for 'light music' or the adjective 'light' as applied to music, which is a staggering omission. Indeed, the origins and first use of 'light music' are shrouded in mystery. The composer Richard Addinsell believed: 'The trouble is that no two people mean the same thing by "light music" ... for "light music" can be both an art form and an art perversion.'[2] The term 'light', is, as Louise Latham in the *Oxford Companion to Music* defined it, 'an adjective applied broadly (often pejoratively) to music deemed of no great intellectual or emotional depth, intended for light entertainment, and usually for orchestra. There is a large repertory of British light music, much of it witty, imaginative, and skilfully orchestrated ... .'[3] Latham is right to praise it for its humour and orchestration, but light music is a genre in which melody (most importantly), emotional buoyancy and a sense of humour all combine to produce a piece of music that raises a smile, is easily enjoyable and does not outstay its welcome. The genre also shares a large amount of common ground with 'serious music' by dint of the fact that light music is almost exclusively scored for orchestra (not used in any 'light way'). Because of its immense popular appeal, light music has often been the victim of snobbery. Light music is an 'umbrella term' for music that appears to be too frivolous and likely to damage the reputation of a 'serious' composer. It can range from symphonic pieces such as Haydn Wood's *May Day* Overture and Coates' *Four Centuries* Suite to mere fripperies such as Torch's *Comic Cuts* and Bucalossi's *The Grasshopper's Dance* to the operettas and musicals of Arthur Sullivan, Vivian Ellis and, dare one say, Andrew Lloyd

---

[1]  Spike Hughes 'Introductory Note', 1955 Light Programme Festival of Music Programme.
[2]  Richard Addinsell quoted in the 11/08/1944 *Radio Times*.
[3]  Latham, Alison (ed.), *The Oxford Companion to Music* (Oxford, 2002), p. 695.

Webber. By its very nature, light music is eclectic. Coates never thought of himself as a light-weight composer, but as a composer of light music. In much the same way, Edward German did not want to be viewed as a 'good *light* composer', but as a composer of 'light *good* music'.[4]

Light music, if considered to be a genre expressing emotional buoyancy, has existed for many centuries without being designated as such. Consider the catches of Purcell and the minuets of Haydn, which are examples of technical dexterity but are undoubtedly light (or indeed vulgar in the case of Purcell) in terms of sentiment. The success of these works clearly demonstrates that in past centuries there was little or no aesthetic distinction made between the 'buoyant' and the 'grave'. By the mid-nineteenth century, the 'light' and 'serious' strands of music were becoming increasingly polarized as there was a growing trend towards a lighter style of writing in the works of Bizet, Rossini (cf. his opera overtures), the Strauss family and Tchaikovsky, often in their opera (especially that of the French school, cf. Massenet, Thomas and Offenbach) and ballet music. The philosopher Theodor Adorno in his essay *Leichte Musik* (translated by Ashton as 'Popular music') talks of light and serious music as initially originating from the same circle; they had both come from the same source but had bifurcated into two polarized semicircles.[5] Perhaps this polarization was strongest in England. Great Britain has constantly had a great volume of light composers, almost to the point that, with certain key exceptions, light music is a British peculiarity. America and Europe have also had their share of light music composers, such as John Philip Sousa, Leroy Anderson, David Rose, Franz Lehár and Paul Linke respectively, but their composers of light music have tended to be more 'serious' composers who have written lighter works; there is not a dynasty of light-music composers as in England.

In England, this concept of writing in a lighter style was swiftly grasped by many composers at the *fin-de-siècle* (such as Arthur Sullivan and Edward German) who then wrote a good deal of lighter music such as operettas, incidental music and concert music. Geoffrey Self, in his history of light music, places Sullivan's overture *Di Ballo* (written for the 1870 Birmingham Festival) as 'the progenitor of a whole of line of light music'.[6] German's dances from *Nell Gwyn, Henry VIII* and *Merrie England* became immensely popular in the early years of the twentieth century. Alongside German, there was a growing army of musicians who were specializing in writing light music, such as Charles Ancliffe, Sydney Baynes, Archibald Joyce, Kenneth Alford, Albert Ketèlbey and John Ansell. By the 1930s, there was a particular flowering of composers, a so-called 'golden age'

---

[4]    Edward German quoted by David Hulme in sleeve notes to *Edward German, Orchestral Works, Volume 2* (Naxos, 8.223726).

[5]    Theodor Adorno, 'Popular Music' in Adorno, Thedor, *Introduction to the Sociology of Music* (New York, 1989), p. 24.

[6]    Geoffrey Self, *Light Music in Britain since 1870* (Aldershot, 2001), p. 10.

that included established names such as Eric Coates, Haydn Wood, Percy Fletcher and Billy Mayerl.

There was nothing 'light' about the education of these composers, they were all educated in exactly the same way as 'serious' composers. They were, however, content to write almost exclusively light music. There were exceptions: Wood wrote a violin and a piano concerto and Phillips two piano concertos (written early in his career). From the start of his student days, Coates chose to write exclusively light-orchestral works. The fillip for the focus of so many composers of light music was a demand for short, tuneful, effervescent miniatures. After the First World War, there was a surge of interest in orchestral music. By October 1923, the music publishers Chappell and Company had disbanded their Ballad Concerts in favour of Popular Orchestral Concerts.[7] The likes of Haydn Wood and Montague Phillips had had great success with their songs during the war and, in the 1920s, Phillips had scored success in light opera with *The Rebel Maid*.

Until the end of the 1930s there were a large number of openings for light composers, not solely with orchestral music. Also popular were ballads (where large money could be made in the 1900s and 1910s), music for brass and military bands, light opera, instrumental music for the amateur market and music for the theatre and music hall.

The revolutions caused by the advent of the cinema and broadcasting brought the need for library or 'mood' music; music that conjured up quickly the mood that was being presented on screen or in the programme. Albert Ketèlbey published a number of pieces for this genre, with titles such as *Mysterious* and *Love's Awakening*. The De Woolf Recorded Music Library was founded in 1927 to provide background music for films. Post war, publishing firms such as Chappells, Boosey & Hawkes, Francis, Day and Hunter and Paxtons all ran flourishing recorded music libraries to provide music for film and broadcasting.

After the Second World War, the focus of light music moved towards providing music for radio, television and film: either using original music or writing music for the recorded music libraries. Light music was still a popular feature on BBC Radio and featured in a whole host of dedicated programmes such as: *Music While You Work*, *Grand Hotel* and *Friday Night is Music Night*. In addition, the rising younger generation, comprising such composers as Charles Williams, Sidney Torch, Ronald Binge, Ernest Tomlinson, Trevor Duncan, Mona Liter, George Melachrino and Robert Farnon continued to provide works for the concert hall, helped in the 1950s by the BBC's Light Music Festivals. By the 1960s and 1970s, light music was in terminal decline and featuring less in radio broadcasts and in the concert hall. The conductor Iain Sutherland commented of these developments that: 'It wasn't that light music was dead, just the BBC were in the process of burying it alive.'[8] Owing to the mass appeal of pop music, the younger generation were not interested in light music and the genre was increasingly alienated from

---

[7]    *Musical Times* 64 (1923), p. 713.

[8]    This remark has been erroneously attributed to Robert Farnon for a number of years.

the contemporary 'classical' music of Boulez, Berio, Birtwistle, Maxwell Davies and Ligeti. There were still several opportunities for concert works, but life was difficult and opportunities scarce for light-music composers. Peter Hope gave up composition in the 1970s, focusing entirely on orchestrations and arrangements (though since 2000 he has returned to composition). It was not until the 1990s that light music began to become more popular on radio, CD (with a landmark series devoted to British Light Music on the Marco Polo label) and to feature more prominently in concert programmes. Today the genre is undergoing a further renaissance with a growing number of composers such as Philip Lane (also a noted record producer), Matthew Curtis and Adam Saunders amongst others who are producing new works and enjoying success in the recording studio.

Even within mainstream British music of the twentieth century, one occasionally catches a glimpse of a lighter style, some may call it lyricism, in the music of composers such as Henry Balfour Gardiner (*Shepherd Fennel's Dance*), Arnold Bax (*Rogue's Comedy Overture*), Arthur Bliss (*Adam Zero*), George Dyson (*Children's Suite*), Gerald Finzi (*Five Bagatelles* for clarinet and piano), E.J. Moeran (*Serenade in G*), and Ralph Vaughan Williams (*English Folk Song Suite*). While these composers are most definitely 'serious' in their outlook, there is at times a degree of lightness beneath the surface. This lighter edge can still be seen today in composers such as Bryan Kelly, Patric Standford and David Lyon, whose work is difficult to pigeonhole.

To understand the wholesale appeal of light music in the twentieth century it is necessary to view the social context of the period and the immense cultural changes that Britain experienced in the first half of the twentieth century. Before broadcasting in 1922, music was everywhere; it was played in parks, hotels, restaurants and tea shops, notably the famous Lyon's Corner Houses, to great effect. The majority of London restaurants employed an orchestra of sorts to perform light music to accompany diners at lunch, afternoon tea and a more substantial programme over the evening meal, a tradition that was still in existence in the 1930s.[9] These ensembles would play a wide variety of music, from rearranged classics to the latest 'hot tune', but most frequently they would play light music. Eugene Goossens remembered, in his autobiography, that when he was in a hotel orchestra, the ensemble was expected to play anything from Liszt to Lehár at a moment's notice.[10]

In Britain during the first-half of the twentieth century, light music was often written for coastal music festivals, ballad concerts, broadcasting or as 'fillers' for concerts; it was designed to appeal to all. When most light music was published, it was often printed with a piano-conductor part (it is exceptionally rare to find a printed full score for any piece of British light music) to enable the conductor to fill in the missing parts at the piano or bolster a weak part; the first violin part usually had general cues to enable direction from the leader in the case of

---

[9]    David Tunley, *The Bel Canto Violin* (Aldershot, 1999), p. 4.

[10]   Eugene Goossens, *Overture and Beginners* (London, 1951), p. 83.

small orchestras. A good deal of light music was published in versions for salon orchestras (orchestras with a vastly reduced or unusual combination of woodwind and brass, an ensemble largely brought about by the cinema), in addition to the standard orchestral edition. Coates' orchestral work was often issued in standard orchestral format (with extensive cues), as well as for military band, piano solo and occasionally a version for small/salon orchestra.

In the interwar period of the twentieth century, there was a vast change to the cultural climate in Britain as LeMahieu has argued:

> In the late nineteenth and early twentieth centuries, the development of popular national daily newspapers, the cinema, the gramophone, and other forms of mass entertainment threatened to upset traditional patterns of British culture, attracting an audience of unprecedented size, this 'mass' or 'commercial' culture – no single term unambiguously defines the phenomenon – was created for profit, dependent upon new technologies, and often dominated by individuals outside the mainstream of British cultural life. Writers, artists, musicians, critics, and their numerous sympathizers responded in a variety of ways. Some retreated into self-conscious isolation from the popular and the profane. Others engaged in detailed polemics against the mass media. Still others embraced new technology and sought to uplift tastes. All these groups struggled against a culture that measured success by popularity rather than aesthetic merit.[11]

During the interwar period, the average working week decreased from fifty-four hours to forty-eight and the average salary, per capita, rose from £1-12-0 in 1913 to £3-10-0 in 1938 – leisure activities were at last within the range of the average man.[12] The early decades of the twentieth century saw a widespread expansion of the press, the extensive adoption of the gramophone; the foundation and phenomenal growth of the BBC; the wide availability of ensembles that performed orchestral music, the twilight of mass sales of sheet music and the foundation of the Performing Right Society (PRS). The 1930s brought the development of what LeMahieu called a 'common culture', a culture shared by all regardless of class.[13]

This was the curious musical world into which Coates emerged as a composer. He may have entered this environment of widespread cultural change with Edwardian musical values, but he consciously and successfully exploited the latest technologies and crazes of the early twentieth century such as the gramophone record, the BBC and the world of dance music. It was his success at exploiting these new media that put him at the forefront of light music, above his competitors.

---

[11]   Dan LeMahieu, *A Culture for Democracy* (Oxford, 1988), pp. 2–3. These changes were also seen, at a more marked level, in popular music of the period.

[12]   James Nott, *Music for the People* (Oxford, 2002), pp. 2–3.

[13]   LeMahieu, p. 227.

# Chapter 2

# A Nottinghamshire Childhood, 1886–1906

Eric Coates was born in the Nottinghamshire town of Hucknall (known as Hucknall Torkard until 1916). Hucknall has had a long and distinguished history dating back to at least the twelfth century, if not well before. The town is situated seven miles northwest of Nottingham in the valley of the River Leen and within easy reach of Newstead Abbey and Sherwood Forest and in close proximity to the counties of Lincolnshire, Derbyshire and Leicestershire. With the advent of the Industrial Revolution, the focus of the town's industry switched from weaving and agriculture to coal mining; the first mines were sunk in the 1860s. Today, the town is famous as the resting place of the poet Lord Byron (who is buried in the parish church) and as the birthplace of Eric Coates.[1]

Coates' father, William Harrison Coates, known as Harrison, was born in June 1851 in Ringwood, Hampshire, where his father, William Thomas Coates, was a draper. Thomas, who originally hailed from Whitchurch in Shropshire, married Emma Harrison in Croydon and lived in Ringwood and Saffron Walden before finally settling in Henley-on-Thames where he became Mayor in 1888.[2] In the late 1860s, Harrison moved to London to study medicine at St. Thomas' Hospital, then in a temporary site whilst the new hospital was built in Lambeth. He qualified as a doctor in 1872, becoming a Member of the Royal College of Surgeons and Licentiate of the Society of Apothecaries. He appears to have commenced his medical career in Saxmundham in Suffolk before moving to Hucknall with his wife Mary, where he was kept busy dealing with the assorted ailments of the large community of miners and colliery accidents. Dr Coates practiced in Hucknall for over forty years and was a well-known and popular figure, known as 't' little doctor' because of his diminutive stature. He retired to Kent until his death in 1935.[3] Outside his busy medical practice, Dr Coates was a highly proficient photographer (whose pictures had graced many local periodicals and books),[4] and a keen breeder of bulldogs. He was also an amateur musician, playing the flute and running St Mary's Church Choir. Coates was always very much in awe of his father and shared his hobby of photography; he became a proficient photographer

---

[1]    Both of these feature in the local heritage trail.

[2]    18/08/1985 Austin Coates to Geoffrey Self. Austin also recalled that his Great-Grandfather was only Mayor of Henley once, not thrice as his father had indicated (Eric Coates, *Suite in Four Movements* (London, 1953), p. 5).

[3]    30/05/1935 *Hucknall Dispatch*. Mary Coates had died in March 1928 aged 77.

[4]    Albert Brecknock, *The Pilgrim Poet: Lord Byron of Newstead* (London: Francis Griffith, 1911). This book has several plates taken by Dr Coates.

himself (the majority of the plates in his autobiography *Suite in Four Movements* were his own photographs).

Coates' mother, Mary Jane Gwyn Coates (née Blower) was born in 1850 in Gwernesney, three miles from Usk in Monmouthshire, where her father, James Blower, was rector of St Michael's Church and an exponent of strict Victorian morals. With a great independence of mind, she left home to become a governess in Herefordshire (the only daughter to leave the household, even after the deaths of their parents in the 1860s). By 1871, Mary was governess to the large family of James Girling (attorney and solicitor) in Tamerton Foliott, Devon. It seems plausible that she later moved with the Girling Family to Suffolk, where she met the young Dr Coates.[5] The two were married on St George's Day 1877 in the market town of Stratford St Andrew. Shortly after their marriage the Coates moved to Hucknall where their first child was born in the following year (Figure 2.1).

Figure 2.1      Dr Harrison and Mrs Mary Coates at Tenter Hill, Hucknall circa
                1920

[5]    There was certainly a James Girling practicing near Saxmundham in the late 1870s. It has not been possible to find positive proof that this was the same James Girling, but it does seem plausible as Girling had his roots in East Anglia.

The Coates eventually had five children Gladys, Gwyn, Meta and Dorothy, with their final child, Eric, descending into the *ménage* on 27 August 1886.[6] Dr and Mrs Coates had originally intended to call their youngest child 'Frank Harrison Coates', but soon changed their minds to 'Eric Francis Harrison Coates'.[7] Within a few years of Coates' arrival the family moved the short distance to a larger house, Tenter Hill, built on the corner of Duke Street and Beardall Street. In many ways, Coates had an idyllic childhood in Hucknall with trips with his father to Southwell and other locations on photographic expeditions. At a young age, he acquired a bicycle and would disappear on expeditions initially with his mother and brother Gwyn, but latterly on his own, as he recalled in 1947:

> I remember how I loved to get away on my own and spend a whole day with no-body knowing where I was, my bicycle, a waterproof cape, sandwiches and a bottle of ginger beer (put up by my mother) and an Ordnance Map borrowed from my father. I wish that all children could spend the kind of life I lived as a child.[8]

The tranquillity of the Coates ménage was interrupted in 1899 when his father, who was always kept busy, was suddenly taken very ill and diagnosed with septic influenza with complications resulting from overwork and was prescribed several months' complete rest.[9] It took Dr Coates nine months to recover followed by a six-week family holiday to Barmouth. This illness must have put considerable strain on family resources with the cost of paying a locum and the patience involved in coping with an invalid, especially one who had hitherto been so active.

The Coates family was very musical and one of Coates' earliest recollections was listening to his mother, an able pianist, playing the piano and singing downstairs whilst he was trying to go to sleep.[10] Indeed, he chose Chopin's Valse in E minor for his appearance on *Desert Island Discs* in 1951 because of its associations with his mother.[11] From his first sighting of the 'queer-looking black box' of Pen Peyton (a family friend), which contained a violin brought to a family party, Coates wanted to learn the violin.[12] A violin was duly procured from the local music shop, run by John Munks, and the young Coates made his first tentative steps. After initial study with a local teacher, Miss Harrington, he went to be tutored by Georg Ellenberger (a former pupil of the violinist Joseph Joachim)

---

[6]   He was baptised 26 February 1887 at St Mary Magdalene's Church, Hucknall.

[7]   Eric Coates' birth certificate. All the Coates' children bore the middle name of Harrison, a tribute to Harrison's mother, Emma, whose maiden name was Harrison.

[8]   29/05/1947 EC to Eric Morley. *GB-HCKl.*

[9]   Eric Coates, *Suite in Four Movements* (autograph), p. 48.

[10]  1935 *Sunray (The Magazine of Hucknall Carnival)*, p. 6.

[11]  20/06/1951 *Desert Island Discs*, broadcast, BBC Light Programme. *GB-Rwac* Desert Island Discs Scripts.

[12]  Coates, p. 7.

and studied harmony and counterpoint with Ralph Horner in Nottingham.[13]
The young Coates would arrange music for the family orchestra (occasionally
augmented by local musicians), as most of the family played an instrument or
sang. The end result must have sounded bizarre given that the family orchestra
consisted of flute, violins, piano, cello and mandolin![14]

Early musical life was hectic for the adolescent Coates: two violin lessons a
week and a harmony lesson, quartet rehearsal, along with travel to Nottingham
by train, practice time and writing exercises for Horner – in all, six half days a
week – in addition to the normal rigours of a young person's academic work.
He was never educated at a school, but at home with a governess,[15] and music
was always the most important aspect of his education. Dr Horner was adamant
that the youthful Coates should not compose until he had a thorough grasp of
all the rudiments of harmony, counterpoint, canon and fugue. However, Coates
managed to steal a few brief moments during his practice schedule to compose
several pieces including a *Romance* for violin Op 1 and a *Berceuse* for viola Op 2
(he later re-used this opus number for the *Ballad* for String Orchestra), both now
lost. He also had a voracious appetite for music and would not only play through
the piano accompaniments of his violin pieces but also the songs of Grieg and
Schubert and the valses of Strauss and Waldteufel, all borrowed from Nottingham
Public Library. One can detect their influence in his first compositions.

On top of his lessons, he was performing more frequently in public. At the age
of ten he was summoned one evening when a soloist at a concert in Nottingham was
delayed by fog and failed to arrive on time. The composer's son, Austin, recalled
the event: 'would Dr Coates allow Master Eric to help out. Master Eric had in fact
gone to bed; he was awakened, dressed and rushed by train to Nottingham where he
played Svendsen's *Romance* with a calm professionalism that astonished many.'[16]
As Coates progressed with his violin playing he was invited to join Ellenberger's
own string quartet in addition to all his other activities.

Coates came to learn the viola almost by accident: Ellenberger wanted to
perform Brahms' Clarinet Quintet with his own quartet and after disastrous results
with a local cleric playing the clarinet part,[17] Ellenberger found Brahms' edition
for solo viola rather than the usual clarinet: Coates was asked to play the solo part,

---

[13]    Ralph Joseph Horner (1848–1926) was born in Wales and studied in Leipzig. He
moved to Nottingham in 1888 to become Lecturer in Music at the university and conducted
various local music groups. Horner obtained a DMus from the University of Durham in
1898. He emigrated to America in 1906, held a number of posts and remained there until his
death. (www.mhs.mb.ca./docs/people/horner_rj.shtml, accessed 17/12/2009.)

[14]    20/06/1951 Eric Coates in *Desert Island Discs* broadcast, BBC Light Programme.

[15]    18/08/1985 Austin Coates to Geoffrey Self. Austin believed that the governess was
present to teach Coates' two sisters and that Eric joined in. Dr Coates seemed to have no
belief that Eric should attend a school.

[16]    Austin Coates, programme 1.

[17]    See Coates, pp. 39–40 for the full story.

although he had never played the viola before. Playing this instrument opened up many avenues for Coates; it was his passport to many a local orchestra, including several performances under the rising conductor Henry Wood in Nottingham. Mixing so much with adults he began to smoke at a relatively young age, a habit that was to become an important creative stimulus and a lifelong pleasure.[18]

With the frequent invitations to perform as a soloist in concerts and engagements with local orchestras, it was not unnatural for Coates to use these outlets to perform several of his early compositions, most notably a *Ballad* for String Orchestra Op 2, first performed in the Albert Hall, Nottingham in late 1904. The performance received reasonable press notices,[19] but the composer later dismissed it in his autobiography as: 'It was an unambitious, youthful attempt, and it did not come off too badly.'[20] Judging by this aside and the fact that the work appears not to have been performed again in his lifetime (it was recorded in 1991), it seems that Coates grew to dislike the *Ballad*.[21] The piece is a set of eight through-composed variations of an original theme. Though it is essentially monothematic, he splits the theme into two parts (part I, bars 1–4 and part II, 4–8); bars 4–8 bear a resemblance to the theme of Elgar's *'Enigma' Variations*, then much in fashion (see Example 2.1).

Example 2.1  *Ballad* for String Orchestra Op 2, bars 1–8

The *Ballad* has all the hallmarks of his later musical style: sectional form, frequent melodic imitation (even if only for two bars, such as in variations 4 and 5), a well-composed main theme and assured string writing. The work shows a slight predilection for mildly unorthodox harmony, as variations 2 and 3 juxtapose

---

[18]   18/08/1985 Austin Coates to Geoffrey Self. Whoever it was who introduced him to the habit also instilled in him a love of Turkish cigarettes, never Virginian.

[19]   Undated, November–December 1904? *Nottingham Guardian*. (Coates Scrapbook 1).

[20]   Coates, pp. 42–3.

[21]   *The Three Elizabeths Suite* (ASV, CDWHL 2053). There is no evidence of the work being performed during Coates' time as a viola professor at the Royal Academy of Music, though his 'Menuetto on an Old Irish Air' was frequently performed.

C minor onto the tonic of G minor. The *Ballad* already shows the sophisticated levels of invention, particularly regarding melody, in which his mind worked.

As Coates approached his twentieth birthday it was becoming apparent that he could no longer continue his life performing in a host of local amateur ensembles and, given his middle-class background, a career would have to be chosen. Coates had already explored the possibility of becoming an orchestral musician, but to no avail. During the ensuing discussions, he escaped for a contemplative break with the Rev. William Harding (a former curate of Hucknall), a parson in the idyllic village of Churcham, near Gloucester, to consider his options. On his return, a family conference was held and the various options were debated. Coates was adamant that he wanted a career in music, but his father was not convinced, despite all the time and money thus far spent on his son's musical education. Ellenberger suggested Coates study in Germany. This was ruled out as Coates' sister, Gladys, had studied the piano in Berlin for several years and on her return never touched the piano again. William Harding suggested that he read for an arts degree at Cambridge and aim for a career in teaching. Dr Coates was in favour of a career in banking, much to Coates' chagrin.

Matters were further complicated by a visit of the cellist Fred Hodgkinson, fresh out of the Royal Academy of Music (RAM) in London, who urged Dr Coates that the Academy would offer Coates the best start for a career as an orchestral musician. Arthur Richards, a local musician who had conducted the premiere of the *Ballad* and a RAM alumnus also applied pressure.[22] Matters were deliberated on slowly and it was finally decided that Coates should go for an audition at the RAM. If he was accepted, it was under the strict proviso that if he had not made sufficient progress within twelve months he would return back to Hucknall and start work in the bank.

Even though, at this juncture, he was keen to pursue a career as a viola player, Coates had not been neglecting composition and had been assembling a portfolio of compositions, mostly now lost, to take to the RAM. During June 1906, he completed *Three Songs for Mezzo Soprano and Orchestra,* Op 10 with texts by Robert Burns. It is believed that these three songs were written as a 'love token' for a Nottingham singer, Lavinia Inman (known as 'Vinnie' to whom the *Songs* are dedicated) with whom he was briefly infatuated. Coates was a frequent visitor to her home in Edwaldton, cycling over from Hucknall.[23]

The *Three Songs* are a delightful, modest set (lasting no more that five minutes) with a distinctly Scottish feel resulting from their use of the 'scotch snap' and quasi-folk-melodies, such as in the opening of the second song, Example 2.2. This Scottish feel was something that he would later capture in the middle movement of *The Three Elizabeths* Suite. The first two songs are harmonically interesting,

---

[22]   It was Richards who officially recommended him to the RAM for an audition. (January 1895–June 1915 RAM Entrance Register. *GB-Lam*).

[23]   02/04/1999 *Hucknall Dispatch*. I am indebted to Harry Smith for drawing my attention to this.

Example 2.2 'The Winter is Past' (*Three Songs for Mezzo-Soprano and Orchestra*), bars 1–6

featuring modulations to the mediant major in 'The Winter is Past' and the distant key of A major (from the tonic of E♭) in the first song. 'The Bonnie Wee Thing' is set in a $\frac{4}{8}$ metre, quite unusual for that period, rather than $\frac{4}{4}$ and marked the start of Coates' use of small denomination time signatures presumably to imply a faster pulse. The orchestral accompaniment, modestly scored for a small orchestra, is skilfully written, but features no doubling of the vocal part (something that Coates often favoured in his later ballads).

In September 1906, armed with these *Songs* and his viola he embarked on a journey to London for an audition at the RAM. He was conscious of everything he had learnt from Ellenberger and Horner and of all the musical experience he had gained. This journey would change the course of his musical life and, apart from regular holidays, he would not return to Hucknall nor ever start work in the bank.

# Chapter 3
# The Royal Academy of Music and Beyond, 1906–1910

Arriving at the RAM on the 20 September 1906, aged nineteen, Coates must have approached the hallowed edifice, then in Hanover Square, with a certain amount of trepidation. After performing on the viola, as one of three viola players auditioning that day, he showed the Principal, Alexander Mackenzie (and a popular composer in his lifetime), his *Three Songs for Mezzo Soprano*. According to his autobiography, *Suite in Four Movements*, Coates was flummoxed by the absence of a singer, having to play the vocal part on his viola, while the accompanist played the piano part. Coates' choice of texts endeared him to the Scottish Principal and Mackenzie prophesied: 'But mark my words, young man, ye'll start as a viola player but ye'll end up as a composer.'[1] He was accepted as a student and his father would have to pay the tuition fees as he was not offered a scholarship to study at the Academy.

It must have been a wrench for Coates to leave the bosom of his family in Hucknall and he lodged with a 'pseudo maiden aunt' (a family friend of Coates' mother) in her house on the High Road, Kilburn.[2] The downside of the accommodation was a forty-minute bus ride twice daily. He was undoubtedly homesick for his family and native Nottinghamshire, but soon grew to love London and made it his home, spending a great deal of time walking around the streets of London on his own.

Founded in 1822 in Tenderden Street, Hanover Square, London (where it remained until 1911, when it moved to its current home in Marylebone), the RAM had a long and distinguished history with many famous students, including popular figures such as Arthur Sullivan and Edward German. By 1906, the RAM was a large institution with over 500 students, most of them female, there to complete their education, and was run on different lines from the Royal College of Music (RCM). All students undertook a first study that guaranteed them two half-hour lessons a week as well as the privilege of being present during other pupils' lessons. A second study, when deemed necessary by the Principal, consisted of a weekly lesson of one hour, partly individual and partly in conjunction with other students. Depending on musical proficiency, students also took an hour's tuition in either the theory of music, harmony and counterpoint, or composition. For

---

[1]  Eric Coates, *Suite in Four Movements* (London, 1953), p. 58.
[2]  Ibid., p. 58.

the most proficient musicians there was also four and a half hours of orchestral practice a week in the college orchestra conducted by Mackenzie.[3]

Coates commenced his studies at the RAM in the Michaelmas term 1906, only four days after his audition, studying viola (as his principal study) under Lionel Tertis, piano (second study) under Sam Hartley Braithwaite (who was only three years his senior) and harmony under Frederick Corder.[4] According to Coates, Mackenzie wanted him to study composition as his first study and viola as his second. Corder had been appointed Professor of Composition at the RAM in 1888 and his pupils included Bax, Bantock and Holbrooke. The young Coates was emphatic that he wanted the viola to be his principal study; after all, he would have to earn his living through performing other composers' work – he could not support himself as a freelance composer.[5] (Many of his light music contemporaries had to support themselves as performing musicians before they could earn their living through composition: Haydn Wood as a violin virtuoso and Montague Phillips as an organist.) Coates had the good fortune to become a pupil of Tertis, the foremost viola player of his generation, producing a characteristic powerful tone and a man who single-handedly expanded the viola's repertoire by commissioning many of the foremost composers of the day to write works for the instrument. In his autobiography, Tertis recalled his first encounter with Coates:

> From the moment I heard him at his first lesson, he had the nucleus of a good viola-player even though his efforts were rather crude, and I took an interest in him at once. His demeanour was of a charming, meek nature, but I was soon to learn that his pecuniary circumstances were of slender proportions and I recollect that whenever I was able, I invited him to take lunch with me and saw to it that he had a good nourishing meal, for he always looked so fragile … . However he developed as a viola-player, and he played extremely well, he could have never attained such a level of eminence, and certainly not affluence, if he had got to the top of the tree as a viola soloist.[6]

Throughout his life, Coates retained a great deal of affection for both Tertis and Corder, but not for his piano professor, Braithwaite, who was nicknamed 'Hartley's Marmalade'. He recalled in an omitted passage from his autobiography that after struggling with Matthay Method in lessons: 'we thereupon settled down to playing each other's compositions to one another for the rest of the term. The Report which followed, under the heading of Pianoforte – Second Study, ran: "Has talent, but will not work".'[7]

---

[3]   1906–07 RAM Prospectus. *GB-Lam*.
[4]   RAM Students' Register G: Lent 1906–Michaelmas 1907, p. 371. *GB-Lam*.
[5]   Coates, p. 58.
[6]   Lionel Tertis, *My Viola and I*, (London, 1974), p. 24.
[7]   Eric Coates, *Suite in Four Movements* (autograph), p. 140.

In his harmony lessons with Corder, it is probable that Coates studied composition, having studied harmony and counterpoint from an early age. In accordance with normal pedagogical procedure at the RAM, all students, especially those wishing to pursue composition, had to register initially for the harmony course in order to qualify. The ardent Wagnerian, Corder, produced a very different breed of composer to that generated by the Brahmsian Charles Stanford at the RCM. Bantock, William Wallace and Bax to a certain degree all absorbed elements of Corder's Wagnerian influenced teaching, but Corder's composition pupils of Coates' period, such as Holbrooke, MacCunn, York Bowen and Montague Phillips, all seemed to have a lighter edge in a handful of their compositions. Many, such as Coates, and to a far lesser degree, Phillips, were content to become light composers. Whether this lightness of style has anything to do with Corder's teaching, or was largely inherent in the pupils is impossible to say. At his first lesson with Corder, Coates showed him his *Three Songs*; they impressed his teacher who suggested that he try his hand at something more ambitious such as the first movement of a symphony. Coates replied that he only wanted to specialize in the lighter type of writing.[8] He was indeed highly fortunate that Corder was in agreement and encouraged him in that vein, although by this stage Coates had not written any light music *per se*.

Coates' interest in light music came from the theatre music of the period (such as Gilbert and Sullivan), playing the lighter works of the nineteenth century (such as Grieg). He obviously knew he had a talent for writing in miniature and a gift for melody. This resolve to write light music (to which he almost exclusively adhered) was something that marked him out from the majority of his lighter contemporaries. Light music figures such as Edward German, Albert Ketèlbey, Haydn Wood, Montague Phillips, Robert Farnon and Ernest Tomlinson all tried their hand at larger, more serious canvasses with varying degrees of success. Perhaps parallels could be drawn with Percy Grainger and Roger Quilter who excelled in writing miniatures, often in a lighter vein.

During Coates' time at the RAM, Montague Phillips and Bertram Walton O'Donnell (subsequently conductor of the BBC Military Band) dominated Academy life, winning all the major competitions and prizes. Coates only managed to win, with a string quartet, the Charles Rube Prize for ensemble playing in 1907 and also a bronze medal for viola playing that year.[9] In many respects, Coates' time at the RAM was well-spent, but he did not have a distinguished student career. Nevertheless, he was a frequent performer in student concerts, especially in chamber music, and a stalwart member of the RAM Student Orchestra.

Coates' perilous financial state changed during his second year at the RAM when, in October 1907, on the news that the existing holder of the Viola Orchestral Scholarship was to leave the Academy, Coates applied for, and was awarded the

---

[8]    Coates, p. 62.

[9]    1907 RAM Prize List. *GB-Lam*. He also received an honourable mention for his harmony.

scholarship.[10] This enabled him to continue for at least another year at the RAM, as initially Dr Coates had only agreed to fund Coates' study for a year. Nevertheless, he still had to earn enough money from small engagements to be able to live in London; during this time he recalled that he played in practically all of London's theatre orchestras.[11] His time as student was never dull with numerous escapades that he recalled in his autobiography such as firing a gun in the RAM gentleman's lavatory, the lengths to which he and three other colleagues went to win the Rube Prize and performing as an orchestral deputy in London's theatres. The most humorous anecdote of his time at the RAM was the formation of the Celtic String Quartet whose one and only concert was beset with numerous incidents.[12]

Even though Coates primarily intended to study the viola at the RAM, he spent a good deal of time on composition. There are several surviving works from his years at the RAM, most notably a set of two violin pieces Op 16 dedicated to a fellow student, Mildred Johns. The first of this set, the more successful, is a minor-mode 'Romance' that shows his ability to write a tender, dreamy melody contrasted with a $\frac{6}{8}$ animato passage. This piece shows an effective grasp of harmony and a fondness for modality and frequent use of the relative major. The second, a will-o'-the-wisp 'Scherzo', demonstrates that he was already more than capable of penning an effective 'light miniature'.

He ploughed much of his compositional energies during his second year at the RAM into the writing of songs. He wrote two sets of songs and a free-standing example, all of which were eventually published. The first set, *Two Songs for Baritone and Orchestra*, were first performed at a RAM Student Concert at Queen's Hall in December 1907. These were well received by the *Musical Times* as: 'two effective songs … "Devon to me" is a robust and manly ditty worthy of publication'.[13] Indeed, the *Songs* were published by Booseys the following year and became Coates' first works in print. When they appeared they must have been a notable encouragement to him as he was troubled with neuritis in his left arm, which he termed 'that gnawing ache', which made playing the viola very difficult. Deep down, he knew that his chances of becoming a 'second Lionel Tertis' were evaporating.[14]

Following closely on the heels of the *Two Songs* was 'The Outlaw's Song', also published by Booseys, which was sung at a RAM Concert in June 1908 sung by Carlton Brough. The *Musical Times* praised the song for its 'elements of

---

[10]   November 1906–June 1910 RAM Minutes of Committee, p. 87. *GB-Lam*.

[11]   Coates, p. 92.

[12]   Ibid., pp. 85–6. This incident was used (slightly adapted) in Bruce Montgomery's script for the 1961 film *Raising the Wind* set in a music college. Montgomery recalled that Coates had told him the story when they met an International Musicians' Association gathering. (David Whittle, *Bruce Montgomery/Edmund Crispin* (Aldershot, 2007), p. 158).

[13]   *Musical Times* 49 (1908), p. 31.

[14]   Coates (autograph), p. 274.

popularity', which, with hindsight, shows that he was already becoming associated with the lighter side of composition.[15]

The second set of songs was the *Four Old English Songs*, with their well-known texts taken from Shakespeare, which were the apogee of his years at the RAM. They were started during his final weeks at the RAM and were finally first performed at a RAM Student Concert on 15 December sung by their dedicatee Gertrude Newson and conducted by Alexander Mackenzie. The *Musical Times* praised their sensitivity and the refined nature of his settings.[16]

The *Four Old English Songs* are wistful songs with instant melodic appeal (see the openings of the first and third songs). While not falling under the banner of great music, they are effective and enjoyable settings of well-known texts. Because of the choice of Shakespeare for the text the songs, like a number of those by Roger Quilter, occupied a curious, hybrid position – they were neither ballads nor high-art songs, but instead straddled both categories. Having orchestrated the accompaniments of numerous songs during 1908, Coates had learnt a good deal and the scoring of the set is highly assured. There is little difference between the piano and orchestral accompaniments (unlike the later *Mill o' Dreams*). The final song, 'It was a Lover' is the best orchestrated song of the set with its deft use of pizzicato strings, occasionally echoed with arco phrases, sparing use of woodwind and splashes of percussion.

After the *Songs'* premiere Coates tried to entice a number of professional singers to perform them and even sent a copy to the soprano Agnes Nicholls. Alas, she never sang them because the composer forgot to attach enough stamps to the parcel and she had to pay an excess postage charge to get hold of them. He fared a lot better with Olga Wood (the first wife of Henry Wood) who liked the *Songs* and sang them at the Proms in September 1909. Coates was no doubt overjoyed at their exposure at such a prestigious occasion and they were well-received. The *Musical Times* pointed out: 'They seemed to increase the well-deserved reputation of a clever young English composer whose ambition does not exceed his powers'.[17] The *Songs* proved to be a favourite item at the Proms, featuring in the 1913, 1930 and 1944 seasons. The Woods also recorded the *Four Songs*, with piano accompaniment, for the Gramophone Company in July 1909, making them Coates' first recorded composition.[18] However, his contact with Mrs Wood was short-lived as she died three months after the performance of the *Songs* at the Proms.

Towards the close of the RAM's mid-summer term of 1908, Coates returned home after a day's work at the RAM to find Tertis waiting for him. Tertis invited him to take his place in a forthcoming concert tour of the Hambourg String Quartet to South Africa during June 1908. Coates accepted the offer with alacrity, resigned

---

[15]   *Musical Times* 49 (1908), p. 532.
[16]   *Musical Times* 50 (1909), p. 31.
[17]   Ibid.
[18]   *Four Old English Songs* (Gramophone Company GC2835 & 03162).

his RAM scholarship and left (though officially he remained a 'harmony' pupil of Corder for another term).[19] After a brief eight-day sojourn in Hucknall (where he completed the *Four Old English Songs*) to break the news of his impending South African tour to his parents, the Hambourg Quartet started intensive rehearsals to learn a dozen quartets for the tour. This period of intensive rehearsal aggravated the neuritis in his left hand, especially of the third and fourth fingers, but the Hambourgs recommended he undergo a course of electrical treatment to cure the problem. This invitation transformed him into a professional musician.

Figure 3.1    The Hambourg String Quartet, Capetown 1908. Jan Hambourg, Boris Hambourg, Orry Corjeac and Eric Coates (left to right)

Little record exists of the Hambourg Quartet, but they were founded in April 1907 by Jan (leader) and Boris (cellist) Hambourg, brothers of the pianist Mark, and gave their inaugural recital in London's Bechstein Hall (see Figure 3.1). They quickly became an established quartet, playing much of the standard repertoire. The Quartet came to an unexplained, abrupt end, not long after the end of the five

[19]    One presumes that he stayed on for another term to secure a performance of his *Four Old English Songs* at the RAM Student Concert at the close of 1908. He also had difficulties in paying for this extra term, possibly because he was financing it himself. (November 1906–June 1910 Minutes of Committee, *GB-Lam*).

subscription concerts at the Aeolian Hall in 1909, perhaps because Boris wanted to emigrate to Canada (he become a Canadian citizen in 1910). For the youthful Coates, working with the Quartet meant not only concerts in London, but also national tours with concerts in other urban centres and even tours abroad. It also meant financial stability, with more time to devote to composition and not having to accept every engagement he was offered.

After their successful South African tour (where they performed over 40 concerts in 20 towns),[20] the Quartet returned to England at the end of August and undertook a number of concerts, culminating in a series of five subscription concerts held at London's Aeolian Hall on Saturday afternoons from 28 November. For the first concert the Hambourgs had invited five composers to write a collective suite based on 'Londonderry Air' for the Quartet entitled *Suite for String Quartet*: The opening movement was by Frank Bridge; 'Scherzo' by Hamilton Harty; 'Variations' by J.D. Davies; 'Menuetto on an Old Irish Air' by Coates; and 'Finale' by York Bowen. Coates relished the chance to be associated with such an array of distinguished composers. After a modest success as a composer of ballads, it no doubt came as a welcome opportunity to write a chamber work. Only Bridge's movement received a favourable review by *The Times* and was subsequently published.[21] The Hambourg Quartet played the work again at a concert to mark a visit by the French composer Vincent d'Indy to London in March 1909. Since that date, the *Suite* appears not have been performed in its entirety.

Coates' contribution to the *Suite* was a lively 'Menuetto', in a ternary structure, which transformed 'Londonderry Air' into a $\frac{3}{4}$ time. The A-section is largely paraphrases of the 'Air' in the tonic (E♭ major), but the B-section is more complex with the 'Air' transposed into G minor and is handled in a more fragmented form. The highlight of the 'Menuetto' is the coda (bar 96) where there is a brief passage of imitation between the first violin and viola (Example 3.1).

The 'Menuetto' is an assured piece of quartet writing that creates a variety of textures through its use of double stopping and pizzicato, frequently employed in the cello part, which gives a lightness of texture to the piece.

After the fifth Hambourg Subscription Concert, Coates continued to be associated with the Quartet for several months until they disbanded. In March 1909, he was pleased to hear that he had been awarded, alongside Montague Phillips, the Associateship Diploma of the RAM (as was the usual practice at the time, diplomas were awarded after one had left).[22] He was also associated with the Cathie and Walenn Quartets, but his most important coup was to join the Beecham Symphony Orchestra.

Thomas Beecham, one of the greatest and most colourful conductors in British musical history, founded his new orchestra in 1909 after he had parted company from the New Symphony Orchestra, The Beecham Orchestra made its debut at

---

[20]   Unknown newspaper. (Coates Scrapbook 1).

[21]   30/11/1908 *The Times*.

[22]   November 1906–June 1910 Minutes of Committee, p. 236. *GB-Lam.*

Example 3.1 'Menuetto on an Old Irish Air', bars 96–104

Queen's Hall on 25 January in a series of six concerts.[23] For this new ensemble, Beecham poached players from his former orchestra, the Queen's Hall Orchestra (QHO) and London Symphony Orchestra (LSO), but also included a host of young players drawn from London's musical academies as well as the likes of Tertis (who for the past five years had abandoned orchestral playing), Eugene Cruft and Albert Sammons (who subsequently became leader of the Orchestra); the average age of the ensemble was twenty-five.[24] Coates presumably joined at its inception through the auspices of Tertis – he was sub-principal to his former teacher. The

---

[23]   John Lucas, *Thomas Beecham* (Woodbridge, 2008), pp. 40-41. The series was purloined by Beecham from the New Symphony Orchestra who Beecham thought inferior to his own ensemble.

[24]   Ibid., p. 40.

early months of the ensemble were very much a 'hand to mouth' existence, but included a number of important first performances of works by Vaughan Williams and Delius including the first complete performance of the latter's *Mass of Life*.[25] Beecham accepted a lucrative offer from Ethel Smyth for the Orchestra to perform in the revival of her opera *The Wreckers* during June 1909. During October, the Beecham Orchestra undertook a mammoth and gruelling tour of Britain: twenty-three concerts in twenty-five days including dates in Exeter, Lancashire and Ireland with seventeen performances of Elgar's First Symphony, which grew progressively shorter on each playing.[26] If Coates' and Tertis' memoirs are to be believed, the tour was never dull, with fireworks being let off from their train every time they passed through Preston, and Beecham throwing light bulbs down lift shafts. At Liverpool's Adelphi Hotel Beecham rotated all the shoes and boots that hotel guests had left outside their rooms leaving little time for the problem to be rectified before the hotel-guests departed on the American boat train.[27] The Orchestra even had its own football team, which challenged several northern football teams, though Coates was not part of the team because of his antipathy to sport. During 1910, Coates also followed Beecham into his operatic ventures, playing at Covent Garden in the first English performance of Strauss' *Elektra* (which sowed the seeds for a life-long love of Strauss' music).[28] At some stage, during Beecham's 1910 season of opera at Covent Garden and His Majesty's Theatre, Coates parted company with the Orchestra, as he recalled in his autobiography:

> There is no doubt that the Beecham 'Pill-harmonic', under its high-tension conductor, was a thing which had to be heard to be believed, but I do not think I should have cared to have ended my days under this temperamental musician, for I am sure my nerves would have suffered as a consequence.[29]

Having suffered from neuritis of the left arm for number of years, the electrical treatment Coates had undergone during his months with Hambourg's had improved it, but as a result of the extra playing with the Beecham Orchestra and Cathie Quartet it was proving to be an even greater barrier. He resorted to all sorts of remedies, such as holding his hand under a cold tap, to be able to carry on performing.[30] It also meant that practising was out of the question. Deep down, Coates realized that the composition of ballads would supplement his income and spare him many hours of painful playing.

---

[25]   Ibid., pp. 40 and 44.

[26]   Ibid., pp. 49–50. Elgar's Symphony was performed in full only on the final night.

[27]   See Tertis pp. 31–3 and Coates, pp. 122–25 for further details.

[28]   Beecham had originally wanted to perform *Salome* but it fell foul of the Lord Chamberlain's office. Strauss conducted the sixth and seventh performances of the *Elektra* (Lucas, pp. 53–6).

[29]   Coates, p. 122.

[30]   Ibid., p. 126.

Despite his burgeoning performing schedule and spurred on by the successes of the songs written during his later months at the RAM, Coates started writing large numbers of ballads; he published ten examples in 1909. As Jeffrey Richards has eloquently summed up: 'The heyday of the ballad was probably between the 1880s and 1920s. An examination of ballads from that period reveals the domination of themes of love, loss, dreams, parting, yearning, regret, separation and memory, with a combination of lilting melodies, an elevated sensibility and deeply felt emotion'.[31] Musically, ballads of this period were characterized by: overt sentimentality; both melodically and harmonically; robust melody; piano accompaniment (though the orchestral ballad later became popular); and various devices to please the audience and test the abilities of the singer, such as long held notes. During the early years of the twentieth century composers were drawn towards ballads because of the possibility of a high financial return from a popular ballad as during this period composers earned their money through sheet music sales. (Haydn Wood was reputed to have earned a six-figure royalty through the sales of 'Roses of Picardy'.) Weatherly, one of the most popular writers of ballad lyrics, had a high opinion of ballads and wrote a justification of his approach in 1926:

> People think ballads are easy to sing. As a matter of fact they are the most difficult of all music to render with true effect. The ballad is simple in words, melody and accompaniment. There is nothing to help out the singer. It depends entirely on the power of expression, the intensity and variety of feeling. It is a question of art, interpretation and personality combined.[32]

One of the major problems with writing ballads was obtaining satisfactory lyrics. In Coates' previous successes he had set texts by deceased authors (Shakespeare and Christina Rossetti). He wrote to John Galsworthy, who was beginning to forge a successful career as a novelist, to ask if he could set one of his latest poems (published in *Punch*) to music, 'Devon to Me'.[33] However it became apparent to Coates that if he wanted to succeed in this genre he would have to secure the services of one of the major lyric writers who provided texts to the likes of Stephen Adams, Hermann Löhr and R. Coningsby Clarke.

Spurred on by the performance of his *Four Old English Songs* at the Proms, Coates decided to write to the doyen of ballad lyric writers, F.E. Weatherly. Despite enjoying a successful career as a barrister (taking silk in 1925) Weatherly had forged a successful second career as a writer of ballad texts, scoring successes with 'The Holy City', 'Danny Boy' and later 'Roses of Picardy' (which was

---

[31]   Jeffery Richards, *Imperialism and Music in England 1876–1953* (Manchester, 2001), p. 343.

[32]   Frederic Weatherly, *Piano and Gown* (London, 1926), p. 120.

[33]   *Punch* appears to have been a favourite location for searching for texts. 'The Old Ships' written in 1919 has a text taken from a poem published in *Punch* which is pasted into the front of the manuscript of the song. *GB-Lcm* Box 184.

reputed to have been offered to, and turned down by, Coates before Haydn Wood made his famous setting).[34] In response to Coates' letter, Weatherly invited him to his house and offered him the lyrics to 'Stone-Cracker John', which Coates accepted with eagerness and on his journey home a melody came into his head that he scrawled down on the back of an envelope. The song was published by Booseys (though Coates stated that Arthur Boosey held back publication for a while because he disliked the song's metre)[35] and taken up by Harry Dearth (one of the leading ballad singers of the day) who eventually sang it at a Ballad Concert at London's Albert Hall.[36] It scored an instant success and sold in high numbers (according to Coates it sold nearly 500,000 copies by 1911),[37] being in the style of, but more refined than, 'Devon to Me' and 'The Outlaw's Song'. The song was soon recorded by Dearth. Coates' only child, Austin, captured the excitement of this development from a family perspective:

> Dr Coates in Hucknall, still really rather worried about his son, was telephoned by an excited neighbour. 'Don't say anything Dr Coates,' he shouted, 'just listen'. The neighbour then put his telephone speaker into the mouth of his gramophone, set the needle on the record and thus my grandfather heard his son's first indication of getting somewhere.[38]

Coates struck up a cordial friendship with Weatherly and the two went on to pen some of the most successful ballads of the 1910s and 1920s together including 'Reuben Ranzo', 'A Dinder Courtship' and 'Green Hills o' Somerset'. During these years, Coates used other librettists (including Arthur Conan Doyle for one song in 1919), but his creations with Weatherly stand out amongst his finest songs. Weatherly went so far in his autobiography to name 'Our Little Home' as his own personal favourite song from the circa 3,000 he had written.[39]

Coates' success with ballad compositions during the late-1910s started him off on a parallel career as a composer and a viola player. Despite his success with ballads he was not in a situation, artistically or financially to become a composer, and had to rely on the viola for his income.

---

[34]   12/11/2005 Gilles Gouset to Michael Payne. Initially, the lyric had been set by Herbert Brewer, but had been rejected by a number of publishers, which was why Weatherly tried to entice other composers (Weatherly, p. 282).

[35]   1935 *Sunray (The Magazine of Hucknall Carnival)*, p. 7 and Coates, p. 119.

[36]   Ibid., p. 119.

[37]   Ibid., p. 168.

[38]   Austin Coates, programme 1.

[39]   Weatherly, p. 283.

# Chapter 4

# The Queen's Hall Orchestra and Miss Black, 1910–1918

After the ephemeral nature of the Beecham Symphony Orchestra and the disbandment of the Hambourg Quartet, Coates was looking for more permanent employment. When an opportunity arose to join the Queen's Hall Orchestra (QHO) in 1910, under Henry Wood, a conductor then at the height of his powers and energy, Coates accepted it with alacrity. He quickly rose to the first desk of the violas and subsequently became the principal of the section in 1912 after the resignation of Siegfried Wertheim (who was also Coates' predecessor in the Hambourg Quartet).[1] While he relished the prestige the position entailed, he hated playing the solos involved, especially the notorious solo viola passage in Strauss' *Don Quixote*.[2]

Coates' membership of the QHO proved to be a vital cultural platform for him in terms of his development as a performer and as a composer. It gave him the opportunity to have his orchestral compositions performed. From its completion in 1893 until its destruction on the night of 10 and 11 May 1941, London's Queen's Hall was the epicentre of musical life in the capital. It was not just a hall, but a cultural icon for the nation; it symbolized Britain's sense of musical confidence before and after the First World War. Many important works, especially by native composers, received their first performances in Queen's Hall and the Gramophone Company used the two halls for recording purposes until the completion of their studios at Abbey Road in 1931. In 1895, Robert Newman founded a series of Promenade Concerts under the unknown conductor, Henry Wood and formed the Queen's Hall Orchestra especially for these concerts. Chappells, the music publishers, were the lessees of Queen's Hall (almost from the hall's foundation) and ran the events. From August 1915, they took over the running of the QHO (it then became the New QHO), after the hounding-out of Edgar Speyer.[3] This was no mean investment on the part of Chappells; it cost them £35,000 a year to keep

---

[1]   It is almost impossible to ascertain the exact dates that Coates was in the QHO, as most of the records of the Queen's Hall have not survived and the surviving concert programmes rarely list the orchestra. Coates was certainly Principal Viola by late 1912 (16/11/1912 Queen's Hall Symphony Concert Programme).

[2]   Eric Coates, *Suite in Four Movements* (London, 1953), p. 138.

[3]   Speyer had helped finance the QHO since 1902. With his patronage, Wood could hold more extensive rehearsals and invite more foreign composers over to London than had hitherto been possible. (Arthur Jacobs *Henry J. Wood* (London, 1994), pp. 84–5).

the New QHO afloat during the years of the First World War, compared to the £4,000 it had cost Speyer before the War.[4] In between Speyer's departure and the arrival of Chappells was an anxious time for members of the QHO, not knowing if the Orchestra was to be disbanded.

Henry Wood brought an interesting and unconventional artistic policy to his programmes, especially in the Promenade Concerts. Besides a staple diet of the core orchestral repertoire (including much Russian music), Wood frequently performed new works by living composers, both native and foreign. As Eugene Goossens, who played in the QHO for four years, pointed out, the QHO had a reputation for the excellence of its sight-reading, often getting to grips with a new work in forty minutes.[5] It was a gruelling schedule working at Queen's Hall as Goossens recalled in his autobiography:

> [I] got a first-hand knowledge of practically the entire symphonic repertoire. Under no other conductor could a more thorough and authentic grounding in orchestral repertory have been obtained … . The season of summer Promenade Concerts … gave me my first sample of real orchestral high-jinks. Ten weeks of nightly three-hour symphony concerts, with three rehearsals a week (and Sunday afternoon concerts thrown in for good measure), is a back-breaking – but worthwhile – experience. Needless to add, we covered the whole gamut of the symphonic repertory during those sixty or more concerts, which invariably began punctually at eight and ended at eleven.[6]

Between November 1912 and March 1915 the QHO gave 220 afternoon concerts, 136 evening concerts on Sundays and 57 ballad concerts.[7]

The QHO attracted a number of the leading instrumental virtuosi of the times and during Coates' time with the ensemble it featured such names as Eugene Goossens, Basil Cameron, Rebecca Clarke (born on the same day in 1886 as Coates) and the young John Barbirolli who all went on to forge successful careers as composers and conductors. In addition to Henry Wood, there were regular guest-conductors and composer-conductors and Coates played under Debussy, Saint-Saëns, Strauss, Scriabin and many native composers such as Parry, Stanford, Elgar, Mackenzie, Smyth, German and Walford Davies. There were also frequent premieres of the latest orchestral works and Coates must have taken part in the notorious first performance of Schoenberg's *Five Orchestral Pieces* in 1912, and

---

[4]    Edgar Speyer quoted in ibid., p. 165.
[5]    03/09/1944 *New York Times*, quoted in David Lamborn, 'Henry Wood and Schoenberg', *The Musical Times* 128 (1987), p. 422.
[6]    Eugene Goossens, *Overture and Beginners*, (London, 1951), pp. 90 and 92.
[7]    William Boosey, *Fifty Years of Music*, (London, 1931), p. 106.

Frank Bridge's *The Sea* in 1915 and the British premiere of Mahler's Seventh Symphony in 1913.[8]

Wood also believed in performing compositions by his own orchestral players,[9] and Coates' first orchestral piece, *Miniature Suite,* was first performed during the 1911 season of Promenade Concerts. Working at Queen's Hall, Coates was able to secure performances of his work by the QHO in their Sunday Concerts and also by the New Queen's Hall Light Orchestra (founded in 1916, with Alick Maclean as conductor) performing at Chappells' Ballad Concerts. It is perhaps inevitable that Coates should have had his music published by Chappells, as his orchestral music was often performed by Chappells' orchestras at Chappells' concerts.[10] As Jacobs has pointed out, Chappells were quite ruthless in promoting their music (especially their ballads, which were often performed in the Promenade Concerts) and pianos, all advertised in the programme complete with their prices.[11]

In addition to his work with the QHO, Coates was also in frequent demand as a viola player with other orchestras and during this decade he would be seen playing in the Royal Philharmonic Society concerts until 1914.[12] With the Royal Philharmonic Society Orchestra he played in the premiere of Elgar's Second Symphony on 24 May 1911.[13] He took part in several of the landmark series of Balfour Gardiner concerts at Queen's Hall (funded by Gardiner) during 1912–1913, which included important premieres of works by Bax, Grainger and Holst. He also took part in a concert of music by the modernist composer Bernard Van Dieren at Wigmore Hall on 20 February 1917 with an audience full of the greatest musical luminaries of London. However, Coates and his viola colleague managed to get lost, but Coates continued to play the final bar continually; he was still playing the final bar when the conductor drew his attention to the fact that the work was over.[14]

The year following his entry into the QHO, Coates' life was to change immeasurably as a result of his infatuation with a female student at the RAM. Judging by the number of pieces written in his youth that were dedicated to ladies,

---

[8]    It is often difficult to pin down exactly who was playing in which concert for two major reasons: first, members of the orchestra were not usually listed on the programmes and, second, the 'deputy system' was rife in London orchestras.

[9]    Henry Wood, *My Life of Music* (London, 1938), p. 79.

[10]    There is no documentary evidence to support this argument, but they certainly played a large part in Coates' early composition career.

[11]    Jacobs, p. 153.

[12]    Cyril Ehrlich, *First Philharmonic* (Oxford, 1995), p. 189. There is little evidence that Coates ever appeared as a soloist in concertos. He infrequently appeared as a soloist in chamber music recitals.

[13]    14/05/1911 Programme of RPS Concert. The programme states that Coates played the viola in the symphony's premiere under the composer. The first performance of Granville Bantock's *Dante and Beatrice* was also given that night.

[14]    Coates, pp.127–8.

Coates appears to have been a ladies man but with limited success. However, on 4 March 1911, a friend encouraged Coates to accompany him to a RAM student concert. Coates was transfixed by an almost seventeen-year-old girl, Phyllis Black, who was performing several recitations, including Tennyson's 'The Mermaid' (see Figure 4.1). It was love at first sight and Coates was besotted. Not one to be easily deterred, Coates went off in pursuit of Phyllis (always known as 'Phyl') the following week with the offer of writing several recitations for speaker and piano. The first was, not surprisingly, a setting of *The Mermaid*. Despite an eight-year age gap, they entered a whirlwind romance.[15] Recollecting his aunt, Phyl's nephew recalled her huge blue eyes, her wonderful sense of humour and the fact that she was always laughing.[16]

Figure 4.1    Miss Phyllis Black, circa 1922. Phyl wrote on the back of this photograph: 'This doleful looking creature is me – when on the stage in the early 20's'

[15]    During this period, Coates wrote six recitations that the two of them performed at various concerts in London. In addition to these pieces, he would perform several viola solos, accompany Phyl on the piano and Phyl would deliver a number of poems.

[16]    Conversation with Francis Freeman, 03/08/2009.

The Black family had lived in a succession of rented houses in North London, often spending the summer in France, where Phyl's artist father had spent a great deal of his early life. They were a family similar to Coates', with five children, each of them artistic in their own way. Phyl's artist father, Francis Black, was a colourful character and Principal of the Camden School of Art. He was a great believer in the state sponsorship of education.[17] Phyl's mother, Anna (known as Annie), had been a pupil of Corder at the RAM when George Macfarren was Principal. Phyl was the fourth of five children and was born on 11 March 1894. After her schooling she entered the RAM in the Michaelmas term of 1910 where her first study was piano (she always professed to be an appalling pianist) and her second was elocution. She left the Academy after two years of study.[18]

It soon became apparent to Eric and Phyl that they wished to be married. However, Phyl's parents were adamantly opposed to the pair marrying after such a short period of acquaintanceship. Phyl's mother wrote to Coates' mother trying to gain her assistance in the matter:

> As she is so young + not "out" in the strict sense of the word, my husband + I could not agree to an engagement at the present. We therefore bound them to wait at least twelve months during which they would get to know each other better.
>
> Eric is very impulsive and we should like a more tried acquaintance before the more serious step is taken.
>
> Please do not think that we do not like Eric. It is simply that we would have been much happier if Phyllis been of an age to know her feelings better. It is so easy to mistake infatuation for love.[19]

The pair continued their clandestine relationship interspersed with occasional 'parental battles' with the Black family, quite ironic given their bohemian nature. The Coates family seemed to be more relaxed about the situation, being distanced from the entanglement. It is believed that Coates wrote his *Evening Doxology* to endear himself to the Black family, staunch members of their local Swedenborgian Church, which would explain the unorthodox choice of text.[20] Phyl's parents

---

[17]  Ibid. Black repeatedly tried to interest the government in funding the Camden School of Art, which London County Council subsequently did. The Camden School of Art took a case to Court in 1899 (Regina vs. Cockerton), reaching the House of Lords. See 06/02/1901 *The Times* 'Ratepayers and the School Board: Costs of Successful Litigation'.

[18]  RAM Student Record 1911–1912. *GB-Lam*. Phyl won a bronze medal for both subjects during her time at the RAM and won a silver medal for elocution.

[19]  Undated (circa 1911) Annie Black to Mary Coates. This letter contained a good deal of crossing out, mostly illegible, which has been omitted here.

[20]  Geoffrey Self, *In Town Tonight* (London, 1986), p. 26. It seems odd that Coates wrote his first religious piece during this period; when he was living in Hucknall, he may

eventually allowed the pair to become engaged in 1912, when Phyl was 18 and Coates was 26.

Relations became strained again at the beginning of 1913 when Phyl's parents took her to their *gîte* in France to escape the attentions of Coates. Almost immediately Coates set off for France to try to keep their engagement alive.[21] In the end Phyl resorted to a desperate and underhand measure, informing her mother: 'You know, Mother, if you do not let us be married now, *one* day you will go up to my room to find that the bed has not been slept in'![22] Phyl's parents capitulated and the pair were given permission to be married.

Eric and Phyllis were finally married on 3 February 1913 at the New Jerusalem Church, Camden Road, London with Phyl's parents acting as witnesses.[23] They moved into Douglas Mansions, a little way out of London's West End where their early married life was chaotic until they established a routine and obtained all the necessary accoutrements to live together. The Coates remained exceptionally close throughout their lives, practically lived in each other's pockets and were devoted to each other. Even after the arrival of their only child they sent him to boarding school at a very early age so that they could remain together. A friend informed Phyl shortly after Coates' death: 'he mentioned that he had celebrated his wedding anniversary by spending the entire evening alone with you, and he wondered how many men who had been married as long as he had would be content to do so'![24]

Phyl was Coates' muse and he often regarded his creative collaborations with her as his finest artistic achievements.[25] He recalled in his autobiography:

> I don't mind settling down to orchestration or some such work which has already been completed in sketch-form, providing I know that it will not be long before Phyl is with me again, but to continue working in solitude usually ends in a state of restlessness which makes any sort of concentration out of the question.[26]

During 1911–13, Coates dedicated almost all his compositions to her, including the romantic 'Intermezzo' in his first orchestral piece.

Shortly after his first meeting with Phyl, Coates started work on an orchestral piece. Indeed, she may have been the inspiration for him turning to an orchestral canvas, trying to prove his mettle as composer. It seems amazing that he had not attempted orchestral works in his student days. According to Coates' autobiography it was Henry Wood who suggested that Coates should write a work for the 1911

---

well have had his father's choir at his disposal.

[21]    Coates, pp. 169–72.

[22]    Ibid., p. 171.

[23]    Coates' Marriage Certificate.

[24]    31/12/1957 PRS to Phyllis Coates. *GB-Lprs*.

[25]    Coates, p. 217.

[26]    Eric Coates, *Suite in Four Movements* (autograph), p. 424.

Proms.[27] Wood must have been convinced by Coates' abilities as a composer to write an orchestral work for such an occasion. Coates decided on a suite of three thematically unconnected movements. Intriguingly, he wrote the concluding valse first (writing valses came easily) completed on 20 August, followed by the 'Children's Dance' and finally the middle movement (dedicated to Phyl) finished on 3 September. One wonders if he chose to include a valse knowing Wood's penchant for 'valse rhythms'.[28] (Figure 4.2)

Figure 4.2      The young composer, Eric Coates, at Tenter Hill during the 1910s

Coates approached the scoring of the Suite with trepidation, choosing a small chamber orchestra, eschewing brass with the exception of two horns, despite the fact that the work would be premiered by a large symphony orchestra. When Booseys published the work, they issued two versions, Coates' original scoring and, later, an expanded orchestration by Percy Fletcher, including two trumpets, three trombones, euphonium, and with an expanded array of percussion instruments.

Coates dedicated the suite to Henry Wood and his orchestral colleagues at the Queen's Hall, and the *Miniature Suite* was first performed by its dedicatees at the Promenade Concerts, with the composer playing amongst the violas. The Suite received an ovation and 'Scène du Bal' had to be repeated.[29] The *Musical Times* reported:

---

[27]    Coates, p. 168.

[28]    Wood, p. 106.

[29]    05/07/1940 EC to Stanford Robinson. *GB-Rwac*.

Mr Coates has previously shown a leaning to toward the light and delicate and 'popular,' but he has never indulged it more decisively and effectively than in this work. The ideas and scoring were full of charm and originality was precluded by the adoption of an idiom that has been exhausted by Johan Strauss and Edward German. As restaurant and theatre entr'acte music, Mr Coates's Suite is equal to the best.[30]

The *Miniature Suite* shows Coates' obvious ability to compose excellent and memorable melodies and his assured grasp of orchestration. Like Ottorino Respighi, a fellow viola player, he learnt the art of orchestration from the heart of the orchestra. The opening 'Children's Dance' is in an expanded binary structure with three key themes. The 'Intermezzo' shows a through-composed monothematic structure, with a violin solo repeated and extended into a romantic climax before subsiding into a hushed coda.[31] The Valse, which shows a clear debt to the valses of Tchaikovsky, is in a varied rondo form (Introduction–A–B–Introduction–A'–C–Bridge–A–D–Coda), but with a good deal of direct repetition of material. The coda, letter J, features Coates' most daring and most exciting passage in the Suite with sudden shifts to the flattened submediant with a gradual accelerando, before an ascending pizzicato arpeggio leads to an 'altered' plagal cadence.

Within the *Miniature Suite*, one can see the traits of orchestration that would become hallmarks of Coates' handling of the orchestra, such as frequent doublings of instruments, doubling the melody on the first violin with the cello, divided strings and the frequent use of pizzicato strings (especially in the cello, as in the opening of the 'Children's Dance'). Nevertheless, the composer does not adopt the structure of each movement of this Suite for his later attempts in the genre. He does, however, use the three-movement structure of a pastoral $\frac{6}{8}$ opening movement, a slow, reflective middle movement and a concluding valse for a number of suites written during the 1920s and 1930s.

However, the *Miniature Suite* does utilize several key ideas that do not often recur in Coates' writing, such as the large use of material in thirds in the latter two movements. The Valse also features a large amount of direct repetition of material; in the direct repeat of the opening until letter B at letter C, the orchestration is not even altered (though the final bar, before letter D, is slightly changed). In his later Suites, he tends to use more material and when sections are repeated they tend to be thematically altered, clothed in different orchestral colours and he never directly repeats passages so close to their original statement. The Suite is a successful and enjoyable work that does not exceed its modest resources and never outlasts its ideas. It gave Coates the confidence to tackle more works for orchestra, when his schedule permitted, and it gave his reputation as a composer an immense boost.

---

[30]   November 1911 *Musical Times*, p. 730.

[31]   The autograph score clearly shows that it was always a violin solo, not a viola solo that was re-written. *GB-Lbh*.

Coates had long held a desire to become an orchestral composer (something the foundation of the PRS in 1914 enabled him to do) and even when composing songs wrote them out on orchestral scoring paper (much to the chagrin of William Boosey, head of Chappells).[32] His approach to orchestration appears to have been largely self-taught. He held strong views that a composer ought to tackle the orchestration of a score himself. After the composition of a piece, usually in short score (the only surviving short score is the manuscript for *Men of Trent*, which shows that he thought on four lines, hinting at the orchestral scoring),[33] he would then turn to orchestration, for him a lengthy process, but one that could be executed in the noisiest of conditions.

In 1934 while discussing his music with a journalist from the *Nottingham Guardian* he expressed his views on orchestration: 'First ... I try to put in a small part for each player. Having performed in orchestras myself, I realise how much more interesting it becomes for the members if they have each have their own little bit. They play the uninteresting parts then with much more pleasure and vigour.'[34] Coates used to say that, in his early days, he had to play so many dull viola parts that he made up his mind that every instrument – including the Cinderella of the orchestra, the viola – should have an interesting part, and that's what makes his orchestrations so colourful.[35]

One can detect influences of the colourful scores of Tchaikovsky, composers of the French Ballet school, hints of the contemporary English composers such as Sullivan, German, Elgar, et al., and his experiences playing in theatre orchestras. From the 1920s, Coates' orchestral scores took on an element of lightness in orchestration, and the orchestral effects in *The Three Bears* and *Cinderella* have a delicacy more redolent of French pointillism, which was occasionally commented on in the press at the time – he was often styled 'the Peter Pan of music'.[36] The conductor Dan Godfrey wrote in his autobiography published in 1924 that Coates 'has a notable lightness of touch and orchestrates his music with quite uncommon skill and fancy. A little more originality in his melody would give him a still higher place, but his music is very popular with our less serious audiences ...'.[37] Other composers of light music of the period, notably Haydn Wood, Montague Phillips and Albert Ketèlbey were effective orchestrators, but none managed to inject the atmosphere of lightness and slickness that Coates imparted to his scores. It was Coates' skills of orchestration that made him one of the finest twentieth-century light-music composers.

---

[32]    Coates, pp. 179–80.

[33]    *GB-Lcm* Box 181.

[34]    29/06/1934 *Nottingham Guardian*.

[35]    Teddy Holmes in Ian Lace, 'Foreword', in Eric Coates, *Suite in Four Movements* (London, 1986), p. viii.

[36]    16/11/1925 *Morning Post*.

[37]    Dan Godfrey, *Memories and Music* (London, 1924), p. 153.

Coates usually scored for double woodwind, either two or four horns, a full brass section of two trumpets and three trombones (the majority of his orchestral music is scored for three trombones). Throughout the 1910s, he responded to the orchestral fashions and standard use of instruments of the period, and included parts for euphonium and cornets instead of trumpets; he was later disparaging about the tone of the cornet.[38] During the 1920s, when he was writing works for coastal orchestras, he often scaled down the woodwind as follows; two flutes and clarinets and one oboe and bassoon, as in the phantasies. This is viewed today as the typical 'light music' combination. No doubt his orchestration was, in part, governed by the size of the country's numerous light orchestras, but also the two standard orchestrations used by Chappells in their orchestral music, especially those pieces that were distributed as part of the various orchestral clubs run by them.

As far as Coates was concerned, he knew the limitations of writing light music, and only in *The Enchanted Garden* did he call for instrumentation beyond the majority of modest orchestras. Many of the pieces are scored so depleted orchestras could perform them with certain instruments marked 'ad lib' and frequent cueing of instruments in the parts. By the 1940s, probably because of orchestral fashions, he began to score for a larger brass section including three trumpets (to obtain triadic fanfares) and the inclusion of the tuba (for pedal points), a notable and worthwhile addition in the later marches.

Coates' scores are often marked by his frequent doublings of instruments, often at the interval of two octaves, though not to the extent of Tchaikovsky and Liszt. This doubling of instruments is best seen in his writing for strings, where rather than use both sets of violins at the top of the orchestral texture, he favours doubling the first violin with the cello (often at an interval of two octaves) as at figure 2 in *Sweet Seventeen,* or the first violin with a high viola (written in the treble clef) such as figure 9 in *Rhodesia March* and figure 20 in 'Rhythm' (*Four Centuries* Suite). Occasionally, in his slower pieces, he treats the strings (except the double bass, which usually supplies the bass, either arco or pizzicato) as a group and places the group with the melody; the lower strings are often at the extremities of their register, with the woodwind providing a countermelody and the brass providing the harmony. The effect can be ethereal as in the close of *By the Sleepy Lagoon*, from figure 6 until the end where the intensity of the high cellos and violas, serenely accompanied by muted brass, conjures up the mythical and soporific paradise of the lagoon, an effect also used in *Summer Afternoon.*

Whilst undoubtedly influenced by the pizzicato bass of the dance band, Coates makes frequent use of the double bass providing the important bass note at the beginning of the bar. This is often played pizzicato, alternating with passages played arco separated by a rest, giving a firm sound, though often doubled by the cellos and bassoon(s). This technique gives his scores their delicacy and the effect is also quite telling within a recording studio.

[38]    10/10/1956 EC to John Lowe. *GB-Rwac*.

In scoring for percussion, Coates usually called for a small section of instruments played by two players. Several of the entr'actes only require one percussionist; *London Calling* March and *The Unknown Singer* dispense with timpani altogether. To inject lightness into the ensemble, he frequently calls for 'bright' percussion instruments such as triangle and glockenspiel (usually marked 'with wooden hammers') or vibraphone to add the necessary brightness. At times, these instruments can give his scores a saccharine sound if listened to constantly, but the effect is often quite luminescent.

By the 1930s, he had begun to write for a more emancipated and expanded percussion section, particularly with the frequent inclusion of the vibraphone in the majority of his orchestral scores written between 1934 and 1941, commencing with *The Three Men* Suite. This was undoubtedly due to its links with the dance band and the effects it could create. Coates was one of the earliest composers to adopt the vibraphone into 'western art' music; the instrument had been adopted by the dance bands from the late 1920s and been used by Havergal Brian and Milhaud. The vibraphone was frequently used in recording sessions in the 1930s and 1940s as an alternative to the glockenspiel, often displacing this instrument in works that called for it.

Even though the orchestra was Coates' métier, composition was a welcome boost to his income as viola player, and he was forced to write commercial music such as ballads, resulting in a steady stream throughout the 1910s. Unlike Haydn Wood and Montague Phillips, who were drawn into ballad-writing to provide songs for their wives (both professional singers), Coates no doubt drifted into this market because it was easier, quicker and more lucrative than orchestral music. During 1911, he published six ballads (mostly with Booseys) including the popular and robust 'Reuben Ranzo'. One ballad, 'Bird's Lullaby', featured a lyric penned by the composer himself (his only song text); he was not the only light-music composer to turn his hand to this; Ketèlbey wrote the lyrics to his song 'Keep Your Toys, Laddie Boy'. He also found time to write a set of six piano pieces for the amateur market, the *Six Short Pieces* (*Without Octaves*).[39] The French titles to several movements show an influence of Tchaikovsky, as too does some of the melodic writing. The French titles were to remain throughout his career in the spelling of waltz and elegy as 'valse' and 'elegie', perhaps because he wanted to recreate the French legerdemain touch rather than embracing German didacticism.

The following year, 1912, Coates composed two short instrumental compositions, *Entr'acte à la Gavotte* and the graceful dance *The Mermaid* (perhaps inspired by Tennyson's poem – a favourite of Eric and Phyl). Both were probably conceived for piano (and dedicated to Phyl) and published initially for piano, but he did orchestrate the *Gavotte*. H.M. Higgs orchestrated *The Mermaid* several years later and there was also and arrangement for military band. The vast

---

[39]   An unusual, but practical title, presumably because he seldom writes any passages in octaves (mostly contained in the final two pieces of the set). Ketèlbey had published his *Six Original Pieces without Octaves* for piano circa 1905.

majority of his output was arranged for military band by important figures such as Dan Godfrey and William Duthoit (who undertook all arrangements from 1937). These two miniatures were written along the lines of entr'actes from operas, such as those of Wolf-Ferrari (who is now exclusively remembered for his entr'actes rather than his operas), and these two vignettes paved the way for Coates to write a good deal of shorter pieces throughout his life.

Both the *Gavotte* and *The Mermaid* were conceived in a similar form: Introduction–A–B–A–C–D–A–(B)–Coda, though the latter reprised the Introduction before the final return of its A-section and did not recapitulate the B-section. The *Gavotte* has a great melodic charm through its quasi-neoclassical feel in the outer sections and use of the mixolydian mode in the trio.

Given the success of the *Miniature Suite*, it is surprising that Coates had to wait two years before writing another work for the Promenade Concerts. During the 1910s, Coates was not the only light-music composer of his generation to feature in the Proms; Haydn Wood and Montague Phillips also had works presented there. The Proms became an important festival for showcasing Coates' orchestral works and songs, and a number of works between 1909 and 1926 received their first performance there. Table 4.1 shows the number of performances Coates received at the Proms, though most of these were concentrated into the 1910s and 1920s.

Table 4.1     List of works by Eric Coates performed at the Promenade Concerts 1909–1956

| Genre | Number of performances | Conducted by Coates | Conducted by others | Premieres |
|---|---|---|---|---|
| Orchestral | 23 | 19 | 4 | 4 |
| Songs with orchestra | 9 | 1 | 8 | 1 |
| Songs with piano | 77 | n/a | n/a | 8 |
| Total | 109 | 20 | 12 | 13 |

Coates' second orchestral work written for the Proms, entitled *Idyll*, was first performed under Wood's direction on 14 October 1913 and was subsequently published by Chappells, the first of Coates' orchestral works to be published by them. What marks the *Idyll* out in his canon is that it is in essence a 'serious' work, albeit tinged with lighter moments (cf. letter D). There is a great debt to Elgar's salon pieces, especially in the variety of countermelodies employed.

The *Idyll* was well-received in the *Musical Times*, though it cast aspersions on the orchestration:

> [it] gave evident pleasure to the large audience. In this, as in the other works already heard, the composer shows himself able to write music which is light, yet refined and musicianly. While one generally knows what is coming next, it

is so pleasant that one does not complain. The effect of the full orchestra for the climax left one with the impression Mr Coates had given them something to do merely because they were on the spot. The music is not such as to demand such resources.[40]

The piece is cast in ternary form with a short bridge passage (letter H, which also recalls the opening introduction) linking the end of the B-section with the reprise of the A-section. The structure is confidently handled with the A-section having three key themes (introduced at letters A, B and C; the opening of the latter is almost an inversion of B) and the B-section one theme (first heard at letter D). The B-section theme is only two bars long and with it Coates introduces a delightful array of effects (through variation of ideas and melodic development), subtle changes of key – usually a third apart – and orchestral effects, especially the flute arpeggios at letter D.

Through his slowly increasing catalogue of work, Coates was beginning to supplement his income as an orchestral musician with royalties from the sale of his sheet music, but like other composers without a private income, the formation of the PRS in 1914 was nothing short of a revolution. It came at the onset of Coates' career as a professional composer and he was one of the first generation of British composers who could reap significant financial benefits from their membership of this august body. The PRS may well have been his fillip to turn to composition as a career knowing he could support his family.[41] Through the PRS, Coates no longer had to rely on the one-off payments and royalty collections from his publishers. The formation of the PRS brought about a radical change in the financial aspirations of composers; they could earn a living by composing orchestral works that, in the past, had proved to be very much a labour of love. As Cyril Ehrlich has noted about the membership of the PRS, 'the composers and authors were, thus, mostly representative of the music-hall and a type of light music at which the English then excelled'.[42] The initial PRS board had a strong light music contingent, including Lionel Monckton (the first Vice-Chairman), Charles Ancliffe and Herman Finck.[43]

Coates was one of the earliest members of the PRS, though not, as some sources suggest, a founder member.[44] He joined the Society in the 'second wave' of membership on 3 May 1914 as member 125.[45] Writing in the 1950s, Coates explained that his initial motive for joining the Society was a suggestion (which was more in the nature of an order) from William Boosey.[46] However, it was not a trouble-free journey: early in 1915 Coates reached a *crise de nerfs* over

---

[40]   November 1913 *Musical Times*, p. 746.

[41]   Coates, p. 182.

[42]   Cyril Ehrlich, *Harmonious Alliance* (Oxford, 1989), p. 17.

[43]   Coates, pp. 16–17.

[44]   Self, p. 30.

[45]   Contract. *GB-Lprs*.

[46]   Coates, p. 180.

his membership of the Society. He remembered: 'what a compensation this sum [his annual royalties] seemed to us when I was receiving almost daily letters from Musical Directors about the country intimating their intentions of cutting my music out of their programmes on account of having associated myself with such an outrageous Trade Union'![47] The level of umbrage was particularly virulent from military band personnel. Coates wrote to Pierre Sarpy (the short-lived PRS Secretary) in January 1915: 'I have decided to resign my Performing Rights [*sic*] Society membership as I find that Artistes will not perform my works if a fee is demanded, therefore it is detrimental to my interests to remain any longer a member.'[48] Sarpy managed to pacify Coates,[49] and by the following month, he had decided to withdraw his resignation.[50] His troubled early relationship with the PRS also suffered another blow over the publication of his latest suite, *From the Countryside*. He had offered the work to Booseys, who accepted it with alacrity after the success of the *Miniature Suite*. However, the publishing house of Boosey was opposed to the PRS, and Arthur Boosey decided that if Coates wished to continue as a member of the PRS he would not publish his new suite but would charge him for the engraving of the plates already produced. This was well beyond the pocket of the impecunious composer and it was only through the *savoir faire* of William Boosey of Chappells that the work was eventually published. William Boosey brokered a deal with the firm of Hawkes (then independent of Booseys and not on cordial terms with their rivals), that they would take over the publication of the work from Booseys and presumably pay for all of the plates thus far engraved. Hawkes eventually issued the Suite in 1915. It is, however, a mystery why Chappells did not publish the *From the Countryside* given the fact that they had recently issued his orchestral *Idyll* and a number of ballads.

Notwithstanding these crises, Coates remained loyal to the PRS and in 1917 received his first royalty cheque for £50,[51] a welcome boost to his income from publishers' royalties, teaching and viola playing. From this juncture, his career went from strength to strength, as did his income from the Society, though it was a number of years before he was amongst the highest earners of the PRS, as can be seen from Table 4.2.

During the summer of 1914, the Coates were holidaying in Barmouth, Wales with 'ten thousand lads and lasses from Lancashire' before the start of the Promenade season, when war was announced.[52] They hurried back to London to find the Promenades cancelled, along with a good number of other concerts and, with the evaporation of Coates' income, soon found themselves in an impecunious state. They sublet their flat in Douglas Mansions and moved to a cheaper flat in

---

[47]   03/06/1945 EC to H.L. Walters. *GB-Lprs*.

[48]   20/01/1915 EC to Pierre Sarpy. *GB-Lprs*.

[49]   21/01/1915 Pierre Sarpy to EC. *GB-Lprs*.

[50]   03/02/1915 EC to PRS. *GB-Lprs*.

[51]   Coates, p. 181.

[52]   Coates, p. 177.

Table 4.2        Comparison of the PRS incomes of Eric Coates, Haydn Wood and Albert Ketèlbey, 1914–1923

| Year | Coates' royalties | Haydn Wood's royalties | Albert Ketèlbey's royalties | Highest earners |
|------|------|------|------|------|
| 1914–17 | £50-0-0 | £75-0-0 | n/a | Lionel Monckton (£150) |
| 1917–18 | £35-0-0 | £150-0-0 | n/a | n/a |
| 1918–19 | £42-10-0 | £157-10-4 | n/a | Nat D. Ayers (£285-7-7) H. Fraser Simpson (£227-10-0) James W. Tate (£277-6-2) |
| 1919–20 | £75-7-2 | £242-13-6 | £50-0-0 | Hermann Löhr (£224-11-8) H. Fraser Simpson (£220-3-9) Haydn Wood (£242-13-6) |
| 1920–21 | £95-1-4 | £256-8-8 | £95-2-10 | Mrs Coleridge-Taylor (£250-9-5) Hermann Löhr (£255-4-6) Haydn Wood (£256-8-8) |
| 1921–22 | £130-2-7 | £201-14-10 | £131-8-11 | Mrs Coleridge-Taylor (£260-8-11) Edward German (£257-5-6) Hermann Löhr (£259-4-6) |
| 1922–23 | £140-15-5 | £227-8-4 | £151-15-1 | Mrs Coleridge-Taylor (£276-10-2) Edward German (£272-0-9) Hermann Löhr (£274-11-11) |

*Source*: Assembled from 1914–1923 Statement of Apportionments. *GB-Lprs*. Ketèlbey did not join the Society until 1918.

Belsize Road in Hampstead. However, it was not long before the value of the arts was recognized and regular concerts resumed. Conscription to the armed services was not compulsory until the 1916 Military Services Act when the steady stream of volunteers dried up, but despite being of 'call-up' age, Coates was deemed unfit for military service (due to his fragile health). Unlike Vaughan Williams and Marcel Dupré, who volunteered for medical duties, Coates remained as a civilian and continued his musical career in London. There appears to have been no animosity towards Coates and his music (as there was to Percy Grainger who fled to America on the outbreak of the First World War). With the gradual disappearance of musicians into the armed forces and the discrimination against German and Austro-Hungarian musicians, Coates was in greater demand. The performance standard and repertoire of the QHO dropped as more personnel left, there was a clamp down on Wood's thirst for new European orchestral music and the regular visits of foreign soloists almost dried up.[53]

---

[53]   Leanne Langley, 'Building an Orchestra, Creating an Audience', in Jenny Doctor & David Wright, *The Proms* (London, 2007), pp. 50 and 52, and Jacobs, p. 154.

One vacancy resulting from the First World Ward was at the RAM, where Coates was invited during 1915 to become a viola professor while James Lockyer was in the Army Service Corps.[54] Whilst his heart was never in pedagogy, the position gave him an opportunity to promote his compositions at the RAM concerts. During his years as a professor, a number of his songs featured at concerts and also his *Menuetto* based on 'Londonderry Air' was played in both its quartet form and in an arrangement for string orchestra (presumably made by Coates) during 1916–19. He also wrote a setting of 'Sigh No More, Ladies' for an RAM production of *Much Ado About Nothing* in 1916. Coates stayed on the RAM's professorial staff until 1922, though it is not clear how much viola teaching he did during the post-war years.[55] He was relieved to be able to relinquish the post.

Despite the onset of war, Coates found time to compose a suite. The idea for the work originated from the conductor Basil Cameron (who became a close friend of Coates whilst he was a violinist in the QHO)[56] who at this stage was in charge of the Torquay Municipal Orchestra prior to joining the army during the First World War in 1915. It is not known when and where the suite received its premiere but it was not until 4 March 1915 that it received its London premiere and even then the first movement had already been heard in the capital.

The *From the Countryside* Suite marked an increase in sophistication from the *Miniature Suite* in structure, construction and orchestration, though it is more uneven than its predecessor. This time, Coates included a full brass section (two cornets and three trombones) and a harp. It is also more pictorial than the *Miniature Suite*; each movement is prefaced by a quotation from Milton's *L'Allegro*. This reliance on pictorial titles was to become a hallmark of Coates' style, as very few of his pieces are totally abstract. *From the Countryside* was his first work of many to focus on pastoral scenes (*Summer Days*, *From Meadow to Mayfair* and *Springtime* Suites and several shorter pieces). He no doubt chose pastoral themes because they were easy to depict musically.

In *From the Countryside* there is again a great debt to Edward German, a fact highlighted by the performance of the Suite at the 1916 Proms when it was programmed alongside the Dances from German's *Henry VIII*. Indeed, when German heard a performance of *From the Countryside* on the radio in 1925 he wrote to his sister complaining that Coates was aping his style: 'Eric Coates is very, very naughty. I heard (wireless) the other night a Suite of his called *From the Countryside* – well, well, well! I'll say no more – simply naughty boy!!'[57]

---

[54]　November 1915 *RAM Club Newsletter*.

[55]　From 1915 Coates' name featured amongst the members of RAM teaching staff in the RAM Prospectus. His name was finally omitted from the list in the 1921–22 RAM Prospectus.

[56]　Coates, p. 146.

[57]　18/01/1925 Edward German to Rachel German quoted in Brian Rees, *A Musical Peacemaker* (Abbotsbrook, 1986), p. 204.

The two outer movements of the Suite are bucolic $\frac{6}{8}$ pastoral dances (a style closely associated with German) and the middle is a valse. 'In the Meadows' has three key themes (first introduced at letters A, B and D respectively), each of them with a rustic, quasi-modal feel, drawn from the ambiguous major/minor tonality. The most successful movement is 'Among the Poppies', which is a slow valse (with its theme scored for the cellos) followed by a fast valse (letter B) with three themes before returning to the slow valse to close. The finale, 'At the Fair', while being the most exciting movement of the Suite, is also the most problematical as it relies heavily on variations of material such as the C-section (five bars after letter E), which lasts until the bridge passage at letter I. There is a large use of the A-section (first heard at letter A), which returns at letters C, J, L and then from letter M onwards all the melodic material is derived from this theme. 'At the Fair' is highly reminiscent of German's 'Merrymakers' Dance' from *Nell Gwyn*, with its vivacious $\frac{6}{8}$ themes and large use of tambourine. *From the Countryside* has never been amongst Coates' most popular works, and even the composer rarely conducted it.

The year following *From the Countryside*, 1915, saw Coates return to a writing a set of songs with *The Mill o' Dreams*. Coates had been publishing songs since 1908, but had only written three sets of songs, none of which could be designated 'song cycles' as they were not designed to be sung as a unit, nor did they have any thematic unity. He had also orchestrated several of his ballads for the various Ballad Concerts (indeed for a number of his songs published by Booseys the orchestral material was advertised on the song; the majority of these accompaniments are now lost). In 1915, he wrote a set of four songs with Nancie Marsland for that year's Promenade Concerts.[58] The songs were frequently sung, indeed they were performed at the Proms in 1915, by Louise Dale, a well-known ballad singer of the period.

The first and third songs of *The Mill o' Dreams* are based around the imagery of the moon. Throughout his career as a songwriter, Coates frequently used the moon as a topic for songs, and indeed in later years he had an interest in astronomy. The orchestral version differs greatly from the piano accompaniment and enhances the songs, not only through the addition of colour, but in subtle changes to the music, such as the addition of violin countermelodies in the *poco animato* passages in 'Back o' the Moon', his trademark pizzicato cellos in 'The Man in the Moon' and the flute and clarinet arpeggios at the close of the first two songs. These changes are most noticeable in the final song, 'Bluebells' in which Coates exchanges the piano right-hand figure for a new pattern, more idiomatic for the strings, with the use of the horns to give the imagery of the bells for the final two verses. The cycle is scored for small orchestra with the two cornets and trombone being employed only in the first song. In a way, the orchestral version of the song cycle is slightly too orchestral, distracting the listener's attention away from the soloist.

---

[58]   They were the only published songs he set to Marsland's lyrics; the other two songs were unpublished and written several years later.

Today, *The Mill o' Dreams* sounds slightly dated owing to its overt sentimentality in both the music (heightened by Coates' frequent use of sevenths and ninths – especially in the opening song) and in Marsland's slightly mawkish text, as in 'The Man in the Moon': 'Is the man in the moon a silversmith,/Who fashions the stars?/And is it true that he pickles them too,/And sells them in jars?' However, these sentiments were very much part of the ballad tradition and, at that time, songs of this ilk could feature in the 'lofty' Promenades in the lighter fare performed on Thursday and Saturday evenings.

The formation of the New Queen's Hall Light Orchestra in 1916, under the conductorship of Alick Maclean, was a highly important event that spurred Coates on to continue writing for the orchestra. This ensemble, originally of 40 players drawn from the New QHO, was designed to cater for the growing demand for light orchestral music at Chappells' Ballad Concerts.[59] The Light Orchestra continued to perform at the Ballad Concerts until 1923, when the concerts, as a result of public request, featured a greatly reduced number of songs and an increased number of orchestral works.[60] Coates joined the viola section of the ensemble for a short while and the Orchestra gave a number of performances of his works over the years. They also recorded a number of his orchestral works for HMV.[61] He formed a close relationship with Maclean that was to prove important to his career. Through his friendship with Maclean, his works were regularly performed by the Light Orchestra, but also by other ensembles that Maclean conducted, especially the Scarborough Spa Orchestra, to which, from 1919, Coates became a regular visitor.[62]

Despite the formation of the Light Orchestra, by 1916 Coates had hit a low patch in composition owing to the gradual decrease of royalties from the sales of his sheet music (he did not receive his first PRS royalties until 1917). He was also bemused at the almost total absence of his music from the Chappells' Ballad Concerts. Chappells were by now his principal publisher. Both Eric and Phyl had thought for some time that someone at Chappells had been obstructing performances of his music at the Ballad Concerts. He had experienced a great degree of difficulty in breaking past the 'ring of established ballad writers', but with the formation of the New Queen's Hall Light Orchestra he had hoped to gain more performances of his orchestral catalogue. One day he was at Chappells' Bond Street shop and heard a director of the company dissuading a well-known tenor from performing any of Coates' songs at ballad concerts. There was little to do except confront William Boosey (the head of the firm) with the matter. This meeting furnished Boosey with enough information to be able to dismiss the director. Within a short space of time, Coates' Valse from the *Miniature Suite* was included in a Chappells' Ballad Concert in February 1916, where it had to

---

[59]   14/12/1915 William Boosey to Alick Maclean. *GB-Lbl* MSMUS200.
[60]   October 1923 *Musical Times*, p. 713.
[61]   The *Miniature Suite*, *Wood Nymphs* and the 'Valse' from the *Summer Days* Suite.
[62]   Coates, p. 190.

be repeated, attracting rave reviews in the press.[63] A number of Coates' songs returned to the Ballad Concerts. William Boosey, or 'The Emperor' as he was often styled, was to be of great importance in Coates' publishing career, as too was Boosey's daughter, Alice. In 1919 Coates set one of Boosey's own lyrics (written under his *nom de plume* William Ackerman) 'An Elizabethan Lullaby'.

Even with his growing confidence in handling orchestral textures, Coates had begun to forge an enviable reputation as a composer of ballads. He was lucky to receive a good number of original lyrics from the doyen of ballad writers, Fred Weatherly. During the 1910s he scored successes with: 'Dinder Courtship', the Somerset-brogue 'Betty and Johnny', 'Green Hills o' Somerset' and 'The Fairytales of Ireland' (dedicated to Coates' mother). It is easy to see why such songs became so popular; the latter two were almost constantly in print throughout Coates' lifetime. There were also more 'serious' attempts such as 'Tell me Where is Fancy Bred?' for a stage production of *The Merchant of Venice*. One of the most successful songs of this period, dedicated to his father-in-law, was 'The Grenadier', which injects humour with its subtle use of 'The British Grenadier'[64] and a delightful touch in verse 3 of an ascending piano motif that illustrates the lascivious look the Grenadier would undoubtedly have wished to give to the passing girl if only he were allowed.

Once performances of Coates' music became more plentiful, especially in the capital, Coates returned to orchestral composition with renewed vigour and during 1917 he found time to write an elfin valse that he styled it a 'valsette', *Wood Nymphs*. One wonders whether he borrowed the title from Sterndale Bennett's overture *The Wood-Nymphs*, which he may well have played under Mackenzie at the RAM. It quickly became a great favourite of orchestras, audiences and the composer who recorded it no less than four times. Almost immediately, the work was taken up by Maclean and the New Queen's Hall Light Orchestra. Coates recalled his fondness for this piece:

> The Valsette never failed to obtain an encore. Whenever we played it, a second play-through was looked on as a foregone conclusion, and on one occasion we had to repeat it three times, making it four performances in all. So often was this piece asked for that Maclean said to me he thought the orchestra could play it blindfolded.[65]

The structure of *Wood Nymphs* bears a close resemblance to *Entr'acte À La Gavotte*, though with its material in triple rather than quadruple time. *Wood Nymphs* also clearly shows Coates' reliance on themes of a regular length (with the exception of the introduction and coda): theme A, 32 bars (letter A + 4 bars);

---

[63]  At the following concert, Maclean included movements from *From the Countryside* and this marked the beginning of the inclusion of Coates' music into the Ballad Concerts.

[64]  Very much like the use of 'The Sailor's Hornpipe' in 'Reuben Ranzo'.

[65]  Coates, p. 188.

B, 32 bars (letter B); C, 16 bars (B + 17 bars); A, 32 bars (letter D). This was something that would become a trademark of his later marches, and no doubt influenced by the structure of the popular songs of the day often consisting of 32-bar choruses.

Given the instant appeal of *Wood Nymphs* it was a forgone conclusion that it would be included in the next season of Promenade concerts. After several weeks in Seaton where the Coates' only worry in the world was the disappearance of Coates' PRS £35 royalty cheque they returned back to London in time for the rehearsals for the Proms.[66] Such was the success of *Wood Nymphs* that it was included in the famous 'Last Night of the Proms' in 1920, the only piece by Coates to appear on that occasion until *Calling All Workers* opened the second half in 2006.

The revolution of the formation of the PRS and the growing popularity of his orchestral scores had begun to sow the seed in his mind that he might be able to earn a living as a freelance composer and the success of his next orchestral work as well as a bizarre twist of fate turned this dream into a reality.

---

[66]   21/07/1918 EC to PRS. *GB-Lprs.*

# PART II
# The Years of Struggle and Triumph

# Chapter 5
# A Freelance Composer, 1918–1922

The years after the end of the First World War were full of struggle and hardship for the Coates given their lack of income, but nonetheless, Coates was beginning to focus more on orchestral music. His final orchestral work to be completed during his years as a professional viola player was somewhat incongruously entitled *Summer Days* (it was written during the winter months of 1918). It had a longer than usual gestation period (presumably due to commitments with the New QHO), with the opening movement, 'In a Country Lane', finished in mid-November and the concluding valse the following January, completed during a sojourn with Coates' family in Hucknall. The first performance of *Summer Days* was probably at the Promenade Concerts on 9 October 1919 under the composer's direction, though several contemporary sources list this as the first London performance. The finale was especially well received and had to be repeated.[1] Alick Maclean once remarked after a concert Coates conducted in Scarborough: 'Well, there you are Eric, you've done it again one-third sitting, two-thirds standing!'[2] *Summer Days* (though only in the piano solo version) bears a dedication to Alick Maclean and one wonders whether he had the honour of launching the work. Later in his career, Coates regretted the use of cornets in A, presumably dictated by the composition of the orchestras playing his works, thinking they sounded 'so plebeian!'[3] *Summer Days* is clearly modelled on the structure of the *Miniature Suite*, following the exact pattern of movements. 'In a Country Lane' resorts to a binary structure with a coda (letter E) recalling the A-section; the B-section (with its theme being a close relative to the A-section) moves towards the relative minor, but as is usual with Coates, the key is never clear-cut.

According to a programme note for a performance in a 1920 performance of the *Summer Days*, written by Rosa Newmarch and Eric Blom, in the middle movement, 'On the Edge of the Lake', subtitled 'Isla of the Waters', the A-section melody was 'suggested by certain lines from a poem of F.E. Weatherly's, and has a certain Scottish flavour'.[4] The movement is structured in ternary form, and the transition back to the A-section (letter C) is handled well, with two bars based on the A-section melody, before the reprise, marked 'grandioso' before a coda (letter D) based on the A-section (opening with an oboe solo reminiscent of letter A). As with the *Miniature Suite*, it is the concluding Valse which is the most

---

[1]   11/10/1919 *Daily Telegraph.*

[2]   Austin Coates, programme 2.

[3]   10/10/1956 EC to John Lowe. *GB-Rwac.*

[4]   24/10/1920 Queen's Hall Sunday Concert Programme.

felicitous movement, characterized by a delightful opening theme at the start of the valse proper. Each of the four themes of the valse contrasts well with its neighbours. The third subject 'tranquillo' (letter B) bears a resemblance to the first in its use of a descending semitone (the first theme uses a descending third).

*Summer Days* went on to become a very popular suite, considerably improving the Coates' precarious finances of the inter-war years. Indeed the Coates' second and third Selsey cottages were named Summer Days Cottage after the work.[5] In Coates' words, the suite was 'literally played to death' during its infancy by orchestras the length and breadth of the country.[6] However by 1940, *Summer Days* had largely fallen out of favour and Coates wrote to Stanford Robinson to encourage him to include the work in his 'Music While You Work' broadcasts.[7]

Until 1919, Coates' twin career as an orchestral musician and composer had been running well in tandem. However, he had always wanted to devote himself solely to composition. (His contemporary Haydn Wood had a similar performing background to Coates, touring the music halls with his wife, accompanying her on the piano and violin. It would not be until 1925 that Wood could afford to become a professional composer.) As far back as 1913, Coates has described his occupation on his marriage certificate as 'musical composer' rather than the more truthful 'orchestral musician'.[8] At the close of the 1918–19 Queen's Hall season, the Coates were revelling in a ten-week holiday on the Suffolk coast before the 1919 Promenade Concerts. While their minds were far away from life at Queen's Hall, he received a letter from Robert Newman, the hall's manager, informing him that Coates' contract as principal viola with the New Queen's Hall Orchestra was to be terminated forthwith. In his autobiography, Coates states that the letter came as a complete shock as there had never been any hint of Wood's dissatisfaction with his services.[9] He was also hurt by the absence of personal intervention by Wood and as a consequence remained slightly bitter towards Wood until the latter's death in 1944. Writing in the 1950s, Coates believed the reason for his dismissal was:

> the deputies I had sent to take my place when I had been invited to conduct the London Symphony Orchestra at the Palladium on Sunday afternoons,[10] and to the rehearsals when my arm was troubling me more than usual. I had certainly

---

[5]   The majority of the Coates' Selsey cottages were named after Coates' compositions: Stonecracker Cottage (after 'Stonecraker John') and Bears Cottage (after *The Three Bears*).

[6]   05/07/1940 EC to Stanford Robinson. *GB-Rwac*.

[7]   Ibid.

[8]   Coates' Marriage Certificate.

[9]   Eric Coates, *Suite in Four Movements* (London, 1953), p. 193.

[10]   The London Symphony Orchestra (LSO) were seriously in the doldrums and performed 'light classics' at the London Palladium and touring suburban halls for rock-bottom rates; though the name of the orchestra was left out of publicity. (Richard Morrison, *Orchestra. The LSO* (London, 2004), pp. 53-4.)

been growing tired of my orchestral life and had already wondered more than once how I could manage to get away from it, but not in this undignified way.[11]

Austin Coates favoured a more dramatic reason, something his father had alluded to in a 1947 interview with the magazine *John Bull*,[12] after a performance of *Wood Nymphs*:

> It brought the house down – it usually did – the audience going on and on demanding an encore. This meant asking Wood's permission and Wood could not be found. The composer gave the valsette a second time and the same thing happened – they wanted to hear it a third time. By now Wood had been located; he had gone up to his private room at the top of Queen's Hall and locked himself in, where no one <u>could</u> ask his position. *Wood Nymphs* was played a third time. A few weeks later came a letter from the orchestra manager saying that Eric Coates' services would not be required for the forthcoming Promenade Concerts.[13]

Henry Wood had always disliked the practice of giving encores. Surely the dismissal cannot have been such a surprise for Coates, since judging by his comments in *Suite in Four Movements* he had often treated his position with a cavalier respect for the high standards that Wood demanded from the Orchestra. Coates recalled one of his absences:

> the programme at the Queen's Hall contained a Rhapsody by Enesco, my *bête noir*, for it has a vile and very tricky viola solo which always rather scared me. So I was doubly relieved when Wood agreed that my services could be dispensed with for one afternoon.
>
> On the following Monday, walking along Oxford Street, I encountered Purcell Jones, the principal 'cello of the Queen's Hall Orchestra, who was notoriously extremely short-sighted. Jones stopped me and said: 'My word, Coates, I've never heard you play that solo as well as you did yesterday afternoon. It was magnificent'![14]

There must have been a growing resentment between Wood and Coates due to Coates' requests to be absent to conduct his orchestral works. Wood had always disliked intensely the practice of sending orchestral deputies to rehearsals and a clampdown by Wood and Newman had caused the formation of the London Symphony Orchestra in 1904 from those who no longer wanted to remain in the QHO. One also wonders if this resentment had something to do with Coates wanting

[11]  Coates, p. 193.

[12]  14/06/1947 *John Bull*.

[13]  Austin Coates, programme 1.

[14]  November 1937, *The Gramophone*, p. 235.

to conduct his music at the Proms. Prior to his dismissal he had only conducted the *From the Countryside* Suite at the 1916 Proms, all the other performances being directed by Wood and the composer acknowledging the applause from the violas. After Coates' dismissal he directed practically all performances of his orchestral music at the Promenades.

Whatever the reasons for Coates' dismissal, the Rubicon had been crossed and a meeting with Newman on the Coates' return from Sussex brought no amendments to the *status quo* apart from a letter from Wood eulogizing Coates' qualities but underlining the fact that Wood wanted a reliable leader of the violas present at every concert and rehearsal. It was not until the 1930s that Coates disclosed the true reason for his departure from the Orchestra, favouring to cloak the saga by informing people that he wanted to spend more time composing.

Whilst Coates' dismissal was in some respects a welcome relief from the day-to-day burden of orchestral work, it did cause certain financial uncertainties, although the Coates merely extended their holiday until the end of August, returning to London for Coates to conduct his new suite, *Summer Days*, at the Proms. Coates recalled the irony: 'I slipped into my dress clothes, strolled along to Queen's Hall, mounted the rostrum, grinned at my successor on my right and conducted the first performance of my 'Summer Days' Suite'.[15] They were fortunate to find, on their return from their extended holiday, a compositional contract from Chappells waiting on their doormat.[16] Coates still had a little income from piecemeal teaching at the RAM and the royalties from his music. Not for the first time in their married life, the Coates were forced to make economies (as they had done on the outbreak of war), so they sublet their flat in Berners Street and relocated to a cheaper flat, in Frognal. It was Phyl who found a way out of their financial problems. She became an actress, a career she had always dreamt of but one her parents violently detested. Her husband effected an introduction to the actress/impresario Lena Ashwell, which kick-started her career on the stage.[17] For the next three years, Coates often neglected composing, frequently accompanying or joining Phyl, whenever possible, on her touring dates with her repertory company, playing a little golf or sightseeing by a hired car.[18] In his autobiography, Coates joked that he was in danger of being known as 'Mr Phyllis Black'.[19] Phyl's theatrical career caused Coates to write a number of songs for theatre productions, including 'Nobody Else but You' for a play Phyl was in and 'Bluebell in Fairyland'.[20] By all accounts, Phyl was a competent actress, moving from one touring production to another, though she occasionally appeared in London's West End. Her infatuation with the stage lasted until 1928 when all the financial pressures were lifted. She

---

[15]   Coates, p. 194.

[16]   Ibid., 195.

[17]   Austin Coates, programme 1.

[18]   Eric Coates, *Suite in Four Movements* (autograph), p. 425.

[19]   Coates, p. 200.

[20]   The published song featured a photograph of Phyl on the front cover.

was persuaded to retire (by declining future offers of work) by Coates as she was a martyr to performance nerves, which caused both of them much anxiety and affected her delicate voice almost to the point of disappearance.[21]

Thankfully, Coates' career began to flourish owing to the popularity of his most recent works *Wood Nymphs* and *Summer Days*. He was also free to adopt a routine of composition when he wanted, rather than slotting his composition in between rehearsals and concerts. Austin Coates recalled his father's working practices:

> Eric Coates' tunes arrived – there is no other word for it – at invariably unexpected moments, during waking hours, seldom if ever after dark, and perversely, never when he was in his writing room. The writing room was for the actual composing, thematic development, orchestration. Tunes and musical ideas occurred elsewhere, and one never knew when.
>
> My father always carried ... [a slim pocket diary] in his breast pocket, for dashing down tunes and ideas, which must be set down immediately lest the next moment they be forgotten.
>
> Then, as soon as he could thereafter, he would go to his writing room, take out a sheet of full-score paper – he never used any other kind – and write out the tune on three staves, showing the bass and harmonies, and allowing for orchestral indications; for his tunes arrived orchestrally. It was not simply the tune; it was also the orchestral sound of it.
>
> After that he would do something else – go for a walk, or do some developing or printing; he was a very good photographer. Then, much later in the day, when he had forgotten the tune, he would go again to his writing room and look at what he had written, seeing it objectively.
>
> If it fitted in with something he was doing, or had been asked to do – and newly-arrived tunes frequently did – he would use it; otherwise it could be put away to be looked at again at a later date. He never threw anything away.[22]

Coates' compositional activities were cushioned to a certain extent when in 1919, aged 33, he entered into an exclusive contract with Chappells.[23] Exactly what form his contract took at this stage is unclear, as the only contract to survive is from 1937–38, and one can only surmise what the previous contracts entailed by looking through his catalogue of works. In 1937–38 (the 'new contract'), he was committed to write one large (such as a suite or an extended, single-movement

[21] Geoffrey Self, *In Town Tonight* (London, 1986), p. 37.

[22] 27/03/1991 Austin Coates to Richard Itter.

[23] 10/07/1942 EC to Louis Dreyfus. *GB-Lcm.*

work) and two smaller orchestral works (such as an entr'acte or march) a year, and one song to qualify for his retaining fee of £300 per annum in addition to all the usual royalties on sales of copies and PRS fees.[24] Coates' contract with Chappells ended in 1940 when he ceased to have a definite contract *per se* with any publishing firm, a freedom he was glad of.[25] However, as generous as the contract was, there was still a shortfall from his income as a viola player.

Coates' contract worked well in tandem with the offers for new works that came from the cross-section of music festivals. The re-establishment of the various musical festivals, especially those promoted by the coastal and spa orchestras, in the years after the First World War, was important for Coates. Not only did he receive a multitude of invitations to conduct, as did many light-music composers, but also numerous requests for new compositions. With the wholesale adoption of the PRS system, the performances by these ensembles generated valuable PRS royalties in addition to those produced by the sales of sheet music. Coates fitted into the world of these orchestras and their festivals as he was prepared to write and conduct performances of his works for the orchestras at Bath, Blackpool, Bournemouth, Brighton, Eastbourne, Folkestone, Harrogate, Scarborough, and Torquay. He generally held these Festivals in high esteem, and adopted their musical values into his artistic credo. Reminiscing in the 1950s, he recalled:

> the English Musical Festivals that were so popular about this time. Those were
> the days when music was not put into categories as it is to-day, or laid out on the
> operating table for dissection, but looked upon simply as music to delight and
> elevate. They were interesting occasions both musically and socially, for people
> flocked from far and wide to hear and see the famous composers and executants
> who had been engaged to appear.[26]

Indeed, this viewpoint was to form the salient argument of his vehement attacks against the snobbery surrounding light music which pervaded the British music scene for a number of years – light music had often appeared in the coastal and spa orchestras' programmes, both in their regular concerts and annual festivals, and it should continue to do so.

At times, Coates was inclined to hold a romanticized notion of the festivals, and after their termination (owing to the onset of the Second World War), he never readjusted to the post-war opportunities available to light music. For him, these regional festivals were the apogee of the widespread adoption and acceptance of light music. The seaside and spa orchestras were a curious phenomenon that he never forgot and he always believed that their *status quo* would one day return and he too would recrudesce with the new post-war generation of composers such as Berkeley, Britten, Rawsthorne, Rubbra, Tippett and Walton (many of whom

---

[24]    12/10/1938 Chappells' Contract. *GB-Lcm*.

[25]    10/07/1942 EC to Louis Dreyfus. *GB-Lcm*.

[26]    Coates, p. 206.

he had met through the auspices of the PRS). However, the BBC's Light Music Festivals of the 1950s enabled him to recapture the ethos of the halcyon music festivals of 1930s and offered opportunities to present premieres of his new works.

He was a frequent visitor to the festivals on the south coast of England. During Dan Godfrey's tenure with the Bournemouth Orchestra, Coates regularly featured in the Easter Festivals of the 1920s, often conducting his own music. He was also an annual visitor to Maclean's Scarborough Spa Orchestra on the north-eastern coast of England, usually conducting for the last four days of August.

Eastbourne, in the south, was by far the most popular venue for premieres. Coates was a frequent guest of Captain Harry Amers, conductor of the Eastbourne Orchestra, and this was perhaps his favourite of all festivals, often accompanied by a stay at the Grand Hotel. By the mid-1930s, the BBC was his desired outlet for first performances, but his latest compositions often made the rounds of the coastal and spa ensembles.

Coates still relied on the popularity and income generated by his ballads. His songs were associated with the likes of Hubert Eisdell, Peter Dawson, Gervase Elwes, Carmen Hill and Stanley Holloway. Like the 1910s, the early 1920s saw large numbers of new ballads produced even though 1920 proved to have been a difficult year with a large number of unpublished songs, including the five-song set *Songs of Arabia: The Garden of Khursu*.[27] Nevertheless, he managed to produce a steady stream of popular 'hits' including 'Brown Eyes Beneath the Moon', 'At Sunset' and 'I Pitch My Lonely Caravan'.[28] In 1921, he tried his hand a writing a song foxtrot inspired by, and dedicated to, the popular dancers Muriel George and Ernest Butcher; the latter also wrote the song's lyrics.

The close of 1919 brought one of Coates' finest song creations, 'Pepita', which also marked the start of the occasional use of popular dance rhythms in his music that was so prevalent in the scores of the latter years of the 1920s. This song was originally written for, and dedicated to, the singer Mischa Léon with orchestral accompaniment. 'Pepita' is a song in which the singer recalls a girlfriend of twenty years ago, which may well have been the reason why Coates sets the song as a Habanera (a forerunner of the tango, and a popular dance at the turn of the twentieth century) and tries to capture an Iberian/Cuban atmosphere. In a programme note for the work's premiere, Coates was praised for his use of orchestral colour, including castanets.[29] The song utilizes two most common Habanera rhythms (the former is used in verses 1 and 3 and on occasions their middle two notes are tied; the latter is used in verse 2) (Example 5.1).

The two patterns are occasionally combined in the second verse. The key structure of the work is relatively sophisticated for a Coates ballad, as it opens in G minor, pulls towards the relative major (B♭), moving to F, then to A minor/ C major for the middle verse, D major for the link between verses 2 and 3 before

---

[27]   *GB-Lcm* Box 184.

[28]   The latter song was the subject of a cartoon in *Punch Magazine*, June 1935.

[29]   25/01/1920 Programme Note in Queen's Hall Sunday Afternoon Concert.

Example 5.1 'Pepita', Habanera patterns

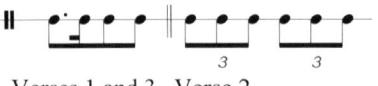

Verses 1 and 3   Verse 2

a return to G minor for verse 3, finally closing in G major for the coda (in which the final two lines of verse three are transposed down a minor third), though this is blurred with the juxtaposition of B major (over a tonic pedal). Alas, the orchestral score has since vanished and it can no longer be heard with orchestral accompaniment.

Even though Coates was now a freelance composer, he spent very little time on composition and the only works that date from 1918–22 are a clutch of songs and the orchestral works *Moresque*, *Joyous Youth* Suite, and a ballet sketch, *Coquette*. The latter is believed to be the middle of three ballet sketches, probably contemporaneous with *Coquette*; though the other two pieces are either lost or were never written.[30] Coates completed the score in May 1920 and it is unknown whether the work was ever performed in Coates' lifetime: certainly it was never published. Taking the eternal *femme fatale* as its subject, it is a brief ternary-form entr'acte along the lines of *À la Gavotte* and *The Mermaid*. However infectious the two themes (the first introduced in the opening, the second in the B-section, starting at the Allegretto after letter B) are, one soon tires of the rhythm of the first subject, Example 5.2, which also invades the second subject.

This problem is also exacerbated by the use of direct repetition of the B-section at letter D (though Coates does alter the ending). *Coquette* is also thickly scored with four horns and two oboes and bassoons, unlike the earlier *Wood Nymphs*,

Example 5.2 *Coquette*, bars 5–12

---

[30]    Sleeve notes by Michael Ponder in *Seventeen Orchestral Miniatures* (ASV, CDWHL 2107).

which gives it a heavier texture. There are several praiseworthy passages, especially in the use of countersubjects (as at letter C), which pave the way for those in the marches of the 1940s.

*Coquette* was one of Coates' very few unpublished pieces. His publishers usually printed his works almost as soon as they were written and on occasions the band parts for the shorter works were ready for use at the first performance (as with *Calling All Workers*).[31] The majority of his unpublished works tend to be juvenilia, songs or works that had copyright implications (*Symphonic Rhapsody after Richard Rodgers*) or scoring problems (*Snowdrop*, which was scored for a theatre orchestra).

Besides his constant absences following Phyl around the country, the major reason for Coates' small output of composition during 1920 was that he had embarked upon the composition of a light opera.[32] There had been many calls in the press for him to embrace the genre, then very much in vogue. No doubt Coates' love of the genre and the fact that he had played the viola in a good many shows meant that he knew the essential ingredients to make a good production. He must also have been conscious of the examples produced by his light-music colleagues Haydn Wood (*Tina* and *Cash on Delivery*), Archibald Joyce (*Toto*, written in conjunction with Merlin Morgan) and Montague Phillips (*The Rebel Maid*). With Phyl's career as an actress, he was spending a good deal of time in the company of theatricals and he had already written several songs for the theatre.

By 1920, he had come into contact with Daisy Fisher and the two of them embarked on writing an operetta entitled *Mary's Orchard*. He had already written two published songs for Chappells with Fisher at the beginning of 1920. Little survives of their production except a handful of completed songs and occasional pages of script and song lyrics, though alas no correspondence of their working relationship. The majority of the completed songs were finished in May–June 1920 and from their variety (as can be seen in Appendix 1) it was to be a large-scale production with a fair-sized cast of principals and chorus. It is impossible from this material to extract a summary of the plot or to even ascertain the subject. During the work's composition, Daisy Fisher stopped writing the lyrics and was replaced by James Heard, though Heard and Coates wrote only three songs for the production together. These songs appear to have been the final work undertaken on this venture and it was left unfinished. One wonders if William Boosey at Chappells had seen the libretto and had dissuaded Coates from continuing with the project; Boosey was notoriously difficult to please on the subject of operetta libretti.[33]

It is a great shame that *Mary's Orchard* failed to reach the stage as the surviving sketches show that Coates had a dramatic flair, somewhat mingled with influences of Sullivan and German, as in the Act I Opening Chorus. There are moments of real

---

[31]   26/08/1940 EC to Stanford Robinson. *GB-Rwac*. However, the printed parts were riddled with errors and not used.

[32]   It is difficult to define exactly what type of production Coates was working on.

[33]   William Boosey, *Fifty Years of Music* (London, 1931), p. 51.

tenderness such as the quartette 'At Dusk' in Act II with its use of flowing melody. Perhaps the most successful of the surviving sketches is the Finale to Act I with its blend of march-like material for the chorus with recitative, an infectious allegretto for Boyle before closing with a delightful slow valse for Boyle, Christina and chorus. Whatever the reason for the failure of *Mary's Orchard*, it was not the music.

Coates was still keen to proceed with an operetta and must have been impressed with the quality of Heard's work, as the two embarked on *All Through My Life*. The title for this production is editorial because none of the surviving material for this production bears any title, librettist or composer. It is only through one of the songs that there is an indication of title and librettist. Nevertheless, Chappells were certainly keen to publish this operetta, as their copyright stamp appears on a number of the sketches. Again, for an unknown reason, the venture failed. It would be some years before Coates would again turn his hand to writing a musical.

With the abandonment of work on his musical, Coates was free to return to his standard realm of composition and produced the second short orchestral vignette of this period – the dance interlude *Moresque*. One of the earliest performances of this was at a Queen's Hall Sunday Concert on 2 October 1921 when it was performed with *Wood Nymphs* and conducted by the composer. In the programme notes for the performance, Rosa Newmarch and Eric Blom noted that both these two miniatures had been originally intended for use as ballet music: *Moresque* was set in a Moorish palace; and *Wood Nymphs* was an elfin ballet.[34] However, they were rarely performed together, especially as the latter completely outshines the former. *Moresque* is notable for its use of a Habanera rhythm in the more relaxed B-section, and builds on Coates' first experimentation with this in the song 'Pepita'.

The Coates were still in financial difficulties and it no doubt came as a welcome relief after the trials and tribulations of living in Frognal to be invited to reside on the upper floor of Phyl's parents' house in St John's Wood in 1921. As was becoming usual, the change of address resulted in a bout of creative inspiration: the suite *Joyous Youth*. This Suite is clearly modelled on the highly successful *Summer Days*, particularly in inspiration and melodic material. Indeed, it could almost be styled *Summer Days II*, though the structure of each movement is markedly different. Coates wrote *Joyous Youth* with Alick Maclean and the Chappells' Ballad Concerts in mind:

> It is not easy to make an effect with an orchestral work on the piano unless you are a competent pianist, but fortunately Maclean's eye perceived in my full-score what my stumbling fingers were trying to achieve. How beautifully he used to present my new works and, like the true artist he was, tried to carry out my wishes down to the smallest detail.[35]

---

[34]   02/10/1921 Queen's Hall Sunday Concert Programme.
[35]   Coates, p. 199.

The opening 'Introduction' is structured in ternary form, with a quasi-folk-music feel with the reprise of the A-section (12 bars after letter F) being a direct repeat of the first A-section. The B-section is a great contrast to the A-section, with the tempo slowed down for the romantic theme (initially scored for solo violin) before a deft bridge passage (letter F) restores the opening mood. The middle movement, 'Serenade' is a monothematic piece based on a 16-bar theme, again with folk-like charm suggested by the blurring of key between G major and E minor, repeated in melodic variants. There is a rare use of two soloists with a dialogue between violin and viola at letter F.

As with the previous three suites, it is the concluding movement that 'steals the show'. The valse presents four key themes before returning to first theme (at letter G in a richer harmonic guise), which is extended by means of a longer than usual coda, from letter J. The final flourish (marked Allegro molto), features an intriguing move to $\frac{6}{8}$ time (an inversion of the *Summer Days* Valse which opens with a $\frac{6}{8}$ passage heralding the first subject in $\frac{3}{4}$), perhaps a reminder of the opening movement, and to the tonic minor in a moment of breathtaking audacity. *Summer Days* has a more immediate and infectious melodic charm, which *Joyous Youth* never surpasses, despite the quality of its material. It was never likely to knock its earlier cousin off its pedestal.

After the completion of the *Joyous Youth* Suite, Coates appears to have had a compositional fallow period, not completing any orchestral canvasses until 1923. Upon relinquishing his teaching post at the RAM in 1922 he was awarded, alongside Lionel Tertis, a Fellowship Diploma of the Academy.[36] It was an honour he was genuinely delighted with, and it was the only honorary award he accepted and used.[37] He was also kept busy with the RAM centenary celebrations in July, with several of his pieces included in the array of festivities. He was also listed amongst the violas (if he did indeed play, as he maintained he had not played his viola since his Queen's Hall days) at the high-profile centenary concert at Queen's Hall on 18 July, for which RAM alumnus Edward German composed his tone poem *The Willow Song*.

The year 1922 proved to be one of immense change with the arrival of the Coates' only child, Austin Francis Harrison Coates, on 16 April. For Eric and Phyl this was both a joy and a major hindrance, as Austin recalled that he was:

> a portent of disaster long before I was born. I would wreck my mother's acting career, while for my father the prospect of a squalling infant in the house whilst he was trying to write music was too awful to contemplate. Worst of all, the

---

[36]   07/07/1922 Minutes of a Management Committee in RAM Minutes of Committee June 1922–April 1924. *GB-Lam.*

[37]   It is not known if he was every offered a national honour. There was an obstacle to Coates' knighthood as the economist Eric Coates had been knighted in 1945. Occasionally the two Eric Coates used to receive each other's post in error.

two of them would no longer be on their own and they had married for no other reason; few first borns have ever been less welcome.[38]

In his parents' defence, Austin's arrival did come at an awkward time because Phyl's career as an actress was in ascendance with repeated offers to appear in London's West End and Coates was beginning to forge an enviable reputation as a light-music composer. Nevertheless, the Coates soon adapted to life as parents, though having a composer for a father was difficult for Austin as he grew older, as it must have been for Elgar's only child Carice. Austin would rarely see his father for more than half an hour each day, unless on holiday when, if Coates could spare the time, he would teach Austin the rudiments of map-reading and astronomy.[39]

Within a few months of Austin's birth, Phyl returned to the stage, appearing in the original cast of Noël Coward's *The Young Idea*, which began rehearsals in August 1922.[40] A nurse was engaged to look after Austin while Phyl was busy touring. There were also lifestyle changes to be made, and within two years of Austin's arrival they had moved to the rural splendour of Hampstead, an environment more suitable for Austin and within commutable distance of central London. However, Coates found it difficult to settle into a structured writing schedule.[41]

Another side effect of Austin's birth was Eric and Phyl's discovery of Selsey (Figure 5.1). During 1922, Coates had succumbed to a virulent attack of pneumonia and they both decided that sea air would be good for him. In the days before the 1956 Clean Air Act, London was thick with pollution and smog, often covered with 'pea-soupers', all bad for Coates' chest. The Coates chose the coastal village of Selsey, then relatively unknown, as he recalled in an omitted passage from his autobiography:

> When we first came to this little place in 1922, such things as charabancs and trippers had not as yet discovered its attraction. The only thing the village had to offer was bathing, fishing and riding, and if you were not interested in these three forms of sport, then the only thing to do was to go into Chichester and do some shopping, take luncheon at the Dolphin and finish up with a visit to the cinema, a place of entertainment which even in those far-away days was very much to the fore in showing the latest in the 'movies'.[42]

During 1922, Phyl rented a small cottage, but in 1923 they acquired their first house in Selsey, Stonecracker Cottage on the East Beech (Phyl took out the lease). For the rest of Coates' life they kept a holiday home on the south coast of England (though they moved further inland during the late 1930s) and finally relocated their second

---

[38]   Austin Coates, programme 1.

[39]   02/08/1986 *Radio Times*.

[40]   Noël Coward, *Present Indicative* (London, 1937), p. 179.

[41]   Coates (autograph), p. 423.

[42]   Ibid., p. 447.

Figure 5.1    A rare moment of informality, Eric and Austin at Selsey, circa 1930

house to Bognor Regis in 1952. The breaks in Selsey soon became invaluable and the Coates spent a good deal of their time there during the summer months and for school holidays. As they became wealthier, they exchanged their houses for larger ones, installing all the creature comforts of their London lifestyle. Selsey was a place to undertake the more workmanlike tasks of music such as orchestrating short scores and making fair copies of compositions. It rarely acted as a place for inspiration or composition; most of his inspiration came on his walks around London. He explained the lure of Selsey: 'Here I can live my own life without being thought eccentric, knowing, at the back of my mind, that there is always the top floor flat to return to at will whenever the desire for change comes over me'.[43] Their houses soon became a Mecca for their friends to visit. Vivian Ellis wrote part of the musical *Jill Darling* (including the hit-song 'I'm on a See-Saw') on Coates' piano at Summer Days Cottage.[44] Coates was not the only creative person active in Selsey. The playwright, R.C. Sherriff (who wrote the screenplay for the film

---

[43]    Coates, p. 210.

[44]    Vivian Ellis, *I'm on a See-Saw* (London, 1953), p. 131.

*The Dam Busters*) wrote a good deal while residing in Selsey with his mother who leased two railway carriages near several of the Coates' first cottages. The ability to establish a second home in Sussex demonstrated how far Coates' fortunes had changed from his days in the QHO.

# Chapter 6
# Maturity and Jazz, 1923–1930

Whilst Coates had already begun to establish a successful career as a composer during the 1910s, during the 1920s he would arrive at full compositional maturity. It was during this period that he could finally stop composing ballads (even though he wrote several of his most popular examples of the genre during these years) and focus almost exclusively on orchestral works. Coates' own success and stability was also mirrored in contemporary politics, as it marked a return to international stability after the First World War. In Britain, Lloyd George had been ousted as Prime Minister leading to the Conservative Party dominating interwar politics.

At the close of 1922, Coates, aged 36, was at work on a short overture provisionally entitled *A New Year Overture*,[1] but as it was only finished on 28 January 1923 and not premiered until 3 March at a Chappells' Ballad Concert, the date precluded the use of the title and it was amended to *The Merrymakers* Overture. Popular singer Peter Dawson was also present and sang two of Coates' songs. The *Merrymakers*, described in the score as 'a miniature overture' was the first work of Coates' that could truthfully bear the title of a masterpiece and with it came the arrival of his mature orchestral style. There is a surer grip on orchestration (with superb writing for horns), succinctness of form and a great melodic charm: a move away from the 'pastorale' Edward German style.

In its melodic construction, *The Merrymakers* owes something to Elgar, whose broad, extended-range melodies are evident in the second subject, whilst those of Edward German are a blueprint for the first subject – the Overture is undeniably conceived for the orchestra. Unusually for Coates, the Overture is cast in a loose sonata-form structure, with a limited development section (bars 93–108). There is a good deal of variation within the exposition and recapitulation.

The second subject (letter D) is one of Coates' finest melodies, broad and majestic. Much is made of the use of the interval of a sixth, which is subsequently extended to an octave (cf. bar 61).

The Overture has traits of Coates' melodic formula with 'self-developing melody'. Instead of directly repeating a melody, or developing it significantly, Coates uses the opening notes or half of the existing phrase, with a new ending with a similar melodic shape to the main-melody. This is clearly demonstrated in the *Television March*, where the second subject (figure 4) is sixteen bars long. This theme opens with a 4-bar phrase, X, which is then repeated down a third, X'. This is then followed by a 3-bar phrase, Y, which is completed by a 4 bar phrase. For the repeat of this theme at figure 5, X is repeated, followed by X" (X' slightly

---

[1]    Geoffrey Self, *In Town Tonight* (London, 1986), p. 36.

altered) and a variant of Y, Y' (which includes an E♮ to give increased harmonic possibilities) and then a new ending to the theme (Example 6.1).

Example 6.1   *Television March*, figure 4. © 1946 Chappell Music Ltd, London, W6 8BS. Reproduced by permission of Faber Music Ltd. All Rights Reserved

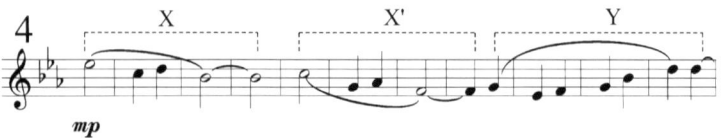

This ploy establishes the melody firmly (especially the opening bars) in the ears of listeners, but the subtle differences between repetitions prevent the listener from tiring of it.

He derives a large proportion of the development section of *The Merrymakers* from a rhythmic cell (bars 93–9), which he modulates through a variety of keys and orchestrations, rather than resorting to a more organic and lengthy development. Despite this, he never does exactly what the listener expects. This is particularly true of the recapitulation of the second subject, which is preceded by a bridge passage over a dominant pedal (bars 140–57), a device garnered from Edward German. This effect leads the listener to expect the subject in a grandiose guise (akin to the recapitulation of the second subject in a Coates march), but Coates starts the subject quietly after a *lunga pausa* and allows the subject to swell most effectively.

It is unfortunate that Coates never wrote another overture, though it would have been difficult to surpass *The Merrymakers*. He was keen to write a 'lively overture' for the BBC's 1954 Light Music Festival and there is a sketch for an Overture in C in Coates' papers that may well date from this period.[2] It certainly left a gap in his compositional oeuvre that he never addressed, especially as his other light-music contemporaries, Haydn Wood wrote eight and Phillips at least four.

Not long after the completion of *The Merrymakers* Overture, the composer recorded it along with *Moresque* with the New Queen's Hall Light Orchestra for Columbia on 23 March 1923.[3] He also recorded his *Joyous Youth* Suite for Vocalion the same month. These were Coates' first gramophone recordings as a conductor, though he may have made gramophone recordings in the 1910s when he was an active viola player (Henry Wood did not make his first orchestral recordings until 1915). As Nott has suggested, the gramophone became one of the most fashionable forms of entertainment for an increasing number of people during the interwar period, though it was less accepted than the cinema or the

---

[2]   17/12/1953 EC to Hubert Clifford. *GB-Rwac*. Sketches, *GB-Lcm* Box 184.

[3]   For all bibliographic details relating to Coates' own recordings see Appendix 1.

radio.[4] Alongside Elgar, Stravinsky (who wrote his Piano Sonata especially for the gramophone; each movement limited to the length of a record), Ketèlbey and German, Coates was one of the first composers to embrace the gramophone record and understand its potential. He continued to make gramophone records until his death in 1957; his final HMV recordings, made four months before his death, were issued posthumously. His ascent to popularity as a composer ran concurrently with the surge of interest in the gramophone, in particular due to the wholesale adoption of electrical recording from 1925 by the majority of recording companies. Subsequently, the two were of mutual benefit to one another and Coates would never have attained his status within the field of light music without his corpus of gramophone records. As Foreman and Foreman have noted, by 1925, eighteen movements from nine of Coates' works had been recorded by a variety of conductors and record labels.[5] He made more recordings as a conductor than his light-music contemporaries (Haydn Wood only recorded two suites and eight orchestral pieces of his own compositions),[6] with the exception of Ketèlbey. Coates' recorded legacy is considerable, amounting to almost seven hours.

How Coates came to be involved in gramophone recording is unclear. One wonders if Albert Ketèlbey, who had worked for a number of years as an arranger and musical director for Columbia, was responsible for enticing Coates to record. Lionel Tertis may have also have helped, having already cut a large number of sides for Columbia. Nevertheless, by 1923 Coates' music was sufficiently popular for record companies to sponsor recordings. Throughout the 1920s and 1930s, Coates recorded exclusively for Columbia and the Gramophone Company (one of whose labels was HMV), apart from his one record for Vocalion, and they ensured that he had a first-rate orchestra. Coates was an ideal composer for the gramophone: he wrote effervescent, popular miniatures that fitted neatly onto single sides of either a 12-inch (which afforded 4 minutes 30 seconds of playback), or a smaller 10-inch disc (which allowed up to 3 minutes 30 seconds).[7] Even his more extended works such as suites split easily into three sides (one per movement), which left a spare side for a miniature. His music fitted so well into the medium that one wonders if he had the gramophone at the back of his mind when he was composing, particularly concerning issues of duration and orchestration.

During the 1920s and 1930s, many of the leading orchestras, particularly the LSO and London Philharmonic Orchestra (LPO), were impecunious and were frequently in the recording studio because of the remuneration this brought.[8]

---

[4]   James Nott, *Music for the People* (Oxford, 2002), p. 13.

[5]   Lewis Foreman & Susan Foreman, *London* (New Haven, 2005), p. 223.

[6]   These were made in batches in 1924, circa 1934 and three sessions in 1935. (12/02/2011 Gilles Gouset to Michael Payne.)

[7]   Timothy Day, *A Century of Recorded Music* (New Haven, 2000), p. 6.

[8]   Richard Morrison, *Orchestra. The LSO* (London, 2004), p. 81. During the 1930s, the standard of the LSO was in decline and the LPO, with whom Coates made the majority of his records in the 1930s, were very much the premier ensemble. (Ibid.)

There was, however, great snobbery attached to making recordings of light music and when recording light music, these orchestras often disguised their identities on the record sleeve as 'Symphony Orchestra' or 'Light Symphony Orchestra' to disassociate themselves from the genre of light music. The orchestras were happy to be associated with 'high art' but when it came to the 'lower art' of light music they were pleased to accept the money it brought, but wanted to be isolated from the finished article.

Like the gramophone, another major development during the 1920s that would alter the course of Coates' musical direction was the formation of the British Broadcasting Corporation in 1922. The spread of the wireless was dramatic and, by 1939, 75 per cent of all households in England had access to a radio set.[9] As Scannell and Cardiff have argued: 'Light music and dance music, which were the bread and butter of broadcasting, particularly during the daytime hours and the late evening, were predictably cheap. Serious music absorbed a high proportion of time and money'.[10] From the foundation of the BBC Coates' music, both songs and orchestral works, had featured in programmes and in February 1925, he was possibly amongst the first composer-conductors to conduct over the airwaves, alongside Percy Fletcher.[11] The BBC took over the financial and artistic responsibilities from Chappells for the 1927 season of Promenade Concerts. The BBC gradually became more important to his work as a composer and, from 1931, gave the majority of first performances of his latest works. Coates remarked, in 1928, on the cumulative effect of the BBC's broadcasts and the influence it had on other outlets of his music: 'Lots of my records have been sold through people first hearing the pieces on the wireless.'[12]

Coates' music occupied a pivotal position within the BBC's output and was comprehensively performed by the BBC's orchestras. It was also used to fill apertures between programmes when required, probably because of its brevity, though it was seldom credited in the *Radio Times*.[13] In a 1935 interview he commented: 'I can't keep pace with the broadcasts of my own works ... as so many are played on the air. I often make a date with myself to stay in and listen, but I usually remember to tune in just as the last notes are coming through ... '.[14] Throughout his life, Coates was a regular broadcaster for the BBC usually conducting, on average, at least two full programmes of his music with the BBC's London orchestras annually. His work for the BBC brought him into contact with

---

[9]    Paddy Scannell & David Cardiff, *A Social History of British Broadcasting: Volume One* (Oxford, 1991), p. 362.

[10]    Ibid., p. 241.

[11]    On 26/02/1925. This is the earliest traced broadcast Coates made for the BBC, though such was the informal nature of the BBC on its formation that he may have made an earlier impromptu broadcast arranged hastily and not duly advertised.

[12]    21/01/1928 *Nottingham Evening News*.

[13]    17/08/1942 EC to Beatrice Harrison. *GB-Lcm*.

[14]    06/12/1935 *Radio Pictorial*.

the BBC conductor Stanford Robinson (who was conductor of the BBC Theatre Orchestra between 1932 and 1946). Coates struck up a cordial friendship with Robinson, universally known throughout the BBC as 'Robbie', a musician with whom he had a lot in common (including photography). Eric Maschwitz recalled Robbie in his autobiography as a man who 'will conduct a musical comedy with the same care and gusto that he devotes to a symphony'.[15] Robinson proved to be a valuable friend, as not only did he promote Coates' music within the BBC, but often performed Coates' music in his broadcasts (frequently meeting with the composer's approval) and offered practical advice over orchestration. This last role had been fulfilled by John Ansell in the 1920s at the Alhambra Theatre (now the Odeon Cinema, Leicester Square) when Ansell's orchestra used to try out Coates' latest compositions during the afternoon matinee.[16]

Coates' ascent to popularity as a composer of light music ran in tandem with the BBC's meteoric rise to prominence with the country. By 1934, the BBC had come to regard him 'as the leading exponent of light music'.[17] There was a symbiosis between Coates and the BBC: the BBC had a crucial need for Coates' music and his status, and Coates for the exposure and support that the BBC was able to offer him. In 1947, one newspaper estimated that the BBC played Coates' music, on average, fifty times a week, in various guises.[18] Probably the greatest assistance that the BBC could provide was the adoption of his music as signature tunes and call-signs; from this juncture, his music was not only wedded to the BBC, but etched into the hearts of generations of British society. For many, even today, over fifty years after his death, his name is indelibly linked with several popular BBC programmes. It was largely because of the BBC, through its regular broadcasts of his music, both under the composer's direction and the BBC staff conductors and through their adoption of Coates' music as signature tunes, that Coates attained his supreme popular status within light music.

As his music was now becoming better known, Coates started to introduce new elements into his orchestral music from the world of popular music. While there were elements of American jazz and ragtime, the two major influences on his work were the 'syncopated style' (as seen in the works of Zez Confrey) and the British dance bands of the 1920s. This was manifested not just in his approach to thematic material and harmony but also in his approach to orchestration and his use of popular dances of the period, especially the foxtrot. These elements, which were popular with a large cross-section of society, were yet another reason for Coates' pre-eminence as a composer over his light-music contemporaries, who were more sparing of their use of 'symphonic syncopation'.

Coates' adoption of this style came through his love of dancing. Both he and Phyl were frequent dancers, taking lessons for most of their life. This love of

---

[15]   Eric Maschwitz, *No Chip on My Shoulder* (London, 1957), p. 65.

[16]   Eric Coates, *Suite in Four Movements* (autograph), p. 453.

[17]   28/02/1934 Kenneth Wright to W.W. Thompson. *GB-Rwac*.

[18]   14/06/1947 *John Bull*.

dance brought him into contact with the arguably the most influential interwar dance-band leader, Jack Hylton. The Coates were frequent visitors to London's Kit-Kat Club, dancing away to the strains of Jack Hylton and his Orchestra. Hylton had clear views about the jazz that would work in Britain: 'Before it [jazz] can be played here it must be modified, *given the British touch*, which Americans and other foreigners never understand … . Symphonic syncopation,[19] which I feel proud to have developed in this country is pre-eminently British.'[20] Even though several members of his band could improvise 'hot jazz', they never did in their influential recordings.[21]

Coates was not the only composer to use jazz in his music: such composers as diverse as Debussy ('Gollywog's Cake-walk', *Children's Corner* 1906–08), Satie ('Ragtime du Paquebot', *Parade*, 1917), Stravinksy and Milhaud's epoch-making ballet (*La Création du Monde*, 1923) all pre-dated Coates. Walton, amongst other English composers, had assimilated elements of jazz into his orchestral works of the 1920s, namely *Façade* and the overture *Portsmouth Point*, after being influenced by the Savoy Band. During 1923–24, Walton was contemplating, and partially sketched, a *Fantasia Concertante* for piano, jazz band and orchestra, which Kennedy suggests may well have been for the Savoy band; Walton was forced to abandon the piece as there would be little future for such a work.[22] Within the sphere of light music, both Albert Ketèlbey and Haydn Wood had integrated ragtime and precursors of jazz into their music: Ketèlbey had written a 'skit' on ragtime in his 1916 novelty *Mind the Slide!* in which the sequence of ragtime melodies are interrupted by an insolent, malapert trombone. Wood also dabbled with the integration of jazz, writing a tango, *Morena*, and the *Jimmy Sale Rag* in the 1910s. Coates was, however, at the vanguard of the integration of jazz into orchestral scores and was one of the first British composers not to parody the style but to use it as an effective part of his music.

Since 1921, Coates had written several song-foxtrots and songs for the London stage. Even though he published several song-foxtrots, he wrote a number of songs under pseudonyms, almost certainly to protect his concert hall reputation. The majority of these songs presumably came his way through Phyl who was still working as an actress. Under the name Ciré he wrote two unpublished songs (both now lost) in 1924: 'Bluebells' for a production at the Aldwich Theatre (which also went touring in a revue entitled *Laughter in Love*); and 'You Keep Haunting Me' sung in cabaret at the Grafton Galleries, London. He was forced to change this *nom de plume* because William Boosey of Chappells disliked

---

[19]    'it represents a pleasing combination of harmony, melody and rhythm in such a way that the musical cravings of a normal person are satisfied'. (Jack Hylton, 'The British Touch', *The Gramophone* 4 (1926–27), p. 145.)

[20]    Ibid., p. 146.

[21]    Catherine Parsonage, *The Evolution of Jazz in England* (Aldershot, 2005), pp. 172 and 199. Jack Hylton's arrangers included Leighton Lucas, Peter Yorke and Paul Fenoulet.

[22]    Michael Kennedy, *A Portrait of Walton* (Oxford, 1989), p. 39.

it, adopting Jack Arnold instead.[23] Under this name he published three songs (through Chappells in 1924 and 1925) 'Diff'rent Somehow' and two songs written for *The Punch Bowl* at London's Duke of York's Theatre (which also featured songs by his light music contemporary Billy Mayerl),[24] 'Ev'ry Minute of Ev'ry Day' and 'K-Naughty Kanute'.[25]

During 1924 and 1925, there were two events that caused Coates to integrate jazz into his orchestral music seriously and this would alter the course of his musical development. First, Jack Hylton invited Coates to London's Ritz Hotel in late-April 1924 to lunch with himself and Maurice Ravel (who was in England to perform in a concert at the Aeolian Hall, including the premiere of *Tzigane*) with a view to asking them to write a work for Hylton's band in their own style.[26] Ravel declined, but later allowed Hylton to make an arrangement of his *Bolero*. Coates recalled his delight in meeting one of his favourite composers, and the difficulty they had in conversing, due to Coates' 'abominable' French and Ravel's 'negligible' English, resorting to sign language a great deal.[27] This engagement must have started Coates thinking about either writing a work for Hylton or producing a work that could be adapted for Hylton's band. Second, early in 1925, the combined forces of the Savoy Hotel gave a series of five concerts at Queen's Hall showcasing the development of jazz and ragtime into the dance music of the day and also including paraphrases of the classics.[28] While no evidence survives that Coates attended these concerts, both Phyl and Eric were regular dancers at the Savoy Hotel and would have presumably have heard about the concerts by word of mouth; they were also well-documented in the press. In addition, the song-foxtrot written that year, 'Rose of Samarkand' (also orchestrated as the second of *Two Light Syncopated Pieces*), was dedicated to Debroy Somers, the well-known leader of the Savoy Orpheans, proving that Coates had come into contact with the Savoy band. Through these concerts, Coates must have seen how popular this type of music was becoming and how he could achieve similar effects by using a standard symphony orchestra in symphonic syncopation.

The result of these two events was *Two Light Syncopated Pieces* written, surprisingly, for the 1925 Promenade Concerts. As Jacobs has stressed, Coates was fortunate that his latest works were performed at the Proms at all, as light music and the ballads had less of an appeal for the audiences and both were gradually being phased out (this purge drastically accelerated when the BBC took the concerts over from Chappells a few years later).[29] Both the *Two Pieces* are

---

[23]   14/05/1924 EC to Charles James. *GB-Lprs*.

[24]   Notably 'Did Tosti Raise his Bowler Hat'. See Peter Dickinson, *Marigold* (Oxford, 1999), pp. 90–94.

[25]   There was also another song for this production entitled 'Oh Yes!', which is now lost.

[26]   Austin Coates, programme 2.

[27]   Coates, p. 154. Coates does not recount that Hylton was present.

[28]   Dickinson, p. 53.

[29]   Arthur Jacobs, *Henry J. Wood* (London, 1994), p. 199.

foxtrots, one slow, 'Moon Magic', and the other, 'Rose of Samarkand', fast; only in 1924 had the fast and slow foxtrots evolved.[30] The latter also appeared separately as a song (with lyrics by Royden Barrie) and it is unclear which originated first, the song or the orchestral piece. The foxtrot, since 1914, had rapidly established itself in the dance halls as one of the pre-eminent dances of the 1920s. The harmonic construction of the *Two Pieces* is very much along dance band lines with frequent occurrences of major seventh and eleventh chords and no significant modulations. The melodic construction of both pieces shows hallmarks of popular dance band melodies with frequent chromatic 'decorating' melodies and the use of muted brass. In 'Moon Magic', the melody at letter A is quite angular, with several leaps of a seventh, syncopated crotchets and chromatic triplets, which are reminiscent of many well-orchestrated dance tunes of the period.

For a large proportion of 'Rose of Samarkand', Coates sustains a 'drum beat', initially a steady crotchet pulse on the tenor drum from letters A to C, which returns from G to I. From J to O the side drum takes the rhythm of the accompaniment of the orchestra, very much a reminder of the function of the drums in a dance band. At times, he treats the orchestra very much as units of sound, as in a dance orchestra, there is the 'saxophone team', the 'brass team' and the 'rhythm team', each represented by different groups of instruments. Furthermore, the instrumentation reflects this, as Coates uses muted brass in bars 33–4, 37–8, 42, 46–50 in the 'Rose of Samarkand'. Later, at figure J, he uses two low clarinets, doubled with cellos, making a sound akin to the saxophone, over which he juxtaposes a solo violin melody – highly reminiscent of the string sound of dance orchestras (if they employed strings, as few did). These two foxtrots marked his wholesale adoption of the jazz idiom into orchestral music and while there are a good number of pieces that do not utilize jazz (or 'syncopated idiom' as Coates preferred to call it), there are traits of it in the orchestrations of most of his pieces. The *Two Light Syncopated Pieces* are important works in Coates' development as a composer and their experimentation with jazz, both in rhythm and in orchestration, was to be of paramount importance in the two next extended works.

The second product of his adoption of a syncopated style was an orchestral phantasy based on Oscar Wilde's short story 'The Selfish Giant', first published in 1888 and very well known at the time. Wilde's story dealt with a group of children who wanted to play in a giant's garden but the giant built a wall condemning the garden to perpetual winter. Eventually spring returns to the garden, the giant's antipathy to the children melts and he finally dies.

Coates had always believed that light music was pictorial and, no doubt inspired by Phyl's story-telling ability, wrote a single movement work around a popular bedtime story, as Austin recalled:

---

[30]    Albert McCarthy, *The Dance Band Era* (Radnor, Philadelphia, 1982), p. 9.

Except on the days when my mother had a matinee she would tell me a story before putting me to bed. She told fairy stories with extraordinary artistry. My father was so fascinated that he would come in from his writing room to listen.[31]

Coates also expounded the importance of Phyl's artistry:

All the same, she [Phyl] has to admit that it was she who, in our early married life when she was still in her 'teens, used to read poetry to me or tell me stories to give me ideas for my music at the times when my "muse" eluded me, and she also has to admit, in this way, she never failed to get me started on some musical project.[32]

Coates chose the term 'phantasy' (anglicized German rather than 'fantasy' or 'fantasie') to describe the work, though the autograph score reveals that he had originally wished to describe the work as a 'fairytale', and adopted phantasy later.[33] During the early twentieth century the genre of phantasy was undergoing a renaissance due to the Cobbett Prize at the RCM (established in 1905) and Cobbett's frequent commissions from composers such as Frank Bridge. For Coates, the phantasy (Haydn Wood styled his single-movement canvasses as rhapsodies) was a miniature symphonic poem and one that could be adapted to the nuances of the fairytale he wished to portray in music. The success of this work sparked off a series of musical fairytales and Coates' choice of well-known stories portrayed in music was another reason of his success over his contemporaries. While others set pictorial situations, very few chose such familiar stories to describe in music.

*The Selfish Giant* was completed in September 1925 and received its premiere in November at the Eastbourne Festival. His usual publishers, Chappells, took fright at the score, fearing it was too difficult, and he was forced to publish the work with Booseys.[34] As a consequence, Booseys invited Sydney Baynes to make unnecessary reductions to Coates' score. Baynes retained the two bassoons and four horns and only removed the second oboe part as well as making numerous minor adjustments to the brass and string parts.

The Phantasy is based on a reduced version of Wilde's story; a synopsis (both pictorial and musical) is included in the score:

Starting with a short introduction, which is meant to depict the desolation of the Giant's Garden, there follows an *Allegro Vivace* which illustrates the North Wind, Hail and Snow making a playground of the Garden. Next comes the Giant's Theme, given out by the brass, depicting the Giant's relentless character. The Theme of Happiness then tries to enter, but is crushed by the Giant's Theme,

---

31    Austin Coates, programme 2.

32    Coates (autograph), p. 462.

33    *GB-Lbh*.

34    Coates, p. 203.

but becoming more insistent it eventually takes possession and after a climax the
Theme of Happiness is heard in full.

Then follows a brief return to the Theme of the North Wind intermingled with the
Giant's Theme:

> The Giant's ill-will is finally silenced by the entrance of the children into his
> garden. The Children's Dance Theme starts hesitatingly, but quickly gains
> confidence and eventually leads into the Theme of Happiness.

> By this time the Giant's heart has melted, Spring wakes in the garden and all
> is peace.

Musically, *The Selfish Giant* is based on two major melodic ideas, the pentatonic
giant's theme, which appears in two guises, the second of which slightly alters
the ending (and shows the influence of jazz in its rhythm; Example 6.2a) and
the theme of happiness (which bears a resemblance to the second subject of *The
Merrymakers* Overture; Example 6.2b).

Inherent in the construction of the giant's theme are influences of the dance
bands: the theme has beats two and three tied, a characteristic of the foxtrot,
along with other popular dances. Coates also calls upon a 'secondary' theme,
the theme of the north wind, first heard at figure 5 (which bears a resemblance
to the first subject of *The Merrymakers* Overture). In *The Selfish Giant*, there
are traits of formula such as the juxtaposition of keys onto one another, often
E♭ major onto the tonic, A minor. This is partially a dramatic device as the giant
is often associated with the 'flattened' world, opposed to the 'pure' world of
the children's A minor/major, though the giant's theme does feature in a minor
key. Coates also introduces two elements into this score that would become a
feature in his later works. The first, jazz, predominately with the foxtrot for the
children's dance (figure 18), but also in its absorption into the harmony and
rhythm, clearly seen at bars 177–86 with the frequent use of off-beat chords
and both major and minor seventh chords, a significant advance from the earlier
*Two Light Syncopated Pieces*. Second, there is a more fundamental assimilation
of the genre in the pentatonic giant's theme; pentatonicism was popular in jazz
scores of the period. A number of his scores feature inherent modality; 'Fresh
Morning' (*Springtime* Suite) has elements of the Phrygian mode and the trio of
*Entr'acte à la Gavotte* features Mixolydian inflexions, prevalent in much British
music of this period. The close of *The Selfish Giant* also features birdsong motifs;
a device that he seems to have been adept at composing. Coates undoubtedly
borrowed the motif from Ketèlbey's *In a Monastery Garden* (published a decade
before *The Selfish Giant*).

Example 6.2  *The Selfish Giant*, Giant's Theme. © Copyright 1926 by Boosey &
Co. Ltd. Reproduced by permission of Boosey and Hawkes Music
Publishers Ltd

(a)  Slow version

(b)  Fast version

(c)  Theme of happiness

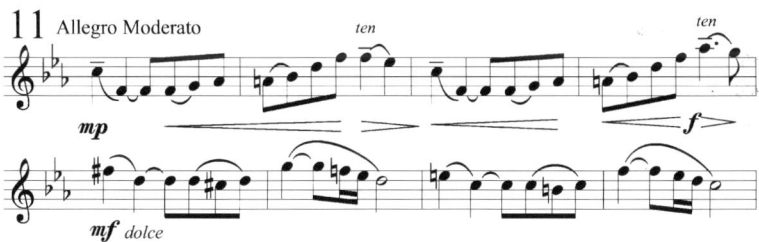

Almost immediately after its composition, *The Selfish Giant* was taken up by
Jack Hylton and his Kit-Kat club band (in an arrangement by Leighton Lucas)[35]
where it was performed in front of a 7,000 strong audience at a London Ballad

---

[35]  Lucas also arranged Coates' *The Three Bears* for Hylton's Band. The score and
parts survive: *GB-LAu*.

Concert at the Albert Hall in a joint performance by the bands of the Kit-Kat Club and Kettner's Restaurant on 20 February 1926.[36]

Hylton and his band also had recorded the Phantasy the previous day with the same forces, though it remains a matter of conjecture whether Coates or Hylton conducted the recording session; it seems most likely that Hylton did, given his tight hold over his ensemble.[37] The Phantasy fitted in with Hylton's 'Symphonic Syncopation', his way of presenting the 'classics' rhythmically paraphrased to suit both the dancer and the listener.[38] *The Selfish Giant* also proved popular with Henry Hall (then working for the LMS Railway at Manchester's Midland Hotel) who also performed it in Manchester; Coates travelled there especially for the concert.[39]

As the result of the immense popularity of *The Selfish Giant*, Coates was soon at work on a successor, this time based on the even more popular staple of bedtime fare, 'Goldilocks and the Three Bears', dedicated to 'Austin on his Fourth Birthday'.[40] According to Coates the choice was presented as an imperative by Austin: 'He gave me no peace until I had set his favourite story to music.'[41] *The Three Bears* Phantasy was completed at the close of May and after losing *The Selfish Giant* to Booseys, Chappells accepted the work with alacrity and published a full score; an unprecedented step for a light work. The first performance was at the Promenade Concerts, conducted by the composer on 7 October 1926. The performance that Coates treasured, however, was a subsequent one in November when he conducted the Phantasy at Eastbourne and Edward Elgar decided to sit amongst the percussion:

> He was quite oblivious that his entry into the orchestra had created a minor sensation among the audience and that during the performance he nearly dried me up by tapping his feet and wagging his head from side to side, to such effect that it was only with the greatest difficulty I managed to keep my mind on directing the orchestra through the cross-rhythms of the foxtrot section in my Phantasy.[42]

*The Three Bears* is pervaded by the use of a leitmotif, verbalizing the phrase 'Who's been sitting in *my* chair' (Example 6.3).

---

[36]   March 1926, *Melody Maker*, p. 11.

[37]   *The Selfish Giant* (HMV, C1253). Several sources credit Coates with the honour of conducting this record.

[38]   Jack Hylton, 'Dance Music of To-Day', *The Musical Times* 67 (1926), p. 800.

[39]   Henry Hall, *Here's to the Next Time* (London, 1955), p. 69.

[40]   Though this only appears in Coates, p. 203, the published full score, orchestral parts and piano solo version do not bear this dedication.

[41]   *The Gramophone* 15 (1936–37), p. 235.

[42]   Coates, p. 206.

Example 6.3   *The Three Bears* Phantasy, leitmotif. © 1926 Chappell Music Ltd,
              London, W6 8BS. Reproduced by permission of Faber Music Ltd.
              All Rights Reserved

This motif forms the basis of the majority of the thematic material and the
countermelody (as in both the slow valses) and can be frequently heard (nearly
100 times) throughout the nine minute duration of the Phantasy. One wonders if
Coates' had Dukas' *The Sorcerer's Apprentice* at the back of his mind, with its
frequent repetition of its main theme. He sets the evergreen story in a pictorial
manner, made more effective by the use of captions in the score, such as the
striking of the clock after letter A (scored for woodwind, harp and glockenspiel)
and Goldilocks knocking on door of the Bears' Cottage after letter E (scored on
the woodblock). Coates' sense of humour is never far away with a three-part fugal
exposition for the arrival of the Three Bears (letter J), each entry being the arrival
of one of the bears and a foxtrot as 'The Three Bears make the best of it and return
home, in the best of humour'. There are also moments of extreme tenderness in
the two slow valses (letters H and T), the latter exquisitely scored for a solo violin.

*The Three Bears*, like its predecessor, proved to be a great favourite with Jack
Hylton. As Coates recalled in 1937:

> On the night when I was conducting the first performance of *The Three Bears* at
> the Queen's Hall, Jack walked into the promenade with my wife. At first he was
> just mildly interested, but when the music got to the rhythmic part it got hold
> of him. To the amusement of people standing near by, he, quite unconsciously,
> began to jig a Charleston, his shoulders swaying, his feet tapping. That was how
> he came to do *The Three Bears* himself.[43]

Aside from *The Three Bears*, 1926 brought three other compositions; a short
intermezzo *By the Tamarisk* and two songs. One of the songs, 'Bird Songs at
Eventide' captured the public's imagination and rapidly became one of Coates'
most popular songs, despite the fact that the popularity of the ballad was in
terminal decline. *By the Tamarisk* was inspired by patches of tamarisk that grew
near the Coates' Selsey cottage. It has moments of great assurance with the key
changes from the tonic of C major to the flattened submediant (letter C) back to
the tonic then to the mediant major (letter D) and returning to the tonic via the
flattened submediant (letter E) are slickly handled with an effortless legerdemain.
Coates saves his most skilful moments until the coda, with a sudden shift toward

---

[43]   November 1937 *The Gramophone*, p. 237.

the flattened submediant (letter I) in a daring chromatic return to the tonic. The final 19 bars of the coda are perhaps the closest he ever came to assimilating the harmonic language of Billy Mayerl.

Coates' schedule of composition rapidly increased in 1927 when he received an invitation from Basil Cameron, who at this stage was briefly the conductor of the Harrogate Municipal Orchestra, for a new work for that year's festival. Coates was apathetic (wanting to spend his time visiting Phyl who was absent with her latest stage play) and repeatedly declined Cameron's invitation.[44] Fortunately, after repeated cajoling from Cameron and the festival committee, an idea for a suite based on the four points of the compass materialized, entitled *The Four Ways* Suite, and he settled down to the composition of his first suite since 1921. It was completed by September and first performed by the Harrogate Orchestra under the composer later that month. Coates had fond memories of the premiere. He recalled:

> The first performance of 'Four Ways' will always bring back a picture of an audience half rising from its seat to stand to attention, owing to the side-drum roll and cymbal crash in the first bars of the opening movement which unintentionally gave the impression of a 'God Save the King' to follow.[45]

There was an abundance of Coates' music at Harrogate during 1927 (undoubtedly because of Cameron's insistence), with ten performances of the *Summer Days* Suite, seven of *Two Light Syncopated Pieces* and five of the *Miniature Suite*, in addition to a healthy number of performances of his other pieces.[46]

Press reception of the new Suite was on the whole positive and much was made of Coates' integration of jazz into the finale. The press lauded his attempt, believing a parody to be more acceptable than the real thing, as the *Daily News* stated: 'If only jazz were as agreeable as Mr Coates makes it out to be there would not be half the outcry against it that there is.'[47] However, after the first performance the same newspaper included an observation about the finale: 'It is ingenious, but Mr Coates has too much native refinement to give a faithful idea of the vulgarities and brutalities of the Charleston or the Black Bottom. All it needs is a few blatant, shrieking discords.'[48]

The Suite is one of Coates' most unique and novel creations and marks, at last, the end of his almost standard (until then) use of a $\frac{6}{8}$ opening movement, a reflective, romantic middle movement and a closing valse. Each of the four movements is based on a point of the compass: 'Northwards' is a march recalling Scotland and using the folk melody 'Ca' the Yowes'; 'Southwards' a valse (possibly thinking of

---

[44]    Coates, p. 204.

[45]    Ibid.

[46]    09/03/2004 George Capel to Michael Payne.

[47]    10/11/1927 *Daily News*.

[48]    24/09/1927 *Daily News*.

the dancehalls and restaurants of London where the Coates danced), with a more Mediterranean feel than the usual French; 'Eastwards' an eastern dance pointing to the Orient; and 'Westwards' a movement entitled 'Rhythm' pointing to America and the Charleston.

'Northwards' holds the distinction of being Coates' first march, though its construction has little in common with his 'March formula' which was adopted in his next-but-one march, 'Knightsbridge'. Intriguingly, 'Northwards' has four themes divided into two subject groups and shows a symmetry of form different to the other marches. 'Northwards' also holds the honour of being Coates' first attempt to integrate 'borrowed material' (letter F), this was something he rarely attempted and here, like his other attempts 'Covent Garden' (*London* Suite) and 'The Man from the Sea' (*The Three Men* Suite) he alters the rhythm and treats the material in his own idiomatic style.

In 'Southwards' Coates alternates between slow and fast valses (as he had done in 'Among the Poppies' (*From the Countryside* Suite). 'Eastwards', like Ketèlbey's *In a Persian Market* (which may well have acted as a model), is full of 'oriental clichés' such as a pentatonic first theme (first heard at bar 5), a 3-beat rhythmic ostinato pattern (letter C) and orchestral effects such as the xylophone (Coates' only use of this instrument) occasionally doubled with piccolo and gong. The finale, 'Westwards: Rhythm' employs one of his favourite dances, the Charleston. It is essentially melodic variants of one theme (first heard in its entirety three bars after letter C), with frequent interruptions and the importance of a rhythmic syncopated pattern (heard in the introduction and later at letter G). As with his other jazz parodies, he assimilates the style effectively (even without the use of a saxophone) and his orchestration is superb.

*The Four Ways* Suite is essentially an unsuccessful work that has not stood the test of time well. This is a result of the large number of interruptions to the melodies; one never feels that a melody flows in this Suite and they are frequently passed between instruments. There is a good deal of repetition of ideas throughout the Suite (especially in 'Northwards' and 'Eastwards'). In addition, with the unsubtle 'Eastern Dance' one feels that Coates could have provided a far more effective movement rather than resorting to musical clichés. Perhaps for these reasons, *The Four Ways* Suite has never been amongst Coates' most popular pieces: though the composer did often include single movements in his BBC broadcasts, he never recorded the work.

Slowly, during the 1920s, Coates was becoming increasingly well-known as a musical establishment figure. In October 1927, he acted as an examiner for the first time for the RCM's Patron's Fund (a fund that offered composers the chance to hear a composition performed). It was a role he undertook until 1933.[49] He was critical of most of the works he examined, berating the composers for their lack of melody and ineffectual orchestration. Rarely did he recommend a work for performance and he was largely out of sympathy for the works of a younger

---

[49]    He examined with either S.P. Waddington or Armstrong Gibbs.

generation. His comments were harsh and acerbic, commenting on a piece by Alan Bush: 'Fearfully dull. No wonder it took 9 months to write. Seventy one pages and not a single bar of inspiration.'[50] Another work was queried for its lack of key signature, as 'this leads to trouble in the end'.[51]

Given his close associations with jazz resulting from *The Four Ways* Suite and other works, Coates was a natural choice for the *Daily Sketch* to invite to write an article for the paper in response to Henry Coward's lecture to the Incorporated Society of Musicians about how 'we must ban jazz'. In the paper, he extolled his love of jazz as a result of dancing: 'the best of modern dance tunes fascinate me immensely, but then I am a keen dancer. Whether they would have the same appeal if I were not a dancer is another matter entirely.'[52] He argued that most critics were dismissive of jazz because they seldom listened to well-orchestrated dance tunes. For him, it was the orchestration of a good dance tune that made it, rather than the tune itself. Further on in the article he went on to justify his approach to the inclusion of jazz in his *The Three Bears*:

> This work has frequently been called the connecting music between jazz and legitimate music. I did not write it with this intention, and was surprised myself when these dance rhythms became so insistent that there was no keeping them out. For this reason, I consider that modern syncopation employed with discretion and occasionally in light orchestral works can be very effective and attractive.[53]

This article demonstrated that Coates was happy to be associated with the *bête noir* of music, jazz. During 1928, he arranged his *The Three Bears* for Jack Payne and the BBC Dance Orchestra, which Coates conducted in a BBC broadcast on 22 May.[54] Later on, he also conducted a full programme of his music including three of his 'jazzier' pieces with the Dance Orchestra on 13 November. Through these broadcasts with the Dance Orchestra, he struck up a friendship with Payne (one of the most influential dance band leaders of the period) who invited him in 1932 to write a foreword to his autobiography *This is Jack Payne*.

Apart from the composition of three songs and two short orchestral miniatures (*Under the Stars* and *Mirage*), 1928 was almost totally devoid of new works. The two miniatures are characterized by luxuriant harmony, building on from *By the Tamarisk*, with the frequent use of sevenths and elevenths, chromatic movement, the use of augmented fifth chords and the dissonances created by melodic

[50]   13/10/1927 RCM Patron's Fund, Examiner's Report. *GB-Lcm*. Coates' comments on Alan Bush's *Symphonic Impression*.

[51]   06/11/1930 RCM Patron's Fund, Examiner's Report. *GB-Lcm*. Coates' comments on Phyllis Tate's *Third and Fourth Movements from a Symphony*.

[52]   07/01/1928 *Daily Sketch*.

[53]   Ibid.

[54]   31/05/28 J.M. Rose-Troup to EC. *GB-Rwac*.

appoggiaturas. The second, and the more successful of the two, is *Under the Stars*, which could almost be a song orchestrated as an entr'acte, as it is effectively verse (bar 9)–chorus (letter B)–verse (letter C)–chorus–verse (letter D)–epilogue (letter E). It also echoes one of Coates' songs with the chorus material introduced in the opening two bars, before the start of the first verse. *Under the Stars* is characterized by a fine scalic first subject (bar 9), which bears a striking resemblance to bars 15–22 of *Mirage*. *Under the Stars* holds the distinction of being the first of his scores to call for a saxophone, though it is not used as a solo instrument, simply adding colour. He may well have used the saxophone and the other instrument associated with jazz, the vibraphone, more extensively during the 1920s and 1930s if they were more readily found in orchestras.

With few new works emanating from his pen, Coates did not neglect the other side of his career as a performer. On 29 January 1929, he made a rare foray into the world of a broadcasting pianist as he accompanied Hubert Eisdell in a selection of his most popular songs and David Wise on the violin, playing the violin and piano versions of *Mirage* and *Under the Stars*. He often included songs in his BBC broadcasts and sometimes these were accompanied on the piano (either a BBC staff accompanist, or, rarely, the composer) or by orchestra. Throughout his life, Coates was very dismissive of his abilities as a pianist, but he clearly must have been up to broadcast standard. Teddy Holmes of Chappells remembered Coates' piano playing abilities: 'When Eric was illustrating a new work on the piano, he had a fantastic habit of singing the various inner counter-melodies, and he could imitate a clarinet or oboe quite beautifully.'[55] He was unhappy in performing his own songs on the piano either in public or on the wireless and by 1933 no longer accompanied singers, apparently being 'too diffident' to play in broadcasts.[56]

The majority of his compositional schedule during 1929 was taken up with the writing of a new fairytale phantasy (and his first major work since *The Four Ways* Suite). This time, the choice of subject was the well-loved 'Cinderella', a subject already dealt with by Rossini, Massenet, Percy Pitt and subsequently by Prokofiev. It marked a spate of single-movement works the following year. *Cinderella* originated as an invitation from the 1929 Eastbourne Festival and, unusually for Coates, was finished nearly three months before the premiere in November. Some of the orchestration was even undertaken during a bridge party at their London flat; Coates abominated bridge.[57] After the first performance, the composer enticed the BBC to broadcast the work under his direction (on 28 January 1930).[58] This placed Coates in an invidious position as *Cinderella* had been used in the score to the film *Symphony in Two Flats* and the film's directors were anxious that the public did not hear Coates' music before the release of the film; Coates had to

---

[55]    Teddy Holmes in Ian Lace, 'Foreword' in Eric Coates, *Suite in Four Movements* (London, 1986), p. viii.

[56]    21/08/1933 Leslie Woodgate to Kenneth Wright. *GB-Rwac*.

[57]    01/07/1934 *Daily Express*.

[58]    17/12/1929 P.J. Tillet to EC. *GB-Rwac*.

write to the BBC to ask them to withdraw the piece from the broadcast, which they did.[59]

Like *The Three Bears*, *Cinderella* is based on a leitmotif that forms the basis of a good proportion of the thematic material, though is not as consistently present like *The Three Bears* (Examples 6.4a and 6.4b).

Example 6.4  *Cinderella* Phantasy. © 1930 Chappell Music Ltd, London, W6 8BS. Reproduced by permission of Faber Music Ltd. All Rights Reserved

(a)  Motif

Cin-de-rel-la

(b)  Bars 1–4

Coates also chooses (as in *The Selfish Giant*) to set only selected parts of the tale. Casting it in a single-movement rhapsodic form depicting the story graphically, Coates handles the structure successfully with many deft touches, such as: the Debussyeque opening (and its altered reprise at letter M), surely homage to Debussy's *Prélude à l'après-midi d'un faune*; the superb valse section (letter F) when Cinderella arrives at the ball, followed by a beautiful, tender slow valse while the Prince and Cinderella dance (letter H), and the adroit way he gradually increases the tempo after this section; the Stravinskyian passage (letter L) when the clock strikes 12 with the trumpets blazing the 'Cinderella motif' over the top; and the march theme (letter P) which returns as the Prince arrives at Cinderella's house and acts as a coda to the phantasy when the Prince and Cinderella depart 'happy ever after.' *Cinderella* also includes subtle touches of humour, such as a piece of slightly ungainly counterpoint when the ugly sisters try to dance at the Ball, 16 bars after letter F.

Coates held his third, and final, phantasy in the highest regard informing the conductor Joseph Lewis: 'I think it is really the best thing I have done ...'.[60] Coates tried in vain to have *Cinderella* included into the 1930 Promenade Concerts (which were now run by the BBC), which marked the start of a number of letters

---

[59]    26/01/1930 EC to P.J. Tillet. *GB-Rwac*.

[60]    13/11/1930 EC to Joseph Lewis. *GB-Rwac*.

sent to the BBC during the 1930s asking for inclusion in the Proms.[61] Adrian Boult (the BBC's recently appointed Director of Music) had to decline as a result of an abundance of British music in that season's programme, though Coates was invited to conduct two of the *Four Old English Songs*.[62] The following year he tried again to have *Cinderella* or his latest suite, *From Meadow to Mayfair*, included but to no avail.

After the completion of *Cinderella*, Coates succumbed to a severe bout of pneumonia and the Coates retreated to Selsey to aid his recovery.[63] On his return to strength he wrote three short piano pieces for Phyl's sister Joan, a professional pianist trained at the RCM under Harold Samuel, the *Three Lyric Pieces*.[64] This was a rare venture into chamber music and his first instrumental pieces since the *Six Short Pieces (Without Octaves)* written nearly 20 years previously. The work shows a marked advance in his writing for the piano. For Coates, the piano was never his *métier* or a natural form of expression. He usually fabricated a piano reduction (and presumably the piano conductor parts) for his orchestral works, but these can often be ungainly and difficult to play. The *Lyric Pieces* are quite different in tone from his orchestral pieces and are quite opulent in their harmony, building on from *Under the Stars* and *Mirage*. The jewel of the set is the fine concluding valse, which owes a clear debt to Tchaikovsky. Sadly the pieces have languished, largely buried since their publication, and deserve a wider audience.

Concurrently with his work on the three piano pieces, he was commissioned by the Columbia Record Company to compose a *Symphonic Rhapsody* based on Richard Rodgers' song 'With a Song in My Heart', primarily for recording purposes.[65] For the composition, he was paid a fee and then assigned the compositional rights to Columbia, the only composition for which he disposed of them.[66] Little is known about the commission, but Coates had a great love for the American song composers of the 1920s, especially Gershwin, Kern and Rodgers.[67] The choice of the Rodgers song for Coates' *Rhapsody* was intriguing as it was first sung in America in early 1929 (in the production *Spring is Here*) and not introduced in England until *Cochran's 1930 Revue* in London in late March 1930;[68] Coates may well have been at work on the *With a Song in My Heart*.

[61]  13/06/1930 EC to Adrian Boult. *GB-Rwac*.

[62]  18/06/1930 Adrian Boult to EC. *GB-Rwac*. On 23/08/1930.

[63]  Coates, p. 216.

[64]  Joan had made her Wigmore Hall debut in the early 1920s and was a regular accompanist to the cellist Thelma Riesse, including a tour to Germany in 1933 with her. She ended her professional career on her marriage in 1938. (Conversation with Francis Freeman, 03/08/2009).

[65]  20/12/39 EC to Reginald Burston. *GB-Rwac*. The song was subsequently used as the signature tune to the BBC radio feature *Family Favourites*.

[66]  Undated PRS Internal Memorandum (circa January 1940). *GB-Lprs*.

[67]  As can be seen in a letter he wrote to the *Radio Times*. (06/03/1936 *Radio Times*.)

[68]  Edward Lea, *The Best of Rodgers and Hart* (London, 1975), p. 25.

*Symphonic Rhapsody After Richard Rodgers* before this latter date. If Columbia had not suggested the song, surely Chappells might have drawn his attention to it, since they published it. Whoever was responsible for the choice, the resulting work is no mere song orchestration.

The composer conducted the recording session (which was also the first performance) in April with the Court Symphony Orchestra for Columbia and the work remained the property of Columbia and was unpublished.[69] During the 1930s, the *Symphonic Rhapsody* attracted occasional performances, with the score and parts being hired directly from Columbia. By the late 1930s the work was receiving several broadcasts and Coates tried to lure Chappells into publishing the work. However, due to the rights being assigned to Columbia and the awkward position of how to define the work for the PRS, as either a joint composition between Rodgers and Coates; or an arrangement by Coates the piece was left unpublished.[70] It is a travesty that such an important and successful work from a 'golden period' should be left unpublished, like the next work written that year.

Rodgers' melody is never far away and Coates amalgamates it into his thematic material. Most of Coates' material is drawn from the opening bar of the chorus ('With a Song in my Heart'), which he uses (often with slight embellishments) as a motif throughout the piece. Example 6.5a shows the motif and Example 6.5b shows one of the subtle ways in which he integrates Rodger's material with his own.

Coates rarely uses whole passages of the song and only on three occasions does he quote the chorus almost directly (letters G, H, and 15 bars after P). The core of the work is the transformation of the song into a valse, initially based on material from the verse (letter J), which then moves into a slow valse before returning, via an accelerando, to the quick valse. As with his subsequent *Second Symphonic Rhapsody*, he introduces his own material (9 bars after letter L), which is highly reminiscent of the opening movement of the *Springtime* Suite.

Almost concurrently with his work on the *Symphonic Rhapsody* Coates was at work on a ballet to form part of a masque, entitled *Charlot's Masquerade* presented by the impresario André Charlot. This masque was to mark the opening of the Cambridge Theatre in London, and was produced by B.A. Mayer and starred Beatrice Lillie. Like Sullivan and German before him, Coates was happy to write music for the theatre. There was another ballet performed alongside Coates', Cyril Scott's *The Masque of the Red Death*. Both ballets were staged by Quentin Tod. Coates was no stranger to Charlot: his song 'Diff'rent Somehow', written and published under his *nom de plume* Jack Arnold, had been composed for Charlot's *1924 Revue* and a ballet based on *The Three Bears* (featuring Betty Oliver as Goldilocks) was staged in his *1928 Revue*. For his subject, no doubt inspired by his early choice of fairytales, he chose 'Snow White and the Seven Dwarfs'. His choice did not meet with approval from the superstitious Charlot,

---

[69]    Only a poor quality copyists score and parts survives, the autograph score being lost. *GB-Lcm* Box 192.

[70]    Undated PRS Internal Memorandum (circa January 1940). *GB-Lprs*.

Example 6.5  *Symphonic Rhapsody after Richard Rodgers*

(a)  Motif

(b)  Letter B

who believed that dwarfs were an ill omen and was horrified at the prospect of the Queen shattering a mirror in rage.[71] Charlot's influence can be seen on the frequent change of title of the ballet which was originally *The Seven Fauns* and became *The Seven Brothers* before being re-titled for the production as *Snowdrop and the Seven Dwarfs*, though the manuscript score bears the title *The Seven Dwarfs*, under which title it was recorded in 1993.[72] However, in the Coates household it was always affectionately known as *Snowdrop*.

Coates finished the score on 6 June and his choice of instrumentation was supremely limited by the composition of the orchestra: single flute, oboe, clarinet, bassoon, two trumpets, single trombone, percussion, harp, two pianos (with the pianist doubling celeste), four violins, two violas, two cellos and a double bass. The masquerade was first presented in an 'out of town' preview in Birmingham on 18 August before moving to London for the official premiere on 4 September; both performances were presumably conducted by the composer.[73] Alas, the production did not run for a great deal of time, transferring to Brighton (where Coates conducted it at the beginning of November).[74] The final performance appears to have been on 6 November when the parts were available for use by the BBC.[75] The BBC were keen to broadcast the Ballet and Kenneth Wright (a member of the BBC's Music Department), who had seen the production in October, approved

[71]  Coates, p. 214.

[72]  *Four Centuries* (ASV, CDWHL 2075).

[73]  04/08/1930 *The Times*.

[74]  17/10/1930 EC to Joseph Lewis. *GB-Rwac*.

[75]  22/10/1930 EC to Joseph Lewis. *GB-Rwac*.

it for broadcast, and set the BBC wheels in motion to secure a performance.[76] However, Charlot would not allow *Snowdrop* to be broadcast until after its run in the theatre, and then provided it was stated that it was from 'Charlot's Masquerade from the Cambridge Theatre'.[77]

The Ballet is structured into two scenes. A brief introduction heralds the arrival of Scene I, set in the Queen's boudoir in her castle. The Queen asks the mirror who is the most beautiful in the land. The mirror replies that Snowdrop is the most beautiful, which enrages the Queen and she breaks the mirror with a candlestick. The Queen sends for Snowdrop to see for herself. Once the Queen has set her eyes on Snowdrop, she orders her from the castle. A bridge passage links to Scene II, which is set in the faun's hut in the forest. Snowdrop enters the hut tired, finds a bed and falls asleep. The First Faun arrives in the hut and sees Snowdrop asleep, beckons the other fauns, who look at her and then depart into the forest. The Queen, disguised as a peddler, arrives at the hut and strangles Snowdrop and leaves. The First Faun returns to the hut and finds her unconscious. He revives her and then departs. The Queen returns disguised as a fruit-seller and sells Snowdrop a poisoned apple, which she eats and again becomes unconscious. The Queen exits triumphantly and later the fauns return jubilantly to find Snowdrop lying on her bed. The First Faun tries to revive her, but believing her to be dead, kisses her, which causes the Faun to turn into a beautiful prince and Snowdrop is brought back from the dead. The Queen and her entourage return and they dance with the fauns. The dancers become exhausted and gradually depart, and Snowdrop and the Prince depart hand-in-hand, leaving the Queen, mad with jealousy, to faint.

Musically, there are eight key themes and a 'motto theme' (heard at the opening), which returns at several strategic points. Theme 5 (heard two bars after letter Q) is clearly associated with Snowdrop and theme 4 with the First Faun (letter M). There is use of several set pieces, such as a Polacca (letter D) and a Gavotte (letter K) and a superb fugue at letter BB, within the 15-minute through-composed structure.

For concert use, Coates sanctioned important cuts, shortening the work by removing the opening until letter I (removing the first three themes) and a short cut between letters W and AA (which removes a brief cadenza and a short grandioso passage).[78] Initially, he had a desire to publish the ballet, although the unique orchestration made this well-nigh impossible (the BBC, however, did present several performances during the early 1930s) and it would have needed to be re-orchestrated for a standard orchestra.[79] It was not until 1938 that the Ballet was recast and published as *The Enchanted Garden* (see Chapter 8 and Appendix 2).

The score of *Snowdrop* was the first to be completed in a new home. When Austin reached school age, his parents decided to send him away to board at a

[76]   15/10/1930 Kenneth Wright to Adrian Boult. *GB-Rwac.*
[77]   22/10/1930 EC to Joseph Lewis. *GB-Rwac.*
[78]   03/12/1930 EC to Joseph Lewis. *GB-Rwac.*
[79]   17/10/1930 EC to Joseph Lewis. *GB-Rwac.*

preparatory school, Seafield School on the south coast of England, before later sending him onto Stowe (where his contemporaries included the actor David Niven and writer and broadcaster Peregrine Worsthorne). Thus, with the absence of a small child, Eric and Phyl could return to their carefree days, dancing and dining in exclusive London restaurants. Austin's initial days at school proved to be particularly traumatic when they received several harrowing letters of heartache from him asking to be removed from school because he hated it so much.[80] Once these difficulties were resolved, Eric and Phyl set about moving from the relative isolation of Hampstead (necessitated by Austin's arrival) to central London with Selsey being used for school holidays due to its proximity to Austin's preparatory school. In the summer of 1930, they signed a lease on a luxury top floor flat in Chiltern Court, Baker Street with views over Regent's Park (Figure 6.1); the previous year's recession had little impact on their finances. Chiltern Court was built by the Metropolitan Railway to offset the cost of building Baker Street Underground Station (situated in the bowels of the flat block). The flats proved popular with London's elite and the residents included authors the authors Arnold Bennett and H.G. Wells. The move can be seen as the summation of how far Coates

Figure 6.1    Eric Coates on the roof of his Baker Street flat during the mid-1930s

---

[80]    Several of these letters survive.

had come since the 1920s and the tremendous personal success that enabled him to live in affluence funded entirely by his composition. In addition, their return prompted Coates to reconsider his attitudes to composition:

> I remember sitting in my writing-room overlooking the Park and glancing back over the seven years we had spent in the Garden Suburb. I realised with rather a shock that, apart from conducting my works a good deal about the country and doing some broadcasts for the BBC at Savoy Hill, my output had scarcely been prolific, which went to prove what I had always thought regarding my lack of desire to compose when away from the actual metropolis.[81]

There followed a steady stream of compositions during the 1930s, less erratic than the 1920s.

The next orchestral work to be completed was a short entr'acte, styled by Coates as a valse serenade, *By the Sleepy Lagoon*. According to Austin, the idea came in Selsey:

> It was inspired by the view, on a warm, still summer evening looking across the "lagoon" from the east beach at Selsey towards Bognor Regis. It's a pebble beach leading steeply down and the sea at that time is the tremendously deep blue of the Pacific. It was that impression, looking across at Bognor, which looked pink – almost like an enchanted city with the blue of the Downs behind it – that gave him the idea for the Sleepy Lagoon.[82]

This short piece enjoyed a modest success, but it was not until the following decade that it gained its unrivalled popularity due to its release as the popular song 'Sleepy Lagoon' and its use in the radio programme *Desert Island Discs* (see Chapter 9). *By the Sleepy Lagoon* was published in two different editions with different plate numbers: 9003 (presumably published first due to its typeface) and 30695, and one wonders whether Coates altered the score after publication. It is impossible to verify this as the autograph for the score is now lost. These two editions are identical except for the characteristic brass interjections (bars 13–14, 16–17, 28–9 and 31–6) that feature in 30695 but not in 9003. In Coates' 1935 recording of the valse serenade, the interjections are present, but in the later recordings, made in 1940 and 1948, the interjections are absent and one must assume this was the effect the composer wanted, hence the re-engraving of the parts.

Besides producing an impressive canon of orchestral works, Coates still produced a stream of ballads, though these were very much the 'final flowering' of his talents in this genre. During the 1930s, he wrote very few songs, and then

---

[81]   Coates, p. 213.

[82]   Austin Coates quoted in Lace, 'Foreword', p. x. A 'blue plaque' now marks the spot on the beach at Selsey.

only because of contractual obligations to Chappells. In 1923, he teamed up with a new lyricist, Royden Barrie (*nom de plume* of Rodney Bennett (father of the composer Richard Rodney Bennett). Bennett was a polymath and had a variety of careers before turning to writing. He began writing the lyrics to popular songs in 1922, starting with Haydn Wood's 'A Brown Bird Singing').[83] Barrie displaced F.E. Weatherly as Coates' chief, but not exclusive, lyric writer. Coates and Barrie went on to write a string of popular songs including 'Summer Afternoon' and 'Bird Songs at Eventide'. The 1930s produced a mere trickle of ballads, with texts by Phyl and Christopher Hassall, but Coates' heart was no longer in this 'limited form of expression' as he termed the genre in his autobiography.[84]

During the 1920s, Coates wrote a number of works that would form the core of his repertoire and consolidated his position within the world of light music. He would build on these successes in the 1930s and the start of a radio programme would alter the course of his life and career forever.

---

[83]   Anthony Meredith, *Richard Rodney Bennett* (London, 2010), p. 8.

[84]   Ibid., pp. 182–3.

# Chapter 7
# Success and Popularity, 1931–1935

Despite their somewhat carefree lifestyle since ensconcing Austin in a boarding school and moving back to central London, both Eric and Phyl were deeply alarmed to hear that Austin had succumbed to an epidemic of measles that swept the south coast during January 1931. As a result of complications, he was forced to undergo an operation and took nearly two years to return to full strength. After his discharge from hospital, Phyl and a nurse tended to Austin at Summer Days Cottage in Selsey. Coates joined the 'other two' (the three Coates *en masse* were often collectively known as 'The Three Bears') whenever his writing and professional commitments allowed, at other times remaining in isolation in London.[1] Gradually his visits became longer as Austin returned to health. It must have been difficult for Coates to write any music, especially when for a short time in 1931 Austin's life hung in the balance. It was not until early 1933 that life returned to normal, Austin returned to school and Eric and Phyl to London.

The ongoing domestic turmoil notwithstanding, Coates miraculously managed to do some writing at the beginning of 1931. As he described in his autobiography:

> I managed to compose an orchestral suite which I called 'From Meadow to Mayfair' and which, as I had adopted London as my home, was intended to be a kind of farewell to my native Nottinghamshire and the pastoral scenes which till than I had felt an urge to describe in music.[2]

For Coates, it was never easy to shake off the lure of Hucknall, despite the fact that he had been resident in London since 1906. Though he had made infrequent visits to Hucknall, London was his spiritual home and the place where inspiration largely struck:

> It was not until we came to live in the heart of London that I was able to shake off my ever-present desire to be wandering about the highways and byways of my native Nottinghamshire. It had been a restless, unsettling feeling, this temptation to get the car out and take the road to the north. But the flat and the view began to take hold of me, and when one day I went up on to the flat roof and saw the vast expanse of the great city spread around me I realised that I had found a new home.[3]

---

[1]  Eric Coates, *Suite in Four Movements* (London, 1953), pp. 216–17.
[2]  Coates, p. 217.
[3]  Ibid., p. 214.

The Suite was the result of an invitation from Captain Amers, conductor of the Eastbourne orchestra, and was officially premiered there on 21 February under the composer's direction, though it had an earlier outing three weeks previously when Coates was conducting at Brighton.[4]

*From Meadow to Mayfair* marked a return to the rustic simplicity of the suites of the 1910s. The most successful movement of the Suite is the valse finale 'Evening in Town', a depiction of restaurant life in London's Mayfair, a favourite spot of Eric and Phyl, which avoids the pizzicato bass part used almost exclusively throughout the first two movements. The Valse has more recurring material than normal with four of the five themes returning. The melodic inspiration burns brightest in this movement and there are several deft touches, especially the start of the C-section in E♭ major (figure 6). Even though the inspiration of the Suite is slightly lacklustre, the work hardly outstays its welcome and each of the movements has a tuneful adroitness that many other composers would find hard to achieve.

Coates recorded the Suite, alongside a superb rendition of *The Merrymakers*, at EMI's Abbey Road Studios on 3 November 1931 making it one of the first recordings to be made there.[5] The studios were officially opened eight days later by Edward Elgar. Coates remained a frequent visitor to this hallowed edifice until he switched allegiance to Columbia/HMV's rival company, Decca.

Later in 1931, he received another invitation from Harry Amers at Eastbourne for a new work for that year's festival, his fourth and final work written for his favourite coastal resort. The resultant composition, *Dancing Nights*, was his first extended freestanding concert valse, drawing on those in the *Summer Days* and *From Meadow to Mayfair* Suites. The work was completed in October 1931 and premiered the following month. The original title of the Valse had been *Autumn Woods* (perhaps closer in spirit to the sentiment of the work than the altered title) which was subsequently altered perhaps because of its propinquity to Bax's *November Woods*.[6] As Geoffrey Self, Coates' first biographer, wryly noted: 'one sometimes wonders if the titles didn't cause more headaches than the music'.[7]

Structurally, *Dancing Nights* shows a more marked expansion of the valse form than those contained in his suites, with the use of eight contrasting themes. The most important of these is introduced 8 bars after letter B and returns at letter R (with a countersubject). The Valse owes a debt to Waldteufel and Tchaikovsky and there are hints of Ravel's *La Valse*. It was never popular in Coates' life as he explained to Stanford Robinson shortly before he (Coates) recorded the work in 1945: 'I was glad that "Dancing Nights" was included in your programmes – it

---

[4]    25/02/1931 *Eastbourne Gazette.*

[5]    Columbia and the Gramophone Company merged in March 1931 to form EMI Ltd.

[6]    The music critic Ernest Kuhe voiced his concerns (privately) over the title. (26/12/1986 Austin Coates to Geoffrey Self.)

[7]    Geoffrey Self, *In Town Tonight* (London, 1986), p. 48.

has not had many performances to date (perhaps the sky-scraping in the 'cellos frightens them!!!)'.[8]

Despite being busy conducting coastal and resort orchestras, such as Eastbourne, Coates was not immune to the orchestral revolution caused by the foundation of the BBC Symphony Orchestra in 1930. For studio broadcasts, the Orchestra was separated into sections for a greater broadcasting flexibility and several of these sections (C and E), alongside the BBC Theatre Orchestra (independent of the BBC Orchestra), became important vehicles for performances of Coates' music during the 1930s. By November 1931, the BBC hierarchy had decided to clamp down on the number of external BBC conductors who were allowed to be invited to conduct the ensemble.[9] Typical of his symbiotic relationship with the BBC, Coates, alongside such luminaries as Henry Wood, Landon Ronald and Constant Lambert, was one of the few allowed to conduct the Orchestra, though he was limited exclusively to light works.

Even before this BBC decision, Coates had conducted the BBC Orchestra (Section C) on 10 August 1931 in the premiere of a short orchestral work, *Lazy Night*; the first of his pieces to be given a first performance by BBC forces. *Lazy Night*, like *By the Sleepy Lagoon*, was another attempt to fuse another form with a valse. *Lazy Night* was published in tandem with another miniature composed at the tail-end of 1931, the Idyll *Summer Afternoon*. *Summer Afternoon* was fashioned from a song, this time one published nearly a decade earlier. Why Coates chose to return to a song that he had written the previous decade is not clear though it is possible he needed to write a new work quickly to fulfil his contract with Chappells or he was lacking inspiration and thought this would be an undemanding task. The Idyll closely adheres to the through-composed structure of the song (Introduction–A (verse 1)–B (verse 2)–Bridge-A (verse 3)–B' (verse 4)), even down to keeping the subtle rhythmic variations of verses 3 and 4 from 1 and 2. However, he eschews the introduction and bridge between verses 2 and 3 from the song in favour of new ones featuring more orchestral colour, although still based on the opening two bars of the first verse. Harmonically, the Idyll remains almost faithful to the song, though with fuller harmony and more countermelodies, until 5 bars after figure 4 when Coates alters and expands the harmony in keeping with its new status as an orchestral entr'acte. *Summer Afternoon* stands up well in its new orchestral guise and one would not guess that it had originated as a song.

One of his largest compositional undertakings of the 1930s came as a result of an invitation from the Torquay Festival of 1932 for an orchestral work. What resulted was a six-movement suite entitled *The Jester at the Wedding* Suite from the Ballet. No other orchestral material was ever written outside these six movements, and one wonders if Coates had envisaged transforming the work into a ballet after the Torquay performance, especially given the propinquity of light music to the ballet. Other works of this period, notably *The Three Bears* and *Cinderella* had

---

[8]    22/04/1945 EC to Stanford Robinson. *GB-Rwac.*

[9]    20/11/1931 Kenneth Wright to Adrian Boult. *GB-Rwac.*

been staged as ballets. Initially, when the invitation came in 1931, Coates was stuck for ideas and Phyl eventually came up with the suggestion of a work based on a jester's hopeless love for a princess. As Coates expounded: 'It was the ideal subject for musical treatment and some of my happiest recollections are of the weeks I spent working out the score and playing over to her the themes and the general lay-out …'.[10] Unsurprisingly, the score is dedicated: 'to Phyllis'. Despite enjoying the period of composition, it took Coates a long time to coax himself into starting work as he informed a newspaper: 'The composition took me about six weeks … It is not so much finding the melodies – I do not have much difficulty with that part – but it is the scoring; orchestration takes a lot of time.'[11] Coates left a month between the completion of the score on 6 March 1932 and the premiere to have the orchestral parts copied and despatched to Torquay. The premiere on 7 April proved one of the highlights of that year's festival, which also included visits from Elgar, Harty and Ethel Smyth. Coates shared the platform with the famous cellist Madame Suggia and there were nearly 1,300 in the audience.[12]

On the publication of the score, Phyl wrote a synopsis for each movement drawn from her original story:

> It is the Princess's wedding-day, and before the Prince comes to the Palace to claim her as his bride she is giving a farewell party to her Court and friends.
>
> 1. *March*. THE PRINCESS ARRIVES.
>
> The guests arrive and the Princess takes her place upon the throne.
>
> 2. *Minuet*. THE DANCE OF THE PAGES. Her pages perform a minuet.
>
> 3. *Humoresque*. THE JESTER. Her young and attractive Jester amuses the guests, and the Princess is fascinated by his charm.
>
> 4. *Valse*. THE DANCE OF THE ORANGE-BLOSSOMS. Her chief ballet-dancer executes a *pas seul* in honour of the approaching wedding.
>
> 5. *Caprice*. THE PRINCESS. The Princess walks among her guests, bidding farewell to each in turn, talking gravely to her grey-haired Chancellor, and laughing gaily with her many young friends.
>
> 6. *Finale*. THE PRINCESS AND THE JESTER. The Princess then turns to the Jester, who has watched her every movement, and with a charming smile she invites him to dance with her, much to the delight of the Court. As they dance, they realize their love for one another, and stand transfixed, during which moment the trumpets are heard heralding the approach of the bridegroom, the Prince. They both realize the impossibility of the situation, and she disengages herself from him, and throwing him a rose from her dress she steps into the royal chair which awaits her, and is carried from the scene (followed by the Court) to the awaiting Prince, leaving the Jester alone, with nothing but the memory of the fragrance of her presence and a rose.

[10]   Coates, p. 217.

[11]   Undated *Westminster Gazette*. (Coates Scrapbook 1.)

[12]   08/04/1932 Unknown Paper. (Coates Scrapbook 1.)

Such was the Coates' delight in the story, that Phyl eventually expanded the work into a short story novel (though it was never published).

Of all the works Coates composed, it is one of the most intriguing in form, cast in six movements with recurring themes, especially in the finale. The form of each movement is not as clear cut as in the majority of his canon. The opening March is a close cousin to the closing march of *Cinderella* (predominately letters P and T of the Phantasy), and is very delicately scored, especially in the A-section (17 bars after letter A) with the subtle interplay of muted brass strings and woodwind (with piano). The Minuet is essentially monothematic, opening with a beguiling melody on the woodwind, continued with a haunting singing motif (letter A), before introducing the princess's theme (which returns in the final two movements) in a cadenza (Example 7.1).

Example 7.1 'Minuet' (*The Jester at the Wedding*), 8 bars after letter B (princess's theme). © 1932 Chappell Music Ltd, London, W6 8BS. Reproduced by permission of Faber Music Ltd. All Rights Reserved

The third movement, Humoresque, handles its complex key structure with subtlety and legerdemain, emigrating to the remote key of B major from its tonic of A♭ major and back again. Both the Valse (a valsette and clone of the earlier *Wood Nymphs*, both in form and melodic content) and Caprice are structured in a varied rondo form (Introduction–A–B–A–C–A–Coda). The Caprice, depicting the Princess, makes full use of the princess's theme (initially presented in $\frac{4}{4}$ time but reworked at letter B into a quasi-valse in $\frac{3}{4}$) and is tinged with hints of Ravel. The Finale is the most pictorial of the movements, opening with echoes of the princess's theme and then breaking into a passionate dance between the Princess and Jester (letter C) before the return of the shortened version of letters D–H from the March (letter E) heralding the return of the Prince. This is subsequently expanded to a climax as the Princess leaves to join the Prince, leaving the Jester alone at letter K with dreams of the Princess (and a coda based on the princess's theme).

One wonders if, in accepting a commission from Torquay, Coates' hands were tied in the matter of orchestration. *The Jester at the Wedding* is scored for double woodwind (though only a single oboe), two horns and limited percussion. The curious addition to the ensemble is an orchestral piano (which he had only used in the earlier theatre score *Snowdrop* out of necessity); surely the harp would have been more effective – unless Coates was forced to use the piano to bolster the woodwind of the Torquay orchestra. Certainly in his 1949 recording of 'Dance of the Orange Blossoms' he dispenses with the piano and does not replace the part with a harp. Despite being pleased with the performance of the Torquay orchestra at the premiere, as Self has noted, a short passage at the close of the Finale that he believes may have defeated the brass technically (since they were tired by this stage in a performance) was omitted on publication.[13] What seems more likely is that the composer changed his mind, since he removed the first three bars of letter L (in the autograph score), which abolished the muted brass fanfares (a rhythmically diminished version of the fanfares from the opening movement), leaving the solo horn, triangle, piano and strings – no doubt a more pleasing aesthetic effect than the original idea – when he published the work. The stylistic importance of this Suite was, however, totally eclipsed by the popularity of his next.

Later in 1932, Coates was at work on another orchestral suite; little did he know that the completion of it and its subsequent recording would change his life and career immeasurably. After the *From Meadow to Mayfair* Suite it seemed natural to encapsulate London in a new suite. Following on from the romantic city-scapes Elgar's *Cockaigne* Overture, Mackenzie's *London Day by Day* Suite, Vaughan Williams' 'London' Symphony and Ketèlbey's *Cockney Suite*, Coates' short *London* Suite pictures three key areas of London viewed from the panorama of his flat: Covent Garden, depicted as an ebullient tarantella; Westminster portrayed as a meditation; and Knightsbridge as a march. The work was completed on 25 November 1932. Some years after the composition of the Suite, the composer provided the following synopsis of the three movements:

"Covent Garden" describes the hurry and bustle in the early morning in London's great fruit & vegetable market (called Covent Garden), which is near-by Covent Garden Opera House, and the second theme is an old English folk-tune introduced to give "local" colour to the music.

"Westminster" is a descriptive scene all around Westminster Abbey: The Houses of Parliament; the river Thames; the stately old buildings which go to make up London's historical tradition; and the chimes at the close of the movement are the exact intervals that one hears before "Big Ben", the clock in the tower of the Houses of Parliament strikes each hour.

---

13   Self, p. 58.

"Knightsbridge" is a picture of one of London's fashionable shopping centers [*sic.*] where is situated the famous Knightsbridge Barracks which house a section of the Brigade of Guards. This movement, with its impression of military flavour, is intended to convey the impression of the Guards passing down this gay thoroughfare on their way to mount guard at Buckingham Palace.[14]

Though the Suite was originally entitled *London Everyday* it was subsequently shortened to *London* perhaps to avoid confusion with Mackenzie's four-movement *London Day by Day*, which was then still in vogue. Legend surrounding the Suite suggests that Coates offered the Suite to Chappells who took fright at the finale, believing it to be beyond the capacity of most amateur orchestras. Nevertheless, they published the Suite the following year (1933). In the meantime, Coates had persuaded the BBC to accept the first performance of the work in a broadcast that was scheduled for 10 January 1933 under Joseph Lewis. Reaction to the Suite was indifferent.

The *London* Suite was also greeted with indifference by Columbia. Anxious to secure a gramophone recording of the work, Coates cajoled Arthur Brooks (the recording manager of Columbia) to listen to Lewis' premiere of the Suite. Much to Coates' chagrin, Brooks telephoned him the following day to inform him that he did not like the work and Columbia would not be interested in recording it.[15] As luck would have it, Coates was due to record his *Two Symphonic Rhapsodies* on 3 March with the LPO and he suggested that it was unfair to judge and dismiss the Suite in one hearing. Coates suggested he could bring the parts for the *London* Suite to the session and if there was time they could record the work.[16]

Chappells suggested that the Suite could be issued as a one-disc record with some judicious pruning to the outer movements leaving 'Westminster' complete despite the composer's preference for presenting 'Knightsbridge' unimpaired.[17] Chappells believed it would be 'Westminster' that would become the popular movement and even thought about only publishing this movement.[18] Coates remained obdurate on the matter and was adamant that 'Knightsbridge should be given in full with other two movements cut'.[19] By 12 o'clock on the day of the recording the *Two Symphonic Rhapsodies* were in 'the can' and, after a short intermission, recording could begin on the *London* Suite. Writing nearly thirty years after the recording, Coates captured the drama of the session:

at 12.22 we started on the first movement of the 'London Suite'. All went fairly smoothly and we managed to get the first two movements completed

---

[14] Undated. EC to Z.J.W. van Schreven. *GB-Lcm*.

[15] Coates, p. 218.

[16] Ibid.

[17] Austin Coates, programme 3.

[18] Coates, p. 219.

[19] Austin Coates, programme 3.

by just on ten minutes to one. We now had only the last movement to record, the 'Knightsbridge March'. At 12.53 we started recording. At 12.54 someone blew a wrong note. At 12.55 we started again. At 12.57 a wax split. I was in despair. Something inside me told me it was absolutely imperative that I should get the disc somehow, and I knew it was now out of the question to achieve a recording before one o'clock. I also knew it was of no use appealing to the recording manager for a few minutes' grace, for every minute overtime meant a considerable increase in the expense of the recording session; and besides, had he not said to me that he did not think much of the new work? So I took my courage in both hands and asked the musicians if they would, as a personal favour to me, spare me a minute or so longer to give me the chance of getting the record. Two signals on the buzzer – we held our breath – the red light glowed and, at three minutes past one o'clock, thanks to a sturdy wax and the good natured gesture on the part of the orchestra, the 'Knightsbridge March', which was to prove to be the biggest seller the Columbia Gramophone Company had ever had, was made.[20]

The recording was issued and went on sale but it was not until 18 November 1933 that the transformation of the March took place. The BBC producer Eric Maschwitz had devised a radio show that showcased talent and popular people who were in London on a Saturday evening. Preparation for the programme was very last minute. Writing years later, Maschwitz recalled that the script of the first programme was not written until the day of transmission.[21] On the day of transmission, it was realized that the show had no signature tune, so Maschwitz sent down an urgent request to the BBC's Gramophone Library for records that had London in the title. After listening to works by Elgar and Haydn Wood, it was soon decided that 'Knightsbridge' fitted the requirements and it was adopted as the signature tune to *In Town Tonight*.[22] Coates takes up the story of the first transmission:

one Saturday evening, deeply absorbed by my camera, I heard Phyl calling me. Reluctantly I dragged myself away from my dark-room and went to see what it was all about. They were playing something on the radio. It was a blare of trumpets. It sounded familiar. We exchanged glances. It was the introduction to the Trio of the Knightsbridge March, my own recording. Looking in the *Radio Times* we discovered the announcement of a new weekly feature entitled 'In Town To-Night' ... . We listened to the broadcast until the fanfare of my march and the few bars of the melody faded out and the half-hour came to a close. 'At any rate', we agreed, 'it cannot do the Suite any harm.'

---

[20]   Coates, p. 219.

[21]   Eric Maschwitz, *No Chip on my Shoulder* (London, 1957), p. 67.

[22]   Ibid.

The telephone started to ring. It appeared that listeners had been in touch with Broadcasting House to ask the title of the tantalising few bars which they had just heard on the radio, and having been told it was by me, they had rung through to the flat to ask for further information about the music. No sooner was the receiver down then the bell rang again … . I resigned myself to coping with the eulogies of complete strangers, ranging from old ladies of eighty down to young ladies in their 'teens, while Phyl looked on and laughed.[23]

The public response to the March was overwhelming and Coates recalled that in the first two weeks of *In Town Tonight* the BBC had over 20,000 requests asking for the title and composer of the March: indeed, they had cards especially printed with the details.[24] The volume of requests is difficult to confirm as the BBC's production files for *In Town Tonight* have been destroyed. Needless to say, both Columbia and Chappells were kept busy producing enough records and copies of the piano edition and orchestral sets to keep up with demands.

The impact on Coates' career was incalculable and cannot be over emphasized as, at the age of forty-six, he moved from the ranks of the moderately successful to the very successful and joined the legion of the minor celebrities, something that he never lost (Figure 7.1). He was always fond of recalling: 'When I wrote

Figure 7.1    Eric and Phyllis Coates attend a Royal Garden Party, 1946

23    Coates, p. 220.
24    Ibid.

the 'London Suite' I moved from the music page to the news page, and it's one of the few moves I have never regretted.'[25] (Eric and Phyl were frequently moving house.) The success of 'Knightsbridge', almost overnight, turned Coates into one of the most successful of all British composers. Thanks, in part to 'Knightsbridge', it was during the 1930s that Coates began to overtake Ketèlbey as Britain's highest earning composer.[26]

There were several upshots of this new burst of fame as Coates recalled in an expunged passage from his autobiography:

> We had to discontinue booking our usual box at the Palladium through being put on "the spot" by Flanagan and Allen, aided and abetted by Richard Crean and the orchestra, who stood up and thundered "Knightsbridge" at us while I stood and bowed my acknowledgements, feeling very foolish, bathed in light, while the audience shouted its approval.[27]

Another side-effect of the popularity came in the form of an invitation from his *alma mater* the RAM to become Benjamin Dale's assistant in teaching composition. As Coates recalled in his autobiography, the RAM must have been totally oblivious to his recent successes:

> "After all, my dear Coates," said the kindly old fellow, "we do not always want to have to work twelve hours a day, and I thought Mr Dale's surplus pupils might be of assistance to you. As I said to the Principal (Sir John B. McEwen): Why not ask Mr Eric Coates to help Mr Dale out. He used to do a bit of writing when he was at the Academy". I thanked him for his offer and gently told him I was afraid that I was too busy to entertain the idea. "Of course, my boy, I expect your viola keeps you too occupied". I had not the heart to tell him that my viola had not been out of its case for nearly twenty years.[28]

As is often the case with works that capture the public's imagination by being at the right place at the right time, there is usually nothing exceptional about their construction. The *London* Suite started life as an ordinary suite but has eclipsed all the others. The opening movement is a vivacious tarantelle based on two subjects, both of which are complex in their construction. The second subject is based on Charles Horn's song, 'Cherry Ripe', using only the first 8 bars of the melody, before being extended with material reminiscent of the song but pure Coates. Also of interest is the way in which he alters the rhythm from the $\frac{4}{4}$ of the song to $\frac{6}{8}$ – a

---

[25]   Eric Coates quoted in 26–27/12/1984 Austin Coates to Geoffrey Self.

[26]   John Sant, *Albert W. Ketèlbey* (Sutton Coldfield, 2000), p. 2.

[27]   Eric Coates, *Suite in Four Movements* (autograph), p. 472.

[28]   Ibid., 475. However, nothing of the invitation survives in the RAM Management Committee Minute Books, *GB-Lam*.

talent seen in the earlier *Menuetto*. On the Suite's publication, he expunged 8 bars from this movement during the reprise of the A-section, 11 bars after letter H.[29]

The finale of the Suite is a robust March, which was Coates' third orchestral attempt at the form (building on the unorthodox structures of those in *The Four Ways* and *The Jester at the Wedding* Suites) and was the first example of what would become his standard march formula (drawing unequivocally on those found in Elgar's epoch-making *Pomp and Circumstance* Marches): Introduction (usually with a foretaste of the A-section and over a dominant pedal)–A-section–B-section (usually in the subdominant)–A-section–B-section (in the tonic, slower than the first statement and in a fuller orchestration)–coda.

As Coates was placing the finishing touches to the *London* Suite in November 1932, the Columbia Record Company, impressed by the success of his previous *Symphonic Rhapsody* based on Richard Rodgers' 'With a Song in my Heart', invited him to compose a new one, though this time based on his own songs. Columbia suggested his most popular song successes of the 1920s: 'I Pitch my Lonely Caravan', 'I Heard you Singing' and 'Birdsongs at Eventide'. According to Coates, Columbia had requested one rhapsody for the three songs, but he responded with two, each with a different character and employing different techniques.[30] The *First Rhapsody* was based on 'I Pitch My Lonely Caravan' and the *Second* on 'Bird Songs at Eventide' and 'I Heard You Singing'. Coates was not alone in this approach to his songs; later the following year Haydn Wood published a song intermezzo based on his tremendously successful song 'Roses of Picardy'.

Structurally, the *Two Symphonic Rhapsodies* are amongst the most formally complex pieces Coates wrote. They are no mere song orchestrations but well-thought-out miniature masterpieces. There is a subtle blend of echoes of the songs, whole verses of the songs and free material. Each *Rhapsody*, like the early one on Rodgers' song, is marked by its use of a motto motif (usually derived from the opening).

In the *First Rhapsody*, Coates strikes an interesting balance between the use of the song and his own new material (first used four bars after letter D). He also chooses to set whole tranches of the song; verse 1 at letter C and verse 2 at letter H (rising to a Tchaikovskyian climax). The coda has a subtle use of material from letters D and E. The opening accompanimental brass triplet is recycled several times, reappearing in bars 2 and 4 of letter B and transformed into a new accompanimental figure at letter F (Example 7.2).

The *Second Rhapsody* is based on two songs; 'Bird Songs at Eventide' (which receives greater treatment helped by its distinctive 'birdsong motif') and the first verse of 'I Heard You Singing' features at letter C. Coates also introduces some new material in the form of a valse (letter G), which culminates in lavish statement of the second verse and coda of 'Birdsongs'.

---

[29]   'Covent Garden' *London* Suite, pp. 22–3. *GB-Lcm* Box 181.

[30]   Coates, p. 218

Example 7.2  *First Symphonic Rhapsody*, rhythmic pattern

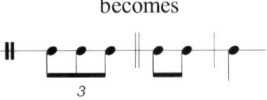

Shortly after the composition of the *Two Symphonic Rhapsodies*, Coates visited Abbey Road Studios on 7 March 1933 to record both the *Rhapsodies* and the *London* Suite. Both the *Rhapsodies* recorded that day differ from the form in which they were eventually published. The *First Rhapsody* featured a soloist, Arthur Firth,[31] singing the first verse of 'I Pitch my Lonely Caravan' two bars after letter C (which is rather high in the tenor's register commencing on a top G); after an orchestral interlude the soloist rejoins after the climax at letter J to sing a brief coda 'sweet dreams of you'. There is no mention of the use of the soloist in the score. Coates may have been under pressure from either Columbia or Chappells to include a part for a singer to boost sales of 'I Pitch my Lonely Caravan'. The *Second Symphonic Rhapsody* featured several performance errors that could have been left in as a result of Coates' haste to record the *London* Suite that morning. There is no use of the tubular bell (4 bars after letter C), or timpani (4 bars after F) and no glockenspiel or tubular bell (2 bars before G). Whilst these are not significant omissions, they are clearly marked in Coates' autograph score.[32]

The *London* Suite was also recorded on the same day as the *Two Symphonic Rhapsodies*. The recording drastically reduced the first two movements so they could be fitted onto a 12-inch disc. 'Covent Garden' had a savage cut from letter C to L which removed the first statement of 'Cherry Ripe' and reduced the playing time from an estimated four minutes to 2 minutes 14 seconds.[33] 'Westminster' began at letter A, removing the introduction and beginning instead with the cello melody. There was a cut from letter C to G, omitting the entire B-section as well as the restatement of the A-section by the full orchestra, but leaving the distinctive coda based on the 'Westminster Chimes', reducing the playing time from an estimated 4 minutes 30 seconds to 1 minute 54 seconds. Thankfully, 'Knightsbridge' was given in full, which proved to be a shrewd move. The first two movements of the *London* Suite were re-recorded in May 1947, presumably because the wax matrix had become worn, and given a new matrix number (CAX 6748-2). They were issued for sale the following month with the original 1933 recording of 'Knightsbridge'.[34] However, there were no shortages of recordings of 'Knightsbridge', with performers ranging from orchestras and dance bands to theatre organists.

---

[31]   One CD release credits the soloist as the Hon. William Brownlaw.

[32]   *GB-Lcm* Box 181.

[33]   The estimated times are taken from those Coates placed on the published scores.

[34]   Michael Smith & Frank Andrews, *The Gramophone Company Limited* (Blandford, 1974), p. 48. The recording session took place on 02/05/1947.

After the cataclysmic success of the 'Knightsbridge' March, Coates had to write another march; the public were expecting it and so too were his publishers. Shrewdly, he left it several months before embarking on the project as he recalled several years after its completion:

> I was not interested in this idea until one day I found myself on London Bridge. It was the first thing in the morning and hundreds of people were walking across the bridge on their way to their daily work. I was amazed at the endless stream. Here were feet – feet – feet – all sorts of feet – all hurrying, all marching briskly about their business – London's business – Britain's business – the business of the Empire. My imagination was fired – the London Bridge March it should be. London Bridge, with its endless rhythm of marching feet. The March is now the Official March of the City of London Police.[35]

Work must have begun on the *London Bridge* March early in 1934 and it is cast in Coates' march formula (as defined by 'Knightsbridge') and the thematic material, as in 'Knightsbridge', does not have the fast/slow variety between the first and second subjects as in those completed in the 1930s and 1940s. The March is based on a short cell verbalizing the title (Example 7.3), which is melodically important as the opening sixth connects both the first and second subjects together.

Example 7.3  *London Bridge*, melodic cell

Lon-don Bridge

The *London Bridge* March bore a dedication to Eric Maschwitz, presumably out of gratitude for choosing 'Knightsbridge' as the signature tune to *In Town Tonight*. Maschwitz was to play an important part in the first performance of the March. A recording session for Columbia had been scheduled for 5 May 1934 with an ad hoc orchestra to record *London Bridge*, *Summer Afternoon* and two movements of *The Jester at the Wedding*. It was decided that the recording of *London Bridge* should be broadcast on *In Town Tonight* as it was made, so the listeners of the programme could hear what went on. Such was the interest in this recording that the Pathé film company recorded the session as well.

The Pathé film, which survives, is a fascinating document as one can see Coates at work in his Chiltern Court flat, introducing the March to radio listeners and finally conducting it.[36] Coates is rather nervous speaking 'live' on the radio, but is in total control of the orchestra. One is stuck by how high his beat is, usually

---

[35]  16/04/1945 EC to E.K. Holmes. *GB-Lcm*.

[36]  1096.24, available from www.britishpathe.com.

on a level with his head and how little he consults his score (there is one moment where he has to turn over three pages at once).

Also recorded the same day (presumably before the film and radio crews descended) were *Summer Afternoon* (coupled with the *London Bridge* March) and two movements from *The Jester at the Wedding* (movements I and IV). Unfortunately, there was a problem with the recording of the March 'The Princess Arrives' (presumably due to difficulties with the wax matrix, a common fault) and the side was re-recorded at a special recording session the following year.

Whilst his career was in the ascendance because of *In Town Tonight*, Coates was becoming increasingly exasperated about the absence of his music from the Promenade Concerts. His music had last featured in the Proms in 1926, before the BBC had taken over their promotion from Chappells. His predicament was addressed through the intervention of his BBC allies Kenneth Wright and Stanford Robinson. In February 1934, Wright informed W.W. Thompson (in charge of planning the Proms): 'I think we are agreed that he holds the leading place in British light music ... [and] we will not be ashamed to put him in some such position with one of his best pieces.'[37] Robinson petitioned Adrian Boult (Director of Music) along similar lines, but was dismissive of other light-music composers:

> I would like to suggest to you that, as the premier light music composer of the day, he might be similarly invited to conduct one of his works this year. There is no-one in the same class as Coates, and his inclusion need not be made as an excuse for anybody else.[38]

As a result, Coates was duly invited to conduct *The Three Bears* phantasy on 8 September 1934 – the composer's second appearance at the concerts since the work's premiere at the festival in 1926.

After his appearance at the Proms, Coates was at work on another Suite, entitled *The Three Men*. The Suite marked the end of a fallow patch of composition he had been suffering from since April. *The Three Men* was written on the request of Eric Maschwitz for a concert of Coates' music to be given in the Concert Hall of Broadcasting House by the composer and the BBC Theatre Orchestra on 28 January 1935. Coates was especially pleased with the premiere of the Suite and subsequently dedicated the Suite to Stanford Robinson and the BBC Theatre Orchestra after the performance.[39] He also informed Eric Maschwitz: 'This is to thank you for giving me such a momentous show last night and also to thank you again for all you have done towards popularising my music ... .'[40] He explained

---

[37]   28/02/1934 Kenneth Wright to W.W. Thompson. *GB-Rwac*. Wright's attitudes towards Coates' music and its entry into the Promenade Concerts were to change markedly over the course of the decade (see Chapter 9).

[38]   31/05/1934 Stanford Robinson to Adrian Boult. *GB-Rwac*.

[39]   29/01/1935 EC to Stanford Robinson. *GB-Rwac*.

[40]   29/01/1935 EC to Eric Maschwitz. *GB-Rwac*.

his inspiration for the Suite in the 1950s: 'I had decided on the idea of describing in music three personalities whom we all know: The Countryman, the Townsman and the Seaman'.[41] The Suite is in his usual three-movement pattern, fast–slow–fast; unusually, no movement is based on a set-piece format such as a march, intermezzo or valse but there are elements of these built into the movements. The first movement, 'Man from the Country' is a bucolic compound duple dance, very much along the lines of the work of Edward German. The form is an attempt to amalgamate variation and ternary forms based around the opening theme (the first subject, though it does not re-enter until bar 98, the start of the B-section) and a second subject given out at figure 2. Table 7.1 shows a brief analysis of the movement and the way its structure uses a hybrid of ternary and variation form.

Table 7.1     Analysis of 'The Man from the Country' (*The Three Men* Suite)

| Section | Passage | Figure |
| --- | --- | --- |
| Introduction – A | Introduction | None |
| | Second theme | 2 |
| | Bridge | 3 |
| B | First variation (of first theme) | 9 bars after 4 |
| | Second variation | 6 |
| | Third variation | 7 |
| | Bridge | 8 |
| A | Introduction | 11 bars after 8 |
| | Second theme | 9 |
| | Extension | 12 |
| | *Coda* | 9 bars after 16 |

The middle movement, 'The-Man-About-Town', is one of the finest middle movements that Coates wrote, and is also one of his best homages to the dance-bands including an extended foxtrot. It portrays a sophisticated London gent on the 'prowl'[42] for an evening's entertainment dancing (a self-portrait of the composer?). There are also elements, especially in the harmony, of Coates' love of the popular American songwriters of the 1930s such as Gershwin, Kern and Rodgers. Peter Dickinson has also noted the movement's propinquity to the harmonic language of Billy Mayerl, especially the passages doubled in fourths, at bars 20–27.[43]

The finale is an orchestral *tour de force* based on the popular sea-shanty, 'When Johnny Comes Down to Hilo'. 'The Man from the Sea', as with the previous movements, is loosely cast in ternary form, with several bridge passages and an extended coda. The first subject is the shanty, which Coates treats in two parts.

---

[41]   Coates, p. 226.

[42]   A term Coates favoured for 'night' excursions. (Coates (autograph), p. 453a.)

[43]   Peter Dickinson, *Marigold* (Oxford, 1999), p. 105.

Bars 7–8 and 15–16 of the shanty are identical to the first three notes of 'Three Blind Mice', which is emphasized in Coates' own rhythmicization of the shanty. As Coates informed listeners in a programme note for a broadcast in 1953:

> Eric Coates wishes to explain to the listeners that it was his original intention only to allow three characters described by the three movements of the Suite to appear in the music. As he was at work on the last movement however, he found that another three characters would insist on coming forward and, try as he might, nothing would keep them out – so they are with us here now, and will be easily recognized as our old friends the "Three Blind Mice"… .[44]

As a result of the inclusion of mice in a work about the sea, he had a letter from an old sea captain assuring him that mice were never to be seen on ships, and if they did get on board they would be eaten by rats! Slightly dumbfounded Coates wrote back to the nautical gentleman to state that even if the mice were doomed to be eaten, they at least had the right of entry onto ships.[45]

He treats 'Three Blind Mice' very much as a secondary theme, exploited in the B-section as a fugal exposition. This was not the only time Coates had used fugue in his works; *The Three Bears* includes a similar fugal exposition. For Coates, trained at the RAM, fugues had been very much part of his training – Quilter used similar fugal elements in *A Children's Overture* – and he did not feel that they were beyond the skills of a 'light-music composer'.

'The Man-from-the-Sea' also shows Coates' attention to detail and humour. In bars 30–38, he provides a woodwind countersubject that could well be a hornpipe, particularly given the trill in bar 36, thus giving the movement a nautical feel. Also, his natural *joie de vivre* shines through in this movement with a brief allusion to the 'The Sailor's Hornpipe', with its inherent affinity to the opening of 'When Johnny' (bars 7–13).

Two days following the premiere of *The Three Men*, Coates recorded a fine performance of the Suite alongside the *Wood Nymphs* for Columbia. Just over a month later, Coates was back at Abbey Road Studios to record *Cinderella* on three sides of 12-inch discs with *By the Sleepy Lagoon* completing the fourth side. The recording, one of his finest, is marked by an absence of cuts, but with a significant rallentando into letter F marking the end of side one. He managed to shave two minutes off the intended playing time of 15 minutes because of his adoption of brisk tempi.

More idiomatic was his recording of *By the Sleepy Lagoon*, the companion side, which was an odd choice for a 12-inch record with a playing time of around 4 minutes 30 seconds; the duration of *By the Sleepy Lagoon* is no greater than 3 minutes 30 seconds. He therefore judiciously fleshed out the piece – the only time that he had to lengthen one of his compositions for recording. *Under the*

---

[44]    Programme notes, attached to 10/05/1953 EC to Miss Happold. *GB-Rwac*.

[45]    05/03/1935 *Liverpool Evening Express*.

*Stars*, *Lazy Night* or a movement from *Four Ways* or *The Jester at the Wedding* would have fitted better onto the disc. In order to make *By the Sleepy Lagoon* fit, he recorded the work as written until figure 7, then inserted a passage, a reprise of figures 3 to 6, scored as a duo for solo violin and harp, (this is taken literally from the piano–conductor score where the solo violin plays the melody line and the harp the two-stave accompaniment with minor adjustments); the combination of the two produces a slightly saccharine effect. The orchestra re-enter at figure 6 and play as written until the end.

With the greater public recognition he received as a result of his records and the success afforded by 'Knightsbridge', May 1935 brought about the first of Coates' outspoken attacks in the press on musical snobbery. He was more vocal about these issues than other light music composers. In an article entitled 'The Highbrow is Ruining Music' in the *Daily Mail* he expounded his views:

> when any competent orchestra plays good light music it invariably scores a success with its audience. The tragedy is that so many of our finest composers either refuse to recognise this or, if they do will not condescend to write music which the public can understand ... . There is nothing degrading in writing for the public. The composition of popular music is no easier than the writing of symphonic works ... . But the hard fact remains that so soon as any music becomes popular, the intellectuals will ban it. Why is it necessary to stuff programmes with great masterpieces? There are three or four in an evening. No wonder concert-goers suffer from aural indigestion ... .[46]

What Coates was arguing was, in effect, that the regular inclusion of a 'light work' in a concert would offer relief in a heavy programme. But he felt that it should be a piece of good light music. As Ketèlbey subsequently wrote:

> is not light music akin to the 'sweets' of a good dinner? The patissier of a high-class kitchen is considered of equal standing to the 'joint' chef, and, I am told, has to have more imagination. I think a light-music composer is, in fact, a musical confectioner, and he can be just as 'serious' about his work as a highbrow composer.[47]

Alas, this was never a barrier light music could break down, as hard as Coates tried, and as the avenues dried up during the 1930s and 1940s, light music moved towards the burgeoning post-war recorded music libraries and into film and radio music rather than concert music. Coates also had a personal grievance against the

---

[46]    14/05/1935 *Daily Mail*. The article was seized on by Henry Morley of the *Hucknall Dispatch* and a précis of the article featured in the newspaper two days later. (16/05/1935 *Hucknall Dispatch*.)

[47]    08/09/1944 *Radio Times*.

'intellectuals' and 'highbrows', perhaps feeling persecuted because his own music was not reaching the heights and the audiences he thought it should.

There were still plenty of avenues open to Coates, especially with the BBC. With the impending silver jubilee celebrations of the coronation of George V in 1935, the BBC invited Coates to write a short work to mark the occasion.[48] Haydn Wood also wrote, and recorded, a *Homage March* for the celebrations. Coates' composition, *Song of Loyalty*, was very much along the lines of a slow movement of a suite or an orchestrated ballad. As he informed the readers of the *Daily Mail* six days before the work's premiere: 'This "Song of Loyalty" is a devotional work in character. Would you sow the seeds in the minds of my kind listeners that they may have to prepare for a shock.'[49] It was first performed in a studio broadcast on 7 May 1935 and on this occasion, as with its recording, (made over a week before its premiere) the closing text was sung by a baritone solo.

A *Song of Loyalty* is constructed in ternary form but rather too much is made of the A-section, which is repeated at letters C and E (with a repeat suggested if the work is to be sung by an audience). For the reprise of the A-section, there was an optional unison choral ending (from letter E) with a sentimental text written by Phyl:

> Within our hearts
> We ask that joy may ever find you,
> May you never lose the light that shines to guide and mind you.
> Within our hearts
> We ask that love may ever bless you.
> May peace and love enfold you
> Is the prayer within our hearts.

However, it is skilfully constructed and designed to be sung by anyone, as the listener hears the melody twice before they sing it and their starting note is heralded by a tubular bell immediately before they start. The work definitely stands up better without the text (as shown in Coates' own 1948 recording), but even then it could still be described as maudlin and not one of his 'top drawer' compositions.

Whilst today it is easy to dismiss the work, during Coates' lifetime the *Song* held a curious position in his oeuvre as he informed the BBC after he conducted a performance of it in 1946:

> It is a strange thing the way in which this last piece seems to "get" some people. Alick Maclean, at Scarborough, told me it was the most effective piece I had ever written and Bertie Lodge, among others, said that the performing of "Song

---

[48]    There was talk that the work was to be dedicated to George V, but no official approach was ever made to Buckingham Palace.

[49]    01/05/1935 *Daily Mail*.

of Loyalty" with chorus was always the signal for the old ladies in the audience to produce pocket handkerchiefs.[50]

1935 brought many guest conducting appearances. In February, Coates visited Liverpool to conduct the Merseyside Symphony Orchestra at St George's Hall. His visit showed off his immense popularity, when, for example, he was autographing scores and records at a Liverpool music shop. The *Birkenhead News* expounded: 'Mr Coatese [*sic*] revealed a cheeriness and good humour when assailed by autograph hunters that put them immediately at their ease.'[51] He was also called upon to accompany several of his songs, a task that he seldom undertook, being too diffident as a keyboard player.

On 21 July 1935, Coates motored to Blackpool to guest conduct on the North Pier during the height of the summer season. He had proved a popular attraction during his first visit in 1932. By a coincidence, Haydn Wood was also conducting at the South Pier and the *Blackpool Gazette and Herald* stated: 'Probably due to the marked difference in the price of seats, Haydn Wood, the prolific Yorkshire composer, had a much larger audience than had Eric Coates'.[52]

On 13 July, Coates was in Hucknall to crown the Carnival Queen. It was presumably his first public engagement in his home town since the meteoric rise of his popularity following *In Town Tonight*. Prior to his visit in June, he wrote a lengthy article for the Carnival's magazine discussing his early life in Hucknall and detailing his musical career thus far.[53] The article proved to be a valuable starting point for his autobiography fifteen years later. The visit proved to be an enormous success as he informed *The Gramophone* a few years later:

> It was a boiling hot day and the market place was jammed with about ten thousand people. When I crowned the Carnival Queen mothers held up their babies to look at me. Old people I didn't know from Adam pressed forward and warmly shook my hand and called me Master Eric.[54]

Coates was back two months later to unveil a photograph in the council chamber marking his visit to that year's carnival, but with characteristic modesty he invited his brother Gwyn to perform the unveiling.[55]

Concluding the variety of engagements carried out in 1935 was an invitation to conduct at three London cinemas, in the 'variety slot' between the main feature. His visits to the New Victoria and the Dominion Theatre, Tottenham Court Road both involved a fifty-piece orchestra, with Coates conducting five of his

---

[50]   11/12/1946 EC to Gwen Williams. *GB-Rwac.*

[51]   16/02/1935 *Birkenhead News.*

[52]   27/07/1935 *Blackpool Gazette and Herald.*

[53]   1935 *Sunray (The Magazine of Hucknall Carnival)*, pp. 5–9.

[54]   November 1937 *The Gramophone*, p. 237.

[55]   12/09/1935 *Hucknall Dispatch.*

pieces. It is believed that the aggregate audience for Coates' 1935 excursions into cinema variety spots was 45,000 people.[56] He was proud of the venture and took a photograph of his name in lights.[57] He returned the following year to the New Victoria Cinema (this time with an orchestra of forty-five) and, again, was well received.

The success of 'Knightsbridge' and *In Town Tonight* had transformed Coates' career and he was kept endlessly busy touring the country making public appearances. Such appearances did divert a great deal of his attention away from composition. However, the by the close of 1935, Coates was at work on another suite which would mark the start of a bold period of experimentation.

---

[56]    07/03/1936 *Belfast News and Letters*.

[57]    See the photograph section of Eric Coates, *Suite in Four Movements* (London, 1986) for the photograph.

# Chapter 8
# A New Direction? 1936–1944

For Coates, the period of 1936–44 was a time of great consolidation, building upon the extraordinary level of popularity afforded him by the tremendous success of the 'Knightsbridge' March. In addition to an increased workload of composition, conducting, broadcasting and recording, it was a period of re-assessment of his compositional direction.

Throughout the winter months of 1935, Coates was working on a new Suite, *London Again*, which was completed on 18 February 1936, after an almost entirely compositionally barren 1935. Given the enormous popularity of the *London* Suite, a sequel was required. This requirement had been partially met by the *London Bridge* March but there was still a demand for another extended work based in the metropolis. Austin Coates, the composer's son, believed: 'Since people were almost certain to say it was "London Again" he thought he might as well strike first and call it that from the beginning.'[1] In the month following the completion of the Suite, Coates took the work along to an informal rehearsal of the BBC Theatre Orchestra under Stanford Robinson. Robbie suggested that Coates add the cellos to the central section of the middle movement (presumably from figure 6, where they double with the clarinets).[2] After the play-through, the orchestral parts went to be engraved and the BBC Theatre Orchestra, under Robinson, gave the first performance at the end of April in a BBC broadcast.

The Suite is cast in Coates' typical three movements, though in contrast to the *London* Suite, *London Again* opens with its march, 'Oxford Street', which depicts the hustle and bustle of London's famous shopping street. It is cast in his usual march formula, though it is marked by frequent chromatic movement in the bass line and the absence of a change in tempo for the B-section (figure 4). The composer described the middle movement, 'Langham Place', as: 'An Elegie written on the notes B.B.C. introducing snatches of "In Town Tonight" and concluding with Big Ben chiming the midnight hour, the signal for Broadcasting House to close-down.'[3] When the Suite was written, *In Town Tonight* was closely associated with both the BBC and with Coates. 'Langham Place' is cast in ternary form with the A-sections relying heavily on the motif $B\flat–B\flat–C$, representing the BBC. Suddenly at figure 4, an increase in tempo (almost doubled), heralds the B-section from the 'Knightsbridge' March in four bar fragments. At figure 6, the triadic fanfares used in 'Knightsbridge' act as a countermelody to the March with

[1]  Austin Coates, programme 3.
[2]  26/03/1936 EC to Stanford Robinson. *GB-Rwac*.
[3]  Programme notes attached to 10/05/53 EC to Miss Happold. *GB-Rwac*.

the BBC motif (transposed) superimposed over the top in a skilful reworking of material and combination of ideas (Example 8.1).

Example 8.1  'Langham Place' (*London Again* Suite), figure 6. © 1936 Chappell
          Music Ltd, London, W6 8BS. Reproduced by permission of Faber
          Music Ltd. All Rights Reserved

The finale, a Valse, depicts the dancing and the gaiety of life in Mayfair and is one of Coates' finest dances whose key structure is quite unorthodox when compared to his earlier valses. 'Mayfair' sticks to G major until figure 10, before a modulation to the dominant (D major), then to F major, using the note A as a pivot, then moving to B♭ before a swift return to D major and back to the tonic (G) at figure 17.

Four days after the premiere of the Suite by the BBC forces, Coates was in the recording studio cutting a disc of the *London Again* Suite and *By the Tamarisk* with the LPO for Columbia. Only the first two movements of the Suite were recorded that day; the finale and the Intermezzo were recorded the following day. *London Again* escaped with only minimal cuts (a short cut in the middle movement from figures 2 to 3 while the Valse began at figure 4, omitting its introduction entirely), whereas *By the Tamarisk* had a completely rewritten ending. Because the Intermezzo lasts approximately 5 minutes 15 seconds it required judicious pruning to fit onto a 12-inch 78rpm disc. Rather than remove any passages from the opening or shorten the recapitulation of the A-section at letter F, he opted to rewrite the extended coda (letter H). He may have felt that the written coda was too protracted to be fashioned into a serviceable conclusion for the piece. The result is a short coda (11 bars, rather than the written 32) based on material from letters F and G – a simple ending compared to the published one.

Coates' second orchestral work of 1936 was composed very reluctantly, following a trip to Ireland. On 7 March 1936, Coates was invited to conduct part of a broadcast by the BBC Northern Ireland Orchestra at the Ulster Hall in Belfast. He arrived feeling distinctly unwell after encountering numerous air pockets on his journey by aeroplane.[4] His discomfort soon vanished on encountering the eminent saxophonist Sigurd Rascher who was performing in the same concert as Coates. He recalled:

> as I sat in the artists' room I heard that lovely limpid tone floating towards me. His playing was silvery and mellow and yet so full of freshness and life. After the concert Rascher told me that he had long being waiting for an opportunity to meet me as he wanted to ask me to write him something for his 'pipe'.[5]

Having made a promise, Coates thought nothing more about the project until a letter arrived one morning, after his return to London, inviting him to compose a work for the 1936 Folkestone Festival. Feeling in a lethargic mood and only wanting to play with his camera, he replied that he would only write something for the Festival if Rascher could be engaged to perform it.[6] Thinking this response would extricate him from the situation in which he found himself, he went off on a tour to conduct his music in Sweden. On his return in June he was horrified to find that the Folkestone Festival Committee had secured the services of Rascher, thus fulfilling their side of the deal. Coates hurriedly settled down to composing the *Saxo-Rhapsody* completing the score at the end of July.

Coates had long been an admirer of the saxophone and had written a small part for the alto saxophone in the late-1920s vignette *Under the Stars*, while the tenor featured in the middle movement of *The Three Men* Suite (that had caught Rascher's attention). In an interview from 1926, Coates believed:

---

[4]   Eric Coates, *Suite in Four Movements* (London, 1953), pp. 226–7. There had also been a murder on the steps of the Town Hall the night before.

[5]   08/01/1937 *Radio Times*.

[6]   Coates, p. 228.

Personally I think the Saxophone has come to stay as a symphony instrument, providing one can find the right musicians to perform upon it. It lends a colouring to an orchestra and its only fault seems to be that, with its beautiful round sweet fullness of tone, it may make some of the other instruments, particularly, perhaps, the Flute and Bassoon, sound very dead.[7]

Notwithstanding Coates' enthusiasm for the instrument, the choice of the saxophone for a concertante work was a courageous decision on his part as it was not a popular choice for contertos during the 1930s. Due to the work of Rascher and others the *status quo* was changing with notable examples by Glazunov and Ibert. Coates must have felt certain that he would secure enough performances of the work to justify the strain of composing a concertante work; it was, after all, outside his usual compositional orbit. During the 1930s there were few professional 'straight' saxophonists who could do the work justice, though Coates no doubt believed that Rascher would incorporate the *Rhapsody* into his repertoire and perform it in his worldwide tours. Despite the paucity of saxophonists, the work was played occasionally during the composer's lifetime (though rarely with Rascher). Rascher did renew his interest in the work in 1954, informing Coates that he was interesting in recording a new performance of the piece.[8] Nothing came of the suggestion.

The *Saxo-Rhapsody*, like the earlier *Idyll*, holds a unique position in Coates' oeuvre as his only orchestral works that are not pictorial or programmatic, but pieces of 'absolute' music. Like Debussy's earlier *Rhapsodie* for alto saxophone, Coates chose to cast his work in a single movement based on a ternary structure showcasing Rascher's lyrical qualities. The work also included numerous passages exploiting the high 'altissimo register' of the saxophone, no doubt at Rascher's request as he was instrumental in expanding the range of the saxophone.

There are three principal themes in the *Saxo-Rhapsody*; the first is introduced in the A-section (figure 2) and the second (figure 5) and third (figure 7) in the B-section. The third subject bears a striking resemblance to the main theme of *A Song of Loyalty* (written the previous year), which possibly accounts for its entry in the violas and cellos at figure 35 as a tribute to King George V (in whose honour it had been written) who had died earlier that year. Another key feature of the work (especially in the reprise of the A-section at figure 29 as a foxtrot) is jazz. As Coates explained in the *Radio Times*: 'Secretly feeling that where there is a saxophone syncopation is never far away, I surreptitiously slipped in a few bars of syncopated rhythm, hoping the classically-minded Sigurd would not mind.'[9] There are several scoring 'tributes' to the dance bands with violins divided into three (figure 2) and muted brass (figure 29).

[7]   March 1926 *Melody Maker*.
[8]   28/04/1954 EC to Sigurd Rascher.
[9]   08/01/1937 *Radio Times*.

The work's significant failing is that the principal three themes are often repeated, perhaps because the work was completed in such a hurry, with little melodic development (though a lot is based upon his technique of 'self-developing melody'), only differing in orchestral textures and countermelodies. Furthermore, there is little exploration of different keys, and the piece adheres closely to the tonic of A♭ major, though, as is usual in Coates' writing, different keys are juxtaposed onto the tonic. In later years, the composer had doubts over the final bars of the *Rhapsody*, feeling that the difference in pitch between the brass and saxophone was too extreme, choosing to perform the alternative printed ending at the 1954 Proms.[10]

Interrupting progress on the *Saxo-Rhapsody* was Coates' first trip abroad as a conductor. Kenneth Wright (of the BBC's Music Department) had invited Adolf Wiklund of Svensk Radiojänst, Sweden to conduct a concert for the BBC. As part of Wiklund's return journey to Sweden, it was decided that Coates should accompany him and conduct a concert of his music in the Swedish capital.[11] Behind the scenes, Wright had been organising a trip of the BBC Orchestra to Sweden and tried to engineer an invitation for Coates to be invited as a guest-conductor. Writing to Nathaniel Broman of Svensk Radiojänst in April 1936, Wright extolled Coates' virtues:

> Knowing of your interest in his music we feel it is the best kind of English light music. I wonder if you would care to engage him to conduct while he is in Stockholm. He conducts well and is engaged to conduct all over England in this way and frequently by the BBC … . Forgive me mentioning this but he is an old friend of mine and a delightful fellow, and I feel sure you and your staff would like to see him.[12]

After Wiklund's concert on 7 June, Coates and the BBC Orchestra travelled to Sweden, and took part in a broadcast concert on 18 June and included the *London Again* Suite. Coates also spent much time sightseeing and being entertained, so much so that he nearly missed the rehearsal for his own broadcast.[13] The tour no doubt did much to bolster his reputation in Sweden and beyond and cemented his reputation as England's premier composer of light music.

After the death of King George V in January 1936 and the subsequent discussion of the Coronation of Edward VIII, *The Observer* ran a small feature on British composers who were writing music for the service in September. The article concluded: 'There is good reason to believe that Mr Eric Coates is to be invited to write the solemn processional march which concludes the service as the

---

[10]    Coates felt that the final note sounded a little remote against the low brass chords. (26/09/1954 EC to Aubyn Ravinski.)

[11]    Coates, p. 228.

[12]    06/04/1936 Kenneth Wright to Nathaniel Broman. *GB-Rwac*.

[13]    Coates, p. 229.

King passes from the Abbey.'[14] The *Nottingham Guardian* reported the following month that Coates had not yet been asked.[15]

It seems unlikely that Walford Davies (Master of the King's Music) would be considering issuing an invitation, although, since the composition of the 'Knightsbridge' March he was clearly associated with the March genre. Austin Coates believed that no official approach was ever made to his father on the issue, but that it was merely speculation created by the media.[16] With the abdication of Edward VIII and the subsequent coronation of George VI the matter was laid to rest and no more was made of Coates' providing any music for the Coronation. Notwithstanding Coates' exclusion, there was a great deal of British new music at the ceremony including Walton's *Crown Imperial* march and music by lighter composers, including Thomas Dunhill (*Canticum Fidei*, used for the entry of Queen Mary into the Abbey) and Edward German (*Coronation March*). There was certainly no mention in the press in 1952–53 of Coates providing any music for the Coronation of Elizabeth II.

Despite the absence of a commission for the Coronation, Coates' professional activities continued unabated. The beginning of 1937 was heralded by a visit to Abbey Road Studios on 15 January to record two discs for HMV with the LSO (though this was simply labelled 'Symphony Orchestra' on the British release of the disc). They recorded the *Saxo-Rhapsody*, with its dedicatee, Rascher, and a new version of *Summer Days*. The impetus to record the *Saxo-Rhapsody* is likely to have come from Rascher himself, who wrote to Coates in November 1936 to inquire when the composer was free to record the work, though the onus fell on Coates to arrange the necessary recording session.[17] Coates believed that the recording was the first time a saxophone had ever been recorded with a symphony orchestra. He also remembered: 'When it was being played in the studio the whole staff turned up in their white coats, their faces a study, to hear what all the noise was about.'[18] The recording is one of Coates' finest and clearly demonstrated Rascher's artistry, though it attracted a scathing review in *The Gramophone*.[19] The recording also features a small concession for the gramophone. At the close of side 1, Coates re-wrote the passage (the bar before figure 17 where the change of side occurred) from repeated triplet quavers to a held chord (Example 8.2a) to enable a more aesthetically pleasing change of side (Example 8.2b).

In addition, he tightens the structure of the work, thus greatly improving it by reducing the introduction where he cuts from the third beat of bar 3 to the forth beat of bar 13. He includes a further cut from figure 22 directly to figure 26, significantly reducing the amount of repetition in the B-section.

---

14    27/09/1936 *The Observer*.

15    Undated (circa October 1936) *Nottingham Guardian*. (Coates Scrapbook 2.)

16    11/11/1985 Austin Coates to Geoffrey Self.

17    18/11/1936 Sigurd Rascher to EC. *GB-Lcm*.

18    November 1937, *The Gramophone*, p. 236.

19    March 1937 *The Gramophone*, p. 427.

Example 8.2  *Saxo-Rhapsody.* © 1936 Chappell Music Ltd, London, W6 8BS.
                Reproduced by permission of Faber Music Ltd. All Rights Reserved

(a)  Two bars before figure 17 (printed)

(b)  Two bars before figure 17, aural transcription of 1937 recording

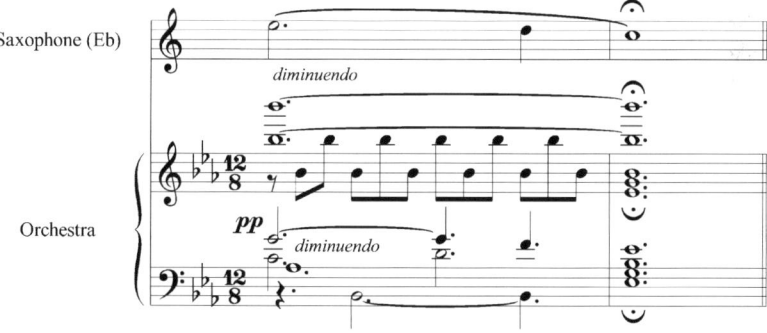

The recording of *Summer Days* Suite was released on a single 12-inch disc, with movements 1 and 2 on side 1 and movement 3 on side 2. To facilitate this, drastic measures were required: the first movement escaped with only one minor omission; but the middle movement was radically cut, from the bar before letter B to seven bars after D, thus expunging the entire middle section; the finale was left intact on the second side. The reason why the work had to be fitted on to a single disc is unclear. It is a shame that such a popular work had to be released with such savage cuts when it surely was more than feasible to produce it on a two-disc set complete with a small *morceau* as a complement. Nevertheless, this new recording of the Suite met with an enthusiastic review in *The Gramophone*, quite different from the review of the first recording of *Summer Days* in 1926.[20]

---

[20]  November 1937 *The Gramophone*, p. 243.

At the close of 1936 the Coates decided to leave Chiltern Court and head across Baker Street to an even grander block of flats, Berkeley Court. Despite the chaos of unpacking, Coates was back at work on another Suite, *Springtime*, which was his major orchestral composition of 1937. After the complexity and sophistication of the previous two suites, *Springtime* was a return to a more pastoral, Edward German-esque vein. As he explained to Harold Lowe, a BBC conductor: 'The work is quite unpretentious and on the lines of my old "Summer Days", so please do not expect to hear anything out-of-the-ordinary.'[21] The work could well have been written ten years previously as a successor to *Summer Days* or *From Meadow to Mayfair*. It marked a brief return to the 'traditional' light-orchestral scoring of two flutes and clarinets and single oboe and bassoon; the only luxury being three horns (made use of in the concluding valse). The Suite might have come as a result of requests from his publishers to write music more performable by amateur and small professional orchestras across the country. *Springtime* was first performed on 15 May, the eve of Coronation Day, in a BBC broadcast that also featured Haydn Wood conducting his *Fantasia: The British Empire*. Coates was fortunate to be associated with both the Coronation and George V's Silver Jubilee, as broadcasting historian Asa Briggs has stated, both of these were the two highlights of interwar broadcasting.[22]

*Springtime* is cast in three movements depicting a spring day: morning, noon and night. The opening movement 'Fresh Morning' is a wonderfully effervescent portrait of a meadow covered in the morning dew. Musically it pays homage to the pastoral $\frac{6}{8}$ style of Edward German. The movement is through-composed and, unusually for Coates in this type of piece, there is an abundance of melodic material with three reoccurring themes. The jewel of the Suite is undoubtedly the finale, 'Dance of the Twilight', one of his finest valses in which there are four main ideas, each repeated with a varied ending.

In contrast to his compositional life, a new development had been happening at home that would disrupt the Coates family for the rest of the year. In April, Phyl had been on a 'voyage of discovery' around the countryside near to Selsey and had found a sixteenth-century house, Ivy Grange. The house, reputed to be haunted, was surrounded by an overgrown garden, five miles upland from Selsey in the small hamlet of Sidlesham and required extensive restoration. She fell in love with the property and quickly convinced Coates that they should purchase the house. Phyl supervised every aspect of the entire project and even made special trips to other houses of the period to find the correct designs for fireplaces and staircases.[23] The Coates finally moved into their new 'holiday home' in October 1937, but there was still much to be done even then, as Coates recalled that there were:

---

[21]    12/06/1937 EC to Harold Lowe. *GB-Rwac*.

[22]    Asa Briggs, *The BBC* (Oxford, 1985), p. 141.

[23]    17/12/1938 *Southern Weekly News*.

No proper foundations, no damp-course, no double walls, no South windows, no hot water, no central heating, no proper drainage, no telephone, all these things had to be rectified. I remember what a song and dance went on over the question of the bath-water and of how we could obviate the running-over of the cess-pool every time any one of us had the temerity to take a bath.[24]

The whole family loved the house, but as Coates recalled: 'it was not practicable to own a house in the country which attracted us so greatly and which, in some ways, interfered with my professional work'.[25]

While work was progressing well on the new house at Sidlesham, Coates was not idle: he conducted two prestigious concerts. The first was on 20 July, when he was invited to perform with the BBC Television Orchestra in a broadcast programme of his music on the BBC's infant television service. However, there were few who could watch his broadcast due to the limited transmission range of the television service before the War.[26]

The second concert, broadcast by the BBC, was on 25 August, when he made a trip to conduct an ensemble of *ad hoc* players (billed as 'Eric Coates and His Orchestra') at the 1937 Radiolympia at Earl's Court (an exhibition devoted to all aspects of the radio from valves to performers). While the show was primarily aimed at wireless enthusiasts, there were numerous events and concerts throughout the duration of the festival. Coates appeared on the same bill as the Dagenham Girl Pipers, swathes of Hammond organs and a troupe of performing poodles!

Despite these excursions into popular events, he still had to provide new music for the masses to fulfil his publishing contract with Chappells. Following his return to a more pastoral vein of composition, his next miniature, written during the summer months of 1937, was the short serenade *For Your Delight*, undoubtedly written to complete that year's publishing contract, as there appears to have been no outside stimulus for its composition. It was one of his finest *morceaux de concert* and dedicated to his friend Burt Godsmark. It was first performed in a studio broadcast of his music in December, having been recorded three months previously alongside the *Springtime* Suite. The composer described *For Your Delight* as: 'very light, nothing to be afraid of'![27] Unusually, for Coates, the Serenade is constructed in rondo form, the material being varied several times (via 'self-developing melody' in each section), before moving onto the next. The Serenade is an infectious piece, felicitously orchestrated and making much use of melodic material in thirds.

Larger compositional projects were afoot during the remainder of 1937. In an interview with *Radio Pictorial* in August, Phyl disclosed that the two of them were

---

[24]   Coates (autograph), pp. 495–7.

[25]   Coates, p. 232.

[26]   By the close of 1937 it was estimated that 2,000 television sets had been sold. (Asa Briggs, *The Golden Age of Wireless* (Oxford, 1965), p. 611.)

[27]   18/10/1937 EC to Kenneth Wright. *GB-Rwac.*

joining forces to write an operetta. The article concluded: 'And now Mrs Coates's libretto of an opera is ready. It only awaits the music by Eric Coates who, after Radiolympia, hopes to retire to the idyllic surroundings of his Selsey home to woo his muse and complete the score.'[28] It was Coates' first serious attempt to compose a musical production since his abortive endeavours of the 1920s. During the early-1930s, Phyl had tried her hand at writing several short stories (most of these were undated but they were all largely written at Chiltern Court) including *The Golden Door* and *The Jester at the Wedding*, *Cherry Trees* (a series of diary entries) and a two-act play, *The Royal Jester*, under the *nom-de-plume* of Leslie Sand.

The operetta was to be a 'romantic melodrama' based on the plot of *The Jester at the Wedding*, which Phyl would expand for the stage.[29] There are no remaining clues as to why the collaboration failed, but Coates was notoriously fastidious over libretti. Writing to librettist, Guy Eden in 1945, Coates explained what he was looking for in a prospective libretto:

> It is so difficult to find just the right kind of theme, and I do not want to write anything in the Old English idiom, for this has been done so beautifully by Edward German and would not bear repetition. I should like a story which is romantic, colourful and which will not date and in asking this I'm afraid I'm asking rather a lot.[30]

Despite Coates' enthusiasm for the operetta, 1937 did see him produce a march, the first freestanding march since *London Bridge* in 1934. According to Austin, his father's inspiration for the work was being taken down the River Clyde in a tugboat owned by his friend John M'Kellar Robertson (Coates enjoyed all things nautical); Coates was captivated by the whole experience and a march ensued.[31] The original title had been 'RNVR – The Reserves' (of which Robertson was a member), but was subsequently changed to *The Seven Seas*. It is the only one of his marches to be in a $\frac{6}{8}$ time signature (favoured by Sousa), and is notable for its long introduction and only one statement of the B-section. *Seven Seas* was re-titled in 1957 as *South Wales and the West*, but this was exactly the same march.

Professionally, 1937 closed with a festive broadcast of his music on the BBC National Programme with the BBC Orchestra (Section E), on 20 December including the premiere of *For Your Delight*. The invitation for the broadcast had been issued in October when Kenneth Wright wrote to enquire if Coates would conduct a broadcast on either Christmas or Boxing Day:

> Most composers have somewhere a sketch of a sort of Carols-and-Bells-Across-the-Snow overture, so where is yours? Being an original sort of fellow you

---

[28]   20/08/1937 *Radio Pictorial*.

[29]   November 1937, *The Gramophone*, p. 237.

[30]   12/09/1945 EC to Guy Eden.

[31]   Undated *Vintage Light Music* 29, p. 3.

may choose to call it Stocking Songs at Eventide or Snowballing Intermezzo from your bandit opera; whatever it is we hereby apply for the privilege of first performance.[32]

Wright's request highlighted a deficiency in Coates' canon of works – he had no music for Christmas (unlike Ketèlbey). Alas, Coates did not rise to the invitation and merely conducted a studio broadcast instead.

The first half of 1938 was punctuated by two important BBC broadcasts. On 31 March, Coates, along with Haydn Wood and Montague Phillips, conducted in a joint concert of light music at the Bath Music Festival; the concert was also broadcast by the BBC. Alongside this light-music concert, the Festival featured a rather eclectic range of musicians including Henry Wood, Malcolm Sargent and Henry Hall and his Orchestra.

His next broadcast, in May, was one of his most unusual, being a spelling competition between officials of the BBC and listeners to the BBC. The two panels were made up of specialists; Coates appeared for the listeners on music – his BBC 'opponent' was musician Joseph Lewis). The listeners proved themselves better at spelling, winning 25 points to the BBC's 22. Coates was praised in the press for spelling 'antirrhinum' correctly, but mis-spelt 'wainscot' and 'pasturage'.[33]

Despite his popularity (with the public) shown by his visits to Bath and Scarborough (during August) and the variety of programmes he appeared on with the BBC, during the late-1930s, Coates entered a period of self-doubt. He decided that he wanted to change direction and produce works in a different style. The deterioration of the international scene and the inevitability of war must have also played its part in his thought process. It is difficult to establish exactly what this 'new direction' was to be, as the only discussion of the matter is a letter from his publishers, Chappells. In November 1938, he had been talking over the matter of his musical future with his publishers and in a follow-up letter, Edwin Goodman encouraged him:

> What I earnestly feel is that it is very important that you should keep the closest contact with the music buying public and not lose the popular market particularly since the advent of "IN TOWN TONIGHT". I personally know how you feel about your compositions and your future work but at the same time I would urge that it is most essential that you do your best to give us some lighter numbers that will carry on the continuity of your success with the large circle of music buyers, in addition to furthering and developing your position in the musically artistic world. It is a nuisance that we have to consider the commercial side of things if we are to carry on but I know you understand and appreciate the situation.[34]

---

[32]   14/10/1937 Kenneth Wright to EC. *GB-Rwac.*

[33]   02/05/1938 *Daily Herald.*

[34]   28/11/1938 Edwin Goodman to EC. *GB-Lcm.*

It seems reasonable to assume that the 'future work' being discussed would demonstrate a move to a more symphonic vein of light music composition, aimed at the standard-sized professional orchestra. Coates had been expanding his compositional vocabulary in the 1930s, especially in *The Jester at the Wedding* with its reuse of material and expansive six-movement structure. He had also pushed boundaries with his jazz-inspired (in parts), larger-scale orchestral works such as *The Three Men* and *London Again* Suites as well as the *Saxo-Rhapsody*. Chappells may not have been enthusiastic to publish these pieces because they were challenging works at the upper limits of what a good amateur orchestra and pianist (in the piano reductions) could manage. It is entirely plausible that this more 'symphonic' style was a response to the critics and that, by trying to push light music further in this symphonic direction, he was trying to change their opinion of light music. He wanted to move away from the constraints of the four-minute, effervescent miniature.

His new idiom is clearly seen in *The Enchanted Garden, The Four Centuries* Suite, *First Meeting* (published for violin and piano) and *The Three Elizabeths* Suite in which he pushed the boundaries of the adjective 'light'. They have a new dimension, and are certainly on a larger scale (demonstrated in an expansion of form, key relationships and thematic material) and use of a more generous orchestra. Whether he had a desire to produce 'symphonic works' along the lines of his contemporary Haydn Wood (Figure 8.1), especially his *May Day Overture*, or had it in his mind to emulate such works as the *Welsh Rhapsody* of Edward German and possibly the Third Orchestral Suite of Tchaikovsky is a matter that is unclear.

Why Coates waited until 1938 before actively pursuing this 'new direction' is not clear: Haydn Wood and Montague Phillips had been writing works like this for a number of years before Coates. They had, to some degree, explored this direction earlier in their careers with their respective symphonies and piano concertos. During the 1930s, Coates had been relying heavily on the BBC orchestras to premiere his new pieces and was beginning to turn his back on the seaside orchestras who had been presenting his works for the first time during the 1920s. The BBC orchestras had adequate rehearsal time, the correct disposition of instruments and could give effective premieres. In addition they would adopt the new pieces into their repertoire and play them frequently, giving Coates' new compositions a wide exposure to a broad cross-section of people.

Even though Coates was keen to embark on a 'new direction', his publishers warned him that there were financial considerations to be taken on board, especially as production costs of music were escalating and overall sales dropping. Goodman stressed that since their last publishing agreement, made in June 1937, Chappells had lost over £399 publishing works he had written since that date alone (this figure did not take into consideration advertising or running costs of the publishing

Figure 8.1    Two light-music greats, Haydn Wood and Eric Coates, in the late
1940s

house).[35] Nevertheless, Coates produced works in both camps as the circumstances
dictated over the next six years.

Coates' 'new direction' was relatively short-lived, lasting from 1938 until
1944. From 1939, he was free from any contractual obligation to provide pieces
for Chappells and his desire to pursue a 'new direction' may well have been a
contributing factor in his decision not to continue his contract; Chappells were
not obliged to publish any of his new works (though they had a 'gentleman's
agreement' that they would have the 'first refusal'). By 1943–44, the ongoing war
must have acted as a damper on any further advancement of the 'new direction'
as the openings for works in the more symphonic vein were becoming rarer. Post
war, Coates had little energy or time and returned to writing short works.

Even though the only epistolary evidence of his 'new direction' dates from
November 1938, Coates must have been contemplating a change of path for some
time, and had begun to move this way well before the letter from Chappells. During
1938, he finally set about rewriting his stage work *Snowdrop* for full orchestra.
The resulting work, a ballet entitled *The Enchanted Garden*, is a piece marked
out by sophistication from the earlier phantasies, which was more symphonic in
construction and orchestration. Even though he termed the work a ballet it was
a symphonic poem, and like *The Jester at the Wedding* it was never intended to

---

[35]    Ibid.

be danced to. Over the years, there had been many requests for Coates to turn *Snowdrop* into an orchestral work, the earliest evidence of which dates back to October 1932 when Stanford Robinson wrote to Coates to enquire when he would get around to rescoring the work for orchestra.[36] Coates replied that he did not think that piece warranted the time and effort to extract a new composition from it, and questioned the number of performances it would obtain.[37] As a result of the constant encouragement from Robbie, Coates decided to re-write *Snowdrop* in 1938. With the advent of Walt Disney's celebrated film of *Snow White and Seven Dwarfs* in 1937, a new plot would have to be found to avoid any artistic or legal altercations with Disney. As he later wrote:

> I remember how Robbie grinned and said it was entirely my own fault for not having done it sooner, although I am certain that this was a blessing in disguise, for the phenomenal success of Disney's portrayal of the delightful Fairy story would have been bound to have put my work in the shade.[38]

The recent acquisition of Ivy Grange in Sidlesham and its garden, a haven for wildlife, provided the ideal inspiration for rewriting the work, as Coates explained to the *Evening Standard*: 'I was inspired to write it by the owls screeching by night and the small birds singing by day in my garden at Sidlesham in Sussex.'[39] The new plot, written by Phyl, had certain similarities to Wilde's 'The Selfish Giant' with its use of animals and the crux of the story being 'good' versus 'evil'. Phyl's plot synopsis was included as a preface to the full score:

> The chief theme of the Ballet is that of the conflict of the Spirits of Light and Darkness in the Garden. After the opening introduction the curtain rises to show the Prince setting out on a journey, bidding farewell to the Princess and leaving her in the care of the animals and birds of the Garden who, to cheer her up, each bring an offering of flowers and fruit which they lay at her feet. During the Ballet the influence of the Evil Spirit of the Garden breaks in from time to time and after gaining strength he and his brood enter to a Tarantelle. The animals surround the Princess to protect her, and the Evil Spirits, in their turn, surround them to try to capture the Princess. The dance becomes faster and faster with the Evil Ones getting closer and closer to the Princess, and just as she is within their grasp the Prince returns holding a flaming sword in his hand with which he disperses the Evil Spirits, after which all is rejoicing and the Garden once more settles down to its peaceful aspect.[40]

---

[36]   07/10/1932 Stanford Robinson to EC. *GB-Rwac*.
[37]   09/12/1932 EC to Stanford Robinson. *GB-Rwac*.
[38]   Coates (autograph), pp. 456–7.
[39]   21/12/1938 *Evening Standard*.
[40]   Plot synopsis by Phyllis Coates.

Work began in earnest after a brief sojourn in Paris (one of the Coates' few personal continental holidays) on 13 June and completed on 1 August, with much of the orchestration carried out in Sidlesham during the summer. Coates scored the work for a larger than normal orchestra, including cor anglais and bass clarinet. His choice of instruments may have been governed by the knowledge of taking the Ballet on an orchestral tour to Europe when he knew he would have a larger orchestra than he would have had in England. The work was offered to the BBC for a first performance and was scheduled to receive its first performance on 3 November with the BBC Orchestra (Section D) under the composer. However, a sudden attack of influenza rendered Coates unfit to conduct the work and Clarence Raybould (who was to direct the rest of the programme) took over the first performance. One orchestral player commented of the switch: 'Thank heavens it's not Coates ... now we shan't have to play so blinkin' quickly.'[41]

Shortly before publication, Coates had discussed the work with Robbie (as he often did) whose comments regarding his music he always valued. As he informed Robinson after a performance of the Ballet in late 1939: 'I expect you noticed I had added the trumpets where you suggested? It certainly was a great improvement.'[42] After various performances of the work, Coates decided to adjust the Ballet before publication, writing to Clarence Raybould in 1939, after it was published: 'I have now brought out this ballet in a slightly shorter form, cutting out all the slow-rhythm section in the middle – I think it has improved it a good deal and it hangs together better ... .'[43]

Though there are many similarities to *Snowdrop*, *The Enchanted Garden* is essentially a new creation recycling many important themes and several passages (notably the tarantella and fugue sections). The Ballet is based on four reoccurring themes (though only three are listed in the preface to the full score) and a number of others used specific sections: the motto theme that represents evil spirits (theme 'M', opening) and that had been the Queen's theme in *Snowdrop*; the theme of happiness (theme A, figure 3), which had been associated with Snowdrop (in the Ballet, Coates places a great deal more emphasis on this theme); the theme of goodness (theme B, figure 6) which represented Snowdrop and the Faun in the stage production; and the fourth, probably representing the Prince (theme E, four bars after figure 33), which was the Faun's theme in *Snowdrop*. The use of a motto theme is akin to *The Three Bears* as it returns at several key points as a quasi-unifying motif, though unlike the Phantasy it does not form the basis of the majority of the melodic material. Appendix 2 shows the structure of the work and its relationship to *Snowdrop*.

As can be seen from Appendix 2, very little material from *Snowdrop* is quoted verbatim. What has been transferred has been significantly altered or extended to take into consideration the expanded orchestral canvas, especially in the fugue

---

[41]   Quoted by Eric Coates in 02/12/1938 *Daily Sketch*.
[42]   16/11/1939 EC to Stanford Robinson. *GB-Rwac*.
[43]   29/09/1939 EC to Clarence Raybould. *GB-Rwac*.

(figure 65 onwards). The coda (figure 93) is completely different in character from the stage production that closes with the Queen fainting from rage.

Coates was adamant that Chappells should publish the ballet with a printed full score, though they were not keen to accede to his request. In the end, he decided to have the full score printed at his own expense. He felt that a work of this complexity merited such a score and the absence of one would be detrimental to the success of the work. However, with the onset of war and the difficulties of obtaining metal, paper and ink the production of the score was delayed until 1946. *The Enchanted Garden* has never been amongst Coates' more popular works, though the composer occasionally aired it in his BBC broadcasts.

*The Enchanted Garden* was one of the few works that Coates never recorded. He did have plans to record it and there is a surviving recording chart amongst his papers.[44] The chart is useful on two counts, as it not only shows where he would have made the cuts in *The Enchanted Garden*, (necessary in order to fit it onto two 78rpm discs) but it also makes it clear that he planned his recordings carefully before going to the studio and knew what cuts and rewrites he would have to make beforehand. The first side featured the opening until figure 18 (4 minutes 10 seconds), the second figure 18 to 42 (4 minutes 5 seconds) with a cut from 23 to 26, side three figure 43 to 71 (4 minutes 5 seconds) with a cut from figure 58 to 60 and the last was figure 71 to the end (4 minutes). This plan is undated and the recording date remains a matter for conjecture.

Almost immediately after the first performance of *The Enchanted Garden*, Coates took the ballet on a conducting tour to Copenhagen, Oslo, Stockholm and Amsterdam in November. The trip proved to be a resounding success and received very positive press notices. To tie in with the British premiere of *The Enchanted Garden* at Bournemouth on his return, the *Daily Telegraph* (on Coates' instructions) printed a brief article quoting various foreign press cuttings.[45] The following year, Phyl wrote to Kenneth Wright: 'We have been told from many different sources from Scandinavia and Holland that Coates' music is their most popular request item, and we were inclined to discredit this, but when we read his press notices we realized that it was probably true.'[46] There was talk at the BBC that a return visit might be engineered in 1939 for Coates to conduct in a tour of different towns around Scandinavia. Alas, the project never came to fruition owing to the joint onsets of war and a decline in Coates' heath.

Shortly before his trip to Europe, Coates was appointed President of the Hucknall Light Orchestra at the beginning of November. The ensemble had been founded in 1924 under the conductorship of Enos Godfrey and the appointment of Coates as President marked the resurgence of the Orchestra after a difficult period, though this was not due to any input on Coates' part.[47] Coates provided

---

[44]    *The Enchanted Garden. GB-Lcm* Box 192.

[45]    17/12/1938 *Daily Telegraph.*

[46]    12/01/1939 Phyllis Coates to Kenneth Wright. *GB-Rwac.*

[47]    04/02/1939 *Hucknall Dispatch.*

the ensemble with a good deal of orchestral sets of his published compositions (he frequently sent sets to the BBC and, in his early days as a freelance composer, donated his pieces to the LSO) to boost their repertoire. It was a valuable link with his hometown and it also kept his name alive in his native Nottinghamshire. He conducted several concerts with the Orchestra and frequently sent them telegrams of good wishes before concerts.

Coates' final composition before the outbreak of the war was a concert valse, *Footlights*. While he had written many valses (as with Tchaikovsky, it was a favourite genre) in his orchestral suites and piano pieces, he had only written one extended concert valse, *Dancing Nights*, which had not been a popular success. There appears to have been no outside stimulus for the *Footlights* Valse, the inspiration simply being Phyl. The title was a nostalgic evocation of their heady days as a young married couple when she was pursuing a career on the stage and the aspiring composer would sit watching his sweetheart hence the original title, *Behind the Footlights*, which was shortened on publication to *Footlights*. The work was premiered in a studio broadcast by the BBC Orchestra (Section E), in June 1939 under the composer, with Garda Hall singing several of his songs.

After the completion of *Footlights*, an article by Haydn Wood entitled 'Fame Can Be a Handicap' appeared in the *Evening News* in June 1939 and Coates felt duty bound to respond to it.[48] In his article, Wood complained about the trappings of fame and how popular works can be despised by the composer. Wood also described one particular difficulty over a performance of his *Variations on a Once Popular Humorous Song*:

> In the course of time I tried to get it included in the programme of a Very Important Concert, but managed to do so only on condition that I conducted it myself! … The regular conductor apparently feared – with some reason – that his position might be jeopardised in the eyes of the higher critical circles if he led his orchestra through the mazes of such a very plebeian tune![49]

Coates felt inclined to respond to Wood's comments in an article entitled 'This Musical Snobbery', printed ten days after Wood's, in which he argued, more cogently than his colleague:

> To my mind, one of the most unfortunate victims of snobbery is the popular composer of the lighter school of music who, no matter how delightful and musicianly his writing may be, finds himself up against the particular difficulty of being classified by the Powers that Be as "Light". This means that he is immediately barred from having his music performed by any but the light and smaller orchestras, and consequently he rarely hears his works played on the proper sized orchestra for which they were written. As Haydn Wood pointed

---

[48]   20/06/1939 *Evening News*.

[49]   Ibid.

out, the writers of symphonies can write a dance tune and it will be performed at a Symphony Concert and acclaimed as "great fun", but woe betide the "Light" writers nowadays if they write a work for full orchestra and aspire to even a Promenade programme. An incredible outlook exists in England and we have taken it upon ourselves to docket music into the two categories "Light" and "Serious" and the two must never meet on the same programme. When one considers much of the badly constructed twaddle that is written under the name "Serious" and much of the well constructed and delightful writing that comes under the name "Light", surely it is about time that we dropped this snobbery and realized that music needs no such classification – it is either "Good" or "Bad". This is well understood on the Continent where one hears the finest symphony orchestras playing both the big symphonic works and also the gayest and most popular melodies.[50]

He went on to extol the virtues of melody, concluding his article:

I know that I shall always be grateful for what popularity my music has achieved and particularly for the success of my "Knightsbridge" March, and I should be a poorer person in several ways if the latter had not "caught on". Yes, I would definitely not like to forego the success of "Knightsbridge" – but then, perhaps my attitude is understandable as I come under the category of "Light".[51]

Whilst Coates had many valid arguments in his article, the world of music was changing and he did not always advance and adapt to new ideas or concert practice. The days were disappearing when he could conduct alongside the leading composers of the day as he had done in the 1920s. Many of the traditional outlets for light music were beginning to vanish and, with the onset of war, were to disappear completely. The reforms brought about by the BBC, both through their various radio stations and orchestras and through the Promenades, had accustomed the public to expect and understand new 'high art' works. Nevertheless, there was still an opening for light music, especially Coates'. It is, however, illuminating to consider that Coates was struggling to obtain performances of his music in what is often thought of as the 'golden age of light music'.

Despite feeling at a disadvantage because of having been branded a 'light-music composer', a major change in Coates' publishing contract made him able to pursue his 'new direction' more fully. After being under an exclusive contract with Chappells since 1919, he terminated his contract with them in April 1940 of his own volition, due to his advancing years and the ongoing war.[52] During his contractual agreement, he had largely been committed to compose one large work,

---

[50]    30/06/1939 *Evening News*. This version of the text is taken from the letter that Coates wrote to the *Evening News* and is in his original pagination. (*GB-Lcm*).

[51]    Ibid.

[52]    10/07/1942 EC to Louis Dreyfus. *GB-Lcm*.

and two smaller orchestral works as well as one song per year to qualify for his generous retaining fee. Coates felt pressurized to be continually producing new works and by this stage of his career, he wanted to compose when he felt a desire to and in any genre he wanted to.[53]

The majority of Coates' inspiration came as a direct result of an invitation for a work, as Austin recounted: 'he hardly ever wrote anything unless there was pressure on him to do so; a new work required for a certain date or in fulfilment of a contract or something of that kind'.[54] He also had a formal approach to composition: 'he couldn't settle down to write music until he was properly dressed in the morning, complete with tie and Harris Tweed coat – and, perhaps a Turkish cigarette'.[55] This freedom from any contractual obligation suited Coates and enabled him to proceed further with his 'new direction' with an idea for a new suite that occurred to him later in 1940.

The genesis of *The Four Centuries* Suite began in September 1940, his fifty-fourth year, and the entire work was conceived *in extremis* when the Coates were temporarily evicted from their Baker Street flat. The incident generated a spark of inspiration, as he later confided in an omitted passage in his autobiography:

> I remember the lovely summer morning in September 1940 when we returned to London, after having been away for a couple of days, to find the building in which we lived surrounded by police and ARP workers (six hundred or so residents had been turned out over night on account of four time-bombs having fallen in the surrounding streets) and we were admitted through the cordon only on condition that we took ten minutes in which to collect the things which we required. On climbing 135 stairs to the top floor (the lifts had been put out of action) we found the flat bathed in sunshine, and this and the peace of my writing-room, added to the knowledge that there were four time-bombs outside in the road likely to go off at any moment, set up such a vibration in my head and caused such a mass of musical ideas to fill my little dark room that it was only with the greatest difficulty I was able to resist temptation to sit down at my piano and relieve the congestion. However, the presence of a burly policeman outside the main entrance, who had permitted us ten minutes to collect our belongings, put a brake on my composing outburst and we reluctantly descended the 135 stairs. Phyl complete with some cherished undergarments under her arm and myself, emptyhanded, cursing at having to leave behind the only two things I wanted to take away with me, the piano and the radiogram.[56]

---

[53]  12/08/1938 Chappells Contract. *GB-Lcm* and 13/07/1942 Edwin Goodman? to EC. *GB-Lcm*. The signature is difficult to decipher, but it likely to be Goodman's.

[54]  Austin Coates, programme 4.

[55]  Austin Coates quoted in Ian Lace, 'Foreword' in Eric Coates, *Suite in Four Movements* (London, 1986), p. vii.

[56]  Coates (autograph), pp. 516–17. Coates is not clear if this was the *Four Centuries* Suite, but he did not compose much in the intervening period, unless he is referring a

Little work was achieved on the score over the winter of 1940 due to Coates
suffering from congestion of the lungs while in May–June 1941 their two-
week notice of permanent eviction from their flat and subsequent relocation to
Amersham caused a further lull in the composition. However, the enemy bombing
raids triggered several ideas for the work and with the move to Amersham in June
1941, which provided both the tranquillity, away from the bombing raids, as well
as the stimulus of the garden, work began on the Suite in earnest. He wrote in his
autobiography:

> The long delay before I was able to put my ideas down had been the means of
> 'Four Centuries' growing in my mind so completely that the actual orchestrating
> was not unlike musical dictation. The writing-room in our temporary house in
> Buckinghamshire, after we had been there a couple of weeks and I had become
> accustomed to its atmosphere, was literally impregnated with musical sounds,
> and the next two months saw me, day in, day out, working on the score ... [I]
> was writing in ideal circumstances.[57]

The Suite was completed on 6 November and depicted dancing in the present
(twentieth) and previous three centuries: the seventeenth century, depicted a
Prelude and Hornpipe; the eighteenth, a Pavane and Tambourin; the nineteenth, a
Valse; while the twentieth, 'Rhythm' is an affectionate tribute to the dance bands.[58]
The scoring also reflects the different centuries: the first movement is scored for
double woodwind, two horns and strings; the second for the same woodwind
forces but with four horns, two trumpets, triangle and tambourine; the Valse is
identical to the previous movement but with the addition of bass clarinet, three
trombones, harp and expanded percussion; and the finale has the second flute
doubling piccolo, three trumpets, three saxophones and a battery of percussion,
but with the absence of the harp. The Suite is to some degree pastiche, but, like
Stanford's Suite for Violin and Orchestra (which also features a tambourin), is a
fusion of 'old' and 'new' styles.

Upon completion, the terpsichorean Suite experienced various problems over
its first performance, publication and the percussion parts of the fourth movement.
Instead of offering the work to Chappells, Coates published the work with Boosey
and Hawkes. He had always retained a special affection for them, as the house of
Boosey had started his publishing career back in 1908:

> It has been for many years an understood thing between Leslie [Boosey] and
> myself that if ever Chappells did not want a work of mine while under contract,

concert overture he wrote during this period which became the first movement of *The Three
Elizabeths* in 1944.
  [57]  Coates, pp. 238–9.
  [58]  It is one of the few orchestral works to ape their style alongside the 'Intermezzo
(Homage to Henry Hall)', of Vaughan Williams' *Partita* for Double String Orchestra.

or if I were ever free, I would give him the opportunity of publishing anything I thought suitable, but he has <u>not</u> pressed me for this even though he knew that my contract with you had been terminated.[59]

An additional factor in luring him to publish the work with Boosey and Hawkes was the promise of the publication of a full score.[60] Nevertheless, it was not all 'plain sailing' and in 1943 he found out that Booseys were printing a condensed score, and as a consequence, sixty-four plates, already engraved, had to be disposed of. There was even talk as to whether the full score would be engraved or photographed.[61]

In January 1942, after he had shown the work to Henry Wood, Coates sent the autograph score to the BBC to see if they would care to undertake the first performance. The BBC retained the score (the only copy) for two months while they decided where to place the work in their schedules. The composer was anxious to secure a performance before publication.[62] The delay also slowed down the publication of the orchestral parts by Boosey and Hawkes. Reginald Thatcher, the BBC's Deputy Director of Music (and in Adrian Boult's absence, the *de facto* head of the music department) was apologetic for the delay when he eventually replied to the composer's letter, but was keen to stress a desire to programme the work for a studio recording at the earliest opportunity. This would alleviate the pressure of a live broadcast if the composer were to conduct the premiere (which pleased Coates as he had not been well).[63] Coates had certain key criteria for the trio of saxophones required for the finale:

> I am somewhat exercising my mind about the quality of the saxophone-players – it is very important that they should know something about dance-band technique and the <u>tenor</u>, in particular, <u>must</u> be able to play a melody like an artist. I think we both know what saxophones can sound like on occasions! When the work is published I am thinking of cueing these parts into another section so as to obviate the danger of being compelled to have inferior players in any future performance.[64]

There was still no final decision as to where the work should be scheduled. In the meantime Stanford Robinson persuaded him that it was better for the composer to hear the work first in somebody else's hands to know how it sounded before tackling it himself. Coates heeded this advice and let Robinson conduct the first

---

[59]   10/07/1942 EC to Louis Dreyfus. *GB-Lcm*.

[60]   For further details, see Chapter 9.

[61]   28/01/1943 Kenneth Wright to Arthur Bliss. *GB-Rwac*.

[62]   04/03/1942 EC to Reginald Thatcher. *GB-Rwac*.

[63]   06/03/1942 Reginald Thatcher to EC. *GB-Rwac*.

[64]   08/03/1942 EC to Reginald Thatcher. *GB-Rwac*.

performance.[65] Robbie championed the work in the BBC and tried to have it included in a 'Saturday 9:53 during June or July'.[66] The work eventually received its first performance on 21 July by the BBC Theatre Orchestra under Robbie, over six months after Coates had sent the work to the BBC. The composer duly stayed at home and listened to the performance on the wireless and was rather pleased with the result.[67] In fact, he was so pleased with the Theatre Orchestra's performance that he worked hard to persuade EMI to record the *Four Centuries*, even if they produced only a hundred pressings for broadcasting purposes, but he failed in the attempt.[68]

Robinson gave the second performance of the Suite on 3 September, hoping to have the printed orchestral parts for his performance, but they were still in their final proof stage. Before this performance, Robbie had suggested an amendment to the string parts of the second movement, which the composer had already altered in the score.[69] However, after the second performance there was a more pressing problem with the Suite that Robinson felt required serious attention, namely the percussion part of the finale. He informed Coates:

> Here is the drum part of the fourth movement of your new Suite as worked out by my drummer, Mr Leslie Lewis, much as he played it last Thursday. It will present no difficulty to any experienced dance band drummer or even the average music-hall one, but it would probably be quite beyond the capacity of the ordinary "straight" drummer and even if he made a shot at it, it would be dangerously "corny". I suggest that you might have it printed as an extra part and put a note at the top that it should only be used with orchestras who have a drummer experienced in dance style. On the other hand, it could hardly be played at the same time as your original S.D. parts, though it could be played in conjunction with your original tympani, triangles and so on. What about adopting this new percussion part as it stands and composing a new tympani, plus triangle and vibraphone part to go with it? This would be practical.[70]

Messers Robinson, Lewis and Coates met two days later to discuss the finale. There is no written outcome of their meeting and it is unclear if Coates acquiesced to their suggestions, as the autograph score is now lost. He certainly heeded Robinson's advice over the layout of the printed full score. Coates was always willing to take on the advice of professional musicians to make his music more practical. It seems likely that Coates adopted the 'new' part into the score, despite the fact this would no doubt require the percussion parts for the finale to be

65    Coates, p. 239.

66    22/05/1942 Stanford Robinson to Assistant Director of Music. *GB-Rwac*.

67    22/07/1942 EC to Stanford Robinson. *GB-Rwac*.

68    17/08/1942 EC to Stanford Robinson. *GB-Rwac*.

69    22/07/1942 EC to Stanford Robinson. *GB-Rwac*.

70    07/09/1942 Stanford Robinson to EC. *GB-Rwac*.

re-engraved, rather than print a separate drum part for those with 'dance band experience'. The issues surrounding this movement show clearly why he wanted a first performance *before* the work was published, as he had already stated to Robinson that the effects he desired to create in the *Four Centuries* Suite 'needed very careful treatment'.[71]

Right from the outset, the work was not yet another 'Eric Coates' Suite', as he informed Stanford Robinson, while writing the Suite, that it: 'may prove to be rather original'.[72] The *Four Centuries* is Coates' masterpiece because in none of his other works does he successfully attempt such a variety of styles, colourful orchestration and exquisite melody. Here, he offers the public (largely uneducated in these styles) something from the past but without exposing the harsher (and less romantic) truth about those earlier periods.

The opening 'Prelude' is essentially a cadenza for solo flute, surely a tribute to Coates' flute-playing father, which represents the spirit of dancing throughout the ages.[73] The flute features prominently in the second movement and has another cadenza in the Valse.[74] The 'Hornpipe' is a real tour de force of contrapuntal writing (in $\frac{2}{4}$ as a hornpipe of the seventeenth century would have been) and is an expansion of his earlier fugal and contrapuntal writing. The 'Hornpipe' is a set of variations, opening with a strict four-part fugal exposition, giving way to a series of twelve variations, each brimming with contrapuntal ingenuity and imitation (especially figure 13 onwards).

The second movement, 'Pavane and Tambourin', is more unified than the first, with the minor-mode 'Pavane' (Coates' only example of a movement or piece totally in a minor key) returning, albeit significantly altered, after the 'Tambourin'. The following 'Tambourin' resembles a baroque keyboard dance as it tends to take the form of a section followed by a varied repetition (very much in the style of the movements in Warlock's effervescent *Capriol Suite*).[75]

The Valse, a dance form that totally epitomized the music of the nineteenth century, is a fine creation and differs markedly from his other valses because of the sheer volume of melodic material. It uses nine separate themes with little repetition; only the A-section returns, five bars after figure 15.

The finale, 'Rhythm', is one of Coates' most ingenious creations and is a superb tribute to the dance bands he loved. He had first used the title and idea of imitating the dance bands at the close of his *Four Ways* Suite of 1928. This time, the movement is a lot more sophisticated, both in its melodic material and orchestration. In the *Four Centuries*, he has assimilated the dance bands' style

---

[71]   23/07/1941 EC to Stanford Robinson. *GB-Rwac*.

[72]   Ibid.

[73]   18/08/1956 Promenade Concert Programme.

[74]   Reminiscent of the flute cadenzas in the 'Valse des Fleurs' from Tchaikovsky's ballet *The Nutcracker*.

[75]   Alongside Duruflé's example in his *Trois Danses*, Coates' is one of the few twentieth century orchestral versions of this dance.

perfectly and often uses instruments or combinations in groups of three (hence the need for three trumpets, three saxophones and three clarinets). It is also one of his finest pieces of orchestration. Coates treats the percussion section more like a drum-kit, with regular patterns for the side drum and suspended cymbal. He creates some truly magical sounds by frequent use of divisi and pizzicato strings (as at figure 6) and Harmon mutes (figure 10) and 'straight' mutes (figure 20) for the trumpets. One of the most skilful aspects of the work is the subtle way in which the saxophones are used, holding their entry back until nearly halfway through the movement. 'Rhythm' opens with a trio of clarinets with the main theme, giving way to the woodwind (*senza* bassoons) at figure 3 while the tenor saxophone finally enters at figure 6; the saxophone chorus is not used *in toto* until figure 10.

Unlike the later *The Three Elizabeths* Suite, the work was not written with a 'thematic unity' (unless one counts the flute cadenzas and solos): it is not designed to be played as a unit. However, the quiet ending of the Valse does cast a slight doubt on this theory, as it segues into the finale rather than a rousing coda bringing the movement to an effervescent conclusion.

Interrupting work on *Four Centuries* was a request from his former viola teacher that took Coates on one of his rare forays into the world of chamber music. In 1942, Lionel Tertis would be celebrating his fiftieth anniversary as a viola player, having entered Trinity College of Music in 1892. During late 1941, he invited Coates to compose a piece to celebrate this milestone. Even though their professional relationship had ended in the 1910s, they remained friends and Coates had loaned Tertis his viola in 1938 when Tertis temporarily retired from playing (he had given his viola away, but soon missed it and borrowed Coates' until he found a more acceptable one). The resulting work was entitled *First Meeting*, scored for viola and piano and was presumably inspired by their first meeting in 1906 at the RAM as master and pupil. The work, despite receiving a warm welcome by Tertis, had an uneasy start and was never played by him after the play-through at the Coates' cottage in Hampstead in November 1941, as Austin Coates recalled:

> After lunch we went into the drawing room, and Tertis and my father played the work ... Tertis played as if he'd known the work all his life – he was sight-reading ... He was so delighted that he insisted on their doing it again. When he left, after tea, we knew it was the last time he would ever play it; and it was.[76]

What Coates thought of the occasion is consigned to history though there appears not to have been any rift between Coates and Tertis. Why the work was not played by in public by Tertis is a mystery. It was not until 1943 that the work appeared in print and then not in its original guise. It was re-scored for violin and now bore a new dedication 'to Austin on his twenty first birthday', rather than to Tertis. All references to Tertis and the viola were removed, though the original title was

---

[76]    14/10/1985 Austin Coates to Geoffrey Self.

retained, which sat incongruously with the amended dedication. Tertis does not mention the piece in the list of works composed for him in his autobiography, *My Viola and I.*[77] The decision to re-score the work may have originated with Chappells who may have decided, in part influenced by the wartime printing restrictions, that it would only be profitable as a violin rather than a viola solo. Austin believed that: "'First Meeting" was never right as a violin piece. If I'd known my father was going to transpose it I would have tried to dissuade him ... .'[78] The work has since been recorded several times in its viola guise, arranged by Michael Ponder. *First Meeting* bears several similarities to the *Saxo-Rhapsody* since both share the use of ternary form, a lyrical atmosphere to show off the soloist and end quietly with an ascent up to the high register of the soloist supported by a low accompaniment.

After the completion of *First Meeting* and *Four Centuries* it would be several years before Coates attempted another work in his 'new direction': a suite. This would prove to be his final excursion down this path and would, furthermore, be his last suite and final extended work. According to Austin Coates, the origins of *The Three Elizabeths* Suite dated back to a visit the Coates made in August–September 1940 to Phyl's 82-year-old mother at Chesham Bois.[79] The trip was made partly because of a need for respite from the Blitz and partly out of concern, as Mrs Black lived alone. During the visit, Coates wrote a concert overture, along the lines of *The Merrymakers*, perhaps to fill a gap in his output. After their return to London a month or so later, Austin recalled:

> Some weeks later, however, I noticed that the score was still lying neatly on his desk; he had done nothing about it. Wasn't he going to show it to his publishers I asked him? No, he didn't think he would. When I asked him why, he gave a curious reply, he said 'I have a feeling it belongs to something else, but I can't think what it is.' I understood exactly what he meant. He had realised that it wasn't a concert overture but the first movement of something and he hadn't got the idea for the other movements. So the stray movement, finished and complete, went into a drawer and there it remained as it turned out for more than three years.[80]

Coates never mentioned in either his autobiography or correspondence of the period that the first movement was written between three and four years before the rest of the Suite. Nevertheless, he was certainly at work on something during the autumn of 1940, as he informed Stanford Robinson in September that he

---

[77]   Lionel Tertis, *My Viola and I* (London, 1974), pp. 171–4.

[78]   14/10/1985 Austin Coates to Geoffrey Self.

[79]   She would eventually live to be 99 and died only a few months before her son-in-law in 1957.

[80]   Austin Coates, programme 4.

was coming to London regularly to try to compose.[81] In the autograph score, the opening movement is dated 3 August 1944 (though work had begun on 19 June), but it could well have been re-written and re-orchestrated for the Suite. However, Austin recounted that on his return from the RAF in 1946:

> My parents were away in the States, but the records of The Three Elizabeths [*sic*] were there, I put them on the gramophone. Halcyon Days was exactly as I remembered him playing it in 1940. The orchestration simply confirmed what I had thought from hearing him play it … . I doubt if a note had been altered.[82]

Austin recalled the genesis of the rest of the Suite:

> Then in the autumn of 1943, in the worst days of the war, in the afternoon mail came a letter from a rector of a parish in Berkshire. I was in the Royal Air Force stationed quite near London and there were occasions when I could get home for a day off, this was one of them. He read the letter very carefully, twice, and then gave it to my mother, who read it and said 'what a wonderful idea' and passed the letter to me. The rector was suggesting that Eric Coates write an orchestral suite about the three Elizabeths in history; Elizabeth Tudor; Elizabeth Glamis, the Queen; and Princess Elizabeth, the Queen to be. I said simply 'yes' and handed it back to him. Enthusiasm could be counter productive. For quite a time he held the letter in front of him, but I could see he was not reading it, he was thinking. Then he said, 'I think I am going to do it'.[83]

The rector in question was Arthur L. Hall, then vicar of Barnes, who was himself quite musical. In his autobiography Coates recalled the delight he felt on receiving Hall's suggestion: 'Gone was my feeling of exhaustion, gone was my fear that I should write no more, forgotten were the air-raid warnings and the 'doodle-bugs'. My imagination was fired.'[84] Work was certainly well under way in October 1943 and Stanford Robinson was eager to peruse the completed score.[85] But then work appeared to stop, and as Austin recounted: 'Stanford Robinson, who had been told about the idea, chivvied him, his publishers chivvied him, eventually even the

---

[81]    11/09/1940 EC to Stanford Robinson. *GB-Rwac*. Coates could have been sketching ideas for the *Four Centuries* Suite, as the work had a long genesis, but the composer himself states that after the initial idea and sketch for the work, nothing further was achieved on the work (Coates, p. 239). Austin was always most emphatic that the first movement of *The Three Elizabeths* had been composed first, even though there is no surviving documentary evidence to support his theory.

[82]    09/03/1986 Austin Coates to Geoffrey Self.

[83]    Austin Coates, programme 4.

[84]    Coates, p. 244.

[85]    03/10/1943 Stanford Robinson to EC.

BBC chivvied him and at last in the spring of 1944 he settled down to it beginning with the second movement.'[86]

According to the *Radio Times* he had sketched the whole Suite in two weeks and spent three months on the orchestration.[87] The orchestration was undertaken during a restorative holiday in Evesham. Coates undertook the task in the Northwick Hotel's bar where he could work in peace until the bar was opened at midday.[88] The score was finally completed on 12 August 1944 and was dedicated, with permission, to Queen Elizabeth, a gesture he decided on in May 1944.[89] During 1944, he wrote several letters to the Queen's Private Secretary to inform the Queen of the work's progress. After he had recorded the Suite in November he sent the Queen a set of the test-pressings before the recording went on sale to the public.[90]

Upon completion of the Suite, he wrote to the BBC to express his desire (perhaps because of its dedication) that the work receive a high-profile premiere in a peak listening slot.[91] Kenneth Wright replied explaining that the Music Department was keen for the work to be presented by the augmented BBC Theatre Orchestra, but not in a *Music for Everybody* programme as suggested by the composer.[92] From this juncture, Victor Hely-Hutchinson (who had just succeeded Arthur Bliss as Director of Music) took a keen interest in the score and he appears to have pushed the work through the various BBC channels. Coates held his new work in the highest esteem. He informed Hely-Hutchinson:

> I think it is important that my Suite receives a good send-off as soon as possible … .
> Regarding the presentation, my tentative suggestion is that you give me, say, a forty-five minute broadcast with an orchestra of not less than between sixty and seventy players (perhaps the occasion calls for the BBC Symphony Orchestra, but I leave this to you), with Stuart Hibberd announcing (this was Ken's [Wright] suggestion) and I would propose commencing with a one-movement work such as "The Enchanted Garden" and concluding with "The Three Elizabeths" which would lend contrast to the broadcast … .[93]

---

[86]   Austin Coates, programme 4. The autograph score states that work started on 19/06/1944 in London, though Coates must have sketched ideas well before this date.

[87]   08/12/1944 *Radio Times.*

[88]   Coates, p. 244.

[89]   23/05/1944 Arthur Penn to EC.

[90]   18/12/1944 EC to Arthur Penn.

[91]   19/09/1944 EC to Kenneth Wright. *GB-Rwac.*

[92]   28/09/1944 Kenneth Wright to EC. *GB-Rwac.*

[93]   15/10/1944 EC to Victor Hely-Hutchinson. *GB-Rwac.* In the end, Coates was invited to conduct just his Suite with the BBC Symphony Orchestra.

Despite the earlier small-scale suggestions for the Suite's premiere, Hely-Hutchinson finally agreed to recommend the work for inclusion in *Music for All*, an unusual slot for a new, light work: [94]

> Unless you can think of a "better 'ole" it had better go into "Music for All". I realise that it does not fit in with your conception of these progs. but I am confident that it won't hurt the appeal & function of the series as a whole … . I am most anxious that it should get in somewhere soon + in a good place. [95]

Hely-Hutchinson also yielded to Coates' suggestion that the work should be given its premiere by the BBC Symphony Orchestra, though even in October (two months before its premiere) the Corporation wished to programme the Suite with the BBC Theatre Orchestra.[96] The last-minute inclusion of the Suite into *Music for All* caused a disagreement between Clarence Raybould, who was to conduct the remainder of the broadcast, and Hely-Hutchinson.[97] The National Symphony Orchestra had recorded it on 14 November, over a month before it received its public premiere. No doubt, like the *Four Centuries* Suite three years earlier, Coates wanted to be sure that the orchestral 'effects' came off successfully before Chappells issued the orchestral material.

The Suite is unique in Coates' output as the three movements are motifically linked, by the 'Elizabeth' motif (a verbalization of Elizabeth), which acts almost as an *idée fixe* for the Suite (Example 8.3).

Example 8.3  *The Three Elizabeths* Suite, 'Elizabeth' motif. © 1945 Chappell Music Ltd, London, W6 8BS. Reproduced by permission of Faber Music Ltd. All Rights Reserved

E - liz-a-beth

In addition, the choice of keys for the movements complement each other: the first movement is in C major; the second opens with a passage in C major before establishing its tonic of G; and the finale opens with an introduction based around

---

[94]   Haydn Wood had been trying for some time to have a work included in 'Music for All' and wrote to the BBC to voice his dissatisfaction. Julian Herbage wryly noted to Hely-Hutchinson, 'I was afraid that, once we included a work by Eric Coates in 'Music for All', we would have an outburst from Haydn Wood, and here it is!' (28/12/1944 Julian Herbage to Victor Hely-Hutchinson. *GB-Rwac* Haydn Wood.)

[95]   27/10/1944 Victor Hely-Hutchinson to Julian Herbage. *GB-Rwac*.

[96]   20/10/1944 Julian Herbage to Victor Hely-Hutchinson. *GB-Rwac*.

[97]   16/11/1944 Clarence Raybould to Julian Herbage. *GB-Rwac*.

G before establishing its tonic of C. Due to this, the Suite is designed (unlike his other Suites) to be played in its entirety, though the movements stand up exceptionally well on their own. The work is an embodiment of his new approach to light music and no other of his works retains this degree of unity.

The middle movement, 'Springtime in Angus', is one of the most tender and perfect pieces that Coates ever wrote. Cast in his ternary 'dynamic arch' form (rising from pianissimo to fortissimo and back down to pianissimo), it acts as a complete tonic to the outer movements and draws inspiration from Delius and Debussy. The movement has a wonderful symmetry of material and a touch of humour with the addition of the cuckoo (replicating Delius' *On Hearing the First Cuckoo in Spring*). The first subject (figure 4) is one of the finest he ever wrote and pays homage to the Scottish roots of the Queen with the use of the Scotch snap rhythm, and the initial accompaniment of a drone on the strings suggesting bagpipes.

The concluding March, 'Youth of Britain', sits oddly with the previous two movements and is slightly too rumbustious after the pastoral splendour of 'Elizabeth of Glamis'. While the March is constructed in his usual march formula, it is slightly more expansive than usual (perhaps paving the way for the later *Rhodesia* March), although it is still in line with his 'new direction' to light music.

The composition of *The Three Elizabeths* Suite brought about the end of his 'new direction' and while *The Enchanted Garden* and *Four Centuries* Suite were seldom played (in comparison to the rest of his output), they were amongst his finest achievements. The tranche of works completed under this banner certainly created a good deal more work for Coates and he might well have continued writing works in this vein had he not suffered a complete breakdown of heath in the late 1940s, though he never returned to the 'new direction' when he returned to complete health in the 1950s. With the onset of war, the ensuing years were difficult for Eric and Phyl, but Coates continued to compose and some of his finest achievements date from the war years.

# PART III
## The Establishment Figure

# Chapter 9

# The War Years, 1939–1945

Following the outbreak of war in 1939, Eric Coates was no longer the carefree, 'Peter-Pan-like' figure, who produced an endless stream of tuneful works, that he had been in the 1920s. It was a period of increasing self-doubt, conflict and struggle to continue writing music. Apart from the two suites *Four Centuries* and *The Three Elizabeths*, Coates focused entirely on miniatures, especially the march, which became exceedingly popular during the war years. During 1939 with the acceleration of rearming, the onset of war had a radicalizing effect on the British public and lead to a marked change in values. Coates declared in his autobiography that during the early months of the Second World War: 'I could not write a note, the incessant air-raid warnings and the 'doodle-bugs' saw to that … . It was all too patent that my writing days were over.'[1] Writing to Stanford Robinson in 1942, he mentioned a change in his compositional psyche: 'It seemed so strange to hear some of my early music again – somehow I do not seem the same person to-day as I was in those days. A good deal of joy seems to have gone out of everything.'[2]

The outbreak of the war was hardly a surprise for the Coates and they chose to remain in London. They were not about to abandon their home in favour of a quieter and safer life in the country. Austin recalled:

> their top floor corner flat, a very high exposed building, all of London spread before them, their windows directly facing the line of the German air approach. Neither of them were in the least concerned about the danger; buildings were bombed and on fire on several sides at various times; and there were smaller firebombs on the roof; they never went near an air raid shelter, they never sheltered at all; but the noise![3]

How Coates managed to produce any compositions during these years is a miracle. Despite all the carnage and destruction around him, nothing seemed to affect or diminish his great gift of melody. There were no works of an outpouring of grief, such as Shostakovich's 'Leningrad' Symphony, since he never experienced the horrors that Shostakovich encountered. As he told the *Evening News*: 'It's very odd, but the noisier the guns the lighter one's music … . On the other hand, I work more slowly. It's rather difficult to shut out of one's mind what is going

---

[1]   Eric Coates, *Suite in Four Movements* (London, 1953), p. 243.

[2]   02/03/1942 EC to Stanford Robinson. *GB-Rwac*.

[3]   Austin Coates, programme 4.

on outside.'[4] Though he soon came to admit that after the initial lack of interest in or support for music at the onset of war, things did generally change for the better, he did, nevertheless, become depressed with the general situation and lack of openings for light music. As Briggs has stressed, 'serious music' gained a wider and more knowledgeable audience during the Second World War (cf. the concerts organized by Myra Hess at the National Gallery); both the Home and Forces programmes considerably increased the amount of broadcast hours of classical and contemporary music.[5]

Since the completion of *Footlights*, midway though 1939, Coates had entered a compositional fallow period, but by November he was at work on a short romance, *Last Love*.[6] Writing to Stanford Robinson, Coates informed him: 'I am in the throes of orchestrating a short Romance – it is extraordinary how difficult it is to make a simple piece interesting to play; there seems to be nothing to work on somehow.'[7] The Romance was completed a week later and despatched to Chappells to be engraved. Robbie invited Coates to conduct the work himself in a broadcast of modern British light music on 8 December (though would not receive a fee).[8] Coates was obliged to decline the invitation owing to a trivial doctor's appointment that could not be cancelled.[9] *Last Love* is, in essence, a 'song without words' and could well have been an orchestrated ballad (like *Summer Afternoon*). It is constructed in ternary form and is essentially monothematic, with the B-section largely a continuation of the A-section, albeit at a faster tempo.

Shortly after the completion of *Last Love*, Coates succumbed to a serious illness that lasted most of January and February 1940. Phyl had contracted influenza and measles and as a result the couple had been largely out of circulation for some time. On Phyl's restoration to health, Coates succumbed to another bout of influenza. Nevertheless, during this period he found time to compose a short work, *I Sing to You*, and to visit the recording studio to record compositions written since his last visit in 1937. *I Sing to You* is very similar to *Last Love*, both in structure (ternary form) and in melodic content, as both rely on two-bar phrases, starting on off-beats and with melodic appoggiaturas, as can be seen by comparing the opening melodies. There are also similarities in the ways in which the first themes are expanded (figure 2 in both pieces). The melodic structures also bear a striking resemblance to the earlier 'Noonday Song' (*Springtime* Suite) (Example 9.1).

Coates was not well enough to conduct the premier of *I Sing to You* in a complete programme of his music broadcast on the Forces Programme, which he was annoyed at having to miss. By the beginning of April, he was showing

---

4    08/11/1940 *Evening News*.

5    Asa Briggs, *The War of Words* (Oxford, 1970), p. 582.

6    Coates, *Suite*, p. 235.

7    16/11/1939 EC to Stanford Robinson. *GB-Rwac*.

8    02/12/1939 Stanford Robinson to EC. *GB-Rwac*.

9    07/12/1939 EC to Stanford Robinson. *GB-Rwac*.

Example 9.1  'Noonday Song' (*Springtime* Suite), *Last Love* and *I Sing to You*,
comparison of A-section melodies.[10] © 1937, © 1939 and © 1940
Chappell Music Ltd, London, W6 8BS. Reproduced by permission
of Faber Music Ltd. All Rights Reserved

some signs of a return to normal strength and had begun to answer correspondence
(Phyl, as usual when he was indisposed, had been dealing with his letters), but
even then he could only walk a hundred yards. The attack of influenza had also left
him deeply dispirited as he informed Stanford Robinson: 'It seems as if I had not

---

[10]  For clarity, all dynamics have been removed and 'Noonday Song' has been
transposed down an octave.

been in touch with the outside world for simply years and years and as for writing any more music! – I do not feel particularly optimistic.'[11]

Owing to the reduction in his compositional schedule, Coates spent more time in the recording studio during the 1940s, often recording his latest compositions almost immediately after he had completed them. He passed the final day of January 1940 conducting four of his most recent works (*Footlights, Last Love, Seven Seas* and *I Sing to You*) for Columbia, with each piece featuring an adjustment to the score. The recording of *Footlights* is marked by the absence of the introduction, commencing abruptly at figure 3, no doubt to reduce the playing time to fit onto a single side of a 12-inch record. *Seven Seas* is one of the very few recordings of a march in which Coates cuts material, in this instance from the second beat 2 bars before figure 6, to the third beat of figure 7.

The recordings of *I Sing to You* and *Last Love* featured changes in orchestration, as in both recordings a vibraphone usually playing in thirds displaces the scored glockenspiel, and has a more expanded role than in the published glockenspiel part. In the opening A-section of *I Sing to You*, Coates scores the glockenspiel to play usually either two crotchets on beats 4 and 1 to intensifying the cadence; or to accentuate beats 2 and 3. In this recording, he replaces the glockenspiel in bars 4–5, 6–7, 9, 10, 12–13, 16–17, 19–20 with the vibraphone and in several cases replaces the single notes with thirds on the vibraphone (complete with motor). In the middle section, the vibraphone plays the notes scored for the glockenspiel and then recreates its role in the reprise of the A-section. The use of the vibraphone was to feature more significantly in his next sortie into the recording studio later that year.

Even though Coates' composition schedule had slowed down during the war years, his back-catalogue was receiving a large number of performances. Unbeknownst to Coates, Haydn Wood wrote to the BBC in March 1940 (though his resentment had begun in 1939) because he felt aggrieved at the lack of exposure his music was receiving on the BBC's airwaves, especially in comparison to that of Coates, as he informed the BBC: 'I depend principally on my broadcasting for my income these days and I feel I must protest against this neglect of my work. Most of the items I have had broadcast for some considerable time have been songs.'[12] An internal memorandum discussed the letter, concluding that: 'actually Eric Coates is in a class by himself as a composer of light orchestral music ...'.[13] Wood had made a comparison of broadcasts of their music (assembled from the *Radio Times*) over three week's worth of programmes. His comparisons make for interesting reading, as they show the level of exposure that Coates was receiving at the time from a wide variety of performers and broadcasts (see Table 9.1).

---

[11]    09/04/1940 EC to Stanford Robinson. *GB-Rwac.*

[12]    07/03/1940 Haydn Wood to Kenneth Wright. *GB-Rwac* Haydn Wood.

[13]    12/04/1939 R. Burns to Adrian Boult. *GB-Rwac* Haydn Wood.

Table 9.1    Haydn Wood's comparisons between broadcasts of his music and Eric Coates' music

| Week commencing | Haydn Wood | Eric Coates |
|---|---|---|
| 25/02/1940 | 'When the Home-Bells Ring Again' (song) | *London Bridge* March |
| | *Supplication* Entr'acte | *From Meadow to Mayfair* Suite (complete) |
| | | 'Bird Songs at Eventide' (song) |
| 03/03/1940 | 'Roses of Picardy' (removed from broadcast) | *By the Sleepy Lagoon* Valse Serenade |
| | | *Footlights* Valse |
| | | *Last Love* (twice) Romance |
| 10/03/1940 | *Life and Love* Overture | *Footlights* Valse |
| | 'A Brown Bird Singing' (song) | 'Knightsbridge' March (*London* Suite) |
| | 'Love's Garden of Roses' (song) | *Seven Seas* March |
| | | *Last Love* Romance |
| | | 'Westwards' (*Four Ways* Suite) |
| | | *Springtime* Suite (complete) |
| | | 'Oxford Street' March (*London Again* Suite) |
| | | Symphonic Rhapsody on 'I Pitch My Lonely Caravan' |
| | | 'Valse' (*Summer Days* Suite) |
| | | *I Sing to You* Souvenir |
| | | *London* Suite (complete) |
| | | 'An Elizabethan Lullaby' (song) |
| | | *Springtime* Suite (complete) |

*Source*: 12/04/1939 R. Burns to Adrian Boult. *GB-Rwac* Haydn Wood.

Certainly, Wood had picked an atypical period, as Coates was conducting on the Forces Programme during the third week, but even without this, Coates still had more performances of orchestral works. Wright wrote to Wood:

> You will realise from looking through the remainder of items this week that they are suggested by all sorts and kinds of people, and this alone should indicate that

they are generally proposals based on the universality of Eric's appeal and the variety in which these popular pieces can be offered.[14]

Wright also demonstrated the universality of Coates' music, as during the week when he wrote his reply to Wood, Coates had music performed by: the BBC Orchestra conducted by Joseph Lewis; a cinema organist; Torquay Municipal Orchestra; Krish Septet; BBC Theatre Orchestra; Northern Orchestra and a military band.[15] This exchange of views between Wood and the BBC clearly showed the value that the BBC placed on Coates' music above others in the field of light music.

Even though performances of his music were plentiful and composition was erratic, Coates was kept busy with a new side to his career and a role that would make him part of the musical establishment. On his return from a fortifying sojourn in Eastbourne in the summer of 1940, Coates embarked on standing for election to the Board of Directors of the PRS. Throughout the 1930s, he had become more involved with the running of the PRS and its various committees, writing letters to *The Times*[16] and sitting on the organising committee of the Congress of Authors' and Composers' Societies held in London during June 1939. In May 1939, Coates was persuaded by Leslie Boosey (the PRS Chairman) to stand for election to the Board, as Coates was anxious that the vacancy, created by the death of Herman Finck, should be filled by a 'real composer.[17]' Haydn Wood also stood for election and Coates was narrowly outvoted.

In 1940, on the resignation of composer Noel Gay, Coates was elected to the PRS Board in June–July, a position he retained until his death in 1957.[18] He relished the opportunities to promote and assist fellow composers of light music. Since its inception, the Board of the PRS had always had a light music contingent, including Lionel Monckton, Charles Ancliffe, and Herman Finck. Coates' participation on the PRS Board and the various committees was usually executed with diligence and humour even when proceedings were dull, as he remembered in his obituary for Arnold Bax: 'when bored by the proceedings, he [Bax] would push his writing-pad towards me with the words: "Eric, draw me a ship!" To which I would oblige by sketching a liner at full steam, and he would add some clouds and a few seagulls.'[19] Coates was responsible for the election of Bax onto the Board in 1945 (he had pleaded with and cajoled Bax to stand for election).[20] The PRS Board were torn between Bax and Walton, but felt that as Bax was Master

---

[14]   12/03/1940 Kenneth Wright to Haydn Wood. *GB-Rwac* Haydn Wood.

[15]   Ibid.

[16]   28/02/1938 *The Times*.

[17]   24/05/1939 EC to Leslie Boosey. *GB-Lprs*.

[18]   Charles James. *The Story of the Performing Right Society* (London, 1951), p. 93.

[19]   Eric Coates, 'Arnold Bax: 1883–1953', in *Music and Letters*, xxxv (1954), p. 7.

[20]   13/04/1945 PRS Secretary to Haydn Wood. *GB-Lprs* Haydn Wood.

of the King's Musick it 'would be ungracious not to invite him and might put the Society in an invidious position'.[21]

Even though his work for the PRS made Coates feel that he was working for his fellow musicians, he still wanted to write something to help the war effort. He stated in his autobiography: 'Writing music in those early days of the war was not a job which received any encouragement from official quarters ...'.[22] He had tried, by writing to Walford Davies (Master of the King's Musick), to recommend that his *Song of Loyalty* may be of some use, perhaps as a reflective anthem.[23] In December 1939, the *Sunday Dispatch* had carried a small story about Coates' ambition to compose a 'war song':

> Last week he was leaving his publishers [Chappells] when he stopped to speak for a few moments to the commissionaire, an old soldier.
>
> A member of the publishing firm saw Coates speaking to the old soldier.
>
> "That's what I like to see" he said, hopefully, "speak to him, Mr Coates and you will get a fine theme for a new war song."
>
> The old soldier turned to Coates. "Don't you write a war song," he said, 'Give us the birds and the fields".[24]

Coates' inspiration had gone through a fallow period since the completion of *I Sing to You*, made more severe by illness and although he received constant requests 'to write something patriotic, but waving Union Jacks not being in my line I could not get up any enthusiasm'.[25] Phyl came to his rescue with a suggestion that he write a piece of music for her and the Red Cross Depot where she went daily to sew hospital supplies.[26] After sitting at his desk in their top floor Baker Street flat looking out over London, he caught sight of the twin towers of Crystal Palace in the distance and inspiration for a march flowed.[27] As he later informed Robinson: 'the picture I had in mind when writing the work is of our cheerful workers, rich and poor alike, hurrying off to their daily job, on foot, on bicycles, in trains and in motor-cars, <u>all</u> with the same wonderful British spirit ...' (Figure 9.1).[28]

After the completion and orchestration of the March in June 1940, he struggled to find a title for the piece until one evening, during a visit to the cinema to see a gangster film (he was rather fond of gangster films) at nearby Madame Tussard's, a policeman bellowed the line 'calling all cars', which became the title of the

[21]   Ibid.

[22]   Coates, *Suite,* p. 235.

[23]   25/09/1939 EC to Walford Davies. *GB-Rwac.*

[24]   31/12/1939 *Sunday Dispatch.*

[25]   30/07/1940 EC to Stanford Robinson. *GB-Rwac.*

[26]   Coates, *Suite,* p. 235.

[27]   Ibid.

[28]   26/08/1940 EC to Stanford Robinson. *GB-Rwac.*

Figure 9.1    'All London before me', Eric Coates on the roof of Berkeley Court,
              late 1930s

new march, neatly switched to *Calling All Workers*.[29] The completed March was
dedicated to 'all workers', though this was soon changed to 'all who work';[30] Phyl
penned the preface to the score: 'To go to one's work with a glad heart, and to do
that work with Earnestness and Goodwill.'

Coates was so pleased with the title that everyone who came into contact with
it was sworn to secrecy.[31] He wrote to Stanford Robinson to invite him, and the
BBC Theatre Orchestra, to give the first performance of the work. He explained:

> I think it is very important that this should be presented as soon as possible ... .
> Perhaps in one of your lovely feature programmes to which everybody listens,
> of course this is if you accept its first performance – and if you like it, to repeat
> it in a 'Music While You Work' broadcast. I am hoping that the latter march
> may be used as a signature to all Workers programmes. I seem to feel that this
> feature has come to stay and it will be continued long after the war is over and
> forgotten.[32]

---

[29]    Coates, *Suite*, p. 235.
[30]    26/08/1940 EC to Stanford Robinson. *GB-Rwac*.
[31]    30/07/1940 EC to Stanford Robinson. *GB-Rwac*.
[32]    Ibid.

The premiere was delayed as the BBC Theatre Orchestra were on holiday for the next two weeks, but Robbie said he would be happy to present it as long as Coates did not mind delaying it until a broadcast public concert at Cheltenham Town Hall on 1 September. From 21 August, the title was well publicized in the press in to prevent anyone misappropriating it (the piano solo version was to go on sale on the day of the premiere) and there were many small press releases giving details of its first performance. Chappells devoted their shop window to Coates with displays of his works, the centrepiece being the new march and details of its premiere.

Coates was immensely pleased with the first performance and wrote to Robbie the following day: 'You will be interested to know that I have already had a number of 'phone calls about your performance last night. My housekeeper tells me she heard several working-men talking about it in the 'bus this morning. It shows that the "man-in-the-street" listens to you and the Theatre Orchestra.'[33] To which Robinson replied: 'I started humming it dozens of times on Monday and in the end had to fine myself 6d. each time to stop it. I hope you will hear it again when we give it an encore on Friday.'[34]

Right from the outset, the March had great popular appeal; a *Gramophone* magazine reviewer stated that he thought it was the 'best piece of war-time music I have heard yet'.[35] *Calling All Workers* was clearly destined to become feted, and it was soon about to receive even greater acclaim in a radio programme. From the moment of its inception, Coates had been keen that *Calling All Workers* be used as a signature tune to all workers' broadcasts.[36] Robinson took up the case for the March's adoption as a signature tune early in August in the BBC, though the suggestion was turned down: 'unless it proves to be particularly apt for the purpose'.[37] Two months later it was adopted as the signature tune to *Music While You Work*.

*Music While You Work* was a programme set up by the BBC, on the suggestion of the War Department, to help increase production in factories by broadcasting cheerful music. The first broadcast of *Music While You Work* was on 23 June 1940, and Coates' *Calling All Workers* was officially adopted as the official signature tune to the series during mid-October. Instead of the opening of the March, as Robinson had suggested, it was the B-section that opened and closed the programme with each ensemble performing it in their own style. The programme proved to be a staggering popular success; overall there were 16,781 editions of the radio show (excluding the later revivals in the 1980s).[38] The BBC liked each ensemble to close

---

[33]  02/09/1940 EC to Stanford Robinson. *GB-Rwac*.

[34]  05/09/1940 Stanford Robinson to EC. *GB-Rwac*.

[35]  October 1940 *The Gramophone*, p. 112.

[36]  30/07/1940 EC to Stanford Robinson. *GB-Rwac*.

[37]  07/08/1940 G.D. Adams to Stanford Robinson. *GB-Rwac*.

[38]  Brian Reynolds, *Music While You Work* (Lewes, 2006), p. 45. This is an approximate figure as during the War the programmes were often cancelled at short notice.

with at least 30 seconds of the trio.[39] These figures must place *Calling All Workers* very high on the list as one of the most-played radio signature tunes, of which Robert Farnon's *Jumping Bean* is believed to be at the top.[40]

Three days before the BBC Theatre Orchestra's premiere of *Calling All Workers*, Coates recorded the work alongside *By the Sleepy Lagoon*. Whilst the March was recorded exactly as written, its companion piece on the disc differs enormously from the score (and also the previous version recorded in 1935). It is one of the few recordings in which Coates departs radically from the printed text. The performing edition used was the later edition (plate number 9003), which omits the characteristic brass interjections in the A-section (before figure 3). Having a vibraphone available at the recording session (*Calling All Workers* calls for the instrument) Coates must have rewritten the glockenspiel part for vibraphone and made a number of significant changes from figure 3. This also fits in with his predilection for the instrument, which lasted from 1935 until 1944: it features in many of his works and recordings (often when it is not scored) of this period. In *By the Sleepy Lagoon*, the single glockenspiel notes are replaced by thirds on the vibraphone. The characteristic acciaccatura at bar 56 is omitted and at the recapitulation of the A-section at figure 5, the single notes are replaced by three-part chords (usually in third or forth inversion). The countermelody (played with the brass) at bars 75–6, 79–80 and 83–4 is omitted in its entirety, though the vibraphone does play several two-part chords in different places to those of the glockenspiel during these bars. All glockenspiel notes in the coda (figure 7) are omitted, with the vibraphone just playing one chord in bar 93. Overall, the effect is strangely tantalizing and the vibraphone enhances the orchestration of this piece. Despite the differences from the score, this is the most popular of Coates' three recordings.

During 1940, with his recent elevation to the Board of the PRS, Coates felt in a position to air his disgust at the BBC's attitudes towards light music. In September 1940, on hearing that his old friend Kenneth Wright had been appointed as the BBC's Director of Overseas Music, an appointment which was to be short-lived, Coates sent him a letter of congratulations. After a brief paragraph eulogizing Wright's appointment, he tangentially sidestepped into a tirade about the BBC's attitudes towards light music and the damage they were doing to it. On receipt of the letter, Wright felt duty bound to append his own comments in the margins (included here in italics inside square brackets):

> Now, my dear Ken, when you start your activities [as Overseas Music Director] I do beg of you to let our foreign friends know that we are not a dull nation musically. I believe that you will only be able to convince them of this if you include in your bag compositions by those composers who write the kind of

---

[39]    Ibid., p. 34. However, if the programme overran, then the trio would not be broadcast, while, if the transmission under-ran, then the ensemble would continuously play the trio until the broadcast was faded out.

[40]    05/06/2005 *The Guv'vor: A Tribute to Robert Farnon*. BBC Radio 2.

thing which it has been the BBC's policy to <u>exclude</u> from certain orchestras and concerts ever since it came into being. How long shall we have to put up with the BBC forcing in the public compositions by intellectual experimentalists? It is <u>this</u> that gives us such a poor name both at home and abroad, and it is an acute form of snobbery. The whole thing boils down to this – is it music, or is it <u>not</u>? [*Eric's world of music stops at Delius & and the less "involved works["]*] *of say, Bliss?*] If it is the latter – then cut it out. Time and again have I heard programmes of so-called representative British music from here and abroad, and <u>no wonder</u> we are dubbed as dull. [*But we are no longer in circles of thinking people! He doesn't <u>know</u>!*]

You probably do know that years ago, before the BBC came into existence, <u>all types</u> of British music were represented at most of our big festivals. This created an incentive for the composer of the lighter school. Do you realize that today the BBC is literally killing the incentive of a composer who writes melody? For instance, if a composer, such as myself writes a work for a large orchestra it is useless for him to expect the BBC to play it more than once in its original form, and he must look to foreign countries for his performances.[41] [*Interesting point.*] As far as the BBC is concerned, if he wants the work to be performed he is almost forced to boil it down to suit the medium of a sextet. What incentive is there for our young composers of the lighter school to bother and master the art of orchestration? I realize that if I were a young man starting my career now I should never have attained such a position I hold today – the BBC's policy would have prevented it. [*I persuaded BBC to include "The Three Bears" in a Prom in a Christmas season – unfortunately it was rather a flop both with the public & the BBC management. The new audience didn't expect or <u>want</u> for that sort of thing.*] Mercifully I have made my name before the advent of this institution and had the good fortune for many years to have my works included in representative concerts of British music, where I found myself appearing on the same platform as Edward Elgar, Granville Bantock, Hamilton Harty, Gustav Holst and Edward German. In those days those in authority were only too <u>pleased</u> to include lighter British works in their programmes, providing that they were written by composers who understand the medium of the orchestra: but today, all this is changed because of the attitudes taken up by the BBC towards light music – others, unfortunately, follow the BBC's lead. Conspicuous absence can be very damning. I am not suggesting that lighter orchestral works be performed at the bigger symphony concerts, but they should be at least represented at concerts such as the Promenades, lighter symphony concerts and such-like. Why must the BBC place composers in <u>categories</u>? [*Because nature often puts them there. Even his own 'Saxo-Rhapsody' is really light music & where he gets "heavier" it is seldom <u>better</u>.*] Cannot they understand that the art of programme building is to give variety – not to give whole programmes of the same fare – which causes

---

[41]   Coates is presumably referring to the first performances of *The Enchanted Garden*.

a form of musical indigestion to the sensitive? Perfect programmes include the sweets and desserts along with the joint and entrée.

Now, my dear Ken, please do not think that I am writing all this to you because I want you to do anything for <u>me personally</u> – I have long ago become reconciled to the BBC's attitude towards my work. Fortunately for me my music is becoming increasingly played by the larger orchestras throughout the world, and it seems only in England that this prejudice towards light music exists. No, the reason for this letter is that I want to see those young composers who follow after me receiving some encouragement, this cannot happen until this unwarrantable snobbery has been put an end to once and for all. I fully expect Dr. Arne, [*He wrote for a much more practical orchestra!*] who has given us so much of our national music, were he alive today, he would be handed over <u>body-and-soul</u> to the tender mercies of Fred Hartley (this is no aspersion of Fred Hartley's work, which is excellent of its kind). Nor do I wish it to be thought that people should be encouraged to have their music played on a large orchestra unless they orchestrate their <u>own</u> <u>works</u>. NO COMPOSER IS WORTHY OF THE NAME UNLESS HE IS A MASTER OF THE ART OF ORCHESTRATION. It will be up to you, in a large measure to see that the composers who know their jobs [*I agree there – always did*] get a square deal.[42]

While Coates' outburst had some similarities to his earlier article in the *Evening News*, it was evidently borne out of a genuine frustration at the BBC and their approach to light music. The core belief that he expressed in this letter was that he believed that apex of all music was orchestral music and that to be a composer one had to master the art of orchestration. Wright's comments may appear to be slightly flippant, but he made valid points about Coates' taste in music, which was definitely conservative and about his firmly rooted standpoint that a work should always be performed by the orchestra it was written for. This was not practical from a broadcasting point of view, as small orchestras were an economical way to fill broadcasting hours.

The letter showed that Coates had failed to move with the times and understand the changes that the BBC and others had made to light music. Nevertheless, the BBC still gave many broadcasts of his music, and as Wright commented four years later: 'Eric Coates is in such a position that we do not look at his music to see whether it is worth broadcasting but to determine the most effective way of dealing with it.'[43]

Despite the lack of openings in prestigious concerts, an invitation to conduct *The Three Bears* with the LSO at the Proms on 17 September 1940 no doubt came as a pleasant surprise; he had last conducted at the Proms in 1934. It was significant that for the 1940 and 1941 seasons the BBC were not in control of

---

[42]    08/09/1940 EC to Kenneth Wright. *GB-Rwac*.
[43]    29/09/1944 Kenneth Wright to Arthur Bliss. *GB-Rwac*.

the Promenade Concerts due to financial worries and they were run through the auspices of the Royal Philharmonic Society. However, the hand of fate dealt him a thwarting blow as, from 7 September, the remainder of the Proms were cancelled because of the ferocity of the enemy bombing raids in London.

Whilst Coates' popularity was escalating to new heights as a result of *Calling All Workers*, in November 1940 he took part in one of Jack Hylton's first acts as a theatrical impresario. Hylton had heard how close the LPO was to financial collapse and set about putting together a rescue package for them. He engaged the orchestra to play a ten-week tour around the country in theatres and music halls, in an egalitarian attempt to bring music to the people. Coates joined the tour in mid-November to guest-conduct (alongside Malcolm Sargent and Basil Cameron) in Glasgow, Manchester and Leeds. As much as he enjoyed the tour and the opportunity to take his music to a wider audience, the trip did not help his precarious state of health. He confided in a passage expunged from his autobiography:

> I think it was a mistake to have taken on so much conducting at a time when I had only just recovered from a sharp attack of congestion of the lungs. This, and the difficult conditions under which we had been touring the country, were the cause of another illness which laid me low for some weeks.[44]

Coates went down with a particularly severe attack of pneumonia that persisted over December and into January 1941 and he was obliged in January to cancel engagements for at least two weeks. Coates recalled the severity of the attack:

> It is not pleasant to have pneumonia at the best times, but to be in bed with a high temperature and enduring cold sweats to a background of falling bombs is nothing short of a nightmare. At the doctor's advice my bed was moved down to a flat on the second floor on the other side of the building. The sense of protection which this arrangement afforded me was somewhat tempered by the risks Phyl ran each time she braved the roof (this was at all hours of the day and night) in order to replenish the hot-water-bottle or bring me sustenance from our flat on the top floor, which unpleasant task fell to her lot through the lift on our side of the block going out of action … . However, all bad things as well as good come to an end, and I was at last able to take the train to fulfil a broadcast for the BBC in Manchester, only to return to take once more to my bed, this time with influenza.[45]

On return from the broadcast from Manchester in February,[46] a far more pressing emergency manifested itself when the Coates received a formal visitation from a

---

[44]   Eric Coates, *Suite in Four Movements* (autograph), pp. 512–13.

[45]   Ibid.

[46]   19/02/1941 BBC Northern Orchestra, Eric Coates. BBC Home Service.

government official informing them that they would soon be evicted from their home in Baker Street. Coates recounted the event with his usual *bonhomie*:

> a Government representative called on us and very courteously gave us fourteen
> days to find a new home. They wished to take over the south and best side
> of the building to house the greatly enlarged staff of a certain department. I
> remember asking the representative what they were proposing to do with our
> three luxurious bathrooms ... .[47]

It was not the first time they had to leave their home, as in September 1940 they were given one hour's notice in the middle of the night due to the threat of four unexploded time bombs close by.[48] They returned over a week later to heavy bombing and a surfeit of delayed correspondence.

In 1941, the eviction was permanent and after much searching, the Coates found a temporary house in Amersham, a good distance from the heart of the metropolis, which was available from 3 May until October. The house provided a welcome respite from the rigours of London and the relative tranquillity of the Buckinghamshire countryside, and the proximity to Phyl's mother (in Chesham Bois) was helpful. By October, they had eventually bought a beautiful eighteenth-century cottage (though with a modern bathroom and central heating) in Hampstead situated on Christchurch Hill with a fine secluded garden. As delightful as the Acrise Cottage was, there were problems, as Coates' piano could not be taken up the stairs; he had always been in the habit of working upstairs, which he found more conducive to concentration. He was forced to work in the downstairs drawing room, conscious of the fact that Austin could hear him work and was barred from listening to the gramophone as this disturbed his father.[49] In addition, Coates still hated being so far out of central London, as he enjoyed walking the streets (where inspiration often came to him), visiting his publishers almost daily and participating in the social scene of London's night life. As he recalled:

> We longed for a flat in Oxford Circus or anything within easy reach of the
> things that mattered to us ... the seven years isolation which we had suffered
> in the Hampstead Garden Suburb, when Austin first descended upon us, was
> as naught to the discomfort we experienced during the one year we existed in
> old Hampstead.[50]

By October 1942, the house was for sale (advertised in *The Times* for £4,950);[51] however, it was not until November they returned to central London. Their new

---

[47]  Coates, *Suite*, pp. 237–8.
[48]  26/06/1940 EC to Arthur Wynn. *GB-Rwac*.
[49]  Coates, *Suite*, p. 241.
[50]  Coates (autograph), *Suite*, p. 523.
[51]  15/10/1942 *The Times*.

flat was in Berkeley Court (from which they had been unceremoniously evicted), but was lower down the block, at number 63. The moved also coincided with a period of inspiration and Coates managed to sketch *The Eighth Army* March. Coates recalled their triumphal return to central London:

> I managed to get through a winter without any serious setbacks thanks to the "life-preserver" and a handwoven scarf that had been sent me by an appreciative admirer as a "thank-you" for my music and which covered my mouth and nose each time I had the temerity to take my walks abroad. This earned me the title of "The Masked Man of Marylebone". Then came September with another attack which left me with the feeling that if I could do this kind of thing in the late summer, the coming winter would in all probability lay me out for life. So I invested in a stock of Scott's Emulsion, and the consuming of gallons of this ancient remedy added to the wearing of the "life-preserver" and the handwoven scarf made it possible for me to live a more or less normal existence.[52]

It was a brave move for Coates to return to the city, but obviously a very necessary one.

The upheaval of the variety of moves around 1941–42 caused a marked increase in composition. Following the completion of *Four Centuries* in November, his next orchestral work was a simple, but effective march. In November 1941, Kenneth Wright wrote to Coates to ask if he would care to compose a signature tune for *Hello Children*, a new BBC children's programme for overseas broadcasting; the March was subsequently used for all overseas children's broadcasts. Wright's requirements were quite specific: 'What we would like is a short bright piece of music which could be recorded by, say, the Theatre Orchestra introducing some well-known airs of our four countries, and possibly (I suggest) "Boys and girls come out to play" thrown in.'[53] What resulted was a standard concert march, originally entitled *This is London Calling*, but published as *London Calling*. The piece was completed quickly and finished by 11 December, less than a month after the invitation. It was dedicated to Coates' godson Alick Mayhew (the grandson of his old friend and champion, Alick Maclean). It was first performed in March 1942, though 'home' audiences did not get the chance to hear the complete work until 13 June. The work is constructed in Coates' usual march formula, though with several notable exceptions: it opens with an inverted pedal and a short B-section (first heard at figure 4) at the same tempo as the A-section. The B-section is one of the finest march melodies he composed.

A few months later the BBC were eager for Coates to produce another work for them, this time a musical. The idea came from the higher echelons of the BBC hierarchy, Basil Nichols (the BBC's Controller of Programmes).[54] Nichols

---

52   Coates (autograph), *Suite*, pp. 527–8.
53   14/11/1941 Kenneth Wright to EC. *GB-Rwac*.
54   21/10/1941 Basil Nichols to Reginald Thatcher. *GB-Rwac*.

suggested that Coates should be formally commissioned to write a production with the writer Geoffrey Bridson (then a BBC employee) as librettist, based around the latter's recent play *Aaron's Field*.[55] The BBC was prepared to pay Coates £150 to undertake the composition of such a project, with the BBC being allowed the privilege of the first performance. Furthermore, the BBC would also pay a similar sum for a librettist if Bridson was unacceptable to Coates.[56] The project does not seem to have come to fruition as a result of a prolonged bout of illness on Coates' part; though the invitation appears to have been relayed to Coates aurally as his standpoint on the project does not survive in any correspondence. Various BBC memoranda kept the proposal alive until 1943, when Coates finally rejected the entire project outright and consigned it to oblivion.[57]

The BBC was not the only outlet for Coates' latest compositions. Towards the close of 1941, he was engaged in the composition of yet another march, *Over to You*. The March was first played by the works band of the Bristol Aeroplane Company conducted by the composer during a lunchtime concert at their factory in December. *Over to You* bears the dedication: 'to all those who make and fly our aircraft'. How Coates came to write a March for an aircraft factory is unclear. He certainly had an affiliation to the airforce, as Austin had recently joined RAF Intelligence (where he befriended the actor Dirk Bogarde).[58] According to the *Bristol Evening World*, Coates was toying with the idea of christening the March 'Beaufighter March' (after the aircraft made at the works), but changed his mind at the last minute.[59] The orchestral version of the March may have been played earlier, but there is little documentary evidence to support this, though the *Radio Times* stated that its first performance took place in a broadcast on 22 February 1942.[60]

In terms of its construction, *Over to You* is constructed on more expanded terms than any other previous marches with three statements of the A-section (figures 1, 5 and 11) and an extra section (figure 7) before the second subject. The repeat of the C-section (the same as the B- or trio section of his other marches) is longer than the usual repetition and is subsequently extended into the coda at figure 17. The key structure of *Over to You* is more sophisticated with a move to the submediant for the C-section (as in the *London Bridge* March, though in this case it is the flattened submediant). This modulation is, to some extent, foreshadowed in the introduction, with the first fanfare centred on D major, acting as a link to the first statement of the C-section, in G major (the submediant) and repeated at figure 10.

Despite the slight flaws of the March, such as repetitions of rhythmic passages and melodic material, *Over to You* started a trend of Coates using three trumpets in

---

[55]   24/10/1941 Basil Nichols to Reginald Thatcher. *GB-Rwac*.

[56]   05/12/1941 D.H. Clarke to Mr Burns. *GB-Rwac*. If Coates chose to stay with Bridson, Bridson would receive a £50 bonus to his BBC salary.

[57]   13/05/1943 Richard Howgill to Copyright Director. *GB-Rwac*.

[58]   Conversation with Francis Freeman, 03/08/2009.

[59]   19/07/1942 *Bristol Evening World*.

[60]   20/02/1942 *Radio Times*.

his marches. This enabled him to obtain triadic fanfares without having to add the first trombone or horn to provide the lower part (cf. 'Knightsbridge' and *Calling All Workers*).[61] Much is made of this in the opening (until figure 1). The reason for his use of three trumpets may well have been because the March (like the later *Salute the Soldier*) was written to be performed by a military band, which would have had three clarinets and three trumpets.

Upon returning from Bristol, Coates succumbed to yet another bout of bronchitis and influenza, which laid him up for some considerable time, though he did manage an orchestration for Stanford Robinson. Robbie invited Coates to orchestrate his song 'I Pitch My Lonely Caravan' for a BBC Theatre Orchestra broadcast at the close of February 1942. This was the second recent orchestration of the song, as Robinson wrote of Coates' previous attempt: 'He will remember we destroyed it after the last broadcast because it was so bad.'[62] The score was finally despatched to Robinson with a small disclaimer: 'I hope you like the orchestration of the song, it was rather a difficult process for me as I could only do a page a day on the account of weakness and the awkward key made matters worse. I hope it will not sound too "growly"!!'[63]

While Coates was still laid up with influenza, a new BBC production was transmitted entitled *Desert Island Discs*, first broadcast on 29 January 1942. The programme, in which famous personalities are metaphorically banished to a desert island and choose eight records to take with them, explaining their reasons, is still a stalwart of Radio 4 and uses *By the Sleepy Lagoon* as its signature tune. The choice of signature tune was made with no input from Coates. Roy Plomley, the show's creator and presenter, initially wanted sounds of the surf-breaking and seagulls, but the producer thought this lacked definition, and they eventually picked three possibilities: *By the Sleepy Lagoon*, *Summer Afternoon* Idyll, both by Coates, and Norman O'Neill's incidental music to *Mary Rose*.[64] In the end they chose *By the Sleepy Lagoon* though *Summer Afternoon* would have been just as effective. The version of *By the Sleepy Lagoon* the BBC initially used for a number of years was Coates' own 1935 recording for Columbia, though latterly the Corporation used its own special recording, complete with seagulls imposed over the top of the music.

*Desert Island Discs* was not the only way in which *By the Sleepy Lagoon* was brought to a wider audience. Towards the close of June 1940, Coates gave his consent for words to be added to the orchestral Valse Serenade by Jack Lawrence (famous for the song 'Yes, My Darling Daughter' amongst others). This was published as 'Sleepy Lagoon' and Coates was overjoyed with the result, writing to Lawrence:

---

[61]   Why he did not score *Calling All Workers* in this way is unclear. In the opening fanfare, the first horn has to begin at the top of its range.

[62]   07/02/1942 Stanford Robinson to Phyllis Coates. *GB-Rwac*.

[63]   20/02/1942 EC to Stanford Robinson. *GB-Rwac*.

[64]   Roy Plomley, *Desert Island Discs* (London, 1975), p. 14.

> I am writing to tell you how delighted I am with your poem. You have set the words to my music so cleverly and one would <u>never</u> suspect that the music had been written first. Up to now I always thought it practically impossible to do a really good work in this way, but after having seen what you have done with my melody, I am beginning to think that "all things are possible"... .[65]

He added a postscript: 'I am wondering whether you have any lyrics by you that would care to send me with an object of setting to music?'[66] With this letter, Coates promptly forgot about the song arrangement until June 1942 when he unexpectedly received a telegram from Max Dreyfus of Chappells' New York office: 'greetings and felicitations to the composer of America's number one song sleepy lagoon [*sic*] ...'.[67] Without knowing it, Coates had gained a huge popular success in America without doing anything; the song was providing good business for the American branch of Chappells.

Despite growing success with *By the Sleepy Lagoon*, in June 1942, Coates entered into correspondence with the eminent cellist Beatrice Harrison, which shows the level of his growing discontent with the BBC and the lack of opportunities he felt available to the light-music composer. In early June 1942 he received a request from Harrison for a work for 'cello and orchestra as she was performing Elgar's Cello Concerto a couple of weeks later with Malcolm Sargent and wanted a small work to compliment Elgar's Concerto.[68] His reply was a letter of anguish complementing his views aired in the *Evening News* in 1939:

> It is very difficult these days to gain adequate performances of ones works on account of the BBC's policy of relegating the "lighter" types of music (how I detest the word "light!") to the tender mercies of a smaller orchestra. It does not matter how much time and thought is put into a work or how big the orchestration, if it is melodious it is practically always cut out of the programmes where it would receive really true presentation. So different to the old days before the BBC took over the "education" of the public and when one was invited to write works for the various Festivals about the country. I have to go abroad to-day to have my music played on the orchestra for which it was written ... . And now with writing something specially for you – nothing would give me greater pleasure, but I very much doubt that whether you would ever get any conductor to conduct it for you. I am blessed with coming under the category of "popular" and "light", and any conductor who is of any standing giving a performance of one of my works runs the risk of being taken off conducting "serious" works, unless he be a man who has the strength of his convictions, and I can honestly

---

[65]   24/06/1940 EC to Jack Lawrence. Lawrence never did add any more words to Coates' music.

[66]   Ibid.

[67]   14/06/1942 Max Dreyfus to EC. *GB-Lcm*.

[68]   05/06/1942 Beatrice Harrison to EC. *GB-Lcm*.

say that I cannot think of many who answer this description. And so you see my difficulties – it all comes down to this country being over-ridden with a form of musical snobbery which there does not seem any way of dealing with. And so I shall have to wait until such time as the "Powers that Be" get it into their dull heads that there is as much musicianship required in the turning out of a good light orchestral work as there is in the producing of the so-called symphonic stuff of which we hear so much on the Radio to-day, before I can give myself the pleasure of writing something for you.[69]

What provoked such an outburst, especially in a letter to someone he did not know well, is a mystery. It seems likely that his ongoing battle over the first performance of his new *Four Centuries* Suite (taking place when the letter was written) and his views on the BBC's attitudes towards his music must have been influences on this tirade. It seems likely that Coates' pre-war tours abroad must have clouded his views of the music in England. His lack of enthusiasm to compose a new concertante work for cello may have been brought about by his experiences with Rascher and Tertis who seldom played 'their' pieces. It may have been a bid not to have Harrison tarnished with the 'light' brush. Whatever the cause of his apathy to compose a new work for her, he never set about it.

Besides the lack of opportunities from concert programmers, Coates was becoming exasperated with his publishers and more particularly with the absence of printed full scores of his larger works. As he explained in a letter to Louis Dreyfus (the head of Chappells) after the publication of his *Four Centuries* Suite in 1943 by Boosey & Hawkes: 'I have never spoken to you about the problems which crop up from time to time in the publishing [of my works] with you... .'[70] Coates' dissatisfaction with Chappells had been growing since 1939 when he was incensed about their initial decision not to engrave the orchestral parts to *The Enchanted Garden* and *Footlights*, but merely to have the parts photographed. He informed them: 'I do not wish to be embarrassed over the publication of these two works and if such is the case will be pleased to relieve you of them.'[71] Chappells repented, and had the parts engraved to avoid losing any of his works to another publisher. Coates was adamant that *The Enchanted Garden*, because of its complexity, needed to be published with a full score, the absence of which he believed would be a grave impediment to obtaining significant performances. He felt, with some justification, that the absence of such was doing irreparable damage to his reputation as a composer, which it was, as many conductors detested conducting from a piano–conductor part. Chappells were not keen to acquiesce to his demands as it was their usual policy not to engrave full scores.

In January 1942, spurred on by a request from Stanford Robinson to borrow the manuscript score of *London* Suite, he vented his frustration: 'I am getting

[69]   17/08/1942 EC to Beatrice Harrison. *GB-Lcm.*
[70]   10/07/1942 EC to Louis Dreyfus. *GB-Lcm.*
[71]   22/06/1939 EC to Edwin Goodman. *GB-Lcm.*

tired of not having my scores in print that I am going to start a campaign that Chappells will have a thousand fits but it will do them all the good in the world. I am definitely "through" with piano-conductors'!!![72] A week later he was able to inform Robinson that Chappells had decided to publish the full score of the *London* Suite followed by *The Jester at the Wedding* and *The Three Men*.[73] The publication of these scores (though in fact a full score of *The Three Men* was never published) during 1942 when ink, metal and paper were in such short supply was testament to Chappells' loyalty to the composer. Despite these disagreements with the firm, he declared in 1946 that Chappells 'is still standing and is still the best firm in England',[74] and remained with them until his death.[75]

In spite of a lack of desire on Coates' part to produce new works, the return to a new flat in Baker Street in November 1942, as with other moves, precipitated a bout of compositional inspiration that resulted in *The Eighth Army* March. As he informed the *Daily Express*: 'I got the idea for it while walking down Oxford-street one day. I wrote the march while the removal men were taking my furniture out of the flat until only the piano was left.'[76] The inspiration of the March was the victory of Montgomery and the Eighth Army over Rommel at the battle of El Alamein at the beginning of November. The dedication was brokered through the auspices of Major Eric Maschwitz who was stationed near Montgomery and managed to secure the appropriate permission for the dedication of the March. There is no surviving correspondence to support the view that the BBC requested or commissioned the March, but it was probably an informal invitation to celebrate the victory of Montgomery. The BBC was keen, as ever, to extract the maximum amount of publicity from their involvement. They invited Coates to their studios to talk about the March before a military band performance and during rehearsals a photographer was present from the *Radio Times* taking pictures.[77] The *Eighth Army* March soon became the signature tune to the BBC's *Salute to the Fighting Forces*. It was also used in the 1943 Ealing film *The Nine Men*, which afforded it a good deal of extra publicity.

After he wrote *Eighth Army*, Coates undertook a break from composition having received a commission from the BBC to write a report on the state of light music broadcast by them, which occupied him during the first five months of 1943. The BBC was undergoing one of its periods of re-evaluation, commissioning reports on the state of its musical output. Besides Coates' *Report on Light Music*, Spike Hughes wrote a report on dance music; Rudolf Bing on studio opera; and Herbert Howells on 'serious' music.[78] As Asa Briggs noted in his august study of broadcasting, the

[72]    07/01/1942 EC to Stanford Robinson. *GB-Rwac*.
[73]    14/01/1942 EC to Stanford Robinson. *GB-Rwac*.
[74]    11/12/1956 EC to Max Dreyfus. *GB-Lcm*.
[75]    Only the hymn 'God's Great Love Abiding' was published elsewhere.
[76]    09/12/1942 *Daily Express*.
[77]    02/12/1942 Hubert Clifford to EC. *GB-Rwac*.
[78]    Briggs, pp. 579, 584 and 742.

BBC was keen to welcome criticism by an outside expert, but was always hesitant and pusillanimous when the time came to act upon external criticisms.[79]

The submission of Coates' report was initially delayed due to a bout of bronchitis on his part. After listening to 168 programmes over a course of three-months (from 7 February to 8 May 1943) and making detailed notes on each, he submitted his findings to the BBC on 22 May.[80] He structured the report in categories dealing with genres of light music and his thoughts on their suitability for broadcasting: Organists (of whom he wrote: 'could it not be insisted upon that organists free themselves from over-sentimentality and play the notes as written? The need for accuracy should continually be being brought home to them …');[81] Military Bands (which he thought were usually too slow and their repertoire characterized by transcriptions of pieces which relied heavily on orchestral colour); Brass Bands (which received praise); Outside Broadcast Orchestras (most of which were dismissed for being too small and their lack of woodwind compensated for by the use of saxophones, thus enabling them to metamorphose into dance orchestras); Small Combinations (which were praised for their versatility but dismissed for their 'eccentric combinations' of instruments and having to have music especially arranged for them); BBC Variety, Revue and Midland Orchestras (all were criticized for their lack of personnel and the Midland in particular for attempting works beyond its capabilities); BBC Scottish and Northern (highly praised but requiring more strings); BBC Theatre Orchestra (Coates had broadcast frequently with this ensemble and knew its failings as well as anybody. Here he called for its augmentation to do full justice to the excellent programmes it already broadcast); BBC Orchestras (criticized for playing music almost exclusively by dead composers); Ballad Concerts (clearly an afterthought, their re-introduction was called for).

Despite his individual criticism of bands and orchestras, the nub of his report was an attack on the fact that the BBC continually favoured the use of small combinations of instruments (such as those run by Fred Hartley) rather than reasonable-sized orchestras with the correct blend of orchestral instruments in their light-music broadcasts. Furthermore, Coates continually attacked the low numbers of strings employed in broadcasts of light music (his only criticism of the BBC Theatre Orchestra). Partly in view of this, and also of the poor standard of the non-BBC orchestras, he called for the foundation of two new orchestras, each of forty-five players, to alleviate this issue.[82] In addition, he felt that, since light-music composers had scored their works for a standard orchestra, they should be heard in their original orchestration not in a reduced or arranged format. What he failed to grasp was that the reason behind the use of small combinations and small numbers of strings was money; it was not financially practical for light music to be played by a full orchestra all of the time. Furthermore, composers such as

---

[79]   Ibid., p. 585.
[80]   27/05/1943 Arthur Bliss to EC. *GB-Rwac*.
[81]   Eric Coates, *Report on Light Music* (1943), p. 5.
[82]   Coates, *Report*, p. 7.

Stravinsky and Hindemith, amongst others, had been experimenting writing for small combinations; Britten wrote a number of significant chamber operas in the 1940s and 1950s.

Coates left his most damming criticism of the BBC until the conclusion of his report, where he expresses an opinion that had been fermenting in his mind for a number of years. He paints a very negative portrait of the BBC's reaction towards, and promotion of, light music in that: 'the public is being rapidly educated to believe that Light Music is of <u>no value whatsoever</u>'.[83] These views may have been clouded by the rather stormy meeting between Coates and Arthur Bliss (the BBC's newly appointed Director of Music) early in May over the latter's non-inclusion of a work of the former's in the Promenade Concerts.[84] Certainly Coates' conclusions in his report about the disappearance of the genuine composers of the school of light music were curiously prophetic of the decline in exposure of light music that was to occur during the 1960s and 1970s, though in defence of the BBC, this was not solely as a result of their attitudes.[85]

Reactions within the BBC to Coates' *Report on Light Music* were mixed; many welcomed it and agreed with his pertinent comments on organists and the lack of string-tone in many of the BBC's orchestras. However, the BBC, in talking through Coates' report at many levels, came to the conclusion that, while there were many relevant and prudent points, it was flawed, as a result of the author's dismissal of small combinations. Kenneth Wright explained that the broadcasts by the small orchestras run by Sandler and Hartley attracted extraordinarily high listening figures – almost double those for programmes by the BBC Theatre Orchestra.[86] All who read the report shied away from the strong conclusions of what he was later to call 'the death knell' sounding for light music and it was promptly forgotten without any effect upon the BBC's policy.[87] Coates never received any official feedback on his report from the BBC, who believed that 'he had no right to be told'.[88] The only positive outcomes were the permanent augmentation of the BBC Theatre Orchestra to 57 players, something that was probably in the pipeline before the submission of his report and, as Briggs pointed out, a concert of light music by the BBC Symphony Orchestra.[89]

Concurrently with Coates' work on the *Report on Light Music* he was embroiled in a serious personal battle with the BBC over his new Suite, the *Four Centuries*, and the embargo on its performance in the 1943 season of Promenade Concerts, a series Coates held in the highest possible esteem. This turbulent episode was not properly resolved and he was forced to involve the BBC's new Director-General

---

[83]   Ibid., p. 15.

[84]   08/05/1943 Arthur Bliss to EC. *GB-Rwac.*

[85]   Coates, *Report*, p. 16.

[86]   31/05/1943 Kenneth Wright to EC. *GB-Rwac.*

[87]   21/05/1944 EC to William Haley. *GB-Rwac.*

[88]   01/07/1944 Kenneth Wright to Basil Nichols. *GB-Rwac.*

[89]   Briggs, p. 581.

the following year. The whole saga demonstrated both the BBC's patrician attitude towards light music and the difficulty that England's premier light-music composer (and also most successful composer) was having in getting his music performed.

The foundations of the problem dated back to late 1941 when Coates had written to the BBC to ask if it would be possible to include his new *Four Centuries* Suite in the 1942 Proms.[90] There were also calls in the press at this time that his music ought to be included in the concerts.[91] Both Messrs Wright and Bliss were totally against its inclusion. Wright dismissed Coates' last appearance at the 'Christmas' Proms with: 'We know what happened when the "Three Bears" went into a Promenade Concert. I had banked on this, but it was a flop – I think because we had by then led the audience to expect something more solid … .'[92] Bliss agreed with Wright, stating that 'it will do his music more harm than good if it goes into a programme of solid music …'.[93] How was Coates ever going to battle against such negative and pretentious attitudes towards his music? In winter 1942–43, Coates had a meeting with Henry Wood who cordially offered to include a new work in the 1943 season of Promenades, to which Coates suggested the *Four Centuries* Suite.[94] Wood had certainly seen the work during its composition when he was asked for his opinion by the composer.[95] In January 1943, while Coates was laid up with bronchitis, Kenneth Wright acted as the composer's emissary and wrote to inform Arthur Bliss of Wood's invitation.[96] Wright was particularly dismissive of the inclusion of the Suite:

> There is some lovely writing in the first two movements. It seems to me that the Suite gets progressively cheaper as the composer progresses down the centuries. That the last movement seems 'vieux jeux' is probably the fault of Jazz rather than Coates, and I doubt whether the Promenade Orchestra could tackle all that tricky stuff even if you wanted it to with the rehearsal difficulties at their disposal.[97]

Bliss appended his stance on the situation to the memorandum: 'I am absolutely against the decision of a Coates suite in the Proms – a retrogression to the Bad

---

[90]    04/12/1941 EC to Unknown. The letter is missing from the BBC's Archives, but its outline is discussed in a memorandum (Undated [December 1941] Kenneth Wright to Arthur Bliss. *GB-Rwac*.)

[91]    22/07/1942 *Evening News*.

[92]    Undated [December 1941] Kenneth Wright to Arthur Bliss. *GB-Rwac*.

[93]    Ibid. Appendage by Arthur Bliss. *GB-Rwac*.

[94]    28/01/1943 Kenneth Wright to Arthur Bliss. *GB-Rwac*.

[95]    29/03/1943 Henry Wood to Julian Herbage. *GB-Rwac* Henry Wood personal.

[96]    28/01/1943 Kenneth Wright to Arthur Bliss. *GB-Rwac*.

[97]    Ibid.

Old Days.'[98] In the meantime, Boosey & Hawkes had sent the full score of the Suite, along with works by others from their catalogue to Sir Henry for his perusal to entice him to include them in that season's concerts.[99] At a Proms planning meeting in March, the inclusion of the Suite was discussed and, writing to Wood after the meeting, Julian Herbage (the BBC's Proms Programmer) stated:

> I had the impression that when we discussed the matter with Mr Bliss he felt that if Eric Coates were to be included, it would open the door to other light music composers, and that this would not be desirable if we are to maintain the present character of the Promenade programmes.[100]

Wood clearly felt that Herbage was mistaken about the tone of the meeting and wrote to him to correct him, still clearly believing in the merits of Coates' Suite:

> I find it difficult to agree that I have a mistaken idea of that conversation that day, but I am equally certain that Mr. Bliss would be the last to exclude any work that I decided it worth while to include – I think this <u>should</u> be included – in a Saturday programme.[101]

Three days later, Wood informed Boosey & Hawkes that a place had been found for the *Four Centuries* Suite, though many of the other works they had sent could not be included because of pressures of time.[102] Knowing of Wood's love of presenting works for the first time, Herbage informed Wood that the Suite had already had two performances by the BBC Theatre Orchestra.[103] With this information, Wood's ardour for the work instantly grew cold.[104] A similar chain of events happened with Arnold Bax that season over his new Seventh Symphony.[105]

News of the removal of the *Four Centuries* Suite reached Coates (he was also provided with copies of the correspondence between Wood and Boosey & Hawkes by the publishers), who was understandably incandescent. In early May, he attended what appears to have been a stormy meeting with Arthur Bliss at the BBC to discuss the matter. Bliss wrote to pacify Coates, with a *soupçon* of flattery, after the meeting:

---

[98]    Note by Arthur Bliss appended to: 28/01/1943 Kenneth Wright to Arthur Bliss. *GB-Rwac*.

[99]    10/04/1943 Henry Wood to Boosey & Hawkes (copy of letter).

[100]   01/04/1943 Julian Herbage to Henry Wood. *GB-Rwac* Henry Wood personal.

[101]   07/04/1943 Henry Wood to Julian Herbage. *GB-Rwac* Henry Wood personal.

[102]   10/04/1943 Henry Wood to Boosey & Hawkes (copy of letter).

[103]   23/04/1943 Julian Herbage to Henry Wood. *GB-Rwac* Henry Wood artists. The Suite was performed in July and September 1942.

[104]   26/04/1943 Henry Wood to Julian Herbage. *GB-Rwac* Henry Wood personal.

[105]   15/05/1943 Henry Wood to W.W. Thompson. *GB-Rwac* Henry Wood artists.

I am unhappy at the impression that may have been left in your mind after our meeting. I hasten to say that it is not true in any way, that we do not consider you a composer serious in intention. We should not have that impertinence, but as programme planners, we have to view the Promenade Season, rightly or wrongly, as specialised in character.

I have a letter from Sir Henry Wood in front of me giving his opinion that the "Four Centuries Suite" is inappropriate to the Promenades to-day, although had it been a first performance, I believe that he would have greatly enjoyed launching it.[106]

Fired on by this letter from Bliss and no doubt of the opinion that he could go no further with the BBC, Coates decided to take the matter up privately with Henry Wood. He believed that the Suite's exclusion was Wood's doing, not a result of the machinations of the BBC's Music Department. [107]

In his reply to Coates' letter (which was delayed because of Wood's illness), Sir Henry stated that he would be happy to include an orchestral work by Coates in the 1944 season as long as it was a first performance. The work would have to be completed by early January 1944 and should be less than 15 minutes as Wood knew that otherwise it would be vetoed by the BBC.[108] Wood's reply did not pacify Coates who did not think that Wood's argument about the non-inclusion of the Suite 'held water' because there were already several works by British composers that had already been performed on the radio. Coates concluded his epistle: 'For a composer of Light Orchestral works to be admitted to the Promenade Concerts is like entering the Kingdom of Heaven.'[109] In Wood's defence he had tried his best to have the *Four Centuries* in the Proms, but he had been obstructed by BBC staff at every opportunity. Nevertheless, Wood was in effect a BBC employee and had to respond to certain of their whims. However, the whole episode was symptomatic of the way that the BBC was turning against light music.

Coates exchanged two more letters with Wood (whose correspondence was being dealt with by Lady Wood),[110] but must have come to the conclusion that there was nothing he could achieve and let the matter rest for the time being. Coates never got round to writing a new work for Henry Wood as through the remainder of 1943 he hit a 'blank patch'.[111]

---

[106]    08/05/1943 Arthur Bliss to EC. *GB-Rwac*. Wood's letter does not survive, if it indeed it was ever written.

[107]    Austin Coates thought that his father's outburst was purely personal. (17/06/1985 Austin Coates to Geoffrey Self.)

[108]    12/06/1943 Henry Wood to EC.

[109]    16/06/1943 EC to Henry Wood.

[110]    18/06/1943 EC to Henry Wood and 22/06/1943 EC to Henry Wood (Lost).

[111]    Coates, *Suite*, p. 242.

After the problems regarding the *Four Centuries* in October 1943, Coates decided that his next altercation with the BBC should be dealt with by his publishers, as they might have more power and influence. Coates' recent ballad, 'Star of God', was fast establishing itself in the song repertoire, but was receiving very few broadcasts. The words were by Fred Weatherly (who had been dead since 1929) and had only recently been found amongst his papers by his wife, who invited Coates to set it.[112] The lyric was believed to have been written during the First World War. Edwin Goodman of Chappells wrote to Arthur Bliss who replied with a typical 'whitewash' answer stating that the song was in an awkward category to place because of its quasi-religious nature.[113] Bliss also discussed the possible intervention of the Director of Religious Broadcasting, but the song was a trivial matter to have to invoke such an august person.[114] It is not clear after this letter whether the song received any more transmissions and the matter was laid to rest, but it did not quell Coates' anger at the BBC.

Perhaps because of the vociferous exchange of letters and his *Report on Light Music* for the BBC, 1943 was a quiet year tempered with illness and almost compositionally barren, dismissed in one sentence in his autobiography with no mention of his activities for and against the BBC.[115]

However, 1944 marked a return to composition with a new orchestral suite, *The Three Elizabeths*, and another march. After the composition of *Eighth Army*, Coates had made a conscious decision not to write any more marches, but a visit to his flat by Sir Harold Mackintosh (owner of the confectionary company and chairman of the National Savings Committee) and Lord Kindersley (president of the committee) during winter 1943–44 caused him to rethink his decision. The pair invited him to write a march for the opening of the Salute the Soldier Campaign, run by the National Savings Committee to raise money for the war effort and held in London's Trafalgar Square. He asked Kindersley and Mackintosh for time to think about the possibility of writing a work for the campaign (presumably the start of delaying tactics designed to extricate himself from the request).[116] A few days later, he was dining in a restaurant when inspiration for a March suddenly came to him and he jotted the themes down on the back of a menu.[117] When Mackintosh returned the following week for the composer's verdict, Coates played him the finished march; as he was leaving, Mackintosh gave Coates a box of his Toffee de Luxe as 'payment' for the March, perhaps making it the only March ever to have been paid for by a box of toffee![118]

---

[112]   07/11/1942 *Evening Standard*.

[113]   22/10/1943 Edwin Goodman to Arthur Bliss. *GB-Rwac*.

[114]   28/10/1943 Arthur Bliss to Edwin Goodman. *GB-Rwac*.

[115]   Coates, *Suite*, p. 242.

[116]   Ibid.

[117]   13/03/1944 *Evening Standard*.

[118]   Coates, *Suite*, p. 242.

Coates donated his share of his royalties from the March (both from the sales of the sheet music and the mechanical rights) to the Army Benevolent Fund and the work was given its orchestral premiere by Stanford Robinson and the BBC Theatre Orchestra, broadcast by the BBC on 4 March. As part of the conditions of writing the March, the composer conducted *Salute the Soldier* in Trafalgar Square with the Band of Scots Guards at the opening ceremony of the campaign on 25 March, which was broadcast by the BBC.[119] He was worried about the weather in March and afraid of catching another cold and 'the idea of a conductor appearing in public looking like an old gentleman who had just got out of bed led to it being agreed that if there was any element which might prove dangerous to the state of my chest, my appearance would be cancelled'.[120] Coates' association with such a high profile organization not only shows how high his reputation as a composer in England was (thanks in part to his recent marches) but yet another reason why his music was more popular than say Haydn Wood, Percy Fletcher and Arthur Wood. Coates' music featured at such prestigious events.

*Salute the Soldier* was recorded, along with *The Eighth Army*, in February but only as a special issue recording, and it never went on sale to the public. The National Savings Committee issued thirty recordings during the Second World War to be played in cinemas and factories to entice potential savers.[121] Various people tried to encourage EMI to issue the record for sale to the general public, as Coates explained in a letter to Lord Kindersley in April:

> My only regret is that the Gramophone Company [EMI] are not sufficiently interested in the National Effort to see fit to issue for sale my recording with the London Symphony Orchestra … . [They] seem to be more interested in importing matrices of "swing-music" from the States to stamp over here in this country than using their resources for National ends … .[122]

It was not the first time he had struggled to get his music recorded by the Gramophone Company, but at least there were copies of the record available for broadcasting.

In Coates' recording, both marches are preceded by a Fanfare. It is unclear whether or not these were penned by Coates, but they do show something of his compositional style, though no manuscript of them survives, nor does Coates refer to them. Nevertheless, he never performed or recorded another composer's work. The *First Fanfare* (preceding *Salute the Soldier*) is based on material derived from the March, whereas the *Second Fanfare* (preceding *The Eighth Army*) is based on free material and makes much use of the three trumpets in triadic arpeggios (a favourite of Coates in his marches).

---

[119]    A copy of which is retained in the BBC archives. *GB-Lbl* BBC T8257.

[120]    Coates, *Suite*, p. 242.

[121]    July 1945 *The Gramophone*, p. 19.

[122]    30/04/1944 EC to Lord Kindersley. *GB-Lcm*.

The difficulties that Coates encountered with EMI were mere bagatelles compared to his ongoing contretemps with the BBC, which, in early 1944, resulted in another exchange of letters; the final time that Coates vented his spleen at the BBC. He had heard that the BBC was to include his *Four Old English Songs*, works closely associated with Henry Wood, in that year's Promenade Concerts.[123] Coates was vexed by their inclusion, as principally he viewed himself as an orchestral composer and the *Songs* were a student work. No doubt driven on by the previous year's fracas with Sir Henry and Arthur Bliss, Coates felt compelled to write the Director-General, William Haley. Austin Coates believed that his father would not have taken the matter any further had he not received numerous telephone calls from people in the music profession who were amazed at the inclusion of his *Songs* in the Proms.[124]

Before embarking on a letter of complaint about the Proms policy, Coates sought advice from his publishers.[125] He eventually sent his epistle to the BBC on 21 May.[126] The finished product was very much a heartfelt plea on behalf of all light-orchestral composers and was a cathartic outburst on a subject close to his heart. After complaining about his own treatment by the BBC with regard to the Proms, Coates questioned the BBC's policy regarding the entry of a light work in the repertoire of the Proms:

> For years I have received, and still receive, embarrassing phone calls from the Press and public asking me why I am not represented at these concerts. There was a time when I felt hurt by the ostracism shown me by the BBC in this respect and when the Press used to approach me with regard to the reason for my non-appearance at these concerts I asked them to refrain from commenting on it in the Press as I felt it would be damaging to my reputation as a composer to publicise the BBC's attitude to my work, and I am sure that you will agree that it is not unnatural, in the circumstances, that I should feel resentment towards the Corporation for its lack of recognition of the School of Light Orchestral Music which I represent.
>
> I have by degrees become accustomed to this state of affairs and I can now quite honestly say that it is completely immaterial to me as to whether I am represented at the Proms or not. What worries me is not the fact of my non-inclusion but the reason for it.[127]

Coates concluded his letter with a stark warning about the BBC's policy:

---

123   Conducted by Basil Cameron on 24/06/1944.
124   17/06/1985 Austin Coates to Geoffrey Self.
125   19/05/1944 Edwin Goodman to EC.
126   21/05/1944 EC to William Haley. *GB-Rwac*.
127   21/05/1944 EC to William Haley. *GB-Rwac*.

If the BBC persists in this attitude towards Light Orchestral Music then the death-knell of this school has already sounded, and I would ask you whether this is the policy of our great British Broadcasting Corporation which, by virtue of its name alone, should be the first to encourage by <u>public</u> <u>performance</u> all that is the best of its type in British music.[128]

After discussing Coates' letter with several key personnel, Haley responded that the Promenades were always special in character and since the BBC had taken over their promotion they had tried hard, and succeeded, to raise the standard and variety of the repertoire to more symphonic proportions; this stance had been pre-echoed by Bliss in an internal BBC memorandum in early 1943.[129] The BBC did not regard light music as 'symphonic' enough for the audiences of the Proms.[130] Haley also reinforced Wood's earlier offer that if Coates had written a short, new work for the 1944 Proms, such as an overture, it would have been accepted with alacrity.[131] Furthermore, as Haley stated, the BBC did have a difficulties in programming music in the Promenades: 'Our problem is not what to include so much as what we leave out'.[132] Haley concluded that due to the ubiquity of light music the BBC did not feel a need to make an effort to promote it: 'Apart from the occasional public appearance by the Theatre and Midland Light Orchestras, we do not feel it is our responsibility to give this kind of music public (concert) performances.'[133] Nevertheless, music by Coates' light-music colleagues featured in the Promenades: Phillips' *Empire March* appeared in the 1942 season and his *In Praise of My Country* (subsequently re-titled *Festival Overture*) featuring in the 1944 season.

In some respects, the Director-General's reply was correct: times were changing and the section of the public who attended the Proms, through the gradual 'education' of audiences by the BBC, were looking for more symphonic and challenging repertoire. Coates was perturbed by the fact that the BBC did not view his music as 'symphonic' enough to be programmed in the Proms, despite the fact that the majority of his music was scored for a full orchestra (which was not in any way handled 'lightly'). It is scandalous that a composer of Coates' reputation and standing could only be included in such concerts with a new piece. He was Britain's most popular and successful composer and unquestionably that alone merited his inclusion in the Proms.

Not appeased by Haley's letter, Coates felt compelled to write to Haley again about the policy of inclusion of lighter works into the Proms. He again concluded his letter with a stark warning for the future of light music: 'I still repeat that I

---

128    Ibid.
129    01/02/1943 Kenneth Wright to Arthur Bliss. *GB-Rwac.*
130    06/06/1944 William Haley to EC. *GB-Rwac.*
131    Ibid.
132    Ibid.
133    Ibid.

think (and many musicians agree with me) that the BBC is absolutely wrong in its attitude towards the best in Light Music, for it is fostering an insidious form of musical snobbery among listeners, teaching them to despise melody.'[134]

It fell to Kenneth Wright to research material for the Director-General's reply.[135] He explained why the BBC had grudgingly included works by Phillips and Dunhill: 'The Montague Phillips March was symphonic in texture rather than achievement ... . Dunhill's "Waltz Suite" was a first performance, which shows how willing we are to stretch our definition for the sake of a first performance by a contemporary British composer.'[136] Wright was also highly critical of the symphonic aspect of Coates' music as: 'some of Eric Coates['] things are scored – some would way [*sic*] <u>over</u>-scored – for large orchestra, but are really sentimental light music for a large number of instruments, e.g., "The Enchanted Garden"'.[137]

With this final exchange the whole saga was closed for Coates; he had tried for a clarification of the BBC's policy, voiced his concerns and tried to change the *status quo* but had failed. He remained bitter towards the BBC for some time in his private views. It was not until the 1954 diamond jubilee of promenade concerts season that he was invited to conduct his *Saxo-Rhapsody*. There were other light-music composers who felt the same way about the BBC, but who had experienced constraints on their artistic freedom. Certainly Coates fared better than many other light-music figures in receiving outlets on the BBC networks and the Proms. This issue reared its head later in 1944 in the *Radio Times* when Haydn Wood felt inclined to reply to an article entitled 'Tastes in Light Music' in September:[138]

> I wonder if it is realised with what difficulties the light-music composer has to contend when he orchestrates his music. For instance, the composer of serious music knows full well that whatever instrument he wishes to include in his score will be available when performed; but not so the composer of light music. The latter has to be chary of including such instruments as a cor anglais, bass clarinet, double bassoon, tuba, or even a harp or celeste, not to mention a third and fourth horn and a couple of drummers. These are all available to the serious composer; and how much easier it is to get one's effects, either delicate or grandiose, with such a galaxy of instruments to call upon! The light composer's music is seldom heard with any of the above-mentioned instruments. On the contrary he has often to be content with incomplete brass and wood-wind sections. This deficiency is overcome by extensive cueing – transferring the passages to other instruments not employed at the time. Cueing is one of the bugbears of the light

[134]  Ibid.

[135]  Undated (circa June 1944) Notes prepared by Kenneth Wright on 12/06/1944 EC to William Haley. *GB-Rwac*. Whether Haley replied to Coates' second letter is unclear, though he may have received 'oral feedback'.

[136]  Ibid.

[137]  Ibid.

[138]  11/08/1944 *Radio Times*, pp. 3–4 and 9.

composer's lot. In these circumstances it is only on special occasions that his music sounds as he conceived it. It is much more interesting and satisfactory to write a score for an outsize symphony orchestra than to juggle with that for a probably depleted light orchestra.[139]

Albert Ketèlbey added to Wood's comments the following week about the problems of duration in the construction of light pieces:

I find that anything over three or four minutes is frowned on as being too long. Consequently the cuts or hurryings, which are made if the piece is a minute or two over, are rather harmful to the design of the piece. This time-limit bogey is a difficulty which highbrow composers do not have to contend with.[140]

These two letters in the *Radio Times* from the two other luminary figures and Coates' own exchange of views with the BBC confirm that there was a growing contention about the outlets available for light music and also the restrictions imposed upon the performance of it by august institutions.

Despite Coates' ongoing frustration at the small window of opportunity for light music at the BBC and beyond, light music was still popular with the public at large. On 16 October 1944, Coates became the subject of a short film. Pathé made a film (around 3 minutes) detailing his career and showing him walking around London cultivating his muse to write a new piece; he sketches a short melody sat on a bench. The film then returns to his Berkeley Court flat showing him reworking his sketches into an orchestral full score (though this is a pretence for the cameras).[141] The score of the film is a montage of three popular compositions. It was not the first time he had been the 'star' of a Pathé film, as they had filmed the recording session of his *London Bridge* March in 1934. This new film was designed to accompany a main feature film in cinemas. It was a boost to his popularity and helped the public to associate the man with the music. Coates was not the only light-music figure to feature in a Pathé film, as in 1946 Haydn Wood was the recipient of a similar honour.[142]

The following month, November, Coates was at Kingsway Hall to record his two most ambitious suites, the *Four Centuries* and *The Three Elizabeths*. The recordings were marked by a 'jumping of ship' to Decca after having recorded almost exclusively for Columbia/HMV since 1923. These two records must have been a source of pride for Coates, especially as he had been trying to tempt EMI to record the *Four Centuries* since its premiere over two years previously. He had a growing discontentment with EMI and came to a gradual realization that the project would never materialize, as he wrote to Stanford Robinson:

---

[139]   01/09/1944 *Radio Times*.

[140]   09/09/1944 *Radio Times*.

[141]   1303.14, available from www.britishpathe.com.

[142]   1392.22, available from www.britishpathe.com.

The Gramophone Company have got themselves into a fearful mess, as you know, through not being long-sighted enough as to lay in a stock of recording material when they saw the war was inevitable. They have always run their business like a lot of amateurs and thought that cheap fox-trot stuff would carry them through any crisis and I very much doubt whether even a war will teach them sense.[143]

Decca chose to release each Suite on two 12-inch records, so cuts would have to be imposed to reduce each movement down to 4 minutes 30 seconds playing time of each side. The 'Hornpipe' lost figures 8 to 15, the 'Pavane' figures 3–5, 'Tambourin' the bar before figure 14 to the last 4 bars, and 'Rhythm' figures 12–20. This reduced the playing time of the Suite down from 22 minutes 30 seconds to 18 minutes. *The Three Elizabeths* escaped with only one cut from figure 16 to 17 in the first movement. Coates shaved 44 seconds off the playing time of 'Springtime in Angus'.

Coates was slightly apprehensive about recording the *Four Centuries*, especially the finale with its trio of saxophones, as he recalled in the 1950s:

My old friend Victor Olof, who was in charge of the orchestras well as balancing, had enlisted for the last movement the services of a well-known team of saxophonists and also a special trumpet player who, at one time or other, had dance band experience. I believe it was the first time that a recognised Symphony Orchestra in this country had departed from the 'straight' and gone over to the 'dance', but it was remarkable (after half an hour's rehearsing to become acquainted with the unfamiliar medium) how quickly the musicians picked up the style. Where jazz is concerned, the tendency over here, on the part of some members of a Symphony Orchestra, is to sit back and smile at something which they think is beneath their notice and needs no rehearsal – so for the first few minutes of the session I had the gravest doubts as to whether I should achieve a recording, for some players showed only too openly their desire to fool about. However, after explaining at some length that the movement was intended to be as a joke and that the effect of a good story was spoilt if you laughed in the telling, they entered into the spirit of the thing ... .[144]

These difficulties notwithstanding, the recording of the last movement of the *Four Centuries* Suite is superb, and the increase of tempo from figure 20 to the end produces an exhilarating effect.

After the recording sessions, during the winter of 1944–45, Coates succumbed to his annual bout of bronchial trouble, which, this year, was worse than normal. By March 1945, he had written to librettist Christopher Hassall informing him of his plan to spend the entire summer in Selsey to try and clear up his chest once and

---

[143]    17/08/1942 EC to Stanford Robinson. *GB-Rwac*.
[144]    Coates, *Suite*, pp. 239–40.

for all; visiting London for a few days every ten days or so.[145] This seemed to have worked and he remained healthy for the rest of the year. Like the rest of the world, the Coates were no doubt relieved about the end of the Second World War, and spent VE Day in the company of Arnold Bax, amongst others, who had a habit of turning up at their flat on 'festive occasions'.[146] They survived the war remarkably unscathed, as he informed the tenor Hubert Eisdell in America in 1947:

> We only had one stone through a window although part of the building was hit on the other side from us and there was a tremendous amount of damage done all round us. We are now in the throes of strikes, shortages and restrictions but are managing to survive with the aid of some wangling!![147]

Despite the ending of the war in Europe, Coates seemed to have little, if any, impetus for the composition of orchestral works. He informed *Everybody's*, in an interview conducted a few weeks before VE Day: 'I was lucky … my position was assured before the rot set in. But I say in all seriousness that any young composer of light music, however talented, has an excessively uphill task to get his works performed and published here today.'[148] This lack of interest for composition was exacerbated by a period of national austerity and a serious breakdown of his health during the immediate post-war years, which lead to a period of wilderness.

---

[145]   12/03/1945 EC to Christopher Hassall. *GB-Cu* Add.8905/10/C/63.

[146]   Coates, 'Arnold Bax'.

[147]   10/01/1947 EC to Hubert Eisdell. *GB-Lcm*.

[148]   May 1945 *Everybody's*.

# Chapter 10

# The Wilderness Years, 1945–1951

In the post-war years Eric Coates produced little of note and at times it appears that he was drifting in a period of wilderness exacerbated by his return from South America in 1948, which resulted in a major breakdown in his health during the remainder of the decade. For many, 1945–51 was a period of austerity under Atlee's Labour Government. While Coates had frequently suffered from compositional 'blank patches'; the post-war years were different, as he had little interest in composition. Coates' decline in health was not the only factor in a lack of compositions during 1945 and 1951. Coates' nephew and godson, Francis Freeman, believes that another aspect was that his uncle was paying a large amount of tax and, therefore, was reluctant to compose for fear that if he wrote another major work he would have to pay even more tax.[1] The tax rates during the early 1940s were drastically increased to pay for the war, and post-war income tax was nine shillings in the pound.[2] As Coffield has pointed out that the post-war rates of tax reached their zenith by 1951 when anyone earning over £5,000 surrendered slightly more than half their income to the government.[3] Coates also lost a good deal of money on his royalties from America as a result of income tax on both sides of the Atlantic. In 1945, he informed one newspaper that he received considerably less than 10 per cent of his American royalties owing to taxation.[4]

Despite Coates' lack of interest in composition, during the late 1940s he was increasingly active in the recording studio. One of his first engagements of peace time was a recording session in October 1945 to record his *Dancing Nights* Valse and the evergreen *The Three Bears*, for Columbia with the LSO. The recording filled important gaps in Coates' discography. It is unclear why *The Three Bears* had to wait so long before it was recorded under the composer's baton. After the Phantasy had been recorded in October, the first side had to be re-recorded just over two months later in December probably because there was a problem with the matrix (CAX 9401-1), which could well have become worn, but there is little difference in the performance of the two sides, though the later recording had slightly lower balance levels (CAX 9401-2).

Coates made a flying visit to Hucknall on 10 May to open the Silver Jubilee Garden Party of the Hucknall British Legion. It must have proved a nostalgic

---

[1]   Conversation with Francis Freeman, 03/08/2009. Coates had aired his views in several interviews with the press.

[2]   Brian Mitchell, *British Historical Statistics* (Cambridge, 1998), p. 645.

[3]   James Coffield, *A Popular History of Taxation* (Harlow, 1970), p. 159.

[4]   May 1945 *Everybody's*.

event as the party was held at Rannoch Lodge on Watnall Road (the street of Coates' birth) and he was presented with a photograph album of Hucknall. As always, he was flabbergasted at the enthusiastic reception he received in Hucknall.

Nearly two years after his last composition, Coates returned to writing with a short march for the BBC. In April 1946, correspondence passed between Cecil Madden (of BBC Television at Alexandra Palace) and Kenneth Wright concerning the possibility of Coates writing a march to be used as the signature tune of BBC Television.[5] Signature tunes played an important part in broadcasting as they opened transmissions and gave the television engineers chance to see if there were any problems before the transmission of programmes began. On the outbreak of war, the BBC's television transmissions ceased, but by 1946 time and finance were ripe for a return to broadcasting. Wright replied recommending that Madden should try the younger generation of composers, such as Arthur Bliss, who would no doubt be cheaper than Coates.[6] In the end, Madden decided Coates would be the best option and wrote to invite him to compose the work.[7] Before he embarked on composing the new signature tune, Coates was keen to stress that before the war the BBC's Television Service were thinking of using 'Oxford Street' (*London Again* Suite) in that capacity.[8] Initially he was not keen to write a complete march, but a trio for a march that could be adapted for BBC use, then developed into a march at a later date.[9] He had informed the *Evening News* in March 1944, after writing the *Salute the Soldier* March, that he intended writing no more marches.[10] Despite his reservations about the genre, he did write a full march. The *Television March* must rank as his most hastily composed piece, as the invitation went out in mid May 1946 and the March had to be completed and recorded for the reopening of the BBC television service on 7 June. There was some concern in the BBC that a recording of the March might not be completed in time.[11] The impending deadline acted as an inspiration rather than a creative barrier.

Coates recalled the compositional process for a newspaper: 'I went for a long walk through the London streets, jotted down a few notes in my musical shorthand, and completed the work in eight days at my Sussex cottage'.[12] As was his usual practice, he refused payment for the March in the knowledge of several years' worth of PRS fees. He informed the *Daily Mail* that he intended not to have the March published, but he soon revoked the decision and it was published

---

[5]    30/04/1946 Kenneth Wright to Cecil Madden. *GB-Rwac*.
[6]    Ibid.
[7]    14/05/1946 Kenneth Wright to Cecil Madden. *GB-Rwac*.
[8]    Ibid.
[9]    Ibid.
[10]   13/03/1944 *Evening News*. He failed.
[11]   22/05/46 Imlay Newbiggin-Watts to Miss Holloway. *GB-Rwac*. The March was recorded on 03/06/1946.
[12]   Eric Coates quoted in 01/06/1946 *Manchester Evening News*.

by Chappells in 1946.[13] By 1948, the BBC felt that the March was too long to be used for the opening of the television service and invited Coates to recompose the piece for them.[14] What resulted was a 60-second fanfare based on themes from the March for which he again eschewed a fee, once more relying on the PRS returns generated by twice daily performances.[15] The *Television March* is a fine composition, cast in Coates' usual march formula, marked by its arresting opening and superb B-section melody at figure 4.

It was not long before the *Television March* was recorded, alongside three others, in July 1946. Two of these recordings were for export only to America for Columbia. Coates' music was gaining rapidly in popularity in the United States, more than that of other light-music composers, because of the impact of the hit song 'Sleepy Lagoon', and this disc was the first exclusive export disc; the second would be made by London (the American branch of Decca) two years later. The choice of repertoire had to include the 'Knightsbridge' March (surprisingly only the second recording under the composer's direction at this stage) and *London Bridge*.

Another distraction from composition was Coates' involvement with the 1946 International Composer's Conference to be held in the United States in October. These conferences not only enabled Coates to act as a plenipotentiary of the PRS speaking up for light music, but also to make numerous friends and musical contacts abroad. Alongside the Coates, the party included William Walton and A.P. Herbert. While the main conference was in Washington, the Coates spent some time in New York (a city he loved).[16] Austin recalled: 'I always remember how delighted he was on his first encounter with a jukebox in New York in 1946 to find that one could put a dime in it and buy silence – which needless to say he promptly did.'[17] He was also invited to conduct a broadcast on CBS radio. A measure of his popularity was that, to compete with his broadcast on CBS, the rival National Broadcasting Company (NBC) played a gramophone recital (broadcast at the same time as the CBS concert) of an almost identical programme.[18]

Coates struck up a friendship with the composer Deems Taylor, President of the American Society of Composers, Authors and Publishers (the American equivalent of the PRS). They discussed the possibility of Coates making a return trip to the USA to undertake a number of engagements. Unfortunately the return trip never materialized owing to illness and other engagements.[19] There were other plans for a second visit to the USA, as towards the close of January 1947, Coates was invited to return to America to conduct an extended concert tour taking in a variety of localities and cities around America including a visit to the Hollywood Bowl.

---

[13]  06/06/1946 *Daily Mail*.

[14]  15/01/1948 R.G. Walford to James Hartley. *GB-Rwac*, Eric Coates copyright.

[15]  18/02/1948 R.G. Walford to EC. *GB-Rwac*, Eric Coates copyright.

[16]  Eric Coates, *Suite in Four Movements* (London, 1953), p. 249.

[17]  27/03/1991 Austin Coates to Richard Itter.

[18]  14/03/1986 Austin Coates to Geoffrey Self.

[19]  25/07/1949 EC to Deems Taylor. *GB-Lcm*.

However, the diffident composer already felt that he had enough home commitments to make it impossible to leave London for longer than four weeks. He did not relish flying, which would make the tour a possibility, and this aversion sealed the fate of the trip. He jokingly chastised Jim Calvert-Fowler, the author of the letter of invitation: 'The picture of you draw of picking one's own oranges is <u>too much</u> when we over here are enduring a beastly cold spell with filthy snow all over the place and two or three minutes of sunshine every week or so, to say nothing of the <u>food</u>'!!![20]

Before he had left for the United States for the 1946 Congress, Coates was full of optimism for what he would achieve on his return. He informed the *Evening News* that he would begin work on a light opera and he also revealed that he would not compose any more suites.[21] This short aside was an important comment as it signalled his lethargy for composition and his powers to be able to sustain a work of a longer duration.

On his return to England, Coates was invited to give several broadcasts in Copenhagen for the Danish Broadcasting Company. He was in two minds about whether or not to cancel his visit because he had returned from the United States with an attack of bronchial asthma, and thought that the travelling would be too taxing, though his doctor recommended that he made the trip. Originally the visit was to be a tour with two concerts in Copenhagen and one each in Arhus and Odense.[22] However, it appears that he only conducted one lengthy broadcast concert on 26 November, which seems to have been a resounding success with the public, but not with the press as he informed readers of his autobiography:

> To this day I do not know how I managed to go through with it. I think the Danish Press had a suspicion that my arrival at the airport smothered in scarves was a 'stunt', the scarves being alluded to as 'a picturesque sight', and, judging by the advance reports, my so-called asthma was nothing more serious than a 'cold'.[23]

Coates returned to a darkened London feeling distinctly unwell, but determined to take himself in hand, as a result of which he embarked on a course of breathing exercises under his next-door neighbour, who was a professor of singing. Through these exercises (much to the scorn of his doctor) and the consumption of vast quantities of Scott's Emulsion, by early spring 1947 he was restored to full health and once again able to undertake engagements (Figure 10.1).[24]

Upon the restoration of his health, he was invited to write a children's hymn for the Hucknall Baptist Church School Anniversary service, to be held on 25 May (Whitsunday) 1947. He wrote to Eric Morley, a local journalist and friend:

---

[20]   27/01/1947 EC to Jim Calvert-Fowler *GB-Lcm*.

[21]   24/08/1946 *Evening News*.

[22]   24/08/1946 *Evening News*.

[23]   Coates, pp. 251–2.

[24]   Ibid., pp. 252–3.

Figure 10.1     The Coates family at war: Eric, Phyllis and Austin Coates at their
temporary home in Hampstead, 1941

'I have written this [Children's Hymn] specially for children; it is quite short and
somewhat on the lighthearted side – I don't think children want to sing anything
too serious.'[25] He wrote both the words and the music as he informed Morley: 'the
words are my own and are meant to be a picture of my early days in Hucknall
when I used to wander about the dusty lanes on my bicycle before motor-cars used
to come along to spoil the peace of the countryside'.[26] The hymn was sung at two
services at the Church by 130 children and an augmented choir conducted by Enos
Godfrey (conductor of the Hucknall Light Orchestra).[27] Coates wished the piece to
be known as 'Children's Hymn: God's Great Love Abiding'.[28] The resulting hymn
is not particularly distinguished and was eventually published in 1956 by Keith
Prowse (presumably the religious nature of the hymn was outside Chappells'
usual publishing remit). Prowse published it in two versions, the original scored
for SATB, and a second for unison voices with a descant and piano.[29] For the
latter, Coates added a short piano introduction, omitted the seventh verse, added

---

[25]   05/05/1947 EC to Eric Morley.

[26]   29/05/1947 EC to Eric Morley. *GB-HCKl.*

[27]   27/05/1947 *Nottingham Guardian.*

[28]   13/05/1947 EC to Eric Morley.

[29]   For publication Coates omitted one of his original eight verses.

a descant from the fourth verse onwards and had the final verse in unison with a slightly expanded accompaniment.

The highlight of 1947 was an International Composer's conference held in London during June (Coates had been on the organizing committee) and the Coates were kept busy with taking delegates on the trips (including a visit to Glyndebourne to see Britten's *Albert Herring*).

The winter of 1947–48 was marked by an absence of Coates' recurrent bouts of bronchitis, which usually made the winter months rather depressing. This was quite unusual considering it was one of severest winters on record. Nevertheless, during this time a project came to fruition that he had been working on intermittently for some time, a musical. The genre was certainly becoming passé with the older light-music composers, but yet was becoming increasing popular thanks to the import of American examples. Work on the project had been intermittent during the 1940s. This time he collaborated with Laurence Howard to write a production based on his story *A Knight of Malta*, a Mediterranean romance set in 1793. By April 1943, Howard had completed a detailed synopsis of the plot, but little in the way of music had been written during this period. Coates appears to have had some doubts over the libretto at this juncture.[30] He invited librettist Christopher Hassall (who had written the libretto to Ivor Novello's *Glamorous Night* and with whom Coates had written several songs) to join Howard and himself to help them finish the production, because Howard had come up against a 'sticky patch'.[31] The following week, Coates wrote to Hassall again: 'So far as I am concerned I would gladly wait a year for you to be free ... . I would rather not do "Malta" at all if I could not work with you. And I learn Laurie [Howard] is as keen to work with you as I am.'[32]

Four months later, Hassall, who was in the Army and posted in Wakefield, but Coates and Howard were still eager that Hassall be involved in the production; both were prepared to commute to Yorkshire to have his input.[33] It is difficult to judge if and when Hassall made any input to the libretto and whether Coates made any progress on the score. Of those surviving sketches, only one is dated. Nevertheless, one suspects that Coates made little musical progress during this period, possibly sketching ideas and waiting for more concrete material before expending the necessary energy and inspiration to produce the full score. There had been some delay on the project, as Coates informed an acquaintance in 1945, but work had resumed in October with the arrival of Howard's completed libretto.[34] In February 1946, Hassall received a letter in which Coates informed him of a serious difference of opinion between Howard and himself:

---

30    12/11/1944 EC to Christopher Hassall. *GB-Cu* Add.8905/10/0/61.
31    Ibid.
32    17/11/1944 EC to Christopher Hassall. *GB-Cu* Add.8905/10/0/62.
33    12/03/1945 EC to Christopher Hassall. *GB-Cu* Add.8905/10/0/63.
34    15/10/1945 EC to Guy Eden.

I think you know what hopes I had of the project but yesterday Laurie [Howard] and I came up against such marked differences of opinion with the regard of working out the book (neither of us feeling we could alter our views) that I realized I could not possibly continue the collaboration.[35]

Such was the level of Howard's umbrage that Coates expected Howard to find another composer for the project.[36] Despite the severity of the disagreement, several weeks after the confrontation Howard wrote to Coates to pacify him: 'I am certain we should all never cease to regret such a tragic breaking-up of a delightful team, especially with such great glory and success for us in near sight'.[37]

Even with this 'olive branch', work on the production was never revived with Howard. The break with Howard notwithstanding, it is not clear why the services of Hassall were cast aside. Coates was still keen to pursue and complete the musical comedy and as far back as 1945 had enlisted the help of Austin (who was, however, was still enlisted in the RAF) to help with the libretto.[38] During the later war years he had temporally abandoned work on *A Knight of Malta*, as in 1945 composer Rutland Boughton suggested that he should look at Margery Sharp's novel *Cluny Brown* published the previous year. Coates set about locating a copy but never got any further. With the return of Austin in October 1946 from his wartime work, production on the 'Malta project' could recommence in earnest. Austin (who had always wanted to write plays) was also a calming influence and an ideal collaborator for his father. From this stage, the project began to take a definite shape, with Austin completing a script and the lyrics for numerous songs. Howard appears to have been relegated to the status of a 'sleeping partner' because of the fact that he had written the book on which the production was based. Coates set many of Austin's lyrics to music, in short score format, planning to orchestrate them closer to the first performance. Most of the surviving material appears to date from this time.

At the beginning of 1948 news of the production reached the BBC via an article on Coates in *Sketch* and they were keen to obtain a first broadcast performance of the work on the Home Service, either as an outside or studio broadcast.[39] More importantly, by 1948 work must have reached a significant stage, as Coates, Austin and Howard almost entered into an agreement with Jack Hylton to present the show at London's His Majesty's Theatre, Haymarket before the end of January 1949.[40]

The proposed contract would run for seven years and gave Hylton exusive rights over the work's performances and broadcasts (both radio and television). Furthermore, Hylton would hold the right to add or adjust scenes as he felt fit and

---

[35]   19/02/1946 EC to Christopher Hassall. *GB-Cu* Add.8905/10/0/64.

[36]   01/03/1946 EC to Christopher Hassall. *GB-Cu* Add.8905/10/0/65.

[37]   03/03/1946 Laurence Howard to EC.

[38]   May 1945 *Everybody's*.

[39]   02/01/1948 Leslie Perowne to Walter Goerh. *GB-Rwac*.

[40]   1948 Contract for *A Knight of Malta*. *GB-Lcm*.

retain one third of the copyright. If the contract had been signed, the surrender of the musical rights would have been a marked departure from the norm for Coates who had always chosen to retain the rights to all his music (the only exception being the *Symphonic Rhapsody after Richard Rodgers*). Regarding payment, the trio would receive £500 on the completion of the work, with 8 per cent of the gross box office takings, rising to 10 per cent after the staging costs had been recovered. The income from the production was to be divided, with Coates and Howard receiving three eighths apiece and Austin two eighths. There were disagreements over contracts and, at the beginning of June 1948, Coates wrote to Hylton to complain about the contract.[41] Just over a week later he wrote to Hylton to inform him that the trio did not want Hylton to stage *A Knight of Malta* as they were not happy with the contract. The reason for the termination was Howard, as Coates explained: 'I am sorry that such a thing should have happened particularly after our years of friendship of so many years standing but the fact that Laurie was adamant and demanded the return of his script left me with no other alternative, whether I had wished to negotiate or not.'[42] In addition, Coates, Austin and Howard were unhappy with the lack of remuneration they would each receive, the lack of rights they would retain and especially Hylton's exclusive holds over performances and broadcasts; Coates would not have endured Hylton's jurisdiction over his music (he was notoriously exacting over this issue).

After the rejection of the contract, little appears to have been done on the project. Early the following year Austin, who was keen to pursue a career in the diplomatic service, was delighted to hear that he had been selected by the Colonial Office for a post in Hong Kong and left England. There was no way that he and his father could communicate effectively enough to produce *A Knight of Malta*, so work was again halted. Two years later, Leon Davey was invited by Chappells (who were trying to help resurrect the project) to produce a new draft of the script in 1950.[43] Teddy Holmes, of Chappells, wrote to Coates: 'I must say I feel very enthusiastic about this new version and will be most interested to know what you and Mrs Coates think'.[44] The new draft of the script has a surviving synopsis of the scenes and from this, it can be seen that it was quite a large-scale production with a large cast and chorus:

**Act I** (* denotes surviving material.)

| | |
|---|---|
| Scene 1 | * Haunted eternally (Rodney) |
| Scene 2 | Opening of a Tunisian Inn Scene (Ensemble) |
| | * Midnight's my Noonday (Tala) |

[41]    01/06/1948 EC to Jack Hylton.
[42]    09/06/1948 EC to Jack Hylton.
[43]    17/04/1950 Teddy Holmes to EC.
[44]    Ibid.

| Scene 3 | Something inside (Bib, Major and Bill) |
|---|---|
| | * Promise (Rodney) |
| | Haunted Eternally + Promise (reprise) (Tala) |
| | I Belong to You (Tala) |
| Scene 4 | Song of the Lacemakers (Ensemble) |
| | Fisherfolk Dance (Ensemble) |
| | Haunted Eternally (Reprise) (Rodney) |
| | Knights return from the Vineyard (Ensemble) |
| | Evening Hymn and Finale (Ensemble) |

**Act II**

| Scene 1 | Opening Hymn (Ensemble) |
|---|---|
| Scene 2 | * The Morning Hymn (Knights) |
| | * Song of Supplication (Rodney) |
| | The Song of Knighthood (Master) |
| | * Rodney's Prayer (Rodney) |
| Scene 3 | You're the Apple of My Eye (Bib, Major and Bill) |
| | The English Way (Tala and Ensemble) |
| | * You've Hypnotised my Heart (Tala) |
| | What Might Have Been (Tala and Rodney) |
| | Knight's Marching Song (Knights) |
| | Fiesta of St George (Ensemble) |
| | Tarantella (Ensemble) |

Certainly some the songs had been composed previously, when Austin was librettist, though it is impossible to attribute the songs to a librettist or to date them but the collaboration was to be short lived; by September 1950, Coates informed J. Ward Mitchell in America:

> You will be interested to hear we are still in the throes of trying to unravel the 'Malta' problem and at the moment come to an impasse all round. My solicitors will not let me proceed with the show until the ownership of the book is proved, and as the author died without so far as we know leaving a will the position is not what one could call clear.[45]

The crux of the legal problems was the unclear ownership of Howard's story *A Knight of Malta*. After Howard's death in March 1949, the rights were passed to Mr Wills as payment for debts incurred by Howard; Coates' solicitors were uneasy for him to proceed any further on the project because Mr Wills was not clear about his ownership rights.[46] Alas, the legal problems were never resolved

---

[45] 07/09/1950 EC to J. Ward Mitchell. *GB-Lcm*.

[46] 06/07/1950 Gery and Brooks [Coates' solicitors] to Chappells. *GB-Lcm*.

and the production was left to languish alongside Coates' other ventures into operetta. Owning to the incomplete nature of the project and the survival of little of the material the work must remain as a historical curiosity. Though if Coates' had finished the work, one wonders how much his reputation would have been enhanced and in which direction his composition would have progressed.

Even though most of Coates' energies during 1948 were channelled into *A Knight of Malta*, it also proved a significant year for gramophone records. In July, Coates returned to Kingsway Hall to record a batch of records for Decca, a handsome set of three records for sole release to the United States on the London label. The choice of repertoire justifiably had to include *By the Sleepy Lagoon* and 'Knightsbridge'. Coates intriguingly included *Song of Loyalty* in its purely orchestral guise and H.M. Higgs' orchestration of 'Bird Songs at Eventide' rather than the symphonic rhapsody based on the song; no doubt the song was as popular in America as it was in England. Each of the three discs were 10 inch, limiting the playing time to around 3 minutes and the recording featured significant alterations to the musical text to fit the pieces on to one side of a record (some more than others; two escaped without any changes). Table 10.1 shows the cuts and changes to the orchestration that Coates was forced to make.

Table 10.1   Cuts made in Coates' 1948 Decca export recording

| Piece | Duration | Playing time | Cuts |
|-------|----------|--------------|------|
| *Song of Loyalty* | 5 minutes | 3 minutes 18 seconds | Starts at bar 4<br>Cut from C to E<br>No repeat of E and F<br>Cut from bar 7 of F into bar 5 of G |
| *By the Sleepy Lagoon* | 3 minutes 30 seconds | 3 minutes 15 seconds | Starts at bar 4<br>Cut from upbeat of figure 5 to upbeat of figure 6 |
| 'Birdsongs at Eventide' (arr. H.M. Higgs) | n/a | 3 minutes 8 seconds | No cuts |
| *Television March* | 3 minutes 25 seconds | 3 minutes 18 seconds | No cuts |
| *Wood Nymphs* Valsette | 3 minutes 30 seconds | 3 minutes 9 seconds | No repeat of D (though repeat of B) |
| 'Knightsbridge' March[*] | 4 minutes 00 seconds | 2 minutes 55 seconds | Starts at letter C<br>Bar 8 of C to bar 5 of D |

[*] Coates' recording of the work starts at the same position as Benjamin Frankel's Special Concert Arrangement of the March, with the A minor fanfares (letter C).

The performance of *By the Sleepy Lagoon* was the most idiosyncratic of his whole discography because of the cuts and alterations. Coates begins his performance at bar 4, halving the introduction during which he introduces a touch of rubato and an unmarked crescendo and diminuendo. At figure 4, he makes more of the tenuto than in the previous two performances by pulling back more. There is a cut from the upbeat of figure 5 to the upbeat of figure 6, reducing the reprise of the A-section. The composer also alters the glockenspiel part from figure 6, with the percussionist playing on different beats of the bar and including notes which do not feature in the printed part. In addition, the final harp arpeggios are inverted so the harpist is playing descending arpeggios rather than ascending as written.

In October 1948, Coates was back at Kingsway Hall to cut another six sides for Decca (this time on three 12-inch discs for the home market) of his two *London* Suites. He had only recorded the *London* Suite once in 1933, and then in a curtailed version, and *London Again* in 1936; both were due a new recording with the increased fidelity of the post-war years. The *London* Suite was recorded with a brief cut in the first movement from H to J and part of 'Knightsbridge', from the eighth bar of letter C to the fifth bar of letter D was removed, which brought it in line with the repeat of this section at letter I. In *London Again*, Coates chose to begin 'Langham Place' at figure 1, eschewing the mysterious introduction, which is vital for introducing the BBC motif. 'Mayfair' is presented as written, but in line with his previous recording he begins at figure 4, omitting the introduction, which reduces the playing time from 5 minutes to just under 4 minutes. There was no real need to impose cuts in either Suite as both could have comfortably fitted on to the space available, but no doubt Coates felt that these cuts tightened up the structure of the works.

With the close of work on *A Knight of Malta* in 1948, he was free to return to his usual gambit of light orchestral works and the first to be completed was a march, *Music Everywhere* on 10 August, shortly before his 62nd birthday. This was a response to an invitation from the broadcasting company Rediffusion, then transmitting in overseas colonies, for a signature tune to occupy a similar position to the *Television March* he had written for the BBC. Coates may well have composed a short call sign scored for four horns, two trumpets and three trombones, which was written in the autograph score, in the same key as the March (Example 10.1);[47] the first subject of the March (figure 1) is based on this short theme. The piece concludes with a coda (figure 12) based on the call sign as if it were designed to end with the call sign, leading straight into the start of broadcasts (though the harmonization in the score was different from that in the call sign).

Nine days after his visit to Hucknall to conduct the Light Orchestra on 5 September, Coates embarked on his final foray abroad as a plenipotentiary of the PRS, this time to Buenos Aires. For Coates, this invitation had come almost as a heaven sent opportunity. Reprieved from his usual winter cold, he had contracted a nasty cough during the summer that nothing seemed to move and he thought that

---

[47]    The manuscript bears a note in Coates' handwriting to copy the call sign separately from the March (*GB-Lcm* Box 181).

Example 10.1   *Music Everywhere* March, call sign

a sea voyage to sunnier climes seemed an ideal tonic.[48] The fifteenth International Confederation of Societies Authors and Composers Conference was held from 11–16 October in Buenos Aires featuring delegates from over twenty different countries.[49] As with the previous trip to New York, Coates was also invited to do a little 'guest-conducting' of his own music. The PRS contingent set sail on 18 September on board the ship Highland Brigade (which the Coates had renamed 'Highland Fling')[50] bound for Argentina. Eric and Phyl were accompanied on the boat by Gerald Hatchman (of the PRS) and A.P. Herbert (who had been furiously studying Spanish for the two weeks prior to the voyage). Leslie Boosey and William Walton travelled independently and joined the party in South America.

While *en route* Coates received a telegram asking to compose a short piece dedicated to the people of Argentina.[51] There was no manuscript paper on board the ship and with a very tight schedule, Coates tactfully declined the offer. On arrival in Montevideo (where the boat had docked) he was invited to give a talk to 400 pupils at the English School, which he declined to do at first, but on relenting found that the experience thoroughly delighted him.[52]

Aside from the routine of the conference, Coates managed to conduct two radio broadcasts: one on Radio Privincio in La Plata; and the other on Radio del Estado in Buenos Aires. Both had been engineered through the auspices of the BBC. Shortly before Coates left England there was some doubt in the BBC whether the broadcasts would take place.[53] Even when Coates arrived at the State Theatre in La Plata for the rehearsal, there were grave doubts about whether the orchestra would arrive, as the broadcast followed a two-day national holiday.[54]

Coates seemed to enjoy the tour and was pleasantly surprised by the reception his music achieved as he informed the BBC: 'They seem to know my music very well out in South America and things like "Knightsbridge" and "Sleepy Lagoon"

---

[48]   Coates, p. 255.

[49]   October 1948 *Musical Opinion*.

[50]   16/09/1948 EC to C.B. McNair. *GB-Rwac*.

[51]   01/10/1948 Cable to Eric Coates. (Coates Scrapbook 3.)

[52]   Coates, p. 255.

[53]   16/07/1948 C.B. McNair to Head of Latin American Service and 21/07/1948 F.B. Thornton to George Hills. *GB-Rwac*.

[54]   Coates, p. 256.

were a kind of "Open Sesame" wherever I went'.[55] The Argentineans subsequently invited Coates to return the following year for a three-month tour, which he dismissed.[56] The after-effects of the journey took a toll on his health (as they had done on his return from the United States in 1946) and he was forbidden to undertake engagements for some months. The attack lasted for the remainder of 1948 and well into 1949, as he informed Deems Taylor in September 1949:

> For the past [*sic*] month (damn this typewriter) I have been having daily injections in my buttocks and then my veins and I am thankful to say I am at last beginning to get better. Have you ever had bronchitis with asthma? I can tell you it's about the most horrible thing you will ever get. And so my doctor will not let me take another sea trip until next year when I shall be completely recovered and my bronchials restored to their normal state.[57]

Another aside to the outbreak of illness was a change of Selsey cottage and a suggestion from Phyl to leave London permanently for Selsey. Owing to the Requisition Act they had lost a previous cottage in 1946. So in 1948, they bought another cottage, Tamarisk Cottage, and lived there for a few months on the south coast, but the environment was not beneficial to Coates' chest and Phyl did not like the exposed position of the cottage, so they reluctantly decided to move back to London. Despite its problems, they loved the cottage and the views across to the Isle of Wight, which were especially good for Coates' telescope; he spent many happy hours watching the ships with his field-glasses.[58] They sold the house quickly, but managed to re-acquire their former chauffeur's cottage as their holiday home. They eventually sold this in 1952, relocating their holiday home to Bognor Regis.[59]

As a consequence of his illness Coates was forced to postpone a conducting tour to the United States, accompanied by Deems Taylor, provisionally planned for May 1949, which included several broadcasts and an engagement with the famous Boston 'Pops Orchestra'. In addition, as a result of recording sessions with Decca, the trip was postponed to October, but looked less likely as time was diminishing to organize such a tour.[60] Because of a further bout of ill health at the close of 1949, his trip was rescheduled for May 1950, but subsequently cancelled yet again owing to the erratic state of his health.[61]

Even with his bronchial trouble, he still managed to 'woo his muse' in composition. The *Valse from the Phantasy 'The Three Bears'* completed in January 1949, is loosely based on the slow valse section (letter H) from his orchestral

---

[55]  28/11/1948 EC to Kenneth Wright. *GB-Rwac*.

[56]  Ibid.

[57]  25/09/1949 EC to Deems Taylor. *GB-Lcm*.

[58]  Eric Coates *Suite in Four Movements* (autograph), p. 575.

[59]  Coates (autograph), pp. 574–76.

[60]  27/04/1949 EC to Arthur Fiedler. *GB-Lcm*.

[61]  26/09/1949 *Nottingham Guardian*.

Phantasy, *The Three Bears*, written 23 years earlier, though it is essentially a new composition.[62] Why he chose to adapt a pre-existing composition is unclear, but with his health problems he may have been struggling to find inspiration.

Another factor in revisiting a former composition was that Coates could have been under some pressure from Chappells to provide library music for their expanding Recorded Music Library, used in broadcasting, and decided that a short piece, especially one based on an existing composition, would be an easy option. His friend Teddy Holmes was in charge of the library at this stage and one wonders if Holmes persuaded Coates to contribute to it. The *Valse* was recorded by Decca for release both as a commercial record and as a piece of library music. Library music for use in the post-war film, television and radio industries was fast becoming a major avenue for light-music composers who had all the necessary skills to excel. Figures such as Charles Williams, Robert Farnon and Trevor Duncan were all providing short miniatures for these libraries. The older figures of light music, such as Coates, Haydn Wood and Montague Phillips, did, to some extent, shy away from this outlet, but allowed their music to be used by these libraries.[63]

The *Valse* has a close affinity with *By the Sleepy Lagoon* in structure, starting with a slow introduction, an A-section, a shorter, slightly faster B-section, a reprise of the A-section and concluding with a short coda with an inverted violin pedal point. The melodic material for the *Valse's* A-section is adapted and extended from the melody from the Phantasy retaining the same overall melodic shape, though the notes are almost totally adjusted (Example 10.2). In the *Valse*, Coates removes the 'three bears' motif' entirely, and replaces it with a countersubject on the flute and oboe in quavers (bars 9–10 and 13–14 onwards) which is a similar idea to the divided first violins at letter I of the Phantasy.

Whilst writing the *Valse*, Coates received a commission for another work. In early 1949, the BBC had decided to give several public concerts as a showcase for light music. These concerts were expanded in the 1950s to be annual, high-profile events at the Royal Festival Hall. The 1949 Festival was largely studio-based and was, in the main, composed of augmented versions of standard broadcasts such as *Grand Hotel*. In order to celebrate the first Festival, Herbert Murrill, the BBC's Director of Music, invited Coates to compose a rhapsody for piano and orchestra. The BBC wanted the completed score in less than two months. Coates informed Murrill:

> I'm afraid it's out of the question – I'm so sorry. I am going out of London in the morning and could not possibly get down to anything until the end of next week and the prospect of being forced to hand over the finished full-score by a

---

[62]   Though the published orchestral parts spell 'phantasy' as 'fantasy', I have adopted Coates' spelling as in the autograph score (*GB-Lcm* Box 181).

[63]   A selection from Coates' *Four Centuries* was recorded for Boosey & Hawkes' Library and Robert Farnon recorded Haydn Wood's *Soliloquy* for Chappells.

stipulated time would not only freeze-up my ideas but would give me writer's cramp as well![64]

Example 10.2    *The Three Bears Phantasy* and *Valse from the Phantasy 'The Three Bears'*, comparison of melodies. © 1926 and © 1949 Chappell Music Ltd, London, W6 8BS. Reproduced by permission of Faber Music Ltd. All Rights Reserved

It was a shame that Coates did not feel able to write a concertante work as it would have been a valuable addition to his canon, perhaps along similar lines to the *Saxo-Rhapsody*.[65] As a consolation, he conducted his *The Three Elizabeths* Suite with the LSO at Kingsway Hall on 28 March as part of the Festival. Haydn Wood conducted the first performance of his own *Festival March* (written for the Festival).

Coates was pleased with the results of the Festival, but his letter of praise to the BBC still had an undercurrent of his past skirmishes with the BBC regarding the Promenade Concerts in 1943 and 1944:

> I am very pleased the Festival went off so well – it's a thing that has been wanted for a long time. You would be surprised if you could see the number of letters I receive every year from complete strangers asking me if I can do anything about getting the BBC to present the best in Light Music on the orchestras for which is was written – perhaps this is the beginning of things to come. Personally I should like to see composers of genuine Loght [*sic*] Orchestral Music represented at such concerts as the Proms, and not being obliged to write a <u>new</u> work every time.[66]

While he was no doubt overjoyed that the BBC appeared to be taking light music seriously, he had to wait until 1953 when the BBC resurrected the Festival.

---

[64]    06/01/1949 EC to Herbert Murrill. *GB-Rwac.*
[65]    14/01/1949 Herbert Murrill to EC. *GB-Rwac.*
[66]    11/04/1949 EC to T.W. Chambers. *GB-Rwac.*

A highlight of 1949 was undoubtedly a visit to Kingsway Hall on 16 July for a busy day recording old works (including *The Three Men* Suite) and his latest two compositions for Decca. All benefited from being recorded in 'FFRR' (full frequency-range recording), which made a significant improvement to the recorded fidelity and meant that for the first time technology could faithfully reproduce the subtle nuances of his orchestral scores. As the noted record producer John Culshaw stated in his autobiography: 'Coates's transparent scoring was particularly effective in demonstrating what the new recording technique could provide.'[67] Indeed, Culshaw went so far as to rate Coates' 'FFRR' recordings from this period as amongst the finest 'FFRR' records made.[68]

The majority of music recorded that day escaped with only minimal cuts and rewrites except *The Three Bears*, which had an important change to the foxtrot section. This rewrite is symptomatic of the 'tinkerings' that Coates made during his recordings of this period, whether it was the addition of vibraphone, or the rewriting of percussion parts. Coates' 1949 performance differs very little from his previous 1946 Columbia recording of the Phantasy, except in one passage. In the foxtrot section (bars 327–52), the brass accompaniment (bars 335–8) is rewritten to become jazzier than the original, complete with the use of 'swing rhythm' (bars 328–30). The major change occurs at 335 when, instead of repeated quaver chords (separated by a quaver rest), the rhythm is altered, adding to the levels of dissonance.

This change to the musical text may well have been a result of the brass section deciding to 'jazz' up the foxtrot as a joke at the recording session; Coates, may well have liked the effect and recorded it as such. If the brass had not 'jazzed up' the passage, it is possible that Coates himself may have rewritten the passage especially for the session. However, what seems most plausible was that Robert Farnon, who was then fast establishing himself in the world of British light music, rewrote the passage for the recording. In a BBC interview, recorded in 2002, Farnon recalled a meeting he had with Coates when they were discussing a 'jazz section' in *The Three Bears*: 'he said, "I can't write jazz, would you mind rewriting this for me?" So I sat down one day and rewrote this little section.'[69] The rewritten passage does bear a resemblance to the style of Farnon. However, Farnon was un-credited on the record-sleeve and Coates never mentioned his assistance, though Farnon recalled they kept it a secret for many years.[70] It seems likely that this passage was updated to appeal to a new generation who were adjusting their musical tastes to the American big band style. Coates was surely trying to make

---

[67]    John Culshaw, *Putting the Record Straight* (London, 1981), p. 52.

[68]    Ibid. Second only to Britten's first recording of his *Serenade for Tenor, Horn and Strings*.

[69]    21/07/2002 *Brian Kay's Light Programme: A Celebration of Robert Farnon's Eighty-Fifth Birthday*. BBC Radio 3.

[70]    Ibid.

his music more relevant to the society he was living in; though ironically, the harmony was identical to the 1926 original.

The final two pieces recorded that day were jointly recorded by Decca and the Chappell Recorded Music Library, hence the joint catalogue number and the unusual matrix prefix of CH. During the late 1940s, Decca held the contract to record library music for Chappells; occasionally they released library-music recordings on the Decca label (including Haydn Wood's *Soliloquy*).[71] The recording of the *Valse* is one of the very few of Coates' performances in which he conducts slower than the prescribed tempo in the score. ($\downarrow$. = 37 rather than the prescribed $\downarrow$. = 48.)

The following month, on 25 September, Coates returned to Hucknall to conduct the Hucknall Light Orchestra in a concert. He conducted in the packed Church Hall, where many had to be turned away. After the ovation at the end of the concert he was presented with an engraved baton marking his links with the Hucknall Light Orchestra.[72]

For many people, Coates' name was still indelibly linked with *In Town Tonight* and on 26 November 1949, Coates was invited to take part in the 500th edition of the programme, alongside the actress Greer Garson, to inform listeners about the genesis of the show's signature tune. Peter Duncan, the producer of the show, recalled the reluctance of the composer to appear, saying 'A composer should only speak through his music'.[73] The broadcast was eventful, as Duncan further recalled regarding the cutting of the cake to celebrate the programme's landmark edition:

> from the depths of someone's pocket, a penknife had been produced and was handed to Eric Coates. As composer of our signature tune, 'Knightsbridge,' we all felt that the honour should go to him. Besides, we had a surprise. Our ingenious outside broadcast engineers had contrived a musical box underneath it. As the knife touched the icing it set up an electrical contact and the opening bars of 'Knightsbridge' tinkled out, discordantly.
>
> 'Hmm, just like I play it,' Eric remarked.[74]

Several months after his appearance on *In Town Tonight*, Coates was at work on another march written to celebrate the fiftieth anniversary of the London town of Holborn becoming a metropolitan borough of London. A full week of celebrations was planned to celebrate this and, at the suggestion of Councillor Betty Moir, Coates was invited to write a March. Being a resident of the borough,

---

[71]   Haydn Wood *Soliloquy* (Decca, F9295). These libraries had been in existence since the days of the silent cinema in the 1910s and 1920s, but there was a rapid acceleration in demand for them after the Second World War owing to the huge expansion of broadcasting.

[72]   26/09/1949 *Nottingham Guardian*.

[73]   Peter Duncan, *In Town Tonight* (London, 1951), p. 9.

[74]   Ibid., p. 8.

Coates was a natural choice for the commissioning of a march and felt he should accede to the request. The composer presented the completed March to the Mayor of Holborn at a ceremony at the Town Hall on 14 June 1950. The presentation of the score occasioned one of the few negative press comments that Coates received. The *Evening Standard* ran an article entitled 'The Composer Who Did Not Play'.[75]

The *Holborn* March was first performed by the BBC Opera Orchestra under the composer, the day before the main celebrations in Holborn. The composer conducted the first public performance with the band of the Irish Guards as part of the Holborn celebrations in Russell Square on 25 June. It was all reminiscent of the first performances of *Salute the Soldier*, but not quite as prestigious.

With the tremendous successes of his previous marches, especially 'Knightsbridge' and *Calling All Workers*, the Borough of Holborn no doubt felt it would be linked to Coates' march and achieve a sort of fame. Alas, *Holborn* is among the weakest he wrote, with the B-section relying too much on repetition of ideas (like *Music Everywhere*).

During 1950, the direction of Coates' composition almost changed direction with the opportunity to write a musical for Paul Whiteman, of the American Broadcasting Company, who wanted to stage a Broadway and London musical production using some of Coates' music.[76] He appointed J. Ward Mitchell as emissary and it was Mitchell who suggested a musical based around Pinero's play *Trelawney of the 'Wells'*.[77] It seems that from the outset that the project would be based on Coates' existing compositions and possibly several songs from the sketches of *A Knight of Malta*,[78] along the lines of Grieg's *Song of Norway*. The project dragged on indefinitely and in August 1951 Coates wrote to Louis Dreyfus at Chappells in New York:

> The position is as follows: I should very much like to do a Musical and there is no doubt that I have enough published music to make more than one show (I have in mind Grieg's 'Song of Norway' in which his music was so beautifully adapted) and I am perfectly willing for my published works to be used in this way (with certain exceptions) providing I have the final word where the adaptation of my music is concerned, also I am quite willing to write new music if this is absolutely necessary, but the amount will have to be confined to certain limits defined by myself. In other words, I am not prepared to write an entirely new show at the moment.

---

[75]   15/06/1950 *Evening Standard*.
[76]   04/04/1950 Paul Whiteman to EC. *GB-Lcm*.
[77]   12/07/1950 EC to J. Ward Mitchell. *GB-Lcm*.
[78]   Ibid.

Possibly you do not know that I have a great many unpublished songs which have never even been sung and which,[79] with alterations here and there in the words and music, would lend themselves admirably to the theatre – I also have several numbers in M/S [manuscript] which were originally intended for a Musical which my son and I were working on and which came to grief over business complications of one Lawrence Howard (who had provided the story). These unpublished numbers were played over the [*sic*] Ward Mitchell when he was in this country some months ago and he was very keen to get hold of them, so much so that he wanted to take them back with him to New York then and there.[80]

While there was a little spirit of optimism for the projected music, Coates was still hesitant to undertake much composition, preferring instead to plunder his 'back catalogue' for material. This decision marks a change in attitude, as he had always dismissed his unpublished works;[81] he had more confidence in his old compositions than in his ability to write new ones.

The year of 1950 was tinged with nostalgia. In June, Coates was invited, along with Haydn Wood, to conduct in a festival of light music in Scarborough, a resort he used to visit annually during Alick Maclean's tenure with the orchestra there. In December, he was invited to conduct *The Three Bears* with the Hallé Orchestra in a concert at the City Hall in Sheffield. According to the *Sheffield Telegraph,* Barbirolli joined the cello section for Coates' Phantasy; apparently the first time in 26 years he had played his instrument in public.[82] For Coates and Sir John it was an event that rekindled their friendship, as it was the first time they had met since their days in the QHO when Coates led the violas and Barbirolli was an aspiring young cellist. To mark the occasion, Barbirolli presented Coates with a baton inscribed: 'to an exquisite musician'.[83] The event led to several other guest-conducting slots with the Hallé and possibly the invitation to write the *Rhodesia* March for their 1953 trip to Bulawayo. Barbirolli played a variety of Coates' music during his tenure with the orchestra.

By all accounts, 1951 appears to have been a quiet year. There was little in the way of composition (nothing was published) and little interest from the press. There was an exchange of letters with Gilbert Vinter, conductor of the BBC Midland Light Orchestra, over the concept of duration that gives an insight into Coates' compositional psyche and thoughts of the period. For some time he had become concerned about the issue of his music being overly long, which was to some extent seen in his recordings of the 1940s, where he removed passages to

---

[79]   Was he referring to the large number of unpublished songs he had written in the 1920s?

[80]   26/08/1951 EC to Louis Dreyfus. *GB-Lcm.*

[81]   09/10/1932 EC to Stanford Robinson. *GB-Rwac.*

[82]   18/12/1950 *Sheffield Telegraph.*

[83]   Ibid.

shorten compositions, not solely to truncate them for the gramophone. Writing to Vinter in May, he stated:

> Speaking once more of 'Four Centuries' – I am afraid I find the first and the last movements a little too long anyhow and if I had written it <u>now</u> I would have cut them both down considerably to bring them into the five-minute limit. Well, as one gets older one becomes less long-winded – in the words of the Immortal Bard: 'Brevity is the soul of wit' – and how <u>right</u> he is.[84]

This 5-minute limit was something he abided by almost entirely in his final batch of compositions.

Nevertheless, June proved a busy month for BBC broadcasts. The first was on 12 June, conducting the BBC Midland Light Orchestra in a programme of his orchestral music in a 45-minute broadcast for the Midland Home Service. Coates enjoyed visits to conduct the Midland Orchestra and relished the chance to play and broadcast his music in the area of his birth. The second was much more prestigious and was the ultimate accolade in spoken word broadcasts; he was invited to be the ninety-second castaway on *Desert Island Discs*, broadcast on 20 June, but recorded five days previously. This third series of the programme also included actor/comedians Stanley Holloway and Jimmy Edwards. As was usual, Roy Plomley, the show's creator and presenter, took the castaway out for lunch to discus the show's content and fashion a script. Coates' musical choices were as follows:

1. Cockaigne Overture (Edward Elgar)
2. 'Pastoral Dance' (*Three Dances from Nell Gwyn*) (Edward German)
3. Violin Concerto in D Minor (Henri Wieniawski), played by Jascha Heifetz
4. *Prélude à L'après-midi d'un faune* (Claude Debussy)
5. Clarinet Quintet in B minor (Johannes Brahms)
6. Valse in E minor (Fredrick Chopin)
7. *Tambourin Chinois* (Fritz Kreisler)
8. 'Valse' (*Four Centuries* Suite), (Eric Coates)

His choices were influenced by his musical upbringing (Chopin and Wieniawski) and performance experiences (Debussy and Elgar). Coates chose to eschew any popular dance melodies, as he thought that: 'their haunting melodies would be <u>far</u> too nostalgic'.[85] He also chose the 'Valse' from the *Four Centuries* Suite (his own recording) because: 'I would like to take one of my own records with me just to remind me, during my enforced isolation, that once upon a time when I lived

[84]    03/05/1951 EC to Gilbert Vinter. *GB-Rwac*, Eric Coates, Midland Light Orchestra.
[85]    20/06/1951 *Desert Island Discs*, broadcast, BBC Light Programme. *GB-Rwac*, Desert Island Discs Scripts.

among my fellow creatures, I used to write music.'[86] Furthermore, Coates also got to take the show's signature tune, *By the Sleepy Lagoon* with him, an added bonus, as it was one of his own compositions.

The immediate post-war years had been difficult and traumatic for Coates because of an appalling run of illness, a feeling of apathy towards composition and the failure of yet another musical production. Nevertheless, he still produced occasional short compositions. However, the onset of the 1950s marked a change in his fortunes with the publication of his autobiography and the production of a march for a film.

---

[86]   Ibid.

# Chapter 11

# Renown at Last, 1951–1955

The completion of both his autobiography and a short orchestral miniature, *The Unknown Singer*, marked a huge change in Coates' life: 1952 marked a return to the halcyon days of the 1930s and throughout the remainder of the 1950s he produced a steady, albeit small, stream of attractive miniatures. This development was partially mirrored in the 1951 General Election, which brought Churchill and the Conservative party out from the wilderness. It also marked, at least outwardly, a return to the values and the 'conventional' style of the 1930s. Coates changed the focus of his music with a simpler approach to form and less influence from dance music. During this period, one march totally obliterated all Coates' previous successes; no mean feat, considering the immense popularity of a number of his compositions. In addition, the publication of his autobiography in 1953 marked him out as an elder statesman of British Music, a fact heightened by the number of interviews on a variety of subjects he gave for the BBC.[1]

Since 1951, Coates had been engaged in writing his memoirs, published in 1953 as *Suite in Four Movements*. The autobiography dated back some years before 1951, as his son Austin recalled for the *Hucknall Dispatch* in 1986: 'After 1941, he was seriously ill with pneumonia and asthma and did not get any better … . Phyl thought he needed another medium and said to him: "You remember those letters you wrote to Eric Morley in Hucknall. Why not have another look at them"'.[2] Coates informed *The Leader* in 1945 that his memoirs were practically finished,[3] though it was not until 1952 that a publisher and a manuscript were ready. The cut-off date for information was 1951, though the typescript of the book does have some information relating to 1952, when, unfortunately, notable works such as *The Dam Busters* March had not yet been written. As a composer, he ingeniously structured the book as a suite with each of the four movements, 'Allegretto Pastorale', 'Lento–Andante–Allegretto', 'Romanza in Modo Variazione' and 'Rondo' reflecting a period of his life.

Before publishing the work, Coates undertook a purge on the material and ejected numerous interesting comments. He informed a Nottinghamshire newspaper of the reasons behind his purge: 'When I wrote my memoirs I read

---

[1]  During the last decade of his life, the BBC invited him to expound his thoughts on topics as diverse as the music of Edward German, Fred Weatherly, Dan Godfrey and 'my friends the composers'.

[2]  05/09/1986 *Hucknall Dispatch*. A number of letters were also written actually written Morley's father, Henry, who was the founder and first editor of the *Hucknall Dispatch*.

[3]  17/11/1945 *The Leader*.

through them again and again and ... I cut out any remarks which seemed unkind about persons I had known. After all people don't want to read insolent comments do they?'[4] The manuscript was eventually finished on 28 August 1952 and published by Heinemann on 3 October 1953 (Austin's first book was also published around the same time)[5] to great critical acclaim. One volume of his seven books of press-cuttings was solely dedicated to the press coverage generated by the publication of the book.[6] Coates was paid a £300 advance on his autobiography and the first two months of sales had generated £312 in royalties for the author alone.[7] The first edition of *Suite in Four Movements* sold out within weeks of publication and had to be reprinted.

The writing of the autobiography was, at times, arduous for him, as he explained in the concluding paragraph from the book: 'Had I known, when I began this book, the time and patience that would be needed in committing my thoughts to paper, I might I have thought twice before embarking on such an undertaking. However, I have learnt my lesson and do not intend to be caught again ... .'[8] Despite his fears, his writing style is far from jejune and his memoirs are delightfully told. The book is an evocative memory largely centred around his youth in Hucknall and early days as a musician in London and includes a rich fund of stories about important figures in British musical life and is a significant document. However, the book is curiously imbalanced with less than 70 pages being devoted to his life as a composer, the preceding 190 dealing with his youth, student and orchestral days.

The BBC were keen to seize an opportunity to broadcast a programme about Coates to coincide with the publication of the autobiography. Two months before the book's release there were several exchanges of letters between Coates and Hubert Clifford (of the BBC's Light Music Department) about the possibility of a programme, but it did not come to fruition and it was not until December that the BBC broadcast four programmes, presented by Stephen Williams.[9] Each edition had a five minute pre-recorded talk by Coates about his life and music.[10]

Concurrent with his work on *Suite in Four Movements* was a remarkable change in the state of his health. In 1950, he was advised by his doctor to cease smoking (he had smoked since he was a child), which he did, and at the same time he lost his creative impulse. One day in 1952, he decided, 'Doctors be damned. I must have a cigarette' and returned to smoking.[11] It rekindled his interest in composition and helped him to return to his former levels of creativity, leading

---

4    24/09/1956 *Nottingham Guardian?* (Coates Scrapbook 6.)
5    Austin Coates, *Invitation to an Eastern Feast.* (London: Hutchison, 1953.)
6    Coates Scrapbook 4.
7    11/07/1954 EC to Peter Watt.
8    Eric Coates, *Suite in Four Movements* (London, 1953), p. 263.
9    24/08/1953 Hubert Clifford to EC. *GB-Rwac.*
10   21/12/1953–24/12/1953 *Eric Coates Remembers*, BBC Light Programme.
11   Eric Coates quoted in 25/01/1985 Austin Coates to Geoffrey Self.

to the composition of *The Unknown Singer*.[12] He informed a newspaper in 1954 of his renewed optimism: 'I feel twice the person I was a few years ago: I can do such a great deal more nowadays.'[13] His return to smoking came during a particularly stressful period, as early in 1952, Phyl was forced into hospital to have an emergency appendectomy. Coates feared for her life, though she was to make a full recovery. He recalled the drama of the events in an omitted passage from his autobiography:

> I was bustled off by the kindly night-sister to the Dorchester while Phyl was being taken into the operating theatre. It was an unpleasant experience sitting in the Grill drinking red wine to keep my strength up knowing that, at that very moment, the surgeon was wrestling with an appendix that ought to have been removed thirty-five years ago.[14]

When Phyl was discharged a few weeks later they decided to relocate to Selsey for Phyl to convalesce in the tranquillity of the south coast. Coates travelled up to London at least one day week on business.[15]

Whilst Phyl was recovering in hospital, an idea for a composition germinated in his mind in the most unusual fashion. Coates reminisced:

> Early one morning, as I slept, I dreamt I heard someone singing from out of a deep wood – it was a lovely soprano voice. I listened to the melody the unseen soprano was singing and to my astonishment, on waking I remembered every note of it. Such a thing had never happened before and I can assure any possible readers that it saved me a great deal of trouble, besides getting me out of an awkward predicament. And so my dream-melody became "The Unknown Singer"... .[16]

The original title had been *A Voice in the Night*. The resulting composition marked a return to the compositional fitness and vigour of the 1930s. *The Unknown Singer* is structured in ternary form (though the recapitulation of the A-section, at figure 15, is much altered and only 18 bars long) and is essentially a set of variations on three themes though none of them are combined.

After the completion of *The Unknown Singer*, John Lowe, conductor of the BBC Midland Light Orchestra, suggested that Coates should conduct its premiere at the 1952 Cheltenham Festival, a festival synonymous with *avant garde* music. That year, the Festival Committee and the BBC were trying an experiment of presenting several light music concerts by the Hallé and the BBC Midland Light Orchestras. Both concerts featured music by Coates, as he recalled that he: 'roused

[12] Geoffrey Self, *In Town Tonight* (London, 1986), p. 91.
[13] 27/04/1954 *Evening Standard*.
[14] Eric Coates *Suite in Four Movements* (autograph), p. 582.
[15] 24/02/1952 EC to Oscar Preuss. *GB-Lcm*.
[16] Coates (autograph), p. 585.

the wrath of the critics by employing a tenor saxophone (I draw a veil over what they said about "The Three Elizabeths")'.[17] Unsurprisingly, the light-music concerts were not a success and the experiment was not repeated. After the Festival in May, the Coates spent a few days basking in the beauty of the Cotswolds.

Compositions of this period are marked by a change of style, becoming simpler in their approach to form and development of melodic material. Ernest Tomlinson recalled an aperçu Coates exchanged with him whilst the two composers were conducting the Bournemouth Symphony Orchestra in November 1956: 'The older I get, the more I realise how important it is to keep things simple.'[18] In these final years, he did try and re-invent his compositional style to a certain degree, as he stated in his autobiography:

> To become old-fashioned or out-of-date I consider to be nothing more nor less than laziness and I think it is important in these days of rapid transit to try and read, see and hear as much as possible of what is happening in this as yet undiscovered world of ours.[19]

In an interview conducted days before his death, he stated: 'I want to write something sweeter and more lyrical.' Compositions dating from these years tend to feature more melodic variation, repetition of themes transposed up or down a third, forth or fifth and a simpler approach to form.

During late 1952, Coates received an invitation from John Barbirolli to write a new work for the gala concert of the Central African Exhibition to be held in Bulawayo, Rhodesia during the summer of 1953. Throughout the 1950s, he received many request for marches and generally only wrote for organizations or people he felt he could not refuse.[20] The Exhibition was to be a grand spectacle to celebrate the centenary of Cecil Rhodes' birth and featured a cornucopia of cultural events including visits by the Hallé Orchestra, John Gielgud and his acting company, Sadler's Wells and a delegation from Covent Garden performing Britten's latest opera, *Gloriana*.[21] It was another high-profile boost to Coates' career and an example of the lofty position that he had attained within the orbit of British music. Forty-six members of the Hallé were performing fourteen concerts during the Festival at the Theatre Royal and Coates' march was to be premiered at the gala concert on 4 July 1953, which coincided with a visit from the Queen Mother and Princess Margaret.[22] Coates decided to write a march for the occasion entitled *The Green Land*, as he explained in an undated programme note about the piece:

[17]   Ibid., p. 585.
[18]   Eric Coates, quoted by Ernest Tomlinson, conversation September 2005.
[19]   Coates (autograph), p. 154.
[20]   *Vintage Light Music* 29, p. 3.
[21]   Jeffrey Richards *Imperialism and Music in England* (Manchester, 2001), p. 208.
[22]   Schedule of the Tour. *GB-Mhallé* 1953 Bulawayo Tour Box.

Written in Eric Coates' straightforward virile style, in the opening section one receives a vivid picture of pioneers striking out into the heart of Rhodesia, their footsteps becoming fainter and fainter as they disappear into the interior. Then comes the second section: a broad hymn-like melody played by the strings, after which we once again hear the steady marching of many people, leading to a repetition of the hymn-tune played by the brass and culminating in a victorious fanfare.[23]

Coates had hoped to travel to Africa for the performance but soon decided against it, leaving it in the capable hands of Sir John. The premiere, with an audience of 3,000 people, went well as Barbirolli informed the composer: 'The March really sounded splendid and had great success. I must say that I thoroughly enjoyed conducting it for you have a real feeling for these things.'[24]

Before the premiere, pressure from the British Government was applied to Coates to change the title of the March because in the view of the Colonial Office, 'green lands' implied jungle, and was not the sort of image that the British Government wanted to promote about a Commonwealth country.[25] As Austin Coates explained to Coates' first biographer:

My father had originally wanted to call it 'The Green Land' but (Sir) Angus Mackintosh, at that time Private Secretary to Olivier Lyttleton (Lord Chandos), Secretary of State for the Colonies, advised against it. In fact, my father, with his memories of South Africa, was right; green means life and cultivation, not jungle. Angus and I became very friendly (and remain so) during Olivier Lyttleton's visit to Hongkong [*sic*] in 1951 … . Thus his ease of access to my father.[26]

Coates amended the title to *Rhodesia,* but the change of name proved to be a curse on the March, as within a few years there was much unrest in Rhodesia and by 1965 Ian Smith's Unilateral Declaration of Independence. With the subsequent renaming of the country to Zimbabwe the title of *Rhodesia* was seen as politically incorrect and performances of the March dried up. Indeed, when *Rhodesia* was first recorded in 1996, it was issued under its original title *The Green Land.*[27]

Despite the hindrance of the title, the March is one of the finest he ever wrote. It is on a larger scale and shares an allegiance with the earlier 'Youth of Britain' March from *The Three Elizabeths* Suite. There is a subtle reuse of the opening introduction in the bridge passage linking the reprise of the B-section to the A-section, 4 bars after figure 18. One can see a debt to Coates' previous marches,

---

[23]   Programme Note. *GB-Lcm* Box M125.

[24]   14/07/1953 John Barbirolli to EC.

[25]   Richards, p. 208.

[26]   17/06/1985 Austin Coates to Geoffrey Self.

[27]   *Seventeen Orchestral Miniatures* (ASV, CDWHL 2107).

but *Rhodesia* feels more Elgarian than the others, as well as showing a hint of Walton.

Given the level of prestige of the premiere of *Rhodesia* it is surprising that Coates never recorded the March. However, in early February 1953, as part of a series of releases by Decca of British music in honour of the Coronation of Elizabeth II, he visited Decca's West Hampstead studios to record his two largest Suites *The Three Elizabeths* and *The Four Centuries* onto LP. The recording quality of these two suites was far superior to their previous recording under the composer in 1944.

Coates' next composition after *Rhodesia* was another March. Athelstan Popkiss, Chief Constable of Nottingham Police wrote to Coates in February 1953 inviting him to write a March for his police band. For a man proud of his Nottinghamshire roots, Coates had produced no music for Nottingham or based on Nottingham folklore. He had been contemplating writing a suite based around Robin Hood in 1935, but when Frederic Curzon wrote his *Robin Hood* Suite, Coates, never one to follow another composer's lead, promptly abandoned the idea.[28] He accepted Popkiss' invitation and had finished the March by May 1953 but was struggling to think of a title. Popkiss suggested *Men of Trent*, which Coates thought a perfect title.[29] As the March was written for a military band, Coates only completed it in short score and sent it to William Duthoit, Chappells' staff arranger for military band and an arranger who had undertaken the vast majority of the arrangements of Coates' orchestral works for military band. Coates had intended to orchestrate the march after Duthoit had completed his work but never got round to it and only arranged a piano solo version. It was left to the conductor Malcolm Nabarro to orchestrate *The Men of Trent* for a 1992 recording, though the absence of an orchestral edition has impeded the popularity of this march.[30] Duthoit completed the orchestration in June and the Band of the Nottingham Police performed it in a broadcast on 2 September. *The Men of Trent* owes something in its structure to the earlier *Over to You* (also first performed by a military band) following a quasi-rondo structure of Introduction–A–B–A–C–C (with countersubject)–A–Coda, with the C-section being the broad melody.

Besides the composition of two marches, 1953 also brought further confirmation of Coates' standing in the world of light music. The BBC were formulating a reading panel for light-music compositions submitted to the BBC and the panel would either reject or accept a composition for broadcasting. Coates was probably the first name on the list. Inviting him to join the panel in November 1953, Clifford wrote:

> We are proposing to institute a reading panel for light music compositions, and we are inviting half a dozen or so people of similar professional status and

---

[28]  18/04/1935 Foster Clark to EC. *GB-Rwac*.

[29]  18/05/1953 Athelstan Popkiss to EC Coates and 19/05/1953 EC to Athelstan Popkiss.

[30]  Various. *Robin Hood Country* (ASV, CDWHL 2069).

integrity to yourself, to meet in groups of three for a maximum of two half days a month. The idea of having seven or eight members is to ensure we can always get three on any occasion. Naturally the names of those accepting would not be disclosed.[31]

Though he was initially hesitant about joining such a panel, Coates nonetheless capitulated and went to several meetings.[32] The Panel eventually included Coates, Montague Phillips, Charles Williams and Frederic Curzon (who worked in the Light Music Department at Boosey & Hawkes). Haydn Wood disliked 'turning other composers' work down' and Montague Phillips resigned early in 1954 because he did not like the idea of censoring music.[33] The panel seems to have been short-lived, lasting until 1955 at the latest, when all records concerning it disappear.

In addition to his work for the BBC, the Corporation were still keen to commission new works and perform Coates' latest compositions. During December 1953, he received a formal invitation from the BBC to compose a new work for the 1954 Light Music Festival being held at the Royal Festival Hall.[34] He had discussed the possibility of writing a work for the Festival after the success of the 1953 celebration.[35] He replied informing the BBC: 'I shall be delighted to accept providing my "muse", which has been a little sluggish of late, wakes up and gives me something worth while writing about. Regarding the nature of the work – I think that something in the nature of a lively overture might meet the case.'[36]

Coates soon extricated himself from the invitation, as by January 1954 he had entered into a partnership with Eric Maschwitz to write a musical that Jack Hylton would present in 1955.[37] The musical was to be entitled *Polly Pryde (Trelawney of the Wells)* based on Pinero's play. It was hoped that this production would be ready by July 1954 (soon deferred until September) and that Patricia Kirkwood would star in it.[38] However, by 24 February Coates was having increased difficulty with his right hand, as a result of writer's cramp (something he had been suffering since

---

[31]   05/11/1953 Hubert Clifford to EC. *GB-Rwac.*

[32]   08/11/1953 EC to Hubert Clifford and 13/11/1953 Hubert Clifford to EC. *GB-Rwac.*

[33]   09/12/1953 Haydn Wood to Hubert Clifford and 13/02/1954 Montague Phillips to Hubert Clifford. *GB-Rwac* Reading Panel.

[34]   14/12/1953 Hubert Clifford to EC. *GB-Rwac.* Montague Phillips, Haydn Wood, Charles Williams and Robert Farnon were also invited to produce works for that year's Festival.

[35]   18/05/1953 Hubert Clifford to EC and 21/05/1953 EC to Hubert Clifford. *GB-Rwac.*

[36]   17/12/1953 EC to Hubert Clifford. *GB-Rwac.*

[37]   19/01/1954 Hubert Clifford to Light Music Office. *GB-Rwac.*

[38]   16/02/1954 Eric Maschwitz to Gery Brooks [Solicitors]. *GB-Lcm* and Eric Maschwitz, *No Chip on my Shoulder* (London, 1957), p. 188.

the late 1940s) and decided that he would have to withdraw from the project.[39] Writing to Maschwitz, Coates stressed that his decision was owing to the fact that the constant pain and strain on himself (whilst orchestrating passages of the production), not to mention all those involved in the production would be too great.[40] This orchestrated material does not survive and one wonders if Coates was giving Maschwitz a false impression that he had written several songs for the production but in reality had not completed anything other than a few sketches. Despite Coates' withdrawal, Maschwitz was eager to pursue the project with another composer, but it never materialized.[41]

Within days of his escape from the ties of *Polly Pryde* Coates returned to the BBC commission for the Light Music Festival. He altered his original idea of an overture to a valse, which he entitled *Sweet Seventeen*.[42] It was an evocation of the halcyon days of his youth when he first met Phyl, who was seventeen. He completed the score at the beginning of April 1954 and dedicated it to 'my beloved Phyl'. One wonders if any of the sketches from *Polly Pryde* were recycled into the Valse. The 1954 Festival was the first to commission new pieces: Haydn Wood wrote his *Gypsy* Suite; Hubert Clifford his *Cowes* Suite; and Farnon his *A la Claire Fontaine*.

*Sweet Seventeen* is the most successful and shortest of Coates' three freestanding concert valses. It has only three themes with a dominance of the first (first heard at figure 3). There is a subtle combination, between figures 10 and 11, of the third subject with a theme derived from the introduction (bar 5 onwards). The Valse features an abundance of broad melodies (figures 3, 8 and 13), as already seen in *Rhodesia* and many sparkling passages of orchestration such as the frequent use of the themes played by the first violin and cello, subtle use of the harp (figure 3) and the valse rhythm given out on three horns and divided violas (figures 4 and 18).

Shortly after the completion of *Sweet Seventeen* in April, the Coates moved permanently away from London to live in their home at Bognor Regis. They had acquired The Holdynge, a large house on the edge of the sea, in March 1953. Given Coates' fragile state of health and the fact that Phyl had not been well since her appendix trouble two years previously, they both thought that a relaxing life away from London would be the key to recovery. This arrangement proved to be too much for Coates who was travelling to London at least one day a week, usually driving the 180 mile round trip himself. In May 1955 they returned to London. The move to Bognor gave him a new lease of compositional life.

The tranquillity of their new home was interrupted a few months later when, in May, Coates received distressing news from the PRS that they had received a letter from novelist and one-time Member of Parliament, Alan Herbert, claiming

---

[39]    24/02/1954 EC to Eric Maschwitz. *GB-Lcm*.

[40]    Ibid.

[41]    Maschwitz, p. 188.

[42]    26/02/1954 Hubert Clifford to R.G. Walford. *GB-Rwac* Eric Coates copyright.

half of the total royalties of *Calling All Workers*.[43] Herbert alleged that he had authored words that were put to the trio melody before the first performance of the March and, as joint author, he was entitled to half the PRS fees.[44] Why Herbert waited until 1954, fourteen years after the composition and publication of the March is unclear. Herbert appears not to have discussed the matter with Coates, whom he knew from their trips abroad with the PRS, as Coates appears to have had no knowledge of Herbert's claims until the PRS forwarded him a copy of Herbert's letter. This claim must have shaken Coates, as between 1951 and 1953 his PRS royalties for the March alone were in the region of £3,500.[45] Nevertheless, he was able to prove that the March was first published on 17 August 1940 and that the vocal form Herbert authored was from a Cochran Revue broadcast in late September and early October 1940. Herbert backed down from the claims but Coates was clearly traumatized by the contretemps. He wrote to H.L. Walter: 'I shall certainly think very hard if any author in the future suggests setting words to any of my music'!![46]

After the worrying news from the PRS, Coates received an invitation for a new march, his eighteenth. The conductor Louis Levy, from Associated British Pictures, invited Coates to write the score for a film entitled *The Dam Busters* directed by Michael Anderson, starring Richard Todd and Michael Redgrave. The film, based on Paul Brickhill's book and Guy Gibson's memoirs, portrayed the development of Barnes Wallis' 'bouncing bomb' and the subsequent bombing raid by 617 Squadron over the Ruhr dams in May 1943.[47] Throughout his career Coates had often received offers to compose film scores; he had written the song 'A Song of the Wild' for Cherry Kearton's adventure film *Wild Life Across the World* in 1923.[48] In 1947, the Press had rumoured that he had turned down a lucrative £10,000 contract to write a film score in America.[49] He may have also been deterred from writing a film score after hearing about the experiences of Arthur Bliss when he was writing his score for *Things to Come*.[50] By the 1950s, many light composers, such as Stanley Black and Phillip Green, were composing film scores instead of concert works. Whatever Coates' reasons, he declined Levy's offer instantly, even

---

[43]   04/05/1954 Alan Herbert to PRS. Copy of letter in *GB-Lcm*.

[44]   Ibid.

[45]   05/05/1954 Broadcasting Department Fees for *Calling All Workers*. *GB-Lprs*.

[46]   19/05/1954 EC to H.L. Walter. *GB-Lprs*.

[47]   Coates greatly enjoyed meeting Barnes Wallis at an RAF Concert at London's Albert Hall on 07/04/1956 where the composer conducted *The Dam Busters* March.

[48]   The front cover of the song featured a photograph from the film. Kearton was a pioneer of wildlife photography and the Coates were frequent visitors at the Kearton's residence where Coates enjoyed hearing Kearton's stories. (Coates (autograph), p. 287.)

[49]   24/12/1947 *Sketch*. Whether the rumour was true remains a matter for conjecture.

[50]   Ian Lace, 'Foreword' in Eric Coates, *Suite in Four Movements* (London, 1986), p. vi.

though he enjoyed reading the script.[51] By 1954, he had neither the inclination nor the patience for the demanding and tiring work for films.

Not easily deterred, Levy enlisted the services of Teddy Holmes of Chappells, and both of them pressurized Coates to write the music. Levy even stressed the national importance of the film, but still Coates declined. They changed their approach and Levy recommended that Holmes approach the composer with the suggestion that he write a concert march that could be incorporated in the film score. However, Coates had beaten them to it, as Austin Coates recalled:

> Teddy rang the composer and explained it. There was a pause at the other end and then to Teddy's astonishment the composer said 'I think I finished it yesterday.' And he had, knowing nothing whatever about the film being made, he had, in a very rare moment, written a concert march without any pressure for him to do so, except that he felt like writing it. He had completed the score literally the day before, all it now needed was a title and at that moment, over the telephone, it   .
> got one, *The Dam Busters*.[52]

*The Dam Busters* March was completed on 14 June 1954 (while filming was still taking place at Elstree Studios) and Coates then passed the manuscript over to Leighton Lucas who was to write the film score. Lucas was no stranger to arranging Coates' music, as, during the 1920s, he had arranged *The Selfish Giant* and *The Three Bears* for Jack Hylton's Band. Coates' March, one of his finest and is cast in his standard march formula. The B-section (figures 3–6 and 10–13 inclusive) shows an allegiance to that of *Rhodesia*, but also bears a passing, though unintentional, resemblance to Roger Quilter's short choral piece, *Freedom*, written over ten years previously.[53] Lucas used very little of Coates' March in his score, indeed the A-section (figures 1–2 and 7–9 inclusive) are not used at all. Instead, Lucas frequently uses the B-section, sometimes in Coates' own orchestration (cf. the opening titles) and sometimes his own (cf. the closing credits). He also frequently uses a motif derived from the B-section in his own material.

Coates was overjoyed with his associations with film, and after seeing some of the rushes in September 1954 wrote to Associated British Pictures informing them:

> There is no doubt that 'THE DAM BUSTERS' is going to be a magnificent film, even from the excerpts we saw the other day it is quite obvious that it is going to make history. The whole production is so <u>direct,</u> so <u>sincere,</u> so <u>simple,</u>

---

[51]   Ibid.

[52]   Austin Coates, programme 4.

[53]   For a more detailed comparison see Valerie Langfield, *Roger Quilter* (Woodbridge, 2002), pp. 195–6.

and in this lies its greatness. I am proud to be associated with you all in this fine achievement.[54]

There was a long gap, nearly a year, in between the completion of the film and the two royal premieres on 16 and 17 May 1955. *The Dam Busters* did not go on general release until September that year. During this time Associated British Pictures worked hard on the publicity, which reached fever pitch by the time of the film's general release.[55] The film attracted rave reviews in the British Press and went on to be Britain's largest box-office success of 1955 (despite the fact it had only been on general release for four months).[56] Though a total flop in America, the film has become one of the most famous of all British war films aided, to some degree, by Coates' March.

Coates' joy with the film was tarnished at the close of 1955. Austin, then living in Hong Kong, demonstrated his usual lavish hospitality by arranging for a group of friends (mainly important government officials) to travel to a local cinema to see the overseas cut of the film. Austin was embarrassed to find that his father's name was omitted from the film's credits (though the music was credited to Lucas) and he cabled his father and Chappells to draw their attention to the matter. His father wrote to film's producer, Robert Clark, to complain: 'you do realise that ... THE DAM BUSTERS MARCH has actually been creditted [*sic*] to another composer'![57] The oversight was partially blamed on the overseas distributors wanting to shorten the film and an employee of Associated British Pictures ticking the wrong box on the paperwork, thereby enabling Coates' name to be removed from the credits.[58] This oversight was rectified in all subsequent overseas editions of the film.

Not only had the film been attracting much press attention since the start of filming in the spring of 1954, but so to had Coates' March. It was published in 1954 and began to gain popularity with the public in late 1954 after performances by Coates with the BBC Midland Light Orchestra on 26 November (probably the March's first public performance) and a subsequent outing on television. To coincide with the film's premiere Sidney Torch recorded Coates' March alongside *Sweet Seventeen* for Parlophone to be released at the same time.[59] Coates also recorded the March himself in 1955. After the film's release, the March went into the 'hit parade' where it remained for some considerable time. The recording by the Central Band of the Royal Air Force enjoyed sales in excess of 200,000 copies.[60] *The Dam Busters* March also received an Ivor Novello Award (administered by

54    12/09/1954 EC to Leslie Frewin.
55    John Ramsden, *The Dam Busters* (London, 2003), pp. 96 and 102.
56    Ibid., p. 112.
57    05/12/1955 EC to Robert Clark.
58    04/11/1955 Robert Clark to EC.
59    (Parlophone, R4084).
60    (HMV, B10877). Peter Martland, *Since Records Began* (London, 1997), p. 230.

the Songwriter's Guild, a society of which Coates had been a founder member) for the best piece of light-orchestral music of 1955. Aged 68, he had written his most popular and enduring success. Whilst composers such as Albert Ketèlbey, Haydn Wood and Robert Farnon all wrote highly popular works, none achieved this level of popularity and Coates was indeed fortunate that this was not his only major success, but the pinnacle of his achievements.

Over the years Coates' March had begun to be used for a variety of different purposes and it was here it began to acquire a patriotic flavour that it was never composed to have; it started out as just another 'ordinary' march. Like 'Knightsbridge' and *Calling All Workers*, *The Dam Busters* had a certain something that totally captivated the British public. Being in the 'pomp and circumstance' tradition, it has become very much part of the core of national works that are known to practically all.

Around the time of the premiere of *The Dam Busters*, Coates made his final visit to America. The trip was brokered through the auspices of an American friend, the playwright Patrick Mahoney, who tried to arrange a meeting with Cole Porter. It was to be a low-key affair with a broadcast for the NBC and interviews with several New York newspapers. Coates was keen to stress that he wished to keep the tour relaxed with very few social engagements so as not to put too much strain on his health.[61] In addition to the tour, Mahoney was trying to persuade Coates to provide incidental music for Maeterlinck's play *The Blue Bird*.[62] Initially the score was to be based on arrangements of his orchestral compositions and songs with several new items (along the lines of a short musical entitled 'Knightsbridge' staged by an American university arranged by William Pitt).[63] Coates was not keen to undertake any work on the project and recommended that Mahoney should adapt Norman O'Neil's score. Mahoney was eager to entice Coates into the project and even informed one American newspaper that Coates was writing several songs for the production, earning himself a rebuke from Coates.[64] The proposal was kept alive until September that year, but Coates was forced to withdraw due to an increasingly hectic schedule and an invitation for a new composition, one that he wanted to undertake.[65]

Some months later, Coates was approached to write a march as a signature for Associated Television (ATV). ATV was part of the newly formed Independent Television Authority and was initially responsible for broadcasting weekday programmes for London and weekend programmes for the Midland regions. Given the success his *Television March* for the BBC, and the large influx of former BBC staff to the commercial television companies, it was perhaps inevitable that he

---

[61]   23/03/1955 EC to Patrick Mahoney. *GB-Lcm*.

[62]   31/03/1955 EC to Patrick Mahoney. *GB-Lcm*.

[63]   08/11/1955 EC to William Pitt. *GB-Lcm*. Pitt was eager to produce a full scale musical arranged from Coates' published music.

[64]   26/09/1955 EC to Patrick Mahoney. *GB-Lcm*.

[65]   Ibid.

would be asked to provide an example for ATV. The march had the inspired title of *Sound and Vision*, a title later used by Briggs for the fourth volume of his history of the BBC.[66] *Sound and Vision* is every bit as enjoyable as the earlier *Television March* and has two memorable themes.

Upon completion of *Sound and Vision* in August–September 1955 Coates recorded the March alongside the justly celebrated *Dam Busters* for Pye, a label more known for its popular music recordings. These were only released on 78rpm discs (a march on each side).[67] The recording of *The Dam Busters* (Coates' only recording of this *marche célèbre*) is the most truncated of his career. He eschews the first statement of the famous B-section melody (figures 3–5), which is initially presented disguised by its dashing countersubject. The recapitulation of the A-section is halved with a cut from the upbeat of figure 7 to the upbeat of figure 8. The March then plays to the coda and instead of the eight-bar modulatory sequence at figure 14 (one of the most thrilling he wrote) is inexplicably expunged, and the March ends rather lamely with held C major chords and the timpani. For this recording there were still time constraints, since it was recorded onto a 78rpm record, but surely Coates was being overly cautious and pruning the work too far.

For the remainder of 1955, there was little time for composition; he was kept rather busy for a man who was approaching 70 years of age, as he outlined to Patrick Mahony:

> My new Commercial TV March was launched last week (I said a few words about it on TV last Saturday); I go up to Birmingham in a few days' time to conduct the City of Birmingham Symphony Orchestra in a concert of my works,[68] and then off to Copenhagen to conduct a concert for the State Radio; after which there are other concerts at Bournemouth and Plymouth, etc. I have been invited by the BBC to write a new work for production at the Royal Festival Hall in the New Year, also a Test Piece for next year's Brass Band Festival but I find it almost impossible to get down to serious writing with all this travelling and conducting.[69]

Coates never got round to writing a brass band test piece. Earlier in 1955, he had adjudicated and conducted a broadcast at a brass band festival in Hanley (including *The Three Bears* Phantasy). He had always steered clear of brass bands and very little of his music was arranged for the medium during his lifetime.

The most important engagement of 1955 was a trip to Copenhagen at the beginning of October that had been arranged with the help of Frank Wade of the BBC's Light Music Department. Wade was fast becoming a useful ally within

---

[66]   Asa Briggs *Sound and Vision* (Oxford, 1979).

[67]   EMI maintained production of 78rpm records until 1961. (Timothy Day *A Century of Recorded Music* (New Haven, 2000), p. 21.)

[68]   01/10/1955.

[69]   26/09/1955 EC to Patrick Mahony. *GB-Lcm*.

the BBC. The trip involved a 75-minute broadcast of Coates' music on 7 October with the Statsradiofonien Symphony Orchestra. He was given a free hand over the programme but the Danish officials requested the *Saxo-Rhapsody*.[70]

The BBC were enthusiastic still to entice Coates to write new music, even in the era of dodecaphony and total serialism. Indeed, they were the driving force behind most of his compositions of the 1950s. Coates received an invitation from the BBC to provide incidental music for a BBC play by Roy Plomley (with lyrics by Henrik Ege) based on *Cinderella*. Wade informed Coates: 'there will be extra music needed for the lyrics. Please, my dear Eric, will you write it for us and confer one further benefit for mankind?'[71] Coates refused and the BBC invited Ernest Tomlinson to provide music for *The Story of Cinderella* broadcast on Christmas Eve. As a proviso of the commission, Tomlinson had to include material from Coates' Phantasy into the score, but in the end, Tomlinson only used the 'Cinderella motif' and a theme from one of the valse passages.[72] This commission marked the start of Tomlinson's career as a freelance composer. For the production Tomlinson wrote a short serenade, which was published after the broadcasts as *Little Serenade* (later to become his most well-known piece) and he subsequently extracted *Fairy Coach* and *Cinderella Waltz* from the score for publication; these pieces became popular in their own right. Coates was impressed by Tomlinson's score and when plans were mooted for a film to be entitled *Eric Coates in London*, Coates was keen for Tomlinson to write the score. Alas the project never materialized due to Coates' death in 1957.[73]

Even though the 1950s marked the rebirth of Coates' compositional prowess, he still had the same underlying doubts from the 1940s seen in his abandonment of *Polly Pryde* and his refusal to undertake the composition of a score for *The Story of Cinderella*. Nevertheless, he undertook a gruelling schedule of engagements that left him little time for composition. He was to continue in a similar vein for the final two years of his life.

---

[70]   26/08/1955 Frank Wade to EC. *GB-Rwac*.
[71]   08/10/1955 Frank Wade to EC. *GB-Rwac*.
[72]   25/10/1955 Light Music Policy Committee Minutes. *GB-Rwac* Light Music.
[73]   Conversation with Ernest Tomlinson, September 2005.

# Chapter 12
# Envoi and Legacy, 1956–1957

Given the development of Coates' career since the composition of *The Dam Busters* March, it was inevitable that he was kept busy with the fame garnered from it. During the final two years of his life he never stopped composing, though he completed little, and kept himself busy with small guest conducting roles.

Throughout 1956, Coates undertook a number of conducting engagements with Charles Groves and the Bournemouth Symphony Orchestra. During the 1950s, he had joined the Management Committee for the Western Orchestra Limited, the parent company of the ensemble; he even wrote a short article for the *Winter Gardens Magazine* reminiscing about Henry Wood's tuning machine.[1] Coates had had a long involvement with the orchestra dating back to Dan Godfrey's tenure. He clearly enjoyed his links with the ensemble, journeying to Plymouth in February 1956 for a concert with the Orchestra. During the 1950s Coates maintained regular conducting visits with the finest professional orchestras, such as the Liverpool Philharmonic (as it then was), the City of Birmingham Symphony and the Hallé.

The BBC were still the major outlet for his orchestral music and in February 1956, the BBC's Light Music Department tried to interest Coates in writing a musical and he was keen to start work as soon as possible.[2] Nothing of the project materialized during 1956 and the following year the BBC tried to make the venture more concrete, suggesting that he join forces with R.C. Sherriff.[3] Coates was happy with the choice of librettist, but was in the throes of problems with cataracts and deferred the project until he felt well enough.[4] Unfortunately, he died before he could commence work. He never did succeed in his life ambition to write a musical despite plenty of offers from differing sources and collaborators. Henry Wood, writing in his autobiography in 1938, stated: 'It is a pity that Coates did not discover some librettist such as Sullivan found in Gilbert, for I am sure he might ... have produced excellent English light operas and operettas.[5]

Throughout the 1950s, the BBC Light Music Festivals had become an important outlet for Coates' music. Each year, since 1953, he had conducted at the Festival and remained grateful for the level of prestige it afforded him, being

---

[1]    April 1955 *Winter Gardens Magazine*.

[2]    14/02/1956 Light Music Policy Committee Minutes. *GB-Rwac* Light Music.

[3]    05/02/1957 Light Music Policy Committee Minutes. *GB-Rwac* Light Music. They also tried to interest Ernest Tomlinson to join forces with Eric Maschwitz, but this project also failed to materialize.

[4]    12/02/1957 Light Music Policy Committee Minutes. *GB-Rwac* Light Music.

[5]    Henry Wood, *My Life of Music* (London, 1938), p. 256.

held in the Royal Festival Hall and broadcast live on the Light Programme. The Festivals also acquainted him with the younger figures of light music such as Ronald Binge, Ernest Tomlinson and Sidney Torch. Besides recording a trailer to advertise the 1956 Festival, Coates had provisionally agreed to perform *The Three Elizabeths* Suite there.[6] However, the BBC invited him to write a new piece for the 1956 Festival. They also informed him that Princess Margaret might well be in attendance for the final concert of the Festival.[7] The Princess had been much in the news during late 1955 having had to forsake her intended husband, the divorced Group Captain Peter Townsend. There was great public sympathy for her plight. He tried to capture this in his Intermezzo, which he was keen to stress was a 'serious work' Coates conducted the work's premiere on 7 July along with a performance of *The Dam Busters*, which, as usual, was well-received.

*Impression of a Princess*, Coates' penultimate orchestral work, is cast very much in the mould of all entr'actes, in ternary form, but is essentially monothematic; the B-section (figures 3–8) being derived entirely from the A-section and presented in a variety of keys and tempi. There is a striking similarity between *The Unknown Singer* and the *Impression of a Princess*, as both employ a saxophone in a semi-soloist role (though the earlier work does so only in the B-section) something that Coates seldom resorted to in the 1920s and 1930s.

In the main theme of *Impression of a Princess* much is made of motif x, and the opening three descending notes (Example 12.1). Also inherent in the theme is the quasi-inversion of x, as x', utilizing the rhythm of x at bars 20–21.

Example 12.1    *Impression of a Princess*, bars 11–16. © 1954 Chappell Music
                Ltd, London, W6 8BS. Reproduced by permission of Faber
                Music Ltd. All Rights Reserved

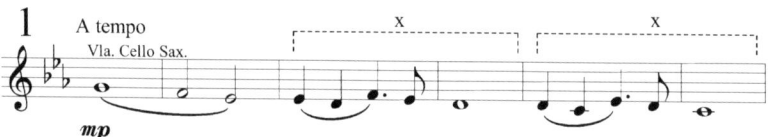

Much is gained through the techniques of 'self-developing melody' and simple variation of the theme. The Intermezzo is an economical construction with all interest being derived from variations of the melody, through change of key and gradual increase of the tempo in the B-section.

Coates marked his seventieth birthday with an appearance at the Proms to conduct the *Four Centuries* Suite on 18 August. He was worried about presenting this difficult work at the Proms (its level of difficulty was one of the previous stumbling blocks when he tried, in vain, to have the work included in the 1943

---

[6]    13/04/1956 BBC Contract and 25/05/1956 Norman Carrell to EC. *GB-Rwac.*
[7]    11/05/1956 *Daily Telegraph.*

season)[8] and he managed to persuade the BBC and Malcolm Sargent (who was to conduct the rest of the concert) to allot him 90 minutes of rehearsal time rather than the hour he had been originally offered.[9]

The concert with the BBC Symphony Orchestra was to be broadcast on the BBC Light Programme and the *Four Centuries* was to open the second half. On the night, Sargent switched the running order so he opened with the 'Theme and Variations' from Tchaikovsky's Third Orchestral Suite. This was an offhand trick by Sargent as both works presented a kaleidoscope of orchestral colour and were difficult and tiring for the orchestra. The switch ensured that Sargent had a fresher, more responsive orchestra. While the performance of *Four Centuries* was far from error-free, it did not, as Austin Coates later recalled, almost collapse in the finale.[10] There was not any outcry in the press, along the lines of the notorious premiere of Tippett's Second Symphony under Adrian Boult in 1958, which, in a live broadcast, broke down several pages into the first movement. Nevertheless, the Suite was well-received by the audience and its reception resulted in an encore of 'Rhythm', and after that:

> Deafening uproar. And again, it went on unabated while my father took two calls. For an awful moment I thought he might have to do it a third time. But he had a wonderful way with an audience. He made a very simple gesture, which without need for a word, said, "Now, I'm going home. So must you." They cheered him till the last instant they could see him.[11]

This was the last occasion that Coates' music features at the Proms until 1989.

During August, various events marked Coates' seventieth birthday. He celebrated the actual day of his birthday quietly with a small party for friends. There was little fuss from the media or the BBC.[12] Columbia released an LP of his music played by the LSO and conducted by Charles Mackerras.[13] The major public celebration was at a broadcast concert from the Albert Hall in Nottingham. The broadcast concert was first discussed in February 1956 and the concert date was set for 26 September, a month after his actual birthday, when it would be broadcast live on the BBC Midland Home Service. This was very much an event to celebrate his Nottinghamshire roots. He only conducted three pieces (for a number of years he found it too much of a strain to conduct full-length concerts).[14] The Albert

---

[8]    01/02/1943 Kenneth Wright to Arthur Bliss. *GB-Rwac*.

[9]    05/06/1956 EC to Miss Wood and 08/06/1956 Miss Wood to EC. *GB-Rwac*.

[10]    Austin Coates quoted in Ian Lace, 'Foreword', in Eric Coates, *Suite in Four Movements* (London, 1986), p. v. Several people who were at the concert have confirmed that it was an adequate performance. BBC Transcription Service also recorded the concert.

[11]    Austin Coates quoted in Lace, p. v.

[12]    18/08/1956 *Newcastle Journal*.

[13]    (Columbia, 33S1092).

[14]    18/08/1956 *Newcastle Journal*.

Hall was full to capacity and when this point was raised with the composer, he nonchalantly replied: 'Yes, when I go to Nottingham I do draw quite a crowd.'[15] He thoroughly enjoyed the evening and wrote to the Head of Midland Region Music, John Lowe:

> we all seemed to become cluttered-up with people, some of whom I had not seen for fifty years; one man in particular claimed to have travelled up and down in the train with me from Hucknall to Nottingham when I used to go into Nottingham for my music lessons <u>fifty-eight</u> years ago! Wasn't it dreadful?[16]

Upon his return from Nottingham, he succumbed to a heavy cold, which debilitated him for several weeks. He also felt lethargic about composition, but during the final months of 1956 he received two requests to write marches. The first came from the independent television regional company, Television Wales and the West (TWW) to provide a march to open their broadcasts. TWW had been established in the autumn of 1956 and would finally begin broadcasting in January 1958. TWW covered South Wales and the west of England, hence Coates' title. After his previous marches for the BBC, Rediffusion and ATV, Coates was readily associated with writing marches for television companies.[17] Like *Sound and Vision*, one wonders if the invitation to compose the work came from Jack Hylton, who owned a stake in TWW.[18] Whether Coates intended to compose a new march for TWW is unclear, but, in fact, he re-titled the earlier *Seven Seas* as *South Wales and the West* and presented it to them. He also re-orchestrated the March, bringing it into line with his standard march orchestration by increasing the woodwind, doubling the horns to four, using three trumpets for triadic fanfares and including a part for tuba (an instrument that, since *Holborn*, had become *de rigueur* in his marches and was useful for sustaining low pedal notes). Alas, he never made a final ink version of the orchestration, instead leaving it in a pencil score, presumably intending to revise his thoughts before performing the march. Chappells issued a piano solo edition of the March, which was merely the piano version of *Seven Seas* with the new title. They did not produce any new orchestral material, because orchestras used the performing material of *Seven Seas*.

Coates received an invitation from Warwick Films to provide a march for use in a film they were producing entitled *High Flight*. The film was directed by John Gilling and starred Ray Milland. It was a film concerned with the training of officer cadets at RAF Cranwell. The project was similar to *The Dam Busters*, with Coates writing a march that Douglas Gamley and Kenneth Jones, the joint composers of the film score, would incorporate into the score. It would seem likely that, after

---

[15]   Eric Coates quoted in Lace, p. vi.

[16]   10/10/1956 EC to John Lowe. *GB-Rwac*.

[17]   It was not all a Coates monopoly. Richard Addinsell wrote his *Southern Rhapsody* for Southern Television who also began broadcasting in 1958.

[18]   Bernard Sendall, *Origin and Foundations* (London, 1982), pp. 210–11.

the success of *The Dam Busters*, he must have been inundated with offers to write film music but the subject of *High Flight* must have appealed to him, as it was the only offer he accepted. There was little chance that the film would be a second *Dam Busters*, and in fact it was universally panned and has been almost totally forgotten; a sad end for Coates' final composition.

Whilst the film was a failure, the March certainly is not. Coates finished the ink score on 2 January 1957, but *High Flight* had to wait until the BBC Light Music Festival in July before it received its official premiere. The A-section (figure 2) makes repeated use of sequences using two ideas, reminiscent of *Salute the Soldier*. It also uses a descending scale figure as a countermelody scored for clarinet and horn, as used in *Sound and Vision*. The B-section (figure 9) has a broad sweeping melody, though contained within an octave, and draws on *Rhodesia* and *The Dam Busters*. Like *Calling All Workers*, when the B-section returns at figure 17, the accompaniment consists of repeated homophonic triplet quavers and the theme, through the use of triplet rhythms rather than dotted, has been has been adapted so as not to clash rhythmically. Intriguingly, it is not the introduction that is recycled to make the coda, but a short modulatory bridge passage (figure 8) that is extended. With Coates' last batch of compositions there is no feeling that he was losing his creative powers. Each piece written from 1952 onwards lives up to the high standards and construction of those of the 1930s.

Shortly after *High Flight* had received its premiere, Coates recorded the March for HMV. Coates' forays into the recording studio were diminishing during the 1950s, primarily because he was not composing at the rate of the 1930s, coupled with the fact that he had recorded the majority of his orchestral canon. Nevertheless, Coates returned to Abbey Road Studios on 16 August 1957 to record three of his latest compositions as well as the *Wood Nymphs* valsette. The recordings were made in stereo but only issued in mono until the re-release of several of the pieces in the CD era.[19] At the time, as was their wont, HMV released the recordings in 78rpm as well as in 45rpm format. As with the previous recordings for Pye each of the three latest compositions received important cuts, again not solely for reasons of space. *High Flight* began at the upbeat to figure 2 and a cut from figure 12 to 15; *Impression of a Princess* began at figure 1 and featured a small cut from figure 10 to 11; *South Wales and the West* started on the upbeat to figure 1 and cut from the upbeat of figure 5 to the upbeat of figure 6. On the 45rpm release, *Wood Nymphs* had its introduction pruned, starting at letter A. However, when the recording was re-released on CD in 1997, that particular cut was reinstated.[20] The proofs of these recordings arrived at Coates' London flat two weeks after the composer's death.

One of the major developments for Coates during 1957 was the formation of the Light Music Society in March, the brainchild of the composer Harry Dexter. Given his reputation, Coates was naturally the first choice for President of the Society, a post that he readily accepted, as he felt: 'that its work will be of benefit

---

[19]   *British Light Music* (EMI, CDM 5665372).
[20]   Ibid.

to music lovers, composers and performers, both professional and amateur'.[21] Spurred on by the success of the BBC's recent Light Music Festivals, he wrote in his foreword to the Society's first Newsletter: 'The inauguration of the Society is undoubtedly a landmark in the history of Light Music and should do much to put this form of musical expression in a place it deserves … . Let us hope the Light Music Society will prove to be an inspiration to composers and, as a result, that the world may be further enriched by their melodies'.[22] His involvement with the Society was, alas, short-lived because of his death, but he was generous in his dealings with the Society, as it was preserving a cause that was close to his heart and one for which he had been fighting since the 1920s.

Even though he was undertaking new roles, Coates' health was giving him cause for concern. During the later months of 1957, he was suffering from cataracts in his eyes. Austin Coates recalled that since late 1956 his father had been complaining of crystals in front of his eyes.[23] This inability to see properly dampened Coates' zest for composition and he never completed any more compositions after *High Flight*, though he was still keen to carry on writing. During October, he was obliged to take life easier in Sussex, as he informed the PRS: 'It's just "one of those things" and there is nothing much one can do about it – it may mean an operation one of these days.'[24] Just over a week later, he was conducting the BBC Concert Orchestra in Norwich, but was struggling to see clearly and had to be assisted in reaching the concert platform, though he was in fine form while conducting the orchestra.[25]

Despite his eyes, he was well enough to take part in the annual St Cecilia's Day Concert at the Royal Festival Hall conducting with Arthur Bliss and Malcolm Arnold. Two days later, alongside Thomas Armstrong and Eileen Joyce, he played the dulcet in the premiere of Arnold's Toy Symphony at the St Cecilia's Day dinner at the Savoy Hotel.[26] This was not the first time he had taken part in such a concert, having performed a toy instrument in a performance of Haydn's Toy Symphony during the celebrations of the 1954 St Cecilia's Day festivities.

Shortly after these celebrations the Coates left London for Sussex (they had recently downsized from their large house on Aldwick Avenue to a smaller house on a neighbouring street). Coates felt unwell on the journey down to Bognor Regis and took the unprecedented step of asking Phyl to drive the rest of the way (he usually drove).[27] Six days later, on 17 December, he suffered a massive stroke and was taken to the Royal West Sussex Hospital, Chichester but never regained consciousness. He died from cerebral thrombosis in the early hours of

[21]   20/04/1957 *The Times*.
[22]   September 1957 *Light Music Society Newsletter*, p. 7.
[23]   Austin Coates in Lace, p. vi.
[24]   11/10/1957 EC to H.L. Water. *GB-Lprs*.
[25]   Austin Coates in Lace, p. vi.
[26]   Anthony Meredith & Paul Harris, *Malcolm Arnold* (London, 2004), p. 158n.
[27]   Lace, p. vii.

21 December 1957 with Phyl by his side.[28] Writing to Christopher Hassall, Phyl described her husband's final days:

> I can only rejoice that dear Eric was released as he would have been paralysed had he lived, and I don't think he could have borne it – he loved life and health … . He never regained consciousness completely, and died gently in his sleep as I held his hand – it was such a wonderful way to go – gentle, as he always was.[29]

His funeral was held on Christmas Eve and Austin was absent (he had become a Special Magistrate in Hong Kong). The BBC Singers under Leslie Woodgate provided musical accompaniment and his ashes were interred at Golders Green Crematorium.[30]

Coates' estate was valued at £53,124-0-3 (£37,458, net), leaving his part-share in their Bognor Regis cottage to Phyl (they rented their London homes) demonstrating that his career as a light-music composer had proved profitable as well as rewarding.[31] As a mark of respect, the BBC broadcast a tribute programme a few weeks after his death, including contributions from Arthur Bliss (Master of the Queen's Musick), Basil Cameron, Sidney Torch and Stanford Robinson.[32] Robinson had also recently recorded a LP of Coates' music, including the first recording of *The Enchanted Garden*, with the Pro Arte Orchestra for Pye, which was released in the early months of 1958 entitled *Tribute to Eric Coates*.[33] In 1960, after initial impetus from Frank Wade (now Head of Light Music at the BBC), Phyl Coates, with financial help from Chappells, established an Eric Coates Composition prize at his *alma mater*, the RAM, for the composition of a piece of light music, which is still awarded.[34]

After her husband's death, Phyl went on to have a long life, dying at the age of 88 in 1982, though unfortunately, her later years were plagued by dementia and she lived with her sister Joan before transferring to a nursing home. Austin continued in the service of the Colonial Office until 1962 when he decided to concentrate on his career as an author, living for a number of years in Hong Kong. Many of his books reflected his love of the East and include a novel set in Macao, *City of Broken Promises*. He retired to Colares, near Sintra in Portugal, where he

---

[28]   Eric Coates' Death Certificate.

[29]   01/01/1958 Phyllis Coates to Christopher Hassall. *GB-Cu* Add.8905/10/C/72.

[30]   As too were Phyl's and Austin's in later years.

[31]   07/03/58 *The Times*. Haydn Wood (died 1959) left £76,770-13-10, Albert Ketèlbey (died 1959), left £28,492-8-7, Billy Mayerl (died 1959) left £20,329-10-8 and Charles Williams (died 1978) left £78,131, all gross. (Values taken from their respective *Dictionary of National Biography* entries.)

[32]   Broadcast on 21/01/1958 on the Light Programme.

[33]   *Tribute to Eric Coates*, (Pye, CML33004).

[34]   The first award was made to Richard Stoker in 1961.

devoted a good deal of his time and money to the legacy of his father's music until his death in 1997.

The death of Eric Coates can be seen as a watershed moment in the history of British light music. Not only had the genre lost its greatest luminary figure, but within the next few years certain cultural changes would begin to render the field archaic and obsolete. The arrival of 'pop music' and rock 'n' roll captured the attentions of the younger generation. Furthermore, the guitars and drums of the pop groups made the orchestra, the standard performance vehicle of light music, seem out of touch and *passé*. With the onset of the 1960s, the BBC's change in attitudes towards light music (seen during William Glock's tenure as Director of Music) and the restructuring of the Home Service, Light and Third Programmes to form Radios 1, 2, 3 and 4 left light music without a broadcasting home. By the 1970s, light music was fast disappearing from broadcasting schedules as well as the concert halls.

Nevertheless, Coates' music still received occasional performances and works such as *The Dam Busters*, *Calling All Workers* and *By the Sleepy Lagoon* kept his name alive whereas those of many of his light-music contemporaries disappeared almost without trace. Coates' centenary year, 1986, saw: an exhibition of Coates memorabilia at Hucknall; concerts in Hucknall and Nottingham (the latter featuring Charles Groves and the BBC Concert Orchestra and subsequently broadcast on Radio 3);[35] Coates (along with Edward German) as 'Composer of the Week' on BBC Radio 3;[36] a four-part appreciation of his life by his son, Austin; a re-issue of his autobiography brought up to date with a foreword and the publication of a biography by Geoffrey Self.

Since then, a resurgence of interest, fuelled by the Light Music Society and the Robert Farnon Society, has led to a great change of fortunes for Coates and light music. Coates has also fared well in the recording studios with many CDs being released in recent years. The composer's own gramophone performances have also fared well on CD and almost all his records (except those made 'acoustically') have been, or are currently, available on disc. These discs (there are more CDs devoted to Coates than any other light music figure) have strengthened his reputation above other figures and given his music a wide audience. The fiftieth anniversary of Coates' death in 2007 brought another outing as 'Composer of the Week' on BBC Radio 3, this time as the sole featured composer. The formation of the Eric Coates Society in Hucknall the following year has done a great deal to promote Coates in his native county.

It is often said that Coates was the 'uncrowned king of British light music'. This is a title that he owed to a variety of factors, most notably because of the quality and delightfulness of his music. In the musical construction of his oeuvre, from his early orchestral songs to the final compositions there is a mastery of melody

---

[35]   27/08/1986. The day also saw the centenary of composer/viola–player Rebecca Clark who also had her own tribute programme.

[36]   25–29/08/1986.

and orchestration that abounds in almost every page. Whilst he was not prolific, generally producing several orchestral pieces each year, one feels that he did not finish and publish a piece until he was completely satisfied. There are very few pieces in his output which do not live up to these high standards. Coates had a gift of giving the public exactly what they desired in orchestral music and infrequently outstayed his welcome. His adoption of the style of the dance band or 'syncopated idiom' as he often termed it, gave his scores a contemporary and popular edge that appealed to both the public and the press, who occasionally styled him 'the Peter-Pan of music'. In addition, he had the good fortune to have composed numerous pieces that achieved cult status through their frequent repetition as signature tunes as well as works such as *The Dam Busters* March that have captured the public's imagination. All these abilities placed him above the other light-music composers.

Coates was a composer with a great sense of commercial acumen. While he obviously possessed great skill as a composer, the reason his music became so successful came from the way in which he exploited it through the latest media. Parallel to his arrival at 'compositional maturity' were both the foundation of the BBC and the wholesale adoption of the techniques of electrical recording. He was lucky to have a symbiotic relationship with the BBC, who often broadcast his music over their networks, thus reaching a wide cross-section of society. Not only did the BBC continually invite Coates to compose new works for them, they adopted several of his pieces as signature tunes, which further raised his profile amongst the public. His relationships with the press were unique for a composer, as he had risen to the ranks of a minor celebrity, and as such often featured in a host of articles and advertisements in the popular press, even if several were of dubious literary and factual content. Of further assistance to his reputation was the foundation of the PRS in 1914, roughly at the same time as he was starting to come to prominence as a composer. The accrued royalties from the multifarious ensembles across England and abroad who performed his music enabled him to devote his time to writing music rather than having to earn a living performing or teaching, as was the case for a number of composers. Coates built up a healthy relationship with these orchestras, which resulted in many invitations to conduct and offers to write new works for them; the highlight for him was the music festival where he would appear on the same platform as many of the most renowned members of the musical profession. These orchestras were invaluable, as they would perform his music to people who might not have come across it before.

All these disparate elements combined to create a composer who had a supremacy over his light-music colleagues, a supremacy that lasts to this day, perhaps because he was content to remain solely a composer of *light* music, a genre that he excelled in and in which he knew his own limitations. It is only with the current resurgence of interest in light music that Eric Coates can be seen more within the context, and in the achievements, of others in that field. Today, Coates is taking his rightful, and well-deserved, position within the field of the major twentieth-century British composers.

# Appendix 1: Work List

This appendix contains:

- Orchestral Works
- Chamber Works
- Instrumental Works
- Choral Works
- Songs
- Operetta Material
- Gramophone Recordings
- Written Works

## Abbreviations

| | |
|---|---|
| Arr | Published arrangement(s) |
| Aut | Location of autograph full score |
| BB | Brass band |
| Cat | Catalogue number |
| Comp | Date of the completion of score where known |
| DB | Dance Band |
| Ded | Dedicated |
| Fp | First performance. Italics denote the earliest traced performance |
| Lab | Label |
| Loc | Location of recording |
| Mat | Matrix |
| MB | Military band |
| Orch | Orchestra |
| Pno | Piano |
| Pub | Year of publication. All works are published by Chappells unless otherwise stated |
| Rec | Date of recording |
| Scr | Scoring |
| WB | Wind band |
| † | Published full score (date of publication) |
| ‡ | Orchestrated by Coates |
| * | Autograph score not in Coates' hand |
| # | Published letter written to a newspaper and co-signed with other composers |

The scoring is given as the following: Flute, Oboe, Clarinet, Bassoon/French Horn, Trumpet, Trombone, Tuba/Percussion/Harp/Strings. Additional instruments are slotted in where applicable.

## Orchestral Works

### Extended Single-movement Works

*Ballad* for String Orchestra Op 2 (Unpublished); comp 23/10/1904; fp November–December 1904, Unknown Orchestra conducted by Arthur Richards, Albert Hall Nottingham; scr String orchestra; aut *GB-Lcm*.

*The Selfish Giant* Phantasy (Boosey); comp September 1925; fp Eastbourne Festival, 15/11/1925, Eastbourne Municipal Orchestra conducted by the composer; scr 2.Piccolo.222/4230/Bass Drum, Cymbals, Glockenspiel, Gong, Side Drum, Tambourine, Tenor Drum, Timpani, Triangle/Harp/Strings; arr MB, Pno; aut *GB-Lbh*.

*The Three Bears* Phantasy comp 22/05/1926; ded 'to Austin, on his fourth birthday';[1] fp Promenade Concert, 07/10/1926, New Queen's Hall Orchestra conducted by the composer; scr 2.Piccolo.121/2230/Bass Drum, Cymbals, Glockenspiel, Gong, Side Drum, Tambourine, Tenor Drum, Timpani, Wood Block/Harp/Strings; arr MB, Pno; aut unknown, † (1929).

*Cinderella* Phantasy comp 09/09/1929; ded 'to the "Cinderella" of our imagination'; fp Eastbourne Festival, 28/11/1929, Eastbourne Municipal Orchestra conducted by the composer; scr 2.Piccolo.121/2230/Bass Drum, Cymbals, Glockenspiel, Side Drum, Small Wood Block, Tambourines, Timpani, Triangle/Harp/Strings; arr Pno; aut *GB-Lcm* (pencil score).

*With a Song in My Heart. Symphonic Rhapsody after Richard Rodgers* (Unpublished); comp 1930; fp Columbia Recording Session, 16/04/1930, The Court Symphony Orchestra conducted by the composer; scr 2122/2230/Bass Drum, Cymbals, Glockenspiel, Timpani, Triangle/Harp/Strings; aut *GB-Lcm*.

*The Seven Dwarfs [Snowdrop]* Ballet (Unpublished); comp 06/06/1930; fp 04/09/1930, Theatre Orchestra conducted by the composer[2] scr 1111/0210/Cymbals, Gong, Tambourine, Triangle/Harp/Celeste/2 Pianos (one piano doubles celesta)/40221 (strings);[3] aut *GB-Lcm*.

---

[1]    The dedication does not appear in any of the published versions of the Phantasy, only in Coates' autobiography (Eric Coates, *Suite in Four Movements* (London, 1953), p. 203.

[2]    The Ballet was performed at an 'out of town' performance on 18/08/1930 in Birmingham before transferring to London.

[3]    There is a short phrase to be sung by the Queen and a passage of dialogue to be spoken by the mirror, which is also doubled by the 'cello.

*Two Symphonic Rhapsodies*
(1) First Symphonic Rhapsody on 'I Pitch My Lonely Caravan at Night'
(2) Second Symphonic Rhapsody on 'Bird Songs at Eventide' and 'I Heard You Singing'
   pub 1933, undated score; fp Columbia Recording Session, 07/03/1933 London Philharmonic Orchestra conducted by the composer; scr 2.Piccolo.121/4230/ Cymbal, Glockenspiel, Gong, Tenor Drum, Timpani, Triangle, Tubular Bell (F♯)/Harp/Strings; aut (1) unknown, (2) *GB-Lcm*.

*Saxo-Rhapsody* comp 30/07/1936; ded 'to Sigurd Rascher'; fp Folkestone Festival, 15/09/1936, Sigurd Rascher (alto saxophone), Folkestone Municipal Orchestra conducted by the composer; scr 2121/2230/Cymbals, Glockenspiel, Tenor Drum, Timpani, Triangle, Vibraphone/Harp/Strings and Solo Alto Saxophone; arr Saxophone and MB, Saxophone and Pno; aut *US-Wc*, † (1954).

*The Enchanted Garden* Ballet comp 01/08/1938; ded 'to Phyl'; fp BBC Broadcast, 03/11/1938 BBC Orchestra (Section D), conducted by Clarence Raybould; scr 3. Piccolo.2.Cor Anglais.2.Bass Clarinet.2/4330/Celesta, Cymbals, Glockenspiel, Gong (of deep tone), Tambourine, Timpani, Triangle, Vibraphone/Harp/ Strings; arr Pno; aut unknown, † (1946).

## Suites

*Miniature Suite* (pub Boosey)
(1) Children's Dance (28/08/1911)
(2) Intermezzo (03/09/1911)
(3) Scène du Bal (20/08/1911)
   comp 03/09/1911; ded. 'to Sir Henry J. Wood and the Queen's Hall Orchestra.' The 'Intermezzo' is dedicated 'to PMB' [Phyllis Black]; fp Promenade Concert, 17/10/1911, Queen's Hall Orchestra conducted by Henry Wood; scr 2.Piccolo.222/2000/Tambourine, Timpani, Triangle/Strings;[4] arr MB, Pno; aut *GB-Lbh*, † (1912).

*From the Countryside* Suite (pub Hawkes)
(1) In the Meadows: Early Morning
(2) Among the Poppies: Afternoon
(3) At the Fair: Evening
   pub 1915; ded. 'to my old friend Basil Cameron'; fp 04/03/1915, New Queen's Hall Light Orchestra 1915, conducted by Alick Maclean (second and third movements only); scr 2.Piccolo.122/2230/Bass Drum, Cymbals, Side Drum, Tambourine, Timpani, Triangle/Harp/Strings; arr Pno; aut unknown, † (1915).

*Summer Days* Suite
(1) Allegretto: In a Country Lane (13/11/1918)
(2) Andante Moderato: On the Edge of a Lake (undated)

---

[4] The Suite was also published in an expanded orchestra (2.Piccolo.222/223.Euphonium.0/ Bass Drum, Cymbals, Side Drum, Tambourine, Timpani, Triangle/Strings) by Percy Fletcher.

(3) Valse: At the Dance (22/01/1919)
  comp 22/01/1919; ded 'to my friend Alick Maclean' (piano solo version only); fp Promenade Concert, 09/10/1919, Queen's Hall Orchestra conducted by the composer; scr 2.Piccolo.222/4230/Bass Drum, Cymbals, Side Drum, Timpani, Triangle/Strings; arr MB, Pno; aut unknown.

*Joyous Youth* Suite
(1) Allegro: Introduction
(2) Allegretto: Serenade
(3) Valse: Joyous Youth
  pub 1921; fp Chappells' Ballad Concert, 1921, New Queen's Light Hall Orchestra conducted by the composer; scr 2.Piccolo.222/4230/Bass Drum, Cymbals, Side Drum, Timpani, Triangle/Strings; arr Pno; aut unknown.

*Four Ways* Suite
(1) Northwards: March (26/08/1927)
(2) Southwards: Valse (28/08/1927)
(3) Eastwards: Eastern Dance (30/08/1927)
(4) Westwards: Rhythm (03/09/1927)
  comp 03/09/1927; fp Harrogate Festival, 23/09/1927, Harrogate Municipal Orchestra conducted by the composer; scr 2.Piccolo.122/2230/Bass Drum, Cymbals, Glockenspiel, Gong, Side Drum, Tambourine, Timpani, Triangle, Wood Block, Xylophone/Strings; arr MB, Pno; aut *GB-Lcm*.

*From Meadow to Mayfair* Suite
(1) In the Country: Rustic Dance
(2) A Song by the Way: Romance
(3) Evening in Town: Valse
  pub 1931; fp 21/02/1931, Eastbourne Municipal Orchestra conducted by the composer; scr 2121/2230/Bass Drum, Cymbals, Glockenspiel, Side Drum, Timpani, Triangle/Strings; arr MB, Pno; aut unknown.

*The Jester at the Wedding* Suite from the Ballet
(1) The Princess Arrives: Tempo di Marcia (19/02/1932)
(2) Dance of the Pages: Minuet (21/02/1932)
(3) The Jester: Humoresque (25/02/1932)
(4) Dance of the Orange Blossom: Valse (01/03/1932)
(5) The Princess: Caprice (02/03/1932)
(6) The Princess and the Jester: Finale (06/03/1932)
  comp 06/03/1932; ded 'to Phyllis'; fp 21/02/1931, Eastbourne Municipal Orchestra conducted by the composer; scr 2122/2230/Bass Drum, Cymbals, Side Drum, Tambourine, Timpani, Triangle/Piano/Strings; arr MB; aut *GB-Lcm*, † (1942).

*London* Suite
(1) Tarantelle: Covent Garden (05/11/1932)
(2) Meditation: Westminster (21/11/1932)
(3) March: Knightsbridge (25/11/1932)

comp 25/11/1932; fp BBC Broadcast, 10/01/1933 BBC Orchestra (Section C), conducted by Joseph Lewis; scr 2.Piccolo.121/2230/Bass Drum, Cymbals, Glockenspiel, Gong, Tambourine, Timpani, Triangle, Tubular Bell (G)/Harp/ Strings; arr MB, Pno; aut *GB-Lcm*, † (1942).

*The Three Men* Suite

(1) The Man from the Country (23/12/1934)
(2) The Man-About-Town (28/12/1934)
(3) The Man from the Sea (02/01/1935)

comp 02/01/1935; ded 'to Stanford Robinson and the BBC Theatre Orchestra'; fp BBC Broadcast, 28/01/1935, BBC Theatre Orchestra conducted by the composer; scr 2.Piccolo.222/222.Tenor Saxophone.2/4230/Bass Drum, Cymbals, Glockenspiel, Gong, Side Drum, Tambourine, Timpani, Triangle, Vibraphone/Harp/Strings; arr MB, Pno; aut *GB-Lcm*.

*London Again* Suite

(1) Oxford Street: March
(2) Langham Place: Elegie
(3) Mayfair: Valse

comp 18/02/1936; fp BBC Broadcast, 26/04/1936, BBC Theatre Orchestra conducted by Stanford Robinson; scr 2222/4230/Bass Drum, Cymbals, Glockenspiel, Gong (of deep tone), Timpani, Triangle, Tubular Bells, Vibraphone/Harp/Strings; arr MB, Pno; aut *GB-Lcm*.

*Springtime* Suite

(1) Fresh Morning: Pastorale
(2) Noonday Song: Romance
(3) Dance in the Twilight: Valse

pub 1937; fp BBC Broadcast, 13/05/1937, BBC Orchestra (Section C), conducted by the composer; scr 2.Piccolo.121/3230/Bass Drum, Cymbals, Glockenspiel, Side Drum, Timpani, Triangle/Harp/Strings; arr MB, Pno; aut unknown.

*Four Centuries* Suite (Boosey & Hawkes)

(1) Seventeenth Century: Prelude and Hornpipe
(2) Eighteenth Century: Pavane and Tambourin
(3) Nineteenth Century: Valse
(4) Twentieth Century: Rhythm

comp 06/11/1941; ded 'to my dear wife'; fp BBC Broadcast, 21/07/1942, BBC Theatre Orchestra conducted by Stanford Robinson; scr 2.Piccolo.22+Bass Clarinet.2/2 Alto Saxophones 1 Tenor Saxophone/4330/Clash Cymbals, Glockenspiel, Gong, Large Cymbal, Side Drum, Small Cymbal, Tambourine, Timpani, Triangle, Vibraphone/Harp/Strings; aut unknown, † (1943).

*The Three Elizabeths* Suite

(1) Halcyon Days (Elizabeth Tudor) (03/08/1944)
(2) Springtime in Angus (Elizabeth of Glamis) (05/08/1944) (post 1953: Springtime in Angus (The Queen Mother))
(3) March – Youth of Britain: The Princess Elizabeth (12/08/1944) (post 1953: March – Youth of Britain March (Queen Elizabeth))

comp 12/08/1944; ded 'dedicated, by permission, to Her Majesty the Queen'; fp BBC Broadcast, 24/12/1944, BBC Symphony Orchestra conducted by the composer; scr 2222/4331/Cymbals, Side Drum, Timpani/Harp/Strings; arr MB, Pno; aut *GB-Lcm* (pencil score), † (1945).

### Marches

*London Bridge* comp 1934; ded 'to Eric Maschwitz'; fp Joint broadcast by the BBC (for *In Town Tonight*) and recording session by Columbia, 05/05/1934, Symphony Orchestra conducted by the composer; scr 2222/4230/Bass Drum, Cymbals, Side Drum, Timpani, Triangle/Harp/Strings; arr MB, Pno, WB; aut *GB-Lcm*.

*The Seven Seas* comp 03/10/1937; ded 'to John M'Kellar Robertson'; fp BBC Broadcast, 21/02/1938 BBC Midland Orchestra conducted by the composer; scr 2121/3230/Bass Drum, Cymbals, Side Drum, Timpani/Strings; arr MB, Pno; aut *GB-Lcm*.

*Calling All Workers* pub 1940; ded 'dedicated to all those who work'; fp BBC Broadcast, 01/09/1940, BBC Theatre Orchestra conducted by Stanford Robinson; scr 2222/2230/Bass Drum, Cymbals, Side Drum, Vibraphone/Strings; arr MB, Pno, WB; aut *GB-Lcm* (pencil sketch).

*Over to You* pub 1941; ded 'to all those who make and fly our aircraft'; fp Bristol Aeroplane Factory Lunchtime Concert, 01/12/1941, The Band of Bristol Aeroplane Company, conducted by the composer; scr 2222/4331/Bass Drums, Cymbals, Side Drum, Tubular Bells, Vibraphone/Strings; arr MB, Pno; aut unknown.

*London Calling* comp 11/12/1941; ded 'to my godson, Alick Mayhew, on his sixth birthday'; fp BBC Broadcast (Latin American Programme), 22/03/1942, BBC Theatre Orchestra conducted by Stanford Robinson; scr 2222/2230/Bass Drum, Cymbals, Glockenspiel, Side Drum, Triangle, Vibraphone/Strings; arr MB, Pno; aut *GB-Lcm*.

*The Eighth Army* pub 1943; ded 'composed at the request of the BBC for their special service for British Forces Overseas, and dedicated, with permission, to General Montgomery, the Officers and Men of the Eighth Army' (piano solo version only); fp BBC Broadcast, 10/12/1942, BBC Northern Orchestra conducted by Maurice Johnstone; scr 2222/2230/Bass Drum, Cymbals, Glockenspiel, Side Drum, Timpani, Triangle/Strings; arr MB, Pno; aut unknown.

*Salute the Soldier* pub 1944; fp *BBC Broadcast, 04/03/1944, BBC Theatre Orchestra conducted by Stanford Robinson*; scr 2222/4330/Cymbals, Glockenspiel, Side Drum, Timpani, Triangle/Strings; arr MB, Pno; aut unknown.

*Television March* pub 1946; fp BBC Recording Session, 03/06/1946, BBC Theatre Orchestra conducted by Harold Lowe (first broadcast on 07/06/1946 for the reopening of BBC Television); scr 2222/4230/Cymbals, Side Drum, Triangle/Strings; arr Pno; aut unknown.

*Music Everywhere* Rediffusion March comp 10/08/1948; fp unknown; scr 2222/4230/Bass Drum, Cymbals, Side Drum, Triangle/Strings; arr Pno; aut *GB-Lcm*.

*Holborn* pub 1950; fp BBC Broadcast, 24/06/1950, BBC Opera Orchestra conducted by the composer; scr 2222/4331/Cymbals, Side Drum, Timpani/ Strings; arr MB, Pno; aut unknown.

*Rhodesia* comp 10/12/1952; ded 'to Sir John Barbirolli and the Hallé Orchestra' (autograph only); fp Gala Concert of the Central African Exhibition in Bulawayo, Rhodesia, 04/07/1953, Hallé Orchestra conducted by John Barbirolli; scr 2222/4331/Bass Drum, Cymbals, Side Drum, Timpani, Triangle/ Strings; arr MB, Pno; aut *GB-Lcm*, † (1953).

*Men of Trent* comp June 1953; fp *BBC Broadcast, 02/09/1953, Nottingham Police Band*; scr MB (arr W.J. Duthoit);[5] aut *GB-Lcm*.

*The Dam Busters* comp 14/06/1954; fp *BBC Broadcast, 26/11/1954, BBC Midland Light Orchestra conducted by the composer*; scr 2222/4331/Cymbals, Glockenspiel, Timpani/Strings; arr BB, MB, Pno; aut *GB-Lcm*.

*Sound and Vision* ATV March comp 29/07/1955; fp *Opening of ATV, 24/09/1955, Unknown Forces*; scr 2222/4331/Cymbals, Glockenspiel, Side Drum, Timpani/ Strings; arr Pno; aut *GB-Lcm*.

*South Wales and the West*;[6] comp 17/12/1956; fp unperformed; scr 2222/4331/ Bass Drum, Cymbals, Side Drum, Timpani/Strings; aut *GB-Lcm*.

*High Flight* comp 02/01/1957; fp BBC Light Programme Music Festival, 06/07/ 1957, BBC Concert Orchestra conducted by the composer; scr 2222/4331/ Bass Drum, Cymbals, Side Drum, Timpani, Triangle/Strings; arr MB, Pno; aut *GB-Lcm*.

### Other Orchestral Works

*Entr'acte à la Gavotte* (Boosey); pub 1912; ded 'to Phyllis'; fp unknown; scr 2.Piccolo.222/2230.Euphonium/Bass Drum, Cymbals, Side Drum, Timpani, Triangle/Strings; arr Pno; aut unknown.

*Idyll* pub 1913; ded 'to my wife' (piano solo version only); fp Promenade Concert, 14/10/1913, Queen's Hall Orchestra conducted by Henry Wood; scr 2122/22(Cornets)3.Euphonium.1/Bass Drum, Cymbals, Timpani, Triangle/ Strings; arr Pno; aut unknown.

*Wood Nymphs* Valsette pub 1918; fp *Chappell's Ballad Concert, 1917, New Queen's Hall Light Orchestra conducted by Alick Maclean*; scr 2222/2230/Bass Drum, Cymbals, Timpani, Triangle/Celesta/Strings; arr MB, Pno; aut unknown.

---

[5]   The march was orchestrated by Malcolm Nabarro.

[6]   This was the re-orchestration of the earlier *Seven Seas* March. The orchestration was never used and when the march was performed and recorded the orchestral parts of *Seven Seas* were used. The piano solo edition was that of the *Seven Seas* with a new title.

*Coquette* Entr'acte (Unpublished); comp 12/05/1920; fp unknown; scr 2.Piccolo.222/42(Cornets)30/Bass Drum, Cymbals, Timpani, Triangle/Strings; aut *GB-Lcm.*

*Moresque* Dance Interlude pub 1921; fp *Sunday Concert, 02/10/1921, New Queen's Hall Orchestra conducted by the composer*; arr MB, Pno; aut unknown.

*The Merrymakers* Miniature Overture comp 28/01/1923; fp Chappells' Ballad Concert, 03/03/1923, New Queen's Hall Light Orchestra conducted by Alick Maclean; scr 2222/4230/ Bass Drum, Cymbals, Glockenspiel, Side Drum, Timpani, Triangle/Strings; arr MB; aut unknown.

*Two Light Syncopated Pieces*

(1) Moon Magic

(2) Rose of Samarkand

Pub 1926; fp Promenade Concert, 05/09/1925, New Queen's Hall Orchestra conducted by the composer; scr 2222/4230/Bass Drum, Cymbals, Side Drum, Tenor Drum, Timpani, Triangle/Strings; arr MB; aut unknown.

*By the Tamarisk* Intermezzo pub 1927; fp Chappells Popular Concert, 12/02/1927, New Queen's Hall Light Orchestra conducted by the composer; scr 1121/2220/ Cymbals, Timpani, Triangle/Strings; arr Pno; aut unknown.

*Mirage* Romance pub 1928; fp unknown; scr 2121/2210/Cymbal, Glockenspiel, Triangle/Harp/Strings; arr Pno, Violin & Pno; aut unknown.

*Under the Stars* (*Sous les Étoiles*) pub 1929; fp unknown; scr 112.1 Alto Saxophone. 1/ 2210/Percussion/Harp/Strings; arr Pno, Violin & Pno; aut unknown.

*By the Sleepy Lagoon* Valse Serenade pub 1930; fp unknown; scr 1121/2220/ Glockenspiel, Triangle/Harp/Strings; arr DB, MB, Pno; aut unknown.

*Summer Afternoon* Idyll (based on the song 'Summer Afternoon'); pub 1932; fp unknown; scr 2.Piccolo.121/2220/Cymbals, Glockenspiel, Timpani, Triangle/ Harp/Strings; arr MB; aut unknown.

*Lazy Night* Valse Romantique pub 1931; fp BBC Broadcast, 10/08/1931, BBC Orchestra conducted by the composer; scr 1121/2220/Cymbals, Glockenspiel, Timpani, Triangle/Strings; aut unknown.

*Dancing Nights* Concert Valse comp 10/10/1931; ded 'to Phyl' (autograph only); fp Eastbourne Festival, 25/11/1931, Eastbourne Municipal Orchestra conducted by the composer; scr 2222/2230/Bass Drum, Cymbals, Glockenspiel, Side Drum, Timpani/Harp/Strings; aut *GB-Lcm.*

*For Your Delight* Serenade pub 1937; ded 'to my good friend Burt Godsmark'; fp BBC Broadcast, 20/12/1937, BBC Orchestra (Section E) conducted by the composer; scr 2121/3230/Cymbals, Glockenspiel, Timpani, Triangle, Vibraphone/Strings; arr Pno; aut unknown.

*Footlights* Concert Valse comp 1939; fp BBC Broadcast, 09/06/1939, BBC Orchestra (Section E) conducted by the composer; scr 2222/4230/Bass Drum, Cymbals, Glockenspiel, Side Drum, Timpani, Triangle, Vibraphone/Harp/ Strings; arr MB, Pno; aut *GB-Lcm.*

*Last Love* Romance pub 1940; fp BBC Broadcast 08/12/1939, BBC Theatre Orchestra conducted by the composer; scr 212+2 Alto Saxophones, 1 Tenor

Saxophone.1/2230/Cymbals, Glockenspiel, Timpani, Vibraphone/Harp/ Strings; aut unknown.

*I Sing to You* (*Je vous ferai une chanson*) Souvenir pub 1940; fp BBC Broadcast, 14/03/1940, BBC Orchestra (Section C) conducted by an unknown conductor; scr 2121/2230/Cymbals, Glockenspiel, Timpani, Triangle, Vibraphone/ Harp/Strings; arr Pno & violin, cello and piano (unpublished); aut *GB-Lcm* (pencil score).

*Valse from the Phantasy 'The Three Bears'* comp 20/01/1949; fp Recording Session, 16/07/1949, Queen's Hall Light Orchestra conducted by the composer; scr 2121/ 2210/Glockenspiel, Timpani/Harp/Strings; aut *GB-Lcm*.[7]

*The Unknown Singer* Interlude comp 24/05/1952; fp Cheltenham Festival, 20/07/1952, BBC Midland Light Orchestra conducted by the composer; scr 222.1 Tenor saxophone.2/ 3230/Glockenspiel, Triangle/Harp/Strings (alternative solo part for Alto Saxophone); arr Pno; aut *GB-Lcm* (pencil sketch).

*Sweet Seventeen* Concert Valse comp 03/04/1954; ded 'for my beloved Phyl'; fp BBC Light Programme Music Festival, 12/06/1954, BBC Concert Orchestra and the London Light Orchestra conducted by the composer; scr 2222/4230/ Cymbals, Glockenspiel, Timpani, Triangle/Harp/Strings; arr MB, Pno; aut *GB-Lcm*, † (1954).

*Impression of a Princess* Intermezzo comp 26/04/1956; ded 'dedicated with permission to HRH Princess Margaret'; fp BBC Light Programme Music Festival, 07/07/1956, BBC Concert Orchestra conducted by the composer; scr 222.1 Alto Saxophone.2/4230/Cymbals, Timpani, Vibraphone/Harp/Strings, Solo Alto Saxophone; arr MB, Pno; aut *GB-Lcm*.

## Chamber Works

*Menuetto* (From *Suite for String Quartet* by different composers) (Unpublished); comp 1908; fp Hambourg String Quartet Subscription Concerts, 28/11/1908, Hambourg String Quartet; scr String quartet; aut *GB-Lcm*.

## Instrumental Works

### *Solo Instrument and Piano*

*Ballad* Op 13, number 1 (Unpublished); comp 09/09/1906; scr Viola or Cello & Pno; aut *GB-Lcm* and *GB-Lbh*.

*Berceuse Op 2* (Unpublished); comp 1904; scr Viola & Pno; aut unknown.

---

[7]   The published piano-conductor part gives the title as *Valse from the Fantasy 'The Three Bears'*, though in the autograph score Coates spelt phantasy in his usual manner.

*First Meeting* Souvenir pub 1943; ded 'to Austin, on his twenty first birthday';
   scr Violin & Pno (originally Viola & Pno); aut unknown.
*Le Dance des Fantômes* Op 28 number 3 (Unpublished); comp undated; ded 'to
   Miss Maud Reudell'; scr Violin & Pno; aut *GB-Lcm*.
*Romance in D Major Op 1* (Unpublished); comp 1902; scr Violin & Pno; aut
   unknown.
*Romance sans Paroles* Op 28 number 2 (Unpublished); comp undated; ded 'to
   Miss Maud Reudell'; scr Violin & Pno; aut *GB-Lcm*.
[*Two Pieces for Violin and Piano*] Op 16 (Unpublished);[8] comp circa 1906–08;
   ded 'to Mildred Johns'; scr Violin & Piano; aut *GB-Lcm*.
(1) Romance
(2) Scherzo

### *Piano*

*The Mermaid* pub 1912; ded 'to Phyllis'; scr Piano; arr MB, Orch (H.M. Higgs);
   aut unknown.
*Six Short Pieces (Without Octaves)* (Boosey); pub 1911; ded 'to Phyllis Black';
   scr Piano; aut *GB-Lbh*.
(1) Prelude
(2) A Little Song
(3) Elégie
(4) Alla Menuetto
(5) Valse
(6) Slumber Song
*Three Lyric Pieces* comp 07/02/1930; ded 'to Joan'; scr Piano; aut unknown.
(1) A Fragment (06/01/1930)
(2) Nocturne (07/02/1930)
(3) Valse (04/02/1930)

### Choral Works

*Come to the Fair* (Unpublished); text Harry Firkin; comp undated; scr ATBarB
   and Piano; aut *GB-Lcm*. (This work is written under the pseudonym of Jack
   Arnold.)
*Evening Doxology* (Unpublished); comp undated, c 1910s; scr Unison voices and
   Organ; aut *GB-Lcm*.
*God's Great Love Abiding* (Keith Prowse); text Eric Coates; comp May 1947,
   pub 1956; fp Baptist Sunday School Anniversary Service, 25/05/1947, the
   Children of Hucknall Baptist Church conducted by Enos Godfrey; scr SATB
   or unison voice(s) and piano; aut Private Collection

---

[8]    This is an editorial title as the manuscript does not bear a title.

*Hymn for the Workers* (Unpublished); text Eric Coates?; comp undated, c1942–45; SATB; aut *GB-Lcm* (music), Private Collection (words).

*A Song of Loyalty* text Phyllis Black; comp 1935; fp BBC Broadcast, 07/05/1935. BBC Orchestra (Section E), Leonard Gowings (Tenor) conducted by the composer; scr 2222/4321/Cymbals, Timpani, Triangle, Bell (G)/Harp/Strings; aut: unknown.[9]

## Songs

### *Songs, Voice and Piano/Orchestra*

*Where songs have been orchestrated the autograph referred to is the orchestral score.*

'All Among the Clover' (Unpublished); text G. Hubi-Newcombe; comp Friday Night, 24/12/1909; ded 'to Mildred Avis'; aut *GB-Lbh*.

'All Mine Own'; text Harold Simpson; pub 1913; ded 'to Phyllis'.

'Always as I Close my Eyes'; text Maud Handfield-Jones; ded 'to Neville'; pub 1929.

'Asphodel'; text Fred Weatherly; comp 31/10/1916, pub 1917.

'At Daybreak' (Enoch & Sons); text F.G. Bowles; pub 1909.

'At Dusk' (Unpublished); text Charles Roff; comp circa 1921–24; aut *GB-Lcm*.

'At Sunset'; text Mrs Charles Hutchins; comp 16/01/1920; fp Promenade Concert, 21/08/1920 George Baker (Baritone) and Frederick Kiddle.

'At Vesper Bell'; text Gunby Hadath; pub 1920.

'Autumn Love' (Unpublished); text Daisy Fisher; comp 17/07/1920; aut *GB-Lcm*.

'The Awakening' (Boosey); text Edward Teschemacher;[10] pub 1912.

'Away in Navarre' (Unpublished); text Edward Lockton; comp circa 1921-24; aut *GB-Lcm*.

'Beautiful Lady Moon'; text Phyllis Black; pub 1934.

'Because I Miss You So'; text Lillian Glanville; pub 1930.

'Betty and Johnny'; text Fred Weatherly; pub 1913.

‡ 'Bird Songs at Eventide';[11] text Royden Barrie;[12] pub 1926; fp Promenade Concert, 09/09/1926, Joseph Hislop (Tenor) and Frederick Kiddle; aut *GB-Lbh*.

'A Bird's Lullaby' (Enoch & Sons); text Eric Coates; pub 1911.

'Blue Sky and White Road'; text Charles Roff; pub 1922; fp Promenade Concert, 18/08/1922 Tudor Davies (Tenor) and Frederick Kiddle.

'Brown Eyes Beneath the Moon'; text Fred Weatherly; pub 1921.

---

[9]    The work can be performed with or without a soloist (tenor) or unison choir, with the verse repeated, by the audience, if desired; aut unknown.

[10]   Edward Teschemacher was the nom-de-plume of Edward Lockton.

[11]   H.M. Higgs arranged this song for orchestra alone.

[12]   Royden Barrie was the *nom de plume* of Rodney Bennett.

'Brown Eyes I Love'; text Lillian Glanville; pub 1926.

'By Mendip Side'; text P.J. O'Reilly; pub 1914.

'By the North Sea'; text Arthur Conan-Doyle; pub 1919; ded 'to Lady Conan-Doyle'.

‡ 'Coloured Fields'; Daisy Fisher; pub 1922; fp 02/12/1922, Maggie Teyte, New Queen's Hall Light Orchestra conducted by the composer; aut unknown.

'Damask Rose' (Boosey); text F.G. Bowles; pub 1908.

'Dick's Quandary'; text Fred Weatherly; pub 1913.

‡ 'A Dinder Courtship' (Boosey); text Fred Weatherly; pub 1912; aut *GB-Lcm*.

'Doubt' (Boosey); text Florence Hedley-Stodden; pub 1929.

'Dreams'; text Fred Weatherly; pub 1917.

'The Dreams of London'; text Almey St. John Adcock; pub 1927.

'Dress Her in White' (Unpublished); text Nancie Marsland; comp circa 1921–24; aut *GB-Lcm*.

‡ *Eight Nursery Rhymes* (Cramer); text traditional; pub 1923; aut *US-Wgu*.

(1) Pussy Cat, Pussy Cat

(2) Mary, Mary, Quite Contrary

(3) Little Boy Blue

(4) Baa, Baa, Black Sheep

(5) Miss Muffet

(6) Pat-a-cake, Pat-a-cake

(7) Hush-a-bye, Baby

(8) New Year's Day

'Eildon Hill' (Boosey); text Fred Weatherly; pub 1914; ded 'to my wife'.

‡ 'An Elizabethan Lullaby'; text William Ackerman [William Boosey]; pub 1919; ded 'to Hubert Earle'; fp 16/01/1919, Louise Dale and the London String Quartet; aut unknown.

'[Ev'rything is Simply Fine and Life is Comp'ly Jolly]'[13] (Unpublished); text Daisy Fisher; comp circa 1921–24; aut *GB-Lcm*.

‡ 'The Fairy Tales of Ireland'; text Edward Lockton; pub 1918; ded 'to my mother'; fp Promenade Concert, 28/09/1918, Carmen Hill (Contralto) and Frederick Kiddle; aut *GB-Lbh*.

'Farmer and I' (Unpublished); text Fred Weatherly; comp 04/12/1909; aut *GB-Lcm*.

‡ *Four Old English Songs for Voice and Orchestra* (Boosey);[14] text William Shakespeare; pub 1909; ded 'to Gertrude Newson'; fp Royal Academy of Music Orchestral Concert, 15/12/1908, Royal Academy of Music Orchestra, Gertrude Newson (Soprano), conducted by Alexander Mackenzie; aut *GB-Lbh*.

(1) Orpheus with his Lute

(2) Under the Greenwood Tree

---

[13]   The manuscript does not bear a title.

[14]   Boosey's also published an orchestration of the *Songs* for String Orchestra.

(3) Who is Sylvia?

(4) It was a Lover and his Lass

*Four Songs of the Air Service* (West & Company); text Edward Lockton; pub 1918.

(1) Ordered Overseas

(2) Five and Twenty Bombers

(3) Billy

(4) The Finest Job of All

'The Fruits of the Earth' (West & Company); text Edward Lockton; pub 1918.

'The Gates of If-ever'; text D. Eardley-Wilmot; pub 1925; fp Promenade Concert, 15/09/1935, Margaret Balfour (Contralto) and Frederick Kiddle.

'The Gates of Spring'; text Fred Weatherly; pub 1909.

'The Golliwog' (Unpublished);[15] text Fred Weatherly; comp unknown; aut *GB-Lcm*.

'Goodbye'; text Irving Caesar; pub 1935.

‡ 'Gorse-Bloom' (Unpublished); text Nancie Marsland; comp undated; aut *GB-Lcm*.

‡ 'The Grenadier'; text Fred Weatherly; pub 1913, orchestrated 19/03/1914; ded 'to Frank H. Black'; aut *GB-Lcm*.

‡ 'Green Hills o' Somerset'; text Fred Weatherly; pub 1915; aut *GB-Lbh*.

'Gwenny' (Boosey); text Fred Weatherly; pub 1909.

'Gypsy Fires' (Unpublished); text Dena Tempest; comp circa 1925–30; aut *GB-Lcm*.

*Headland Love Songs* (Unpublished); text Florence Attenborough; comp 23/11/1908; aut *GB-Lbh*.

(1) Wonder

(2) Doubt

(3) Triumph

'A Heart from Kerry' (Unpublished); text Fred Weatherly; comp 21/03/1909; ded 'to EO' [Elsie Owen]; aut *GB-Lbh*.

'The Heart You Love is Calling You' (Keith Prowse); text Edward Lockton; pub 1918.

'Here is the Shade', An Interlude (Unpublished); text Royden Barrie; comp undated; aut *GB-Lcm*.

'Home-Along'; text Arthur L. Salmon; pub 1931.

'Homeward to You'; text Royden Barrie; pub 1928.

'The Hour of Love'; text Harold Simpson; pub 1914.

'A House Love Made for You and Me'; text Gordon Johnstone; pub 1932.

'I'd Like' (Unpublished); text Gladys Davidson; comp 22/04/1920; aut *GB-Lcm*.

'I'm Lonely', Valse Song; text Gordon McConnell; pub 1928.[16]

'I'm Wanting You'; text Gunby Hadath; comp 26/12/1919, pub 1921.

---

[15]  The manuscript is un-texted and incomplete.

[16]  Chappells published an orchestration of this song by Max Irwin.

‡ 'I Heard You Singing'; text Royden Barrie; pub 1923; aut *GB-Lbh*.

'I Know a Little Chalêt' (Unpublished); text May Awoose; comp undated; aut
    *GB-Lcm*.

'I Looked For You'; text Phyllis Black; pub 1933.

‡ 'I Pitch My Lonely Caravan at Night'; text Annette Horley; pub 1921; aut *GB-Lbh*.

'If I Follow where my Heart's Goin'' (Unpublished); text Katrina Bogosoff; comp
    30/05/1921; aut *GB-Lcm*.

'If Stars Were Tears'; text Frank Eyton; pub 1932.

'If You Were My Little Boy' (Boosey); text Edward Teschemacher; pub 1911; ded
    'to Marie Novello'.

'In the Hush of Dawn' (Unpublished); text E. Milton Kench; comp 23/11/1908;
    ded 'to the writer of the words'; aut *GB-Lcm*.

'In Town'; text Dorothy Dickinson; pub 1924.

'In Wessex Lane' (Unpublished); text P.J. O'Reilly; comp 15/05/1909; ded 'to
    Phyllis'; aut *GB-Lbh*.

'The Inconstant Lover' (Unpublished); text Daisy Fisher; comp circa 1921–24;
    aut *GB-Lcm*.

'A Japanese Farewell'; text G. Douglas Furber; pub 1914.

'June's First Rose'; text Edward Lockton; pub 1922.

'Just Now and Then' (Unpublished); text Dorothy Dickinson; comp undated; aut
    *GB-Lcm*.

‡ *Lace and Porcelain*, Three Old World Songs (Boosey); text Harold Simpson;
    comp 08/05/1910; ded 'to my friend Ivor Foster'; aut *GB-Lcm*.

(1) Love is Every Maiden's Joy

(2) Strephon and Amaryllis (Going to the Fair)

(3) A Cavalier Love Song

'Land of my Heart'; text Fred Weatherly; pub 1917.

'Lily of the Valley' (Unpublished); text Edward Lockton; comp 11/05/1921; aut
    *GB-Lcm*.

'The Little Girl I Love' (Boosey); text Fred Weatherly; pub 1910; ded 'to GN'
    [Gertrude Newson].

'The Little Green Balcony'; text Royden Barrie; pub 1925.

'Little House of Dreams' (Unpublished); text Royden Barrie; comp circa 1921–
    24; aut *GB-Lcm*.

'Little Lady of the Moon'; text Fred Weatherly; pub 1928.

'Little Love' (Boosey); text G. Hubi-Newcombe; pub 1910; ded 'to Mildred Avis'.

'A Little Love Affair' (Unpublished); text Daisy Fisher; comp undated; aut *GB-
    Lcm*.

'Little Snoozy Coon'; text Royden Barrie; pub 1925.

'The Little Sweet Shop'; text Edward Teschemacher; pub 1913.

'Love Among the Daffodils' (Boosey); text Edward Teschemacher; pub 1909; ded
    'to Ada Forest'.

'Love's Fantasy' (Boosey); text Fred Weatherly; pub 1911; ded 'to PMB' [Phyllis
    Black].

'The Lowland Sea' (Boosey); text C. Upton; pub 1909.

'The Maid and the Moon'; text Eileen Price-Evans; pub 1918.

'Marry Me, Nancy Do!'; text Fred Weatherly; pub 1914.

'May Day Dance'; text M. Byron; pub 1909.

'Melanie'; text Fred Weatherly; pub 1913; fp Chappells' Ballad Concert, 08/11/1913 sung by Hubert Eisdell; ded 'to my wife'.

'Mendin' Roadways'; text Dena Tempest; pub 1923; fp Promenade Concert, 01/10/1923, Malcolm McEachern (Bass) and Frederick Kiddle.

‡ *The Mill o' Dreams*; text Nancie Marsland; pub 1915; ded 'to Phyl';[17] fp *Promenade Concert, 25/09/1915, New Queen's Hall Orchestra, Louise Dale (voice), conducted by Henry Wood*; aut \**GB-Lbh*.

(1) Back o' the Moon

(2) Dream o' Nights

(3) The Man in the Moon

(4) Blue Bells

'Molly Malone' (Unpublished); text G. Hubi-Newcombe; comp undated; aut *GB-Lbh*.

'The Moon-Boat' (Boosey); text Fred Weatherly; pub 1911; ded 'to PMB' [Phyllis Black].

'Moon-Daisies'; text Fred Weatherly; pub 1921; fp Promenade Concert, 23/08/1921, Mischa Léon (tenor) and Frederick Kiddle (piano).

'Moonland Dreams' (Boosey); text Fred Weatherly; pub 1914.

'Mother England's Brewing' (Boosey); text Harold Simpson; pub 1911; ded 'to PMB' [Phyllis Black].

'Music of the Night'; text Phyllis Black; pub 1934.

'My Lady Comes' (Unpublished); text Fred Weatherly; comp 12/07/1912; aut *GB-Lcm*.

'My Prayers Take Wing' (West & Company); text Fred Weatherly; pub 1918.

'A Nest in Arcady' (Cary & Company); text Edward Lockton; pub 1919.

‡ 'Nobody Else But You', Song Fox-Trot; text Daisy Fisher; pub 1923; ded 'to "Phyl"'; aut *GB-Lcm*.

'The Old Ships' (Unpublished); text C. Fox-Smith; comp 05/12/1919; aut *GB-Lcm*.

'An Old World Garden'; text Eric Chilman; pub 1916.

'Ole Dear'; text Dorothy Dickinson; pub 1922.

'The One White Rose' (Unpublished); text Fred Weatherly; comp 17/05/1919; aut *GB-Lcm*.

'Our Little Home'; Fred Weatherly; pub 1917.

‡ 'The Outlaw's Song' (Boosey); text J. Baillie; pub 1908; ded 'to Carlton Brough'; fp Royal Academy of Music Student Concert, 24/06/1908, Carlton Brough (baritone), Royal Academy of Music Orchestra conducted by Alexander Mackenzie; aut: unknown.

'The Palaces of Roses'; text Harold Simpson; pub 1916.

---

[17]    Marsland's text is dedicated 'to my husband'.

'Passion-Flower'; text Gertrude Wiskin; pub 1921.

‡ 'Pepita'; text G. Douglas Furber; pub 1920; ded 'to M. Mischa-Léon'; fp Queen's Hall Sunday Afternoon Concert, 25/01/1920, Mischa-Léon and the New Queen's Hall Orchestra conducted by the composer; aut unknown.

'Pierrette's Song' (Boosey); text Fred Weatherly; pub 1913.

'Princess of the Dawn'; text Christopher Hassall; pub 1938.

'Ratcatcher Richard' (Unpublished); text Fred Weatherly; comp 17/07/1911; ded 'to my friend Harry Dearth'; aut *GB-Lbh*.

'Red, Red Rose' (Unpublished); text Ruth Dappin; comp 12/07/1920; aut *GB-Lcm*.

'Reuben Ranzo' (Boosey); text Fred Weatherly; pub 1911.

'Rise Up and Reach the Stars'; text Winifred May; pub 1933.

'The Road of Dreams' (Unpublished); text Royden Barrie; comp undated; aut *GB-Lcm*.

'Rose of Mine'; text Edward Teschemacher; pub 1912; ded 'to Phyllis'.

. 'Rose of Samarkand', Song Foxtrot;[18] text Royden Barrie; pub 1925; ded 'to Debroy Somers'.

'Rose of the World'; text Helen Taylor; pub 1914.

‡ 'Roses all the Way', Song Foxtrot; text Ernest Butcher; pub 1921; ded 'to Muriel George and Ernest Butcher'; aut: unknown.

'Roses of Peace' (West & Company); text E. Barker; pub 1919.

'Sally and I and the Daylight' (Keith Prowse); text Fred Weatherly; pub 1918.

'The Scent of Lilac'; text Winifred May; pub 1954.

‡ 'Sea Rapture (An Impression)'; text Emeric Hulme Beaman; pub 1924; aut *GB-Lcm*.

'Seasons Please' (Unpublished); text Fred Weatherly; comp 20/12/1918; aut *GB-Lcm*.

'Ship of Dream'; text Winifred van Noorden; pub 1933.

‡ 'Sigh no More, Ladies'; text William Shakespeare; comp 09/05/1916; ded 'to Acton Bond'; fp A performance of *Much Ado About Nothing* at the Royal Academy of Music, 02/06/1916, unknown forces; aut *GB-Lcm*.

'Since Yesterday'; text Anne Page; pub 04/01/1920.

'Smile Again' (Unpublished); text Dorothy Dickinson; comp undated; aut *GB-Lcm*.

'Smile all you Can' (Unpublished); text Dorothy Dickinson; comp undated; aut *GB-Lcm*.

‡ 'A Song of Summer'; text Lady Joan Verney; pub 1943; aut *GB-Lbh*.

'Song of the Little Folk'; text Jennie Dunbar; pub 1925.

'A Song of the Wild'; text Edward Lockton; pub 1923.

'A Song Remembered'; text Royden Barrie; pub 1927.

*Songs from Arabia: The Garden of Khusru* (Unpublished); text Edward Lockton; comp 17/02/1920; aut *GB-Lcm*.

(1) Dawn Song (15/02/1920)

---

[18]    This song was used in the second of Coates' *Two Light Syncopated Pieces* written at the same time.

(2) On the Blue of the Water (15/02/1920)
(3) The Garden of Khusru (15/02/1920)
(4) You Came From Desert Places (15/02/1920)
(5) The Golden House (17/02/1920)
*Songs of a Simple Fellow* (Unpublished);[19] text Dorothy Dickinson; comp undated; aut *GB-Lcm*.
(1) In Town
(2) Ain't It Beautiful
(3) Weather
(3) Lurcher
(4) Thinkin' of You (Unwritten, but marked on the title page)
'Star of God'; text Fred Weatherly; pub 1942.
'The Stars Above' (Cary & Company); text Haydn H. Morris; pub 1919.
'Stars and a Crescent Moon'; text Phyllis Black; pub 1932; fp BBC Broadcast, 10/08/1931, Dorothy Bennett (soprano) and the composer (piano).
'Stone-Cracker John' (Boosey); text Fred Weatherly; pub 1909; ded 'to my friend William Samuel'.
'The Stream-Enchanted' (Unpublished); text Royden Barrie; comp circa 1925–30; aut *GB-Lcm*.
'Summer Afternoon';[20] text Royden Barrie; pub 1924.
‡ 'Sweet-and-Twenty'; text William Shakespeare; pub 1912; ded 'to Phyllis'; aut *GB-Lcm*.
'Sweet Phyllis' (Boosey); text Fred Weatherly; pub 1909; ded 'to Phyllis'.
'Tell me Where is Fancy Bred?' (Boosey); text William Shakespeare (*The Merchant of Venice*); pub 1912; ded 'to Annie Child'; fp Production of *The Merchant of Venice* at Caldecote Towers, 06/07/1912.
'Thinkin' of You'; text Dorothy Dickinson; pub 1922.
'This is the House that Jack Built' (Unpublished); text Dena Tempest; comp undated; *GB-Lcm*.
'Three Sailormen and Me' (Unpublished); text Edward Lockton; comp 07/04/1918; aut *GB-Lcm*.
‡ *Three Songs for Mezzo-Soprano and Orchestra* Op 10 (Unpublished); text Robert Burns; comp 09/06/1906 (piano score); ded 'to Vinnie Inman'; aut *GB-Lcm* (orchestral score) & *GB-NO* (piano score).
(1) My Love is Like a Red, Red Rose (02/06/1906)
(2) The Winter is Past (08/06/1906)
(3) The Bonnie Wee Thing (09/06/1906)
*Three Songs from Op 11* (Unpublished); text (1) and (2) Percy Shelly (3) William Syle; comp 14/09/1906; ded:(1) and (2) 'composed expressly for and dedicated to Sybil Welsh (3) 'to Celia Welsh'; aut Private Collection.

---

[19] There are two songs marked number three.
[20] Coates transformed this song into an orchestral idyll, *Summer Afternoon*, published in 1932.

1) Loves Philosophy Op 11 number 3 (26/08/1906)
2) To a Maiden Op 11 number 4 (26/08/1906)
3) Tit-for-Tat Op 11 number 6 (14/09/1906)
'Through All the Ages'; text Fred Weatherly; pub 1919; fp Promenade Concert, 13/09/1919, George Baker (baritone) and Frederick Kiddle.
'Today is Ours'; text Frank Eyton; pub 1940.
‡ *Two Songs for Baritone* (Boosey); text (1) G. Roberts, (2) John Galsworthy; pub 1907; ded 'to Percy Driver'; fp Royal Academy of Music Orchestral Concert, 12/12/1907, Royal Academy of Music Orchestra, Percy Driver (baritone) conducted by Alexander Mackenzie; aut unknown.
(1) Swedish Love Song
(2) Devon to Me
'Violets' from *Two Little Flower Songs* (Unpublished);[21] text E.B. [E. Brown]; comp undated; ded 'to E.O.' [Elsie Owen]; aut *GB-Lbh*.
'Waiting for the Spring' (Enoch & Sons); text Fred Weatherly; pub 1910.
‡ 'When I am Dead' (Boosey); text Christina Rossetti; ded 'to my friend Carlton Brough'; pub 1908; aut unknown.
'When the Robin Goes a-Singing'; text Harold Simpson; pub 1910.
'When We Two Went a-Maying' (Boosey); text E. Brown; pub 1908; ded E.O. [Elsie Owen].
'The White Winding Road'; text Daisy Fisher; comp 15/02/1920.
'Why I Sigh for the Moon' (Unpublished); text Daisy Fisher; comp circa 1921–24; *GB-Lcm*.
'The Widow of Penzance' (Boosey); text Harold Simpson; pub 1916.
'Wind on the World' (Unpublished); text Anne Page; comp undated; *GB-Lcm*.
'Yearning'; text Royden Barrie; pub 1924.
'You are my Rose'; text Christopher Hassall; pub 1938.
'You Come No More'; text Daisy Fisher; pub 1920.
'The Young Lover'; text Royden Barrie; pub 1930.
'Your Heart is Like a Golden Fair' (Boosey); text E. Brown; pub 1909; ded 'to Elsie Owen'.
'Your Love'; text Fred Weatherly; pub 1917.
‡ 'Your Name'; text Christopher Hassall; pub 1938; aut *GB-Lbh*.
'Yours and Mine' (Cary & Company); text Edward Lockton; pub 1918.
'Yvette' (Enoch & Sons); text Fred Weatherly; pub 1909; ded 'to EO' [Elsie Owen].

### Songs Written under a Nom de Plume

All songs are by Jack Arnold unless otherwise stated
'Bluebells' (Unpublished); text unknown; comp circa 1924; aut unknown. (Written under the *nom de plume* Ciré.)
‡ 'The Challenge' (Unpublished); text Daisy Fisher; comp undated; aut *GB-Lcm*.

---

21   The second song may not have been written.

'Diff'rent Somehow'; text Gordon McConnell; pub 1924.

'Ev'ry Minute of Ev'ry Day'; text Elsie May Skeet; pub 1924; ded 'This song was written for, and sung by, 'Miss Norah Blaney and Mr Michael Cole in 'The Punch Bowl' in an Archibald de Bear Production.

'K-Naughty Kanute'; text Elsie May Skeet; pub 1925; ded 'This song was written for, and sung by, 'Miss Norah Blaney and Mr Michael Cole in "The Punch Bowl" in an Archibald de Bear Production'.

'Oh Yes!' (Unpublished); text unknown; comp 1924; aut unknown.

'Purple Heather' (Unpublished); text Daisy Fisher; comp undated; aut *GB-Lcm*.

'You Keep Haunting Me' (Unpublished); text unknown; comp circa 1924; fp Cabaret at the Grafton Galleries, London, April 1924; aut: unknown. (Written under the *nom de plume* Ciré.)

### *Arrangements of Coates' Orchestral Works as Songs*

'God is our Strength and Refuge' (*The Dam Busters* March); (Chappells and Jubilate Hymns); text Richard Bewes; pub 1994.

'Loyal Hearts' ('Springtime in Angus' *The Three Elizabeths* Suite); text A.C. Wood; pub 1963.

'Our Flag Shall Fly' (*The Dam Busters* March); text David Nash Williams; pub 2009.

'Proudly with High Endeavour' (*The Dam Busters* March); text Carlene Mair; pub 1956.

'Sleepy Lagoon' (*By the Sleepy Lagoon*); text Jack Lawrence; pub 1940.

### *Recitations with Music*

Scored for Reciter and Piano

'Fairies' (Unpublished); text W. Allingham; comp circa 1911; fp British Society of Composers Concert, 18/12/1911, Phyllis Black and Eric Coates; aut: unknown.

'The Highwayman' (Unpublished); text Alfred Noyes; comp circa 1911–12; fp Social Union Concert, 19/11/1912, Phyllis Black and Eric Coates; aut: unknown.

'The Lamplighter' (Unpublished); text Robert Louis Stevenson; comp circa 1911; fp British Society of Composers Concert, 18/12/1911, Phyllis Black and Eric Coates; aut: unknown.

'The Mermaid' (Unpublished); text Alfred Tennyson; comp 02/03/1911; aut *GB-Lcm*.

*Two Recitations with Piano* (Unpublished); text (1) Eugène Field, (2) Robert Louis Stevenson; comp (1) 18/10/1911, (2) 20/10/1911; ded 'to Miss Phyllis Black'; aut *GB-Lcm*.

(1) Little Boy Blue
(2) My Treasures

'Wynken, Blynken and Nod' (Unpublished); text Eugène Field; comp circa 1911–
  12; fp Social Union Concert, 19/11/1912, Phyllis Black and Eric Coates; aut:
  unknown.


**Operetta Material**

All material is unpublished and housed at *GB-Lcm* unless otherwise stated.

### *Mary's Orchard*
*(1) Libretto: Daisy Fisher, Music: Eric Coates*

**Act I:**

| | |
|---|---|
| Introduction: | Introduction |
| Opening Chorus: | Little Louise, Big Louise (05/06/1920) |
| Solo: | Wouldn't it Just Be Beautiful (Miss Smith) (01/06/1920) |
| Duet: | I Think You're a Perfect Treat (Miss Smith and Boyle) (18/06/1920) |
| Solo: | The Call of the West (Latimer) (13/06/1920) |
| Solo: | Deep Within Each Women's Heart (Christina) (10/06/1920) |
| Duet: | Moonshine (Christina and Latimer) (18/06/1920) |
| Duet: | No 10. A Happy Place (Mary and Chester) |
| Quartette: | No. 7. Take it Early |
| Trio: | Money Can't Buy Everything (Latimer, Wyndham, Boyle) |
| * Solo: | Walk into my Chorus (Delevanti) |
| Duet: | No 4. Featherin' a Nest (Joe and Martha) |
| Quartette: | Ghost Quartet |
| Solo: | No 5. Sometimes (Mary) |
| Duet: | No 6. Fate (Freddie and Suzette) |
| Finale: | (09/06/1920) |

**Act II**

| | |
|---|---|
| * Opening Chorus: | Untitled |
| Duet: | I've Not Known You Long (Allison and Wyndham) (31/05/1920) |
| Duet: | It Can Never Be (Boyle and Delevanti) (11/06/1920) |
| Duet: | I Don't Care (Christina and Latimer) (30/05/1920) |
| Quartette: | At Dusk (Christina, Allison, Latimer, Wyndham) (08/06/1920) |
| Solo: | The Call of the West (Chester) |
| Solo: | I Hadn't Got a Notion (Boyle?) |
| Solo: | I'm in Love (Allison) |
| Solo: | I Discover (Latimer) |
| * Finale: | Untitled |

**Act III**

| | |
|---|---|
| Opening Chorus: | Let us Tread a Merry Measure (19/06/1920) |
| Solo: | Pierette (Christina) (17/06/1920) |
| Solo: | Don't be Afraid Little Ladies (Delevanti) |
| Trio: | (Boyle, Miss Smith, Delevanti) |

**Unknown**

| | |
|---|---|
| Duet: | (Mary and Chester) |
| Solo: | Willow Woods (Christina) |
| Duet: | [The Time has Seemed so Long to Me] (Cynthia and Colin) |

*(2) Libretto: James Heard, Music: Eric Coates*

| | |
|---|---|
| Duet: | My Kisses Were Wages (Allison and Sir Wyndham) |
| Chorus: | Entrance and Chorus of Servants (Boyle and Servants) |
| Quintette: | (Allison, Aunt Emily, Delevanti and Sir Wyndham) |

*All Through My Life*[22]
*Libretto: Unknown, Music: Eric Coates*

| | |
|---|---|
| No 1 | Opening Chorus: When the President Presides |
| No 2 | Act I Scene 2 Margaretta's Ballad |
| No 3 | Act I Scene 2 Mazurka (Louise) |
| No 4 | 'This Must be You' (Pierre and Margaretta) |
| No 5 | Act I Scene 2 [All though my life] (Margaretta) |
| No 6 | Romance (Pierre) |
| No 7 | Can This Be True (Louise and Paul) |
| No 8 | Peter and Paul |
| No 9 | Promise |
| No 10 | Colonel Potshott (Paul, Pierre and Cadets) |
| No 12 | Trio & Chorus [Crossed out in pencil] 'You're mad if you marry a Soldier' |
| | Untexted song (Paul) |

*A Knight of Malta*
*After a story by Laurence Howard, Libretto: Austin Coates, Music: Eric Coates*

Entrance of Montagu
Flower Song
Haunted Eternally
I've Tried to Disbelieve
I Shan't Enjoy Myself Till Things Are Done My Way (Melody only) (Private Collection)

---

[22] Editorial title.

Knight's Change
March of the Knights of Malta
Morning Hymn
Midnight's My Noon Day
Oh Can You Take (Melody only) (Private Collection)
Promise
Promise (Act II) (Melody only) (Private Collection)
Responses
Request Serenade (17/04/1947) (Private Collection)
Rodney's Prayer
Song of Supplication
You've Hypnotised my Heart
Various sketches of melodic material all undated and un-texted

### *Miscellaneous*
*Librettist, where known, is in brackets*

Ghost's Song †
[Heads of Tails] (Boyle and Delevanti) (Sketch)
* I Love You So (Cynthia and Colin)
I've Been Looking for You (Duet), (James Heard)
I've Come Out
Joe Peppercorn's Song (Act I, No 3)
Simplicity (Daisy Fisher)
The New Poor (Wyndham, Aunt Ellen, Allison, Act I)
[Your Memory is a Useful Thing to Lose] (Act II, Boyle) (Sketch)


### Gramophone Recordings

All recordings are conducted by the composer. Orchestras in brackets are the names given on the record label. Catalogue numbers in brackets are for USA/ overseas release.

### *Acoustic Recordings (78rpm)*
*The Merrymakers* Overture & *Moresque* Dance Interlude; New Queen's Hall Light
    Orchestra; rec 23/03/1923; lab Columbia; cat L1529; mat 76919 & 76922.
*Joyous Youth* Suite & 'At the Dance' (*Summer Days* Suite); Aeolian Orchestra; rec
    March 1923; lab Vocalion; cat DO2151 & 2152; mat unknown.

### *Electric Recordings (78rpm)*
*Summer Days* Suite & *Wood Nymphs* Valsette; New Queen's Hall Light Orchestra;
    rec 24/08/1926; lab Columbia; cat L1812 & 1813; mat Wax 1854, 1855, &
    1856; loc Wigmore Hall.

*With a Song in My Heart. Symphonic Rhapsody after Richard Rodgers*; The Court Symphony Orchestra; rec 16/04/1930; lab Columbia; cat DX63; mat 5537-1 & 5538-1.

*The Merrymakers* Overture & *From Meadow to Mayfair* Suite; London Symphony Orchestra; rec 03/11/1931; lab HMV; cat C2448 & 2449; mat 2B2007-1, 2008-2, 2009-2 & 2010-2; loc Abbey Road Studios.

*Two Symphonic Rhapsodies*; London Philharmonic Orchestra with Arthur Firth (baritone) for the *Second Rhapsody* (Symphony Orchestra); rec 07/03/1933; lab Columbia; cat DX454; mat CAX6746-2 & 6747-1; loc Abbey Road Studios.

*London* Suite; London Philharmonic Orchestra (Symphony Orchestra); rec 07/03/1933; lab Columbia; cat DX470; mat CAX6748-1 & 6749-2; loc Abbey Road Studios.[23]

*London Bridge* March & *Summer Afternoon* Idyll; Symphony Orchestra; rec 05/05/1934; lab; Columbia; cat DB1382; mat 14469-2 & 14470-2; loc Abbey Road Studios.

'The Princess Arrives' & 'Dance of the Orange Blossom' (*The Jester at the Wedding* Suite from the Ballet); Symphony Orchestra; rec 05/05/1934; lab Columbia; cat (1) not released, (2) DB1505;[24] mat (1) CA14476 & (2) CA14477-1; loc Abbey Road Studios.

*The Three Men* Suite & *Wood Nymphs* Valsette; London Philharmonic Orchestra (The Light Symphony Orchestra); rec 30/01/1935; lab HMV; cat C2722 & 2723; mat 2EA972-1, 973-1, 974-1 & 975-2; loc Abbey Road Studios.

*Cinderella* Phantasy & *By the Sleepy Lagoon* Valse Serenade; London Philharmonic Orchestra (Symphony Orchestra); rec 04/03/1935; lab Columbia; cat DX711 & 712; mat CAX7452-1, 7453-2, 7454-1 & 7455-2; loc Abbey Road Studios.

*A Song of Loyalty* & 'Song by the Way' (*From Meadow to Mayfair* Suite); Symphony Orchestra with Lance Fairfax (baritone for *A Song of Loyalty*); rec 26/04/1935; lab Columbia; cat DX690; mat CAX7530-1 & 7529-1.

'The Princess Arrives' (*The Jester at the Wedding* Suite from the Ballet); London Philharmonic Orchestra (Symphony Orchestra); rec 04/05/1935; lab Columbia; cat DB1505; mat CA14476-4; loc Abbey Road Studios.

*London Again* Suite & *By the Tamarisk* Intermezzo; London Philharmonic Orchestra (Symphony Orchestra); rec 30/04/1936 ('Oxford Street' & 'Langham Place') & 01/05/1936 ('Mayfair'); lab Columbia; cat DX736-737; mat CAX7783-1, 7784-2, 7785-1 & 7786-2.

*Saxo-Rhapsody*; London Symphony Orchestra, Sigurd Rascher (alto saxophone); rec 15/01/1937; lab HMV; cat C2891; mat 2EA4617-2 & 4618-2; loc Abbey Road Studios.

---

[23]  'Covent Garden' and 'Westminster' were re-recorded on 02/05/1947 (with a new matrix number of CAX 6748-2) and issued (with the original pressing of 'Knightsbridge') the following month.

[24]  The recording of 'Dance of the Orange Blossom' was issued in 1935 with a new recording of 'The Princess Arrives'.

*Summer Days* Suite; London Symphony Orchestra (Light Symphony Orchestra); rec 15/01/1937; lab HMV; cat C2901; mat 2EA4619-1 & 4620-1; loc Abbey Road Studios.

*Springtime* Suite & *For Your Delight* Serenade; The Light Symphony Orchestra; rec 14/09/1937; lab HMV; cat C2926&2927; mat 2EA5353-1, 5354-1, 5355-1 & 5356-1.

*Footlights* Concert Valse & *Last Love* Romance; The Light Symphony Orchestra; rec 31/01/1940; lab Columbia; cat DX966; mat CAX8715-2 & 8716-1; loc Abbey Road Studios.

*The Seven Seas* March & *I Sing to You* Souvenir; The Light Symphony Orchestra; rec 31/01/1940; lab Columbia; cat DB1904; mat CA17823-1 & 17824-1; loc Abbey Road Studios.

*By the Sleepy Lagoon* Valse Serenade & *Calling All Workers* March; Symphony Orchestra; rec 27/08/1940; lab Columbia; cat DB1945; mat CA18124-1 & 18125-1.

*Fanfare Number One* and *Salute the Soldier* March & *Fanfare Number Two* and *The Eighth Army* March; London Symphony Orchestra; rec 01/02/1944; lab HMV; cat JG213 & 214; mat CTPX12587-1 & 12588-1; loc Abbey Road Studios.

*The Four Centuries* Suite; National Symphony Orchestra; rec 10/11/1944; lab Decca; cat AK 1273 & 1274; mat AR 8750-4, 8751-4, 8752-2 & 8753-2; loc Kingsway Hall.

*The Three Elizabeths* Suite; National Symphony Orchestra; rec 14/11/1944; lab Decca; cat AK1109 & 1110; mat AR8859-2, 8860-2, 8861-1 & 8862-2; loc Kingsway Hall.

*Dancing Nights* Concert Valse; London Symphony Orchestra; rec 03/10/1945; lab Columbia; cat DB2345; mat CA19871-1 & 18972-1; loc Kingsway Hall.

*The Three Bears* Phantasy; London Symphony Orchestra; rec 03/10/1945; lab Columbia; cat DX1217; mat CAX9401-1 & 9402-3; loc Kingsway Hall.[25]

*Television March* & *London Calling* March; London Symphony Orchestra; rec 19/07/1946; lab Columbia; cat DB2233 (17607D); mat CA20138 & 20139; loc Abbey Road Studios.

*London* Suite & *London Again* Suite; New Symphony Orchestra; rec 07/10/1948; lab Decca; cat AK2072, 2073 & 2074; mat AR12652, 12653, 12644 & 12655; loc Kingsway Hall.

*The Three Men* Suite & 'Dance of the Orange Blossom' (*The Jester at the Wedding*); New Symphony Orchestra; rec 16/07/1949; lab Decca; cat AK2436 & 2437; mat AR3515, 3516, 3517 & 3518; loc Kingsway Hall.

*The Three Bears* Phantasy; New Symphony Orchestra; rec 16/07/1949; lab Decca; cat K2280; mat AR12513 & 13514; loc Kingsway Hall.

---

[25]    The first side was re-recorded on 14/12/1945 possibly due to wear on the matrix (CAX9401-2).

*Valse from the Phantasy 'The Three Bears'* & *Music Everywhere* March; New Symphony Orchestra; rec 16/07/1949; lab Decca and Chappells; cat F9157 (Decca), C363 (Chappells); mat DR13519 & 13520 (Decca) and CH41-1 & 42-1 (Chappells); loc Kingsway Hall.

*Sound and Vision* March & *The Dam Busters* March; Concert Orchestra; rec 1955; lab Pye (Nixa); cat N18003; mat XX1004-A2 & 1004-B2.

### Long Play Records

*London* Suite & *The Three Elizabeths* Suite; Philharmonia; rec circa 03-10/04/1947; EMI (Special Recordings Department); cat EPZ 14; mat 6CTP14555 & 14556. (Recorded on a 16-inch disc).

*London* Suite & *London Again* Suite; London Philharmonic Orchestra (Philharmonic Promenade Orchestra); rec 29 & 30/09/1952; lab Parlophone; cat PMD1004; mat XE57; loc Abbey Road Studios.

*The Three Elizabeths* Suite & *The Four Centuries* Suite; New Symphony Orchestra; rec 03 & 04/02/1953; lab Decca; cat LK4056; loc West Hampstead Studios.

*High Flight* March & *Impression of a Princess* & *Wood Nymphs* Valsette & *South Wales and the West* March; Eric Coates and his Orchestra; rec 16/08/1957; lab HMV; cat 7EG8333; loc Abbey Road Studios.[26]

### Export Recordings

*London Bridge* March & 'Knightsbridge' March (*London* Suite); London Symphony Orchestra; rec 19/07/1946; Columbia; cat 72597D; mat CAX9620 & 9621; loc Abbey Road Studios.

*A Song of Loyalty* & *Bird Songs at Eventide* (arranged H.M. Higgs) & *By the Sleepy Lagoon* Valse Serenade & *Television March* & *Wood Nymphs* Valsette & 'Knightsbridge' March (*London* Suite); New Symphony Orchestra; rec 26/06/1948; lab London (Decca); cat R10047, 10048 & 10049; mat DR12461-1, 12462-1, 12463-1, 12464-1, 12465-2 & 12466-4; loc Kingsway Hall.

## Written Works

### Books

'Foreword' *This is Jack Payne* by Jack Payne; pub Sampson Low, Marsden & Company, 1932.

*Report on Light Music Presented to the BBC on 22/05/1943* (Unpublished); aut GB-Rwac.

---

[26]   This recording was also released on 2 78rpm disc; cat POP386 and 418; mat OEA19017-1, 19018-1, 19019-1 & 19020-1

*Suite in Four Movements* by Eric Coates; pub Heinnemann,1953; reprinted Thames 1986;[27] ded 'to the other two' [Phyl and Austin]; aut *GB-Lcm*.

### Articles

Arnold Bax (1883–1953); pub *Music and Letters*, January, 1954; aut *GB-Lcm*.

Eric Coates Writes an Appreciation of Sigurd Rascher; pub *Radio Times*, 08/01/1937; aut *GB-Lcm*.

Fair Play for Jazz; pub *Music for All*, March 1927.

Foreword; pub *Light Music Society Magazine*, September 1957.

From Meadow to Mayfair; pub *Sunray (The Magazine of Hucknall Carnival)*, 1935; aut *GB-Lcm*.

How Do You Like Your Music By Eric Coates; pub *Liverpool Evening News*, 05/03/1935.

How to Write Songs; pub *Musical News*, circa 1928.

Is Light Music a Dying Art?; pub *Radio Times*, circa 1942.

A Meal to Remember; pub *John Bull*, 30/11/1947?

Misadventure and Intonation; pub *Winter Garden's Society Magazine*, April 1955.

Taking Jazz Seriously; pub *Daily Sketch*, 07/01/1928.

The Highbrow is Ruining Music; pub *Daily Mail*, 14/05/1935.

This Musical Snobbery; pub *Evening News*, 30/06/1939; aut *GB-Lcm*.

### Published Letters

\# A Canadian Bill; pub *The Times*, 28/02/1938.

\# Copyright Bill; pub *The Times*, 27/03/1956.

\# The Copyright Bill: Grave Injustices in Proposals; pub *The Times*, 16/10/1956.

\# The Copyright Bill Proposal: Music for 'Social Service Bodies' pub *The Times*, 07/12/1955.

Dance Tunes and Crooners; pub *Radio Times*, 06/03/1936.

A Famous Notts. Composer; pub *Nottinghamshire Guardian*, October 1936.

The Light Music Society; pub *The Musical Times* and *Music and Musicians*, June, 1957.

The Light Music Society; pub *The Times*, 20/04/1957.

Musical Copyright; pub *The Times?*, 16/04/1928.

\# Record Royalties; pub *The Times*, 02/07/1956.

### Significant Interviews and Miscellaneous

Eric Coates by W.S. Meadmore; pub *The Gramophone*, November 1937.

Masterpiece Music Selected and Edited by Eric Coates; pub 1937–38. This was a sixteen-part set (originally billed as a twenty-part set) of popular pieces for piano, though each volume contained one piece for violin and piano as well as several songs. Whilst the magazine states that the pieces were selected and

---

[27]   The second edition was printed with a Foreword by Ian Lace with contributions by Austin Coates

edited by Coates (including a lengthy two-page introduction to each edition), it is likely that the magazine used Coates' name and all the work was done by a 'shadow' editor. There was an earlier edition of *Masterpiece Music* edited by Percy Pitt.

Our Interview Gallery, No 21: Mr. Eric Coates; pub *The Performing Right Gazette*, January 1928.

# Appendix 2: The Use of Material from *Snowdrop* in *The Enchanted Garden*

| Figure | Theme/Section (The Enchanted Garden) | Key | Tempo | Material (rehearsal letter) used from Snowdrop |
|---|---|---|---|---|
| Opening | Motto | F | Maestoso | I |
| 3 | A | F | Andante moderato | J, expanded |
| 6 | B | F | Poco meno mosso | Q + 3 bars, expanded and altered |
| 8 | C | A♭ | Allegro | New |
| 11 | A' | A♭ | | New |
| 13 | Bridge | A♭ | | New |
| 14 | A'' | A♭ | Più mosso | New |
| 18 | D (similarities to figure 11 and A) | A♭ | Poco meno mosso | New |
| 20 | Bridge (based on B) | A♭ | | New |
| 21 | B | C | Moderato | New |
| 23 | Motto (direct repetition of opening) | F | Tempo I | I |
| 26 | Bridge (based on A) | F | Andante moderato | New |
| 27 + 3 bars | Valse (link to A) | F | Tempo di valse | G, altered and expanded |
| 32 | Bridge (violin cadenza) | F | | New |
| 33 + 3 bars | E | F–C–G | Allegretto ($\quarternote$ = 84) | M, altered and U altered (figures 34–35) |
| 42 | B | A | Allegretto ($\dottedquarternote$ = 108) – Poco più mosso | Q + 3 bars |
| 48 | E (with hints of motto) | G–B♭–f–D, | Allegro molto | T, significantly altered |
| 54 | Bridge with new idea F | C–G | | New |
| 56 | B | B♭ | Molto meno mosso | New |
| 57 | Bridge (cello solo) based on second half of B | G | | Y |
| 58 | B | C | Grandioso | Z |
| 60 | Motto (shortened to 8 bars) | C | Tempo I | AA |

| | | | | |
|---|---|---|---|---|
| 61 | Bridge in $\frac{6}{8}$ | C | Allegro | New |
| 65 | Fugue on G | A | Allegro molto | BB onwards, but reworked |
| 75 | Fragmentation of G | a–f | Presto (Figure 83) | HH + 5 bars, but reworked and expanded, especially the Presto section |
| 88 | End of Tarentelle. Motto theme with fuller orchestration and chromatic scales | F | Tempo I | New |
| 91 | A (As figure 3, though altered) | F | Andante moderato | New |
| 93 | Coda with hints of A, B, C and motto (figure 95) | F | Meno mosso | New quiet ending, as *Snowdrop* ends with a climax based on motto and with 'pseudo' birdsongs |

# Select Bibliography

**Primary Sources**

*Boosey and Hawkes, London (GB-Lbh)*

Manuscript Collection
Song File

*BBC Written Archives Centre, Reading (*GB-Rwac*)*

BBC WAC RCONT 1 Eric Coates file 1, 1928–1935
BBC WAC RCONT 1 Eric Coates file 2, 1936–1939
BBC WAC RCONT 1 Eric Coates file 3, 1940–1942
BBC WAC RCONT 1 Eric Coates file 4, 1943–1948
BBC WAC RCONT 1 Eric Coates file 5, 1949–1957
BBC WAC RCONT 1 Eric Coates Copyright File, December 1941–1962
BBC WAC RCONT 1 Eric Coates Midland Light Orchestra File 1, 1951
BBC WAC RCONT 1 Eric Coates file II, 1947 (Music General)
R27/172/1 – Light Music (file 1, 1939–1943)
R27/172/2 – Light Music (file 2, 1944–1946)
R27/172/3 – Light Music (file 3a, 1947–1948)
R27/172/4 – Light Music (file 3b, 1949–1952)
R27/172/5 – Light Music (file 4, 1953–1954)
R27/774/1 – Light Music (file 5, 1955–1957)
R27/774/2 – Light Music (file 6, 1958–1962)
R27/947/1 – Light Music (file 7, 1963–1965)
R27/798/1 – Light Music (file 8, 1966–1968)
R27/176/1 – Light Music – Reading Panel (1953–1954)
R27/173/1 – Light Music – Direction Meeting, Minutes (1954)
R27/174/1 – Light Music – Policy Conference (1953)
R27/175/1 – Light Music – Producers' Meetings (1954)
R27/801/1 – Light Music Policy Meetings – Minutes (file 2, 1955–1957)
R27/801/2 – Light Music Policy Meeting Minutes (file 3, 1958–1961)
BBC WAC S133/18/7 Special Collections. Plomley, Roy 'Desert Island Discs' (Scripts 91–109)
BBC WAC RCONT 1 Haydn Wood file 1, 1929–1939
BBC WAC RCONT 1 Haydn Wood file 2, 1940–1942
BBC WAC RCONT 1 Haydn Wood file 3a, 1944
BBC WAC RCONT 1 Sir Henry Wood Personal File 6, July 1938–1944

BBC WAC RCONT 1 Sir Henry Wood Artists File 2a, 1942–June 1943

*British Library (*GB-Lbl*)*

Add.52364 Rutland Boughton Collection
MS.MUS 198–200, 202 and 204 Alick Maclean Collection
Add. 57484 Eric Parker Collection
Add.70605 Roger Quilter Collection
MS.339 Royal Philharmonic Society Collection

*Cambridge University, Christopher Hassall Collection (*GB-Cu*)*

Add.8905/10/C/59-Add.8905/10/C/73. Correspondence between Christopher Hassall
    and Eric Coates

*City of Birmingham Symphony Orchestra, Birmingham*

Programme Archive

*Hallé Orchestra, Manchester (GB-Mhallé)*

1953 Bulawayo Tour Box
Press Cuttings File
Programme Archive

*Hucknall Public Library, Nottinghamshire (*GB-HCKl*)*

Eric Coates files and press cuttings

*Jack Hylton Archive, Lancaster University*

Jack Hylton Orchestral Material
Jack Hylton's Press Cuttings

*National Sound Archive, London (*GB-Lbl*)*

26/08/1943 *Eric Coates Conducts the BBC Theatre Orchestra*. CDA6277
25/03/1944 *Eric Coates Conducts Salute the Soldier*. T8257.
26/08/1948 *Around and About. One-Hundredth Anniversary Programme*. BBC
    Midland Home Service
26/11/1949 *In Town Tonight*. BBC Home Service. LP14060
05, 12, 19, 26/08/1986 *Eric Coates – King of Light Music*. Programmes 1–4. BBC
    Radio 2 PLN622/86ZA0396-PLN622/86ZA0399

*Performing Right Society, London (*GB-Lprs*)*

Eric Coates file 1
Eric Coates file 2
Statement of Apportionments 1917–1923.
Haydn Wood file 1

*Private Collections*

Correspondence between Geoffrey Self and Austin Coates
Eric Coates' Scrapbooks
General correspondence of Eric Coates

*Royal Academy of Music, London (*GB-Lam*)*

January 1895–June 1915 Entrance Archive
Minutes of the Board of Directors June 1920–March 1933
Minutes of Committee November 1906–June 1910, June 1922–April 1924,
    21/03/1951–30/03/1960
Student Record 1911–1912
Students Register G: Lent 1906–Michaelmas 1907
Prize List July 1907
RAM Club Magazines February 1908–March 1958
RAM Prospectuses 1906–1923

*Royal College of Music, London (*GB-Lcm*)*

Centre for Performance History, Queen's Hall Boxes 1907–1935
Eric Coates Archive, boxes 181–92 and M125 and M127
Patron's Fund Records

## Secondary Source Material

Anon., 'Syncopation and Dance Band News', *Melody Maker and British Metronome*, March 1926, 11–13.
Adorno, Theodor, 'Popular Music', in *Introduction to the Sociology of Music*, trans. Aston, E.B. (New York: Continuum, 1989).
Banfield, Stephen, *Sensibility and English Song* (Cambridge: Cambridge University Press, 1985).
— (ed.), *The Blackwell History of Music in Britain, Volume 6: The Twentieth Century* (Oxford: Basil Blackwell, 1995).
Barker, Duncan, *The Music of Sir Alexander Campbell Mackenzie (1847–1935): A Critical Study* (PhD Dissertation, University of Durham, 1999).

Bax, Arnold (ed. Lewis Forman), *Farewell My Youth and Other Writings by Arnold Bax* (Aldershot: Scolar Press, 1992).

Bliss, Arthur, *As I Remember* (London: Thames, 1989).

Boosey, William, *Fifty Years in Music* (London: Ernest Benn, 1931).

Brecknock, Albert, *The Pilgrim Poet: Lord Byron of Newstead* (London: Francis Griffith, 1911).

Briggs, Asa, *The Birth of Broadcasting* (Oxford: Oxford University Press, 1961).

— *The Golden Age of Wireless* (Oxford: Oxford University Press, 1965).

— *The War of Words* (Oxford: Oxford University Press, 1970).

— *Sound and Vision* (Oxford: Oxford University Press, 1979).

— *The BBC: The First Fifty Years* (Oxford: Oxford University Press, 1985).

— *Competition* (Oxford: Oxford University Press, 1995).

Brook, Donald, *Conductors' Gallery: Biographical Sketches of Well-Known Conductors Including Notes on the Leading Symphony Orchestras, and a Short Biography of the Late Sir Henry Wood* (London: Rockcliffe, 1945).

Cannell, John, *In Town To-Night: The Story of the Popular BBC Feature Told from Within* (London: George Harper and Company, 1935).

Carey, Mike, *Sailing By: The Ronald Binge Story* (Derby: Tranters, 2000).

Coates, Austin, *Invitation to an Eastern Feast.* (London: Hutchison, 1953).

— *Myself as a Mandarin: Memoirs of a Special Magistrate* (London: Frederick Muller, 1968).

Coates, Eric, *Report on Light Music* (Unpublished, 1943).

— *Suite in Four Movements* (London: Heinemann, 1953).

— 'Arnold Bax: 1883–1953', in *Music and Letters*, xxxv (1954), 7.

— *Suite in Four Movements* (London: Thames, 1986).

Coffield, James, *A Popular History of Taxation: From Ancient to Modern Times* (Harlow: Longman, 1970).

Cole, Hugo, 'Light Music – Serious Music', *The Musical Times* 97 (1956), 521–2.

Coward, Noël, *Present Indicative* (London: Heinemann, 1937).

Cox, David, *The Henry Wood Proms* (London: British Broadcasting Corporation, 1980).

Culshaw, John, *Putting the Record Straight* (London: Secker and Warburg, 1981).

Day, Timothy, *A Century of Recorded Music: Listening to Musical History* (New Haven: Yale University Press, 2000).

Dickinson, Peter, *Marigold: The Music of Billy Mayerl* (Oxford: Oxford University Press, 1999).

Doctor, Jennifer, *The BBC and Ultra-Modern Music, 1922–1936: Shaping a Nation's Taste* (Cambridge: Cambridge University Press, 1999).

Duncan, Peter, *In Town Tonight* (London: Werner Laurie, 1951).

Ehrlich, Cyril, *Harmonious Alliance: A History of the Performing Right Society* (Oxford: Oxford University Press, 1989).

— *First Philharmonic: A History of the Royal Philharmonic Society* (Oxford: Clarendon Press, 1995).

Elkin, Robert, *Queen's Hall 1893–1941* (London: Rider and Company, 1944).

Ellis, Vivian, *I'm on a See-Saw* (London: Michael Joseph, 1953).

Foreman, Lewis, *Bax: A Composer and His Times* (Woodbridge: Boydell Press, 2007).

Foreman, Lewis & Foreman, Susan, *London: A Musical Gazetteer* (New Haven: Yale University Press, 2005).

Godfrey, Dan, *Memories and Music: Thirty-Five Years of Conducting* (London: Hutchinson, 1924).

Goossens, Eugene, *Overture and Beginners: A Musical Autobiography* (London: Methuen, 1951).

Greer, David, 'Hamilton Harty Manuscripts', *The Music Review* 47 (1986–87), 238–52.

Griffith, Anthony, 'The 78 Era', in *The Elgar Edition: The Complete Electrical Recordings of Sir Edward Elgar, Volume 3*. EMI: CDS 7 54568 2, 1993.

Hall, Henry, *Here's To The Next Time: The Autobiography of Henry Hall* (London: Odhams Press, 1955).

Hughes, Meirion & Stradling, Robert, *The English Musical Renaissance 1840–1940: Constructing a National Music* (Manchester: Manchester University Press, 2001).

Hughes, Spike, 'Introductory Note', *1955 Light Programme Festival of Music Concert Programme*, 1.

Hustwitt, Mark, 'Caught in a Whirlpool of Aching Sound: The Production of Dance Music in Britain in the 1920s', *Popular Music* 3 (1983), 3–31.

Hylton, Jack, 'Dance Music of To-Day', *The Musical Times* 67 (1926), 799–800.

—— 'The British Touch' *The Gramophone* 4 (1926–27), 145–6.

Ingham, Richard (ed.), *The Cambridge Companion to the Saxophone* (Cambridge: Cambridge University Press, 1998).

Jacobs, Arthur, *Henry J. Wood: Maker of the Proms* (London: Methuen, 1994).

James, Charles, *The Story of the Performing Right Society: An Association of Composers, Authors and Publishers of Music* (London: Performing Right Society, 1951).

Johnson, Peter, 'The Legacy of Recordings', in Rinck, John (ed.), *Musical Performance: A Guide to Understanding* (Cambridge: Cambridge University Press, 2002).

Kennedy, Michael, *A Portrait of Walton* (Oxford: Oxford University Press, 1989).

—— *The Life of Elgar* (Cambridge: Cambridge University Press, 2004).

Kenyon, Nicholas, *The BBC Symphony Orchestra: The First Fifty Years 1930–1980* (London: British Broadcasting Corporation, 1981).

Knox, Collie, *It Might Have Been* (London: Chapman Hall, 1938).

Lace, Ian, 'Foreword', in Coates, Eric, *Suite in Four Movements* (London: Thames, 1986).

—— *Eric Coates and Sussex*. (Transcript of BBC radio programme 'The Enchanted Garden'), www.musicweb-international.com/coates/sussex.htm (1997).

Lambert, Constant, *Music Ho! A Study of Music in Decline* (London: Hogarth Press, 1985).

Lamborn, David, 'Henry Wood and Schoenberg', *The Musical Times* 128 (1987), 422–6.

Langfield, Valerie, *Roger Quilter: His Life and Music* (Woodbridge: Boydell Press, 2002).

Langley, Leanne, 'Building an Orchestra, Creating an Audience: Robert Newman and the Queen's Hall Promenade Concerts, 1895–1926', in Doctor, Jenny & Wright, David (eds), *The Proms: A New History* (London: Thames & Hudson, 2007).

Latham, Alison (ed.), *The Oxford Companion to Music* (Oxford: Oxford University Press, 2002).

Lea, Edward, *The Best of Rodgers and Hart* (London: Chappell and Company, 1975).

LeMahieu, Dan, *A Culture for Democracy: Mass Communication and the Cultivated Mind in Britain Between the Wars* (Oxford: Clarendon Press, 1988).

Lloyd, Stephen, *Sir Dan Godfrey: Champion of British Music* (London: Thames, 1995).

Lucas, John, *Thomas Beecham: An Obsession with Music* (Woodbridge: Boydell Press, 2008).

McCarthy, Albert, *The Dance Band Era: The Dancing Decades from Ragtime to Swing: 1910–1950* (Radnor, Philadelphia: Chiltern Book Company, 1982).

Mackenzie, Alexander, *A Musician's Narrative*. London (Cassel and Company, 1927).

Mair, Carlene (ed.), *The Chappell Story 1811–1961* (London: Chappell and Company, 1961).

Martland, Peter, *Since Records Began: EMI The First Hundred Years* (London: B.T. Batsford, 1997).

Maschwitz, Eric, *No Chip on my Shoulder* (London: Herbert Jenkins, 1957).

Meadmore, W.S., 'Eric Coates', *The Gramophone* 15 (1936–37), 235–7.

Meredith, Anthony, *Richard Rodney Bennett: The Complete Musician* (London: Omnibus Press, 2010).

Meredith, Anthony & Harris, Paul, *Malcolm Arnold, Rogue Genius: The Life and Music of Britain's Most Misunderstood Composer* (Norwich: Thames/Elkin, 2004).

Mitchell, Alistair & Poulton, Alan, *A Chronicle of First Broadcast Performances of Musical Works in the United Kingdom, 1923–1996* (Ashgate: Aldershot, 2001).

Mitchell, Brian, *British Historical Statistics* (Cambridge: Cambridge University Press, 1988).

Moore, Jerrold, *Elgar on Record: The Composer and the Gramophone* (Oxford: Oxford University Press, 1974).

Morrison, Richard, *Orchestra. The LSO: A Century of Triumph and Turbulence* (London: Faber and Faber, 2004).

Norris, Gerald, *A Musical Gazetteer of Great Britain and Ireland* (Newton Abbott: David and Charles, 1981).

Nott, James, *Music for the People: Popular Music and Dance in Interwar Britain* (Oxford: Oxford University Press, 2002).

Parsonage, Catherine, *The Evolution of Jazz in Britain 1880–1935* (Aldershot: Ashgate, 2005).

Payne, Jack, *This Is Jack Payne* (London: Sampson, Low, Marston and Company, 1932).

— *Signature Tune* (London: Stanley Paul & Co, [1947]).

Payne, Michael, *'The Man Who Writes Tunes': An Assessment of the Work of Eric Coates (1886–1957) and his Role Within British Light Music* (PhD Dissertation, University of Durham, 2007).

Plomley, Roy, *Desert Island Discs* (London: William Kimber, 1975).

Ramsden, John, *The Dam Busters* (London: I.B. Tauris, 2003).

Rees, Brian, *A Musical Peacemaker: The Life and Music of Sir Edward German* (Abbotsbrook: Kensal Press, 1986).

Reid, Charles, *John Barbirolli: A Biography* (London: Hamish Hamilton, 1971).

Reynolds, Brian, *Music While You Work: An Era in Broadcasting* (Lewes: Book Guild, 2006).

Richards, Jeffery, *Imperialism and Music in Britain 1876–1953* (Manchester: Manchester University Press, 2001).

Russell, Dave, *Popular Music in England 1840–1914: A Social History* (Manchester: Manchester University Press, 1987).

Rust, Brian & Walker, Edward, *British Dance Bands 1912–1939* (London: Storyville Publications, 1973).

Sadie, Stanley (ed.) *The New Grove Dictionary of Music and Musicians* (Oxford: Grove, 2001).

Sant, John, *Albert W. Ketèlbey (1875–1959): From the Sanctuary of his Heart* (Sutton Coldfield: Manifold Publishing, 2000).

Scannell, Paddy & Cardiff, David, *A Social History of British Broadcasting. Volume One, 1922 – 1939: Serving the Nation* (Oxford: Basil Blackwell, 1991).

Scott, Derek, 'Light Music and Easy Listening', in Cook, Nicolas & Pople, Anthony, *Cambridge History of Music: Twentieth Century* (Cambridge: Cambridge University Press, 2004).

Scowcroft, Phillip, *British Light Music – A Personal Gallery of Twentieth Century Composers* (London: Thames, 1997).

Secrest, Meryle, *Somewhere for Me: A Biography of Richard Rodgers* (London: Bloomsbury, 2001).

Self, Geoffrey, *In Town Tonight: A Centenary Study of the Life and Music of Eric Coates* (London: Thames, 1986).

— *Light Music in Britain Since 1870* (Aldershot: Ashgate, 2001).

Sendall, Bernard, *Origin and Foundation, 1946–1962. Independent Television in Britain, Volume I* (London: Macmillan, 1982).

Smith, Ann (ed.), *The Life of Henry Morley and the Birth of the Hucknall Dispatch* (Southwell: Private Printing, 2003).

Smith, Harry, *Hucknall 'Looking Back'* (Brimscombe Port: Tempus Publishing, 2000).

— *Hucknall and District* (Brimscombe Port: Tempus Publishing, 2003).

Smith, Michael & Andrews, Frank, *The Gramophone Company Limited. 'His Master's Voice' Recordings, Plum Label 'C' Series 12 Inch* (Blandford: Oakwood Press, 1974).

Smith, Michael et al., *Columbia Gramophone Company Ltd. 'DX' & 'YBX' prefixed catalogue series of 12 inch 78 rpm discs 1930–1959: A Discography* (Wells-Next-the-Sea: City of London Phonograph and Gramophone Society, 2007).

Tertis, Lionel, *My Viola and I: A Complete Autobiography* (London: Paul Elek, 1974).

Tomlinson, Ernest, 'Foreword', in Scowcroft, Philip, *British Light Music: A Personal Gallery of Twentieth Century Composers* (London: Thames, 1997).

Tunley, David, *The Bel Canto Violin: The Life and Times of Alfredo Campoli 1906–1991* (Aldershot: Ashgate, 1999).

Upton, Stuart, *Eric Coates: A Biographical Discography Covering All Known 78 Recordings, Plus a List of All Important LP Releases, Reissues etc.* (West Wickham: Vintage Light Music Society, 1980).

Wallace, Helen, *Boosey and Hawkes: The Publishing Story* (London: Boosey and Hawkes, 2007).

Weatherly, Frederic, *Piano and Gown* (London: G.P. Putnam, 1926).

White, John, *Lionel Tertis: The First Great Virtuoso of the Viola* (Woodbridge: Boydell Press, 2006).

Whittle, David, *Bruce Montgomery/Edmund Crispin: A Life in Music and Books* (Aldershot: Ashgate, 2007).

Wood, Henry, *My Life of Music* (London: Victor Gollancz, 1938).


The following periodicals have been of invaluable assistance:
*BBC Year Books* (Published by the BBC).
Hucknall Dispatch.
*Musical Times*.
*Radio Times*.


The following websites have been of invaluable assistance:
BBC Proms Archive Database (www.bbc.co.uk/proms/archive/search/).
*Dictionary of National Biography* (ed. H.C.G. Matthew and B. Harrison) (Oxford: Oxford University Press, 2004) (www.oxforddnb.com).
*The Gramophone* Magazine (www.gramophone.net).
The Times Digital Archive (www.infotrac.galegroup.com).

**Radio and Television Programmes**

26/08/1948 *Around and About*. BBC Midland Home Service.
26/11/1949 *In Town Tonight*: BBC Home Service.
05, 12, 19, 26/08/1986 *Eric Coates – King of Light Music*. Written and presented by Austin Coates. BBC Radio 2.

21/07/2002 *Brian Kay's Light Programme*: A Celebration of Robert Farnon's Eighty-Fifth Birthday. BBC Radio 3.

14/09/2002 *The Music Factory*: Music While You Work. BBC Radio 4.

16/09/2004 *Brian Kay's Light Programme*: A Celebration of Ernest Tomlinson's Eightieth Birthday. BBC Radio 3.

05/06/2005 *The Guv'nor: A Tribute to Robert Farnon*. Written by Russell Davies and presented by David Jacobs. BBC Radio 2.

08/10/2005 *Music For Everybody!* BBC 4 Television.

24–28/12/2007 *Composer of the Week*: Eric Coates. BBC Radio 3.

23/02/2008 *King of Light Music* [Tribute to Eric Coates]. BBC Radio 4.

25/01/2011 *Tales from the Stave*. BBC Radio 4.

18/06/2011 *Archive on 4*: The Light Music Festival. BBC Radio 4.

25/06/2011 *Music Matters:* Whatever Happened to Light Music? BBC Radio 3.

26/06/2011 *Light Music Signature Tunes*. BBC Radio 3.

26/06/2011 *Discovering Music:* Eric Coates. BBC Radio 3.

Date unknown *British Composers in Sussex*: Eric Coates. BBC Radio Sussex. Written, presented and produced by Ian Lace.

# Index

Made in the
USA
Middletown, DE